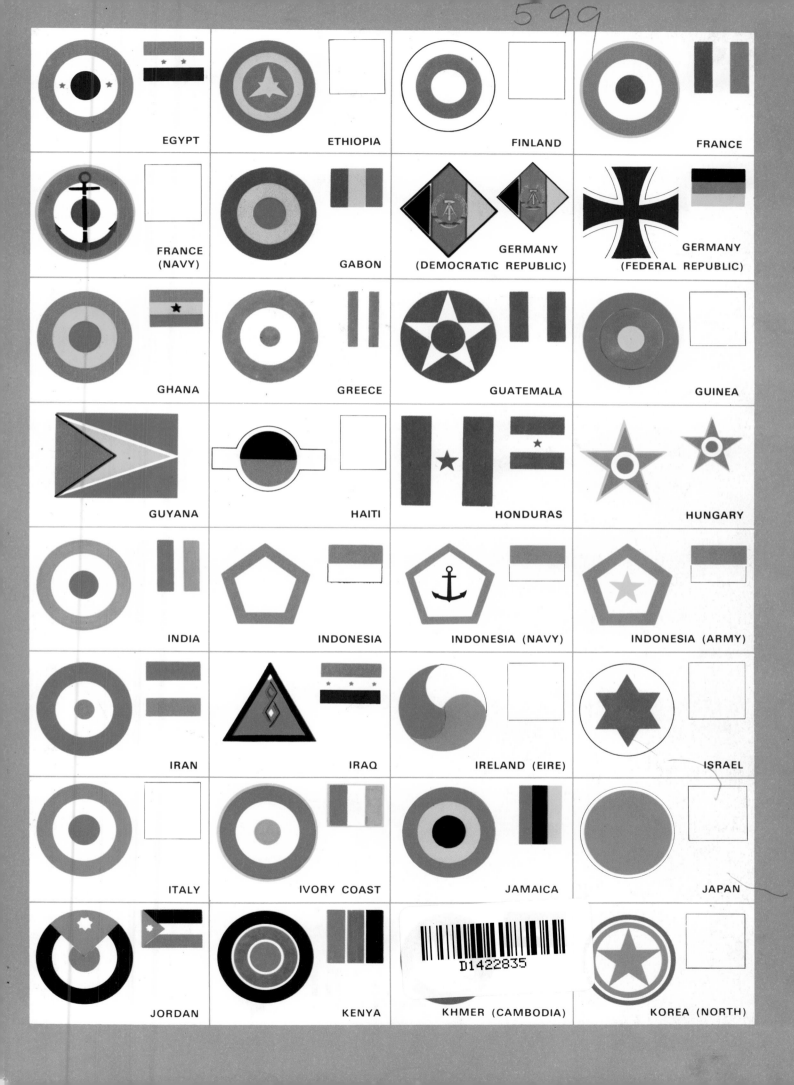

599

EGYPT

ETHIOPIA

FINLAND

FRANCE

FRANCE (NAVY)

GABON

GERMANY (DEMOCRATIC REPUBLIC)

GERMANY (FEDERAL REPUBLIC)

GHANA

GREECE

GUATEMALA

GUINEA

GUYANA

HAITI

HONDURAS

HUNGARY

INDIA

INDONESIA

INDONESIA (NAVY)

INDONESIA (ARMY)

IRAN

IRAQ

IRELAND (EIRE)

ISRAEL

ITALY

IVORY COAST

JAMAICA

JAPAN

JORDAN

KENYA

KHMER (CAMBODIA)

KOREA (NORTH)

The Encyclopedia of

AIR WARFARE

a **Salamander** book

Published by
SPRING BOOKS
London New York Sydney
Toronto

The Encyclopedia of AIR WARFARE

A SALAMANDER BOOK

This edition published 1975 by
The Hamlyn Publishing Group Ltd
London · New York · Sydney · Toronto
Astronaut House, Feltham,
Middlesex, England.

ISBN 0 600 33112 1

© Salamander Books Ltd 1974
52 James Street
London W1R 5FD
United Kingdom

Fourth impression 1977

Filmset by
Photoprint Plates Ltd, Rayleigh
Essex, England

Reproduced by
City Engraving Ltd, Hull
Yorkshire, England

Printed in Belgium by
Henri Proost, Turnhout,
Belgium.

All correspondence concerning the
content of this volume should be
addressed to Salamander Books Limited.

CREDITS

Iain Parsons: Editor
Faulkner/Marks Partnership: Design
Jonathan Moore: Photo research
ARKA Cartographics Ltd: Maps and
diagrams
Pilot Press: Aircraft drawings pages
65–165; 174–239; 248–253 © Pilot
Press
County Studios Ltd: Aircraft drawings
pages 8–64; 166–173; 240–247

CONTENTS

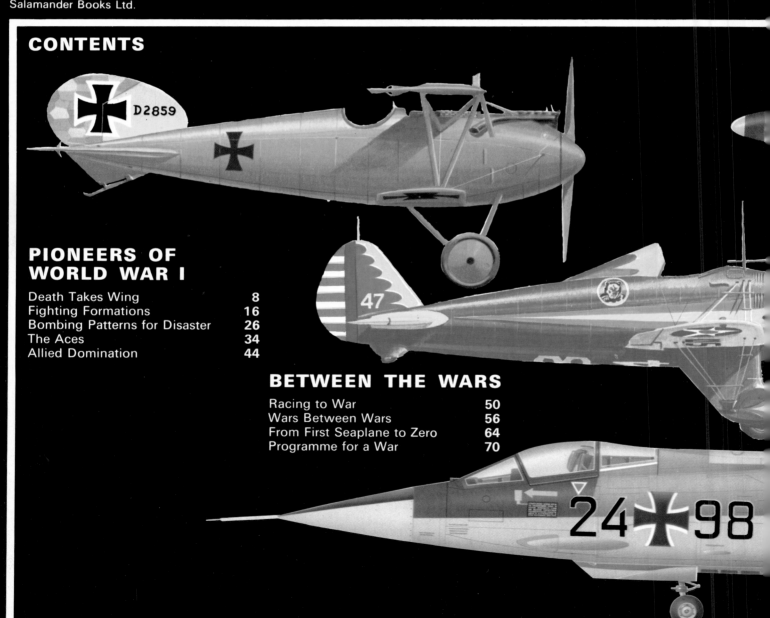

PIONEERS OF WORLD WAR I

BETWEEN THE WARS

THE AUTHORS

Christopher Chant, M.A. (Oxon)
Vastly experienced as an editor and contributor to a number of authoritative comprehensive weekly publications devoted to the history of both World Wars, a specialist in the aviation history of World War I on which he has written numerous articles.

Richard Humble, M.A. (Oxon)
A former editor and managing editor of two extensive series publications on the history of World War II and the author of several books on World War II, a subject of which he has made a special study.

Air Commodore John F. Davis, O.B.E., D.F.C., A.F.C., M.A. (Oxon)
A veteran of World War II, a former experimental flyer who has formulated and taught the strategy and tactics of air warfare, a contributor to specialist journals on Middle East affairs and the author of numerous articles on air and defence matters for a leading British newspaper.

Captain Donald Macintyre, D.S.O., D.S.C.
An ace U-boat 'killer' in World War II and a former Fleet Air Arm pilot, now one of the world's foremost naval historians and the author of numerous books on maritime history and World War II subjects.

Bill Gunston
A former World War II R.A.F. pilot and one of the most prolific and respected of authors on scientific and aviation subjects, a frequent broadcaster, the author of numerous books, and contributor to leading international aviation and defence periodicals.

By Air Vice-Marshal S.W.B. Menaul, C.B., C.B.E., D.F.C., A.F.C. Director-General, Royal United Services Institute of Defence Studies, Whitehall, London.

If the conquest of the air—the third dimension—was slow in coming, its subsequent development has been rapid and dramatic. In just over seventy years, following the first powered flight by the Wright brothers in 1903, man has penetrated the stratosphere, ascended into outer space and soft landed on the moon. Unmanned spacecraft have photographed Mars, Venus and other planets, and no corner of the earth is today hidden from the prying eye of the reconnaissance satellite. The dreams and designs of Leonardo da Vinci have been fulfilled; yet there is more to come. The conquest of space is not complete.

When Alcock and Brown made the first aeroplane crossing of the Atlantic on June 15, 1919, in a Vickers Vimy aeroplane in 16 hours 27 minutes, who would have foretold that on September 1, 1974, as a curtain-raiser to the international aerospace show at Farnborough, a United States Lockheed SR 71 military reconnaissance aircraft would cross the Atlantic between New York and London in 1 hour 55 minutes. Two world wars in the first half of this century undoubtedly gave additional stimulus to the development of air power, and inevitably the advances in technology inherent in military aviation requirements were reflected in the design and construction of civil aircraft. The supersonic Concorde is but the first of a new generation of civil aircraft.

This book recounts the evolution of the aeroplane and other vehicles of air warfare in a new and attractive form. It is not a comprehensive history of air warfare, nor indeed could it be, since that would require volumes, and in any event is available elsewhere. It is, rather, an up-to-date chronology of the conquest of the air and the development of air warfare from the

earliest days, against a background of the more dramatic events on which particular aerial vehicles have imprinted their image. The Albatros, Sopwith Camels and the Zeppelin are associated with World War I; the Hurricanes and the Spitfires will for ever more be synonymous with the Battle of Britain; the Lancasters, Halifaxes and B 17s with the Battle of Germany, while in more recent times the Skyhawks, Phantoms, MiG 21s and SU 7s are indelibly imprinted on the Yom Kippur War of 1973. Other great battles are used to illustrate developments in aerial warfare tactics and the application of new technology in weapon design and delivery systems.

Air warfare has its romantic as well as its more sinister aspects, and this book contains an admirable selection of both. It provides a compact and valuable reference document for the student of air warfare and a nostalgic reminder to older aviators everywhere of the joys of controlled flight in peacetime and its dangers and exhilaration in war. The illustrations are particularly attractive and the text is liberally spiced with anecdotes of the famous and the not so famous. The influence of air power at sea, as well as over land battles, is well illustrated by reference to some of the more deadly encounters in the Atlantic, Arctic Ocean and Pacific in World War II, while the Korean War, events in Vietnam, and the Middle East War of October 1973 are used to good effect to remind the Western democracies of the rapid progress made by the Soviet Union in the field of aerospace technology in recent years. The MiG 25 (Foxbat) and the supersonic bomber (Backfire) are equal to anything the West possesses.

This is an admirable book, from which everyone interested in the conquest of the air and the battles that have been fought in it over such a short span of time should derive much enjoyment.

S.W.B. MENAU

September 1974

DEATH

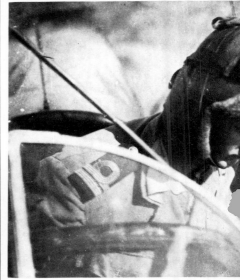

In 1903 the Wright brothers achieved the first powered flight, in 1911 men took to the air for the first time with the express intention of killing and so wrote the first chapter in the history of air warfare. It had taken Man only eight years to turn the realisation of an idyllic dream, the freedom of the skies, into an instrument of death. It would be only three more years until the first real war in the air. According to the military strategists of both sides, World War I would be quickly won on the ground. Air power did not enter into their thinking. Though air forces were small and poorly equipped and their aims were limited, even confused, the two sides formed up against each other and, under the stimulus of war, their new and vital role evolved. But warplanes were just the latest twist in a fascinating story that had begun about a thousand years before the birth of Christ.

The realisation of the dream of flight has proved tantalisingly difficult, although the separate elements to make it possible have existed for centuries: the kite, the prototype for an aircraft wing, since about 1000 BC and the airscrew, in the form of windmill rotors and toy helicopters, since about AD 1300. But through a variety of circumstances the invention of the true flying machine had to wait until the 20th Century. This is not to say, however, that strides in the right direction were not made: Leonardo da Vinci, for example, between 1485 and 1510 came to understand many of the aspects of flight. But the majority was still convinced that the way to achieve flight was by slavish imitation of the birds. Many brave, or perhaps foolhardy, men, wearing an imitation of a bird's wings, leapt from towers and cliffs to death or injury in pursuit of this false dream.

As well as the doers there were the thinkers, men such as Francesco Lana de Terzi, who in 1670 wrote in his native Italy of his visions of fleets of aircraft that could fly over cities and hurl vast numbers of missiles down onto the defenceless citizens below. A little later, though, in 1709, a Portuguese priest named Lourenzo de Guzmao was successful in his experiments with model gliders and hot-air balloons. Thereafter the practical expression of the urge to fly waned until the arrival of the Montgolfier brothers, Jacques Etienne and Joseph Michel, in 1783.

Hot air lift-off

As professional paper makers, the two brothers noticed that paper bags filled with hot air rose. They did not understand that this was the result of the less dense and consequently lighter air trying to rise

takes wing

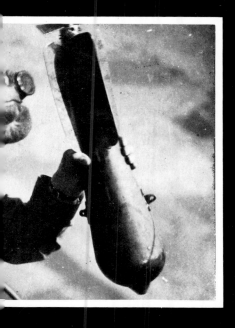

and carrying the bag with it, but did realise the practical implications. They built several experimental models, and on October 15, 1783, launched the first man-carrying model. Word of the brothers' successes had preceded them to Paris in the latter half of 1783, and French scientists there decided to improve on the Montgolfier type of balloon.

The result was J. A. C. Charles' hydrogen-filled balloon, which flew for the first time on December 1 of that same year. Although the Montgolfiers had opened up the way, it was Charles' balloon that was more important, relying as it did on hydrogen, a light gas, rather than ordinary air 'lightened' by heat. Future developments in ballooning, and thence airships, were centred on the use of a light gas rather than hot air.

The French were quick to realise the martial possibilities of the balloon, and a balloon unit was raised in the army. This was instrumental in securing the French victory at Fleurus in 1794, but Napoleon failed to see that the use of tethered balloons for observation purposes could be further enhanced and ordered the dissolution of the balloon unit. Later, in the 19th Century, other military men were not as short-sighted,

and balloons played a small, but increasingly important, part in the American Civil War (1861–1865), the siege of Paris in 1871–1872, and the British expeditions to Bechuanaland and the Sudan in the last quarter of the century. Balloons were also used with some success in the Boer War by Major B. F. S. Baden-Powell.

The first Zeppelin

The balloon is intrinsically a clumsy device, however, as it must either be tethered or be at the mercy of the winds. Naturally enough, efforts were made throughout the 19th Century to provide balloons with some form of motive power, so that they might manoeuvre in the air, but the necessary power source was not yet available. Some progress was made, though, and it was realised that the spherical shape of the balloon was a considerable hindrance, offering as it did great resistance to the air. Gradually the spherical shape of the gas envelope was elongated into a cigar shape that gave far greater manoeuvrability.

So far there was no practical power source light enough in weight and with the

necessary power in existence. But in 1885 and 1886 two Germans, Carl Benz and Gottlieb Daimler, developed practical petrol engines, and from this point onward progress with airships, as the elongated balloons came to be known, and aircraft became increasingly rapid. Here at last was an engine that was capable of development

---

Far left: First flight. In December 1903, Orville Wright's flight at Kitty Hawk N.C. meant that aviation was born.

Centre left: Primitive bombing. In October 1911, the first bombs were dropped from an aircraft over Tripoli and air warfare was a deadly reality.

Left: Fighting Formations. This picture of S.E. 5as, taken only months before the end of World War I, gives some indication of how quickly air forces developed under the stimulus of combat.

Right: The grim reality. After fighter attack the helpless crew of a Caquot balloon plummet earthwards—the deadly result of war in the air.

---

into a powerful motive force at a relatively low weight.

Although the first nearly practical airship, La France, had been flown with an electric motor driving a huge bow propeller just before the invention of the petrol engine, it was not until 1900 that the airship, in its true form, with a rigid rather than semi-rigid structure, became a practical invention. That year Graf von Zeppelin flew his first giant rigid airship over Lake Constance; the next year Alberto Santos-Dumont, an expatriate Brazilian, navigated his miniscule No. 6 round the Eiffel Tower; and in 1903 the Lebaudy brothers produced the world's first truly practical airship. This flew a distance of 38 miles on November 12, 1903.

Wright brothers' breakthrough

But shortly after this an event of far more importance was to take place in the United States. After years of painstaking research and experimental work with kites, tethered gliders and then free gliders, the Wright brothers of Dayton, Ohio, were ready to try their first powered flying machine. On December 17, 1903, Orville Wright made the world's first powered, sustained, and controlled flight in a heavier-than-air machine, the **Flyer**. Although the newspapers were informed, however, the event had little or no impact in the US and was flatly disbelieved in Europe. Discouraged, but not deterred, the Wrights persevered in secrecy during the next two years and produced an aircraft capable of staying in the air for over half an hour. Finally, in 1905, after repeated attempts to interest the authorities in their machine, the Wrights retired from flying for a short period.

Meanwhile, the Europeans, confident that they led the world in the development of flying machines, were slowly groping their way forward. On November 12, 1907, **Santos Dumont** flew his extraordinary **14-bis** in the first powered flight in Europe, and on January 13, 1908, Henri Farman flew his **Voisin-Farman I-bis** round a one kilometre circle at Issy, France and thereby ushered in the age of true flight in Europe.

From then on flying was an accepted fact, and became increasingly popular as a sport. A great flying meeting was held at Rheims in August 1909. Spurred to action by the claims of European aviators, the Wright brothers had decided to re-enter the lists, and late in 1908 Wilbur Wright travelled to France with an example of the **Wright A**. His flying was a sensation, and far outstripped anything that the Europeans had achieved. At the same time Orville Wright was showing a similar machine to the US Army at Fort Myer, with considerable success. It was marred only by the death of a Lieutenant Selfridge in an accident on September 17—the first death in the history of powered flight.

Spurred on by Wilbur's achievements, the French in particular made great strides in 1909: the aviation week at Rheims was a great success and in July of that year Louis Bleriot flew the English Channel, an event that had vast popular impact and great significance—England had to think beyond a purely marine defence!

Air forces and bombing contests

By now the military authorities could no longer deny the capabilities of aircraft, and slowly the European powers began to assemble motley assortments of aircraft to scout for their armies. Progress was slow, most technical developments being left to private citizens. In Germany interest centred on the vast **Zeppelin** airships that had at last proved their practicability after public subscription had enabled Zeppelin to continue with his pioneering work. But in France and Britain, the two other major aeronautical powers, more attention was devoted to aeroplanes. So, by 1912 what can be regarded as true air forces were in being, and aircraft were being developed specially for the military. Such machines as the British **Royal Aircraft Factory's B.E. 2**, which was destined to play so important a part in the forthcoming war, were direct results of the growing military interest in aircraft. However, machines such as the **Sopwith Tabloid** and **Morane Saulnier Type N** reflected the needs in private enterprise of high speeds for racing and similar refinements in performance.

As yet the military authorities had formulated no precise role for aircraft, and so aircraft were not ordered with any particular specifications in mind, except that they be tractable and capable of scouting for the army or the navy. There

was thus little standardisation of types and their attendant spares, which was to prove a great strain in the opening months of the war. Little experimental work had been done in the fields of aircraft armament or of bombing, although contests in this latter field had become very popular at flying meetings in the last two years of peace.

But the first use of aircraft in war had preceded even these contests. This occurred on October 23, 1911, when the Italian Captain Piazza, flying a **Bleriot**, made a reconnaissance flight over the Turkish positions at Azizia in Tripoli at the beginning of the Italo-Turkish War. Soon afterwards the first bombing raids were made, resulting in Turkish claims of war crimes against a hospital.

When the First World War broke out in the late summer of 1914, the generals on both sides fondly imagined that their carefully laid plans would ensure victory for their own armies in a matter of a few months. The

war was to be like a modernised version of the Franco-Prussian War of 1870–1871. The Germans, however, had built on their experience in 1870 with a properly organised and trained general staff and planned in detail an operation (the Schlieffen Plan) which came within an ace of winning the war for them. This was a daring and courageous scheme to knock France out of the war by sending the German armies sweeping round through Belgium and northern France to encircle Paris, cut off the major portion of the French army from reinforcement, and compel the French government to surrender.

'Race to the Sea'

But the plan needed a man of nerve and decision to control it, and the general at the head of the German army, Helmuth von Moltke (nephew of the Moltke who

---

Below: A Farman M.F.7, the famous 'Longhorn', in flight. Although used operationally in the first days of the war, the Longhorn was soon relegated to the more suitable task of training—and occasionally killing—novice pilots. In 1915 its front-line duties were assumed by the M.F.11, soon dubbed the 'Shorthorn' for its short landing skids. The 'Shorthorn' had a single tailplane, with twin rudders, unlike the 'Longhorn', which featured a biplane tail unit.

had won the Franco-Prussian War), was singularly lacking in these characteristics—indeed he allowed his senior subordinates on the all-important right wing of the great sweeping movement to dictate an alteration of the basic plan. By this their tired armies would not push on round the west of Paris to cut off the French capital, but cut inside Paris and advance to the Marne. The French and British, retreating in some disorder, at last saw a chance for their forces to counterattack. While a force from Paris took the Germans in flank, the front facing the Germans was reorganised and attacked northwards. It was the end of German hopes of knocking France out of the war in one swift blow. With their lines of communication overextended, the Germans were compelled to pull back from the Marne.

From this developed the German retreat that has since become known as the 'Race to the Sea', which finally established the front line that resulted in the stagnation of the next four years of trench warfare. It was the trench warfare that was at last to force senior commanders on both sides to think more deeply about the role of their aircraft.

As we have seen, the first heavier-than-air craft had flown only 11 years before the outbreak of war, and although the fledgling aircraft of 1914 showed remarkable improvement in performance over the types of only three years before, the art of flying was still very much in its infancy. The load that could be carried was small, reliability was low, and flying at all depended on the clemency of the weather. Thus the type of task that could be undertaken by the aircraft of 1914 was very restricted, and commanders were right in assessing the basic role as reconnaissance. Although correct, however, this interpretation of the aircraft's role was very short-sighted. For it was clear that as the performance and capabilities of aircraft had improved dramatically since the great air meeting at Rheims in 1909, the next few years would also bring about further improvements, especially when the stimulus of war was applied.

Lack of Vision

The result of this lack of forethought was that the basic groundwork and organisation for efficient air arms was not laid. As the weapon was a new one, distrusted by senior commanders, there were no commanders of middle to senior rank capable of taking over the administration. The only answer was to promote the captains and majors already in air services to fairly senior command. They at least knew what was in their new commands, but they did not have the training to utilise the power of command to the full; nor did they have the authority to deal firmly with other commanders with whom they were now supposedly equal. The air arm was the junior service and subordinated to the armies of all combatant powers. Moreover, most new commanders were unwilling to risk their charges with things like machine guns and bombs, and so the enthusiasm of the more aggressive and imaginative pilot officers was severely curbed.

In this matter even the air services' own commanders were short-sighted. For it was clear that if it was worthwhile sending out aircraft to gather reconnaissance information, it was also worth the effort to prevent the information being collected or delivered. Looked at thus, in the light of reason, it should have been patently clear that air combat of one form or another was inevitable. To attempt to prevent it would merely give the other side an advantage—as did in fact happen. A further point that makes it even less credible that the authorities should not have seen what was inevitable was the fact that the practicability of the war being carried into the air had been made apparent long before the war.

Experimental work in the fitting of machine guns to aircraft had been carried out, but not persevered with, in Germany and France before the war; similar experiments had been carried out on a private basis in Britain and the United States; bombing trials had proved a popular attraction at pre-war flying shows, and live tests had been carried out in January 1911 by a Wright aircraft off San Francisco. Results had not been spectacularly successful, but it should have been realised that the whole art was still in its infancy. What was needed was greater help from the authorities.

Britain's Early Warplanes

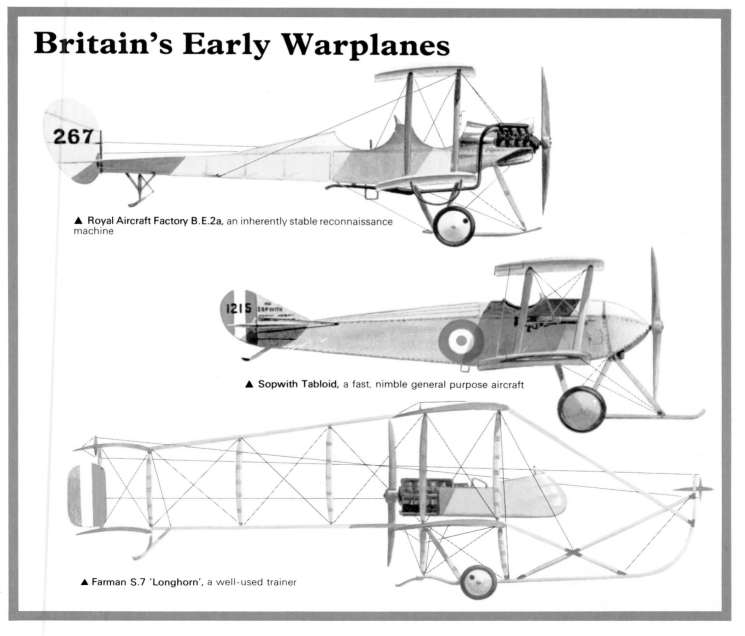

▲ Royal Aircraft Factory B.E.2a, an inherently stable reconnaissance machine

▲ Sopwith Tabloid, a fast, nimble general purpose aircraft

▲ Farman S.7 'Longhorn', a well-used trainer

Vulnerable Zeppelins

Be that as it may, at the beginning of the war in 1914, the airmen of both sides were ill-prepared to undertake anything but the most elementary reconnaissance missions, for which they also had not been trained. The largest of the air forces was that of Germany, which had been expanded considerably in the two years before the war. This air force was divided into two parts, the Imperial German Military Aviation Service and the Imperial German Naval Air Service. As can be seen from the table of comparative air strengths, much of Germany's expansion programme had been devoted to Zeppelins, from which much was expected in the way of tactical and strategic reconnaissance (for the great airships had considerable range and a good ceiling). But the Germans had consistently ignored the fact of the Zeppelins' vulnerability—each ship was filled with highly inflammable gas, and to obtain worthwhile tactical results, the ships would have to descend to the altitudes at which they could be hit by artillery fire.

Of Germany's aircraft strength, about half was made up of **Taube** (Dove) type monoplanes, a stable type developed by the Austrian Etrich and built under licence in Germany. The rest of Germany's machines were mostly **LVG**, **Aviatik** and **Albatros** tractor biplanes. The basic tactical formation was the *Fliegerabteilung* (Flight) of six aircraft. There were 41 of these, 34 assigned to army and corps commanders as *Feld-fliegerabteilungen* (Field Flights) and the other seven to important fortresses as *Festungfliegerabteilungen* (Fortress Flights). These last each had a strength of only four aircraft. Administrative control was exercised by the *Inspektion der Fliegertruppen* (Aviation Inspectorate) under Major Wilhelm Siegert. In March 1915 the growth in importance of the air force was reflected in the authorisation of the office of *Chef des Feldflieger* (Head of Field Aviation), the first of which was Major Hermann Thomsen.

Next in size to the German air force was that of France, the *Aviation Militaire*, which was run by the Directorate of Aeronautics at French General Headquarters. At the head of this was initially *Commandant* (Major) Barres, who was later succeeded by Commandant du Peuty. Tactical organisation was into *escadrilles* (squadrons) of six aircraft each for two-seater units and four aircraft each in single-seater units. Equipment was mostly manufactured by the firms Bleriot, Deperdussin, Farman, Morane-Saulnier, and Voisin.

The French go for agility

It is worth noting here that there was a considerable difference in the types of aircraft flown by the French and by the Germans. French machines fell into two basic categories: the light, agile single-seaters and the heavy, intrinsically stable two seaters. This reflects the dual nature of French aeronautical thinking. Before the arrival of Wilbur Wright on his tour of Europe in 1908, French aircraft had developed along the lines that the machine should be able to fly itself, and the pilot should merely steer it, as a chauffeur would a car. This philosophy had resulted in the lumbering types produced by Voisin and Farman. The other school of thought, which had been greatly influenced by the thinking of the Wright brothers, was that true flight could only be achieved in an aircraft that was basically unstable, and needed the pilot to fly it the whole time, as a rider controls his horse. This entirely different philosophy resulted in the more agile types produced by Deperdussin, Bleriot, and Morane-Saulnier. Another factor affecting the whole design philosophy was that of the type of engine to be used.

In the larger machines there was a tendency towards the conventional, water-cooled inline engine, which developed considerable power; in the lighter types the tendency was towards the rotary type developed by the Frenchman Seguin. In this the cylinders are disposed radially around the crankshaft, thus much reducing the length of the engine. Unlike the ordinary radial engine, however, in the rotary the cylinders revolve around the crankshaft, which is bolted to the airframe. The propeller is bolted to the revolving crank-

---

The two sides. Though World War I involved more than just the major powers they were in fact the only nations engaged in the war in the air.

The Alignments of the European Powers at the outbreak of World War 1

THE CENTRAL POWERS

STATES REMAINING NEUTRAL ON THE OUTBREAK OF WAR, AND LATER JOINING THE ALLIED POWERS

THE ALLIED POWERS

NEUTRAL STATES

0   200   400 MILES

case. Such rotary engines are light, mechanically simple and compact, which made them very popular with the designers of the 'rider' school. Rotary-powered types were noted for their manoeuvrability.

German attention to detail

German design philosophy had much in common with the French 'chauffeur' school. The petrol engine had been invented in Germany, and great strides had been made in turning it into a reliable, powerful propulsion unit. The Germans could thus concentrate on heavy, fast, but not particularly agile, tractor biplanes. The chief difference between the German and French schools was that the Germans paid far more attention to the detail design of aspects such as streamlining, whereas the French were still quite content with their ponderous pusher biplanes, with their lower speeds and complicated rigging.

The British air force was also divided into two sections, the Royal Flying Corps and the Royal Naval Air Service. The Royal Flying Corps, which had initially had a military and a naval wing, had been founded in April 1912, but in July 1914 the RNAS had been established as an independent air force under naval control. Basic tactical organisation of the RFC was into squadrons each of three flights of four aircraft. Above squadrons came wings and brigades. In the RNAS, organisation was into flights, squadrons and wings. Command of the RFC was at first in the hands of Brig.-General Sir David Henderson, but in August 1915 he was succeeded by Colonel Hugh Trenchard.

The aircraft flown by the RFC were probably the most mixed assortment of any in the air forces involved in the opening stages of the First World War. In August, 1914 the total operational strength of the British air arm amounted to 56 aircraft, mostly consisting of B.E. 2's of various types, **Avro 504's Farman Longhorns, Bleriot XI's** and sundry **Bristol Scouts,** Morane-Saulniers, and Sopwith Tabloids. Unlike the French and Germans, the British did not even attempt to assemble squadrons with anything like homogeneity of types, often allocating one fast single-seater or 'scout' to a squadron equipped otherwise with a miscellany of slower reconnaissance types.

Britain relies on France

As can easily be seen, the British relied heavily on French types, and this was particularly unfortunate. It meant in the opening stages of the war that the RFC was forced to rely on French production capacity for replacements and reinforcements at a time when it was stretched to capacity meeting the needs of its own air force. In fact it was not until 1916 that the British aircraft industry began to be able to meet the requirements of the ever-expanding

EARLY AVIATION RECORDS

	Speed	Distance	Altitude
1909	47.85 mph (Blériot on a Blériot XII)	145.59 miles (Henry Farman on a Farman)	1,486 ft (Latham on an Antoinette)
1910	68.2 mph (Leblanc on a 100-hp Blériot)	363.34 miles (Tabuteau on a 60-hp Maurice Farman)	10,476 ft (Legagneux on a 50-hp Blériot)
1911	82.73 mph (Nieuport on a Nieuport monoplane)	449.2 miles (Gobé on a Nieuport monoplane)	12,828 ft (Harros on a Blériot XI)
1912	108.12 mph (Védrines on a Deperdussin)	628.15 miles (Fourny on a Maurice Farman)	18,405 ft (Garros on a Morane-Saulnier)
1913	126.67 mph (Prévost on a Deperdussin)	634.54 miles (Seguin on a Henry Farman)	20,079 ft (Legagneux on a Nieuport)
1914	No official records.		

Germany's First 'War-birds'

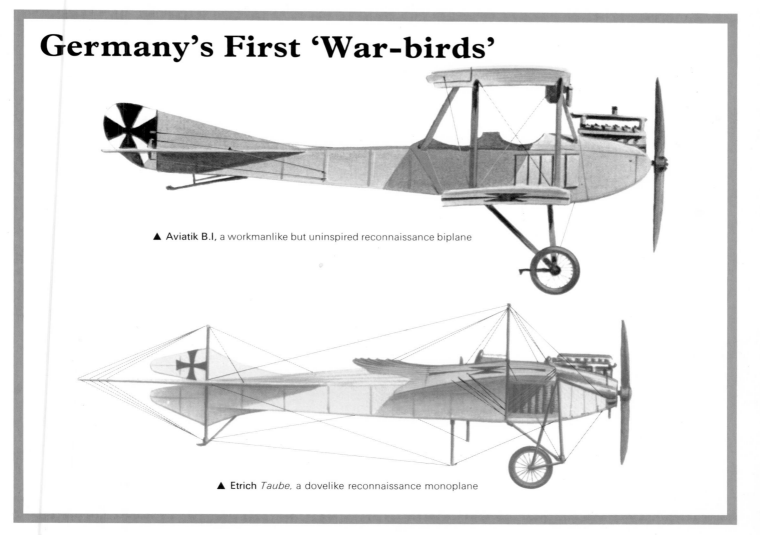

▲ Aviatik B.I, a workmanlike but uninspired reconnaissance biplane

▲ Etrich *Taube*, a dovelike reconnaissance monoplane

PERFORMANCE OF PRINCIPAL AIRCRAFT IN SERVICE 1914

Type	Engine	Max. Speed	Ceiling	Endurance	Load/armament	Function
Albatros B.II (Germany)	100-hp	65 mph at sea level	9,840 ft	4 hours	1 observer	Reconnaissance
Etrich 'Taube' (Austria-Hungary and Germany)	100-hp	71½ mph at sea level	9,840 ft	4 hours	1 observer	Reconnaissance
Blériot XI-2 (France)	70-hp	66 mph at sea level	13,000 ft	3½ hours	1 observer/ small arms	Reconnaissance and artillery spotting
Farman M.F.11 (France)	100-hp	66 mph at sea level	12,500 ft	3¾ hours	1 observer	Reconnaissance
Morane-Saulnier N (France)	80-hp	102 mph at 6,500 ft	13,125 ft	1½ hours	Pilot/ machine gun	Scout
Bristol Scout (Britain)	110-hp	110 mph at sea level	16,400 ft	2 hours	Pilot/ small arms	Scout
Royal Aircraft Factory B.E.2b (Britain)	70-hp	70 mph at sea level	10,000 ft	3 hours	Observer	Reconnaissance

The Machines of the *Aviation Militaire*

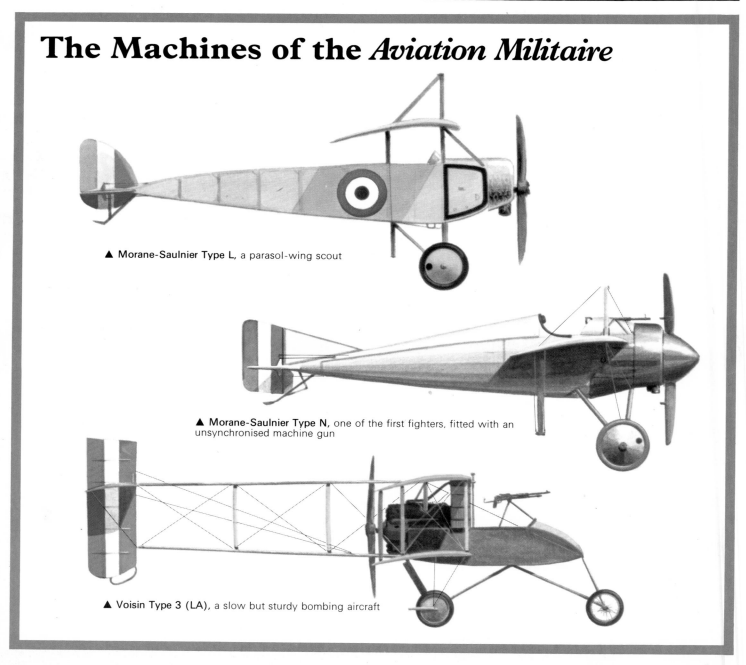

▲ Morane-Saulnier Type L, a parasol-wing scout

▲ Morane-Saulnier Type N, one of the first fighters, fitted with an unsynchronised machine gun

▲ Voisin Type 3 (LA), a slow but sturdy bombing aircraft

Royal Flying Corps.

Probably the best type of indigenous British design serving with the RFC was the B.E. 2, and even this provides evidence of the lack of thought in the design of aircraft. The type had been designed by Geoffrey de Havilland at the Royal Aircraft Factory at Farnborough in 1912 but, being a government-designed type, was not allowed to take part in the Military Aeroplane Competition at Larkhill in August 1912. The winner of the competition, a **Cody** biplane with 70 per cent more power, was clearly an inferior design, and the B.E. 2 was ordered into production.

The B.E. 2 was a clean tractor biplane, powered with a 70-hp Renault engine, and had at the time an excellent all-round performance. Anticipating that the type's function would be scouting, de Havilland designed his machine to be intrinsically stable, so that the observer might have a steady view. But the observer was placed in the front cockpit, from where his view was restricted by the wings above and below him, a multitude of bracing wires, and the fuselage around him. Had he been placed in the rear cockpit, his task could have been carried out more easily and more efficiently.

Yet by the standards of 1914 the **B.E. 2b**, the latest model, was still a good machine.

Air power in the balance. At the outbreak of the war, Britain and France were ill-equipped for an air war. Germany, and Russia were better prepared.

It was kept in production far too long, however, for it was incapable of being turned into the kind of fighting machine that was needed in 1915. The gunner-cum-observer was still positioned in the front cockpit, where he could not use his machine gun to advantage, and the type was too stable to be manoeuvred away from hostile planes. The story of the B.E. 2 is thus an example of the lack of foresight on the part of the authorities before the war. The aircraft did well what it was intended to do, but the whole specification was shortsighted.

Russia's bomber breakthrough

The air forces of the other countries involved in 1914 were small and ill-equipped. On the Allied side were Belgium and Russia. Belgium had no aircraft manufacturing capacity of her own and, after most of the country had been overrun by the Germans, France became the main source of supply for the small but efficient Belgian air force. As with the rest of Imperial Russia's war effort, her aircraft industry was poorly organised, but nonetheless capable of producing 40 aircraft a month, many of them French types built under license. So Russia's air force relied mainly on the French for the supply of its replacements.

However, it is worth noting that from the summer of 1916 on Russian designers did produce some interesting and capable machines such as the **Anatra D** and

Lyebed 12. However, most important of all was the gigantic **Sikorsky Ilya Mouromets**, the world's first four-engined bomber. This was evolved from the earlier **Bolshoi 'Baltiski'** and **Russkii Vityaz** types, and first flew in December 1911. It was ordered into production for the Imperial Russian Air Service, and proved a most successful type. Eighty were built, and of the six lost, only one was shot down, and then after disposing of three of its attackers. The type had a wing span of over 100 feet, and was capable of carrying a load of over 1,200 lbs of bombs—at a time when the aircraft operating over the Western Front found their performance severely reduced if their load included a machine gun.

On the German side was Austria-Hungary, which had only a small air force and aircraft industry. Yet although little of note was achieved by Austro-Hungarian airmen, several advanced types were produced in the foundering Hapsburg Empire. Among these were the **Lloyd C** type reconnaissance biplanes, and the **Phönix D** type biplane fighters.

These then were the air forces and the aircraft with which the combatants entered into the First World War. Some were excellent machines, and were to prove their worth in the months and years to come. Others were to prove totally inadequate under the stress of war and be quickly abandoned. It was to be a war of unforeseen dimensions and characteristics that were to help forge a weapon that, for better or worse, dominates the world today.

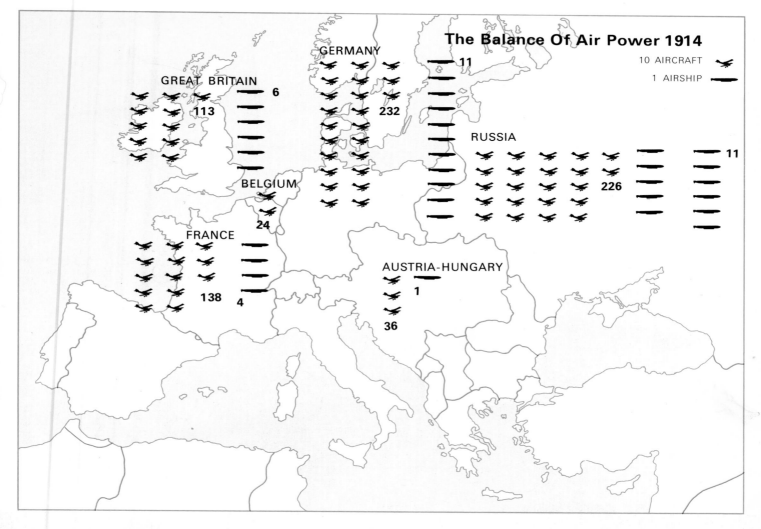

FIGHTING FORMATIONS

World War I was pre-planned by the Generals to last only six months, but their strategies took no account of the part that aircraft could play. Within months, aerial reconnaissance had proved decisive in halting the German advance. But fighting tactics were non-existent and it was not until 1916 that air warfare was dramatically changed from a spasmodic affair into a planned strategy.

The First World War was hardly three weeks old when the first victory in the history of air warfare was scored. On August 25 a flight of three RFC aircraft from No. 2 Squadron, under the command of Lieutenant H. D. Harvey-Kelly, spotted a German **Taube** reconnoitring the French lines south of Mons. Harvey-Kelly immediately closed in on the German machine and positioned himself just behind his rudder. The two other British machines took up station on each side of the German. No little disconcerted by the proximity of the British aircraft the pilot put down the nose of his machine and attempted to dive away. But the three Britons stuck to him. Unable to escape, the German pilot put his machine down in the first place he could and fled. The British also landed, and having searched in vain for the German set fire to his aircraft and took off.

It was a small beginning, perhaps a humorous one, but it was a clear portent that the war was going to spread to the air, and that as on land and at sea, it was to be the courage of the individual that was to be the deciding factor. Although this was the first air victory of the war, aircraft had already played a small, but significant, part in operations. As the Allies fell back in front of the great German drive towards Paris, the British decided to make a stand at Mons. A short, furious battle followed, and the British halted the Germans on August 22. During the night, however, the French to the south of the British pulled back, leaving the British flank exposed. On the morning of the next day the Germans found this gap in the Allied line and started to push on through it. A British reconnaissance machine spotted what was happening, luckily, and was able to report back in time to allow the British Expeditionary Force to disengage and pull back before it was outflanked and cut-off.

It was to be this type of humdrum work that became the air forces' most vital task in the years to come. Although later machines were able to carry a reasonable bomb-load, little could be done apart from

local tactical damage, and so reconnaissance and spotting for the artillery continued to occupy the time of most squadrons. Although the fighter pilots achieved far greater fame and publicity, it must always be borne in mind that the role of the fighter was essentially defensive in the First World War.

The most important targets

They either protected their own reconnaissance types from the attentions of the enemy's fighters, or, conversely, attempted to destroy the enemy's reconnaissance aircraft to prevent information about their own side's dispositions and intentions from being relayed back to the enemy's high command. It was, therefore, the lowly reconnaissance machines that were the most important targets of the war. Although greater 'glamour' has become attached to the pilots who excelled in fighter *versus* fighter combat (and admittedly it was the most difficult form of air combat), it was the airmen who manned the two-seater reconnaissance types who served their countries the better. Nor was it easy to shoot down a two-seater: many of them were agile, well-armed machines, and many a fighter pilot came to grief by underestimating the defensive firepower of what he considered an easy victim.

Although the reconnaissance over Mons had paid-off handsomely, there was to be a similar occasion on September 3 which had much more far-reaching implications. For on this date a French reconnaissance machine spotted that the Germans were no longer racing round the west of Paris, but had cut inside the capital to the east and thus exposed their right flank to a French counterblow from the capital itself. The result was the all-important battle of the Marne, which halted the Germans at the furthest point they reached into France during the whole war. The Germans now pulled back in their turn, and after two months of desperate marching and fighting established themselves along the line that

with a few variations of a minor nature was to constitute the notorious Western Front of the First World War.

With the establishment of a static front line, the task of aircraft became at once both more easy and more difficult. It became more easy as bases could be set up immediately behind the important sectors of the front, and pilots soon became familiar with their sectors, thus being able to spot anything out of the ordinary with greater ease. It became more difficult as the opposition was able to predict where and when reconnaissance machines would cross the lines, and could thus position their anti-aircraft guns (now becoming an increasingly important weapon) and fighter patrols to inflict the maximum damage on the intruders. One other factor must always be remembered when considering the air operations on the Western Front in the First World War.

Blowing in the wind

The front line ran basically from north to south from the Belgian coast near Ostend to the Swiss frontier near Basle, with the German armies on the eastern side of the lines. The prevailing wind, particularly over the northern part of the line, where most air operations took place, is a westerly one, and this had considerable importance. In the days when average aircraft speeds were as low as 60 to 70 miles an hour, Allied aircraft returning from the German side of the lines often had to battle against a head wind that reduced their speed over the ground to perhaps only 30 miles an hour. If the aircraft were damaged, air speed could be much lower, when speed in returning to base with a wounded crew member or leaking fuel tanks was a matter of life and death.

The wind also tended to drift patrols over the lines, where the German fighters could pounce on them from a position of superiority. It is clear, therefore, that the prevailing westerly wind was greatly detrimental to the Allied effort. It was, of course, very useful to the Germans, who would normally have the aid of the wind in returning to their own side of the lines. It was not an infrequent sight to men on the ground to see Allied aircraft struggling back to the west at 40 miles an hour with German machines going the other way at 100 miles an hour.

As the Allies and the Germans struggled to secure the greater advantage after the Battle of the Marne, there occurred on

Great Fighters of the War

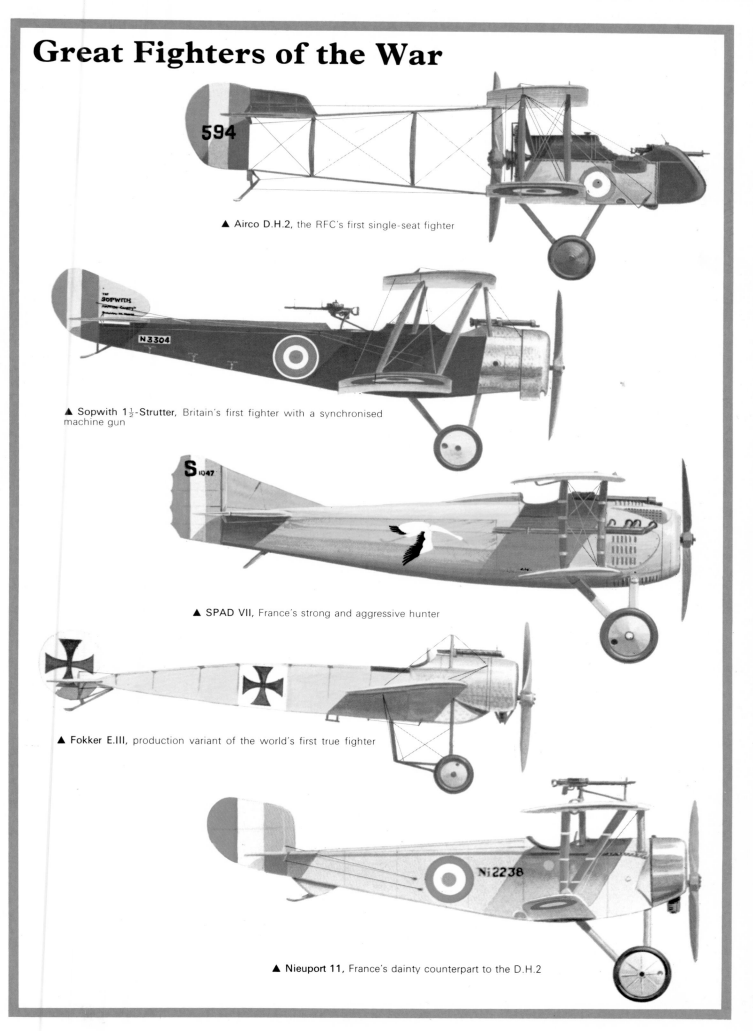

▲ **Airco D.H.2,** the RFC's first single-seat fighter

▲ **Sopwith 1½-Strutter,** Britain's first fighter with a synchronised machine gun

▲ **SPAD VII,** France's strong and aggressive hunter

▲ **Fokker E.III,** production variant of the world's first true fighter

▲ **Nieuport 11,** France's dainty counterpart to the D.H.2

October 5 the first true aerial combat in which the machine gun played the decisive part. It had become clear in the opening weeks of the war that aerial combat was going to take place, and the French had taken the initiative in providing armament for their larger two-seaters whose performance would not be unduly handicapped by the extra weight and drag of a machine gun. As yet there was no provision for a fixed machine gun fired by the pilot, so the gun carried was a flexibly-mounted one in the charge of the observer. On the 5th a French **Voisin**, piloted by Joseph Frantz, with Sergeant Louis Quenault, a mechanic, as observer, spotted a German **Aviatik** two-seater reconnoitring the French lines. Frantz closed in on the interloper and after a short battle Quenault succeeded in downing the German machine.

Right: An Airco de Havilland 2 makes a low pass over the camera. This type equipped the RFC's first homogeneous fighter squadron early in 1916, and soon achieved fame for its part in eliminating the 'Fokker Scourge'. In the absence of an interrupter gear, de Havilland designed a pusher biplane of compact dimensions, with the Lewis gun on a semi-flexible (later fixed) mount in the front of the nacelle. The D.H.2 was only an interim measure, but was kept in service well into 1917 for lack of a suitable replacement.

Below right: Major Lanoe G. Hawker, VC. While a Captain, Hawker had won his VC for shooting down three armed German machines with a carbine from his Bristol Scout. Flying a D.H.2, he became the 11th victim to fall to Germany's rising star of 1916, Manfred von Richthofen.

Left: The final word—a Bristol F.2B. It had both forward and rearward firing guns.
Below: The next stage in evolution. Tractors replace pushers and a Lewis gun is fitted to the top wing of a Nieuport to fire over the propeller disc.

Another problem that was becoming increasingly difficult was that of aircraft identification, which had been virtually non-existent at the beginning of the war. But with growing numbers of aircraft operating over the front, it was now important to distinguish the aircraft of one power from those of another. This was necessary not only so that aircrew could tell machines of their own side from those of the other, but also to prevent troops on the ground from firing at their own machines. Infantry, however, had the disconcerting habit throughout the war of firing indiscriminately at any aircraft that flew near to them, regardless of markings.

The French had by October solved their problem by ordering that the traditional

Early British Fighters

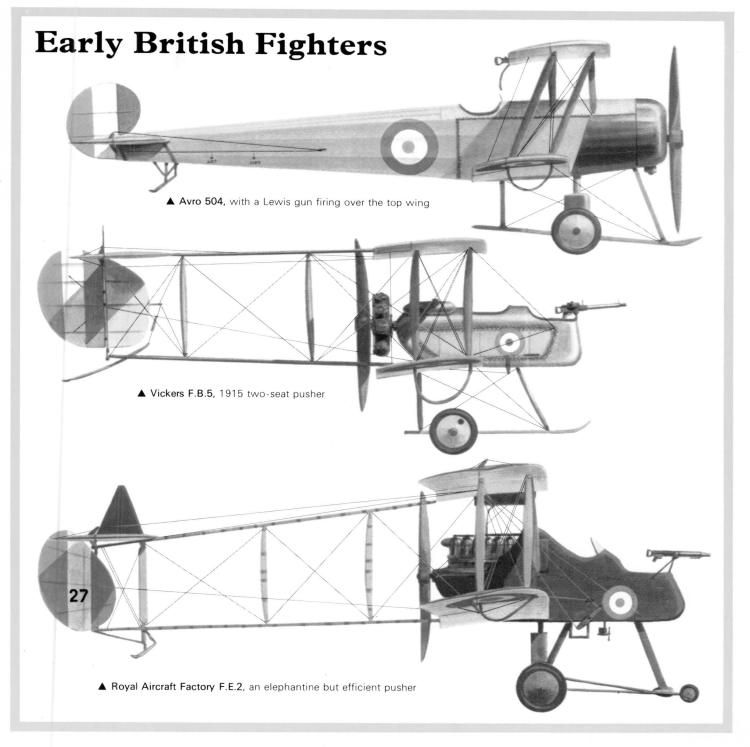

▲ Avro 504, with a Lewis gun firing over the top wing

▲ Vickers F.B.5, 1915 two-seat pusher

▲ Royal Aircraft Factory F.E.2, an elephantine but efficient pusher

cocarde (cockade) of red, white and blue be painted on the wings of their aircraft. The Germans also solved their problem by painting a black cross *patée* on the wings and rudder. The British had a harder time of it. At first a small Union Jack was painted in easily seen positions, and when this was found to be unrecognisable, BEF headquarters ordered that the largest possible flag be painted across the full chord of the wings. At a distance, though, it was possible to confuse this large Union Jack marking with the German cross *patée* insignia. The British therefore decided to adopt the roundel type of marking like the French, but with the order of the colours reversed to red in the centre, white in the middle, and blue on the outside. These markings were finalised in November 1914.

Armed encounters, usually indecisive, were by now becoming relatively frequent, and considerable thought was being devoted to the problems of air combat. It was realised that the best solution was a forward-firing gun, but in tractor aircraft the propeller was in the way. The obvious solution was to fit a machine gun in the forward part of the nacelle of a pusher type, such as the Voisin flown by Franz and the British **Vickers F.B. 5 Gunbus**. This was the first aircraft to be designed as a fighting machine from the start, and was a compact two-seater, of pusher biplane configuration. The observer was accommodated in the front of the boot-like nacelle, and armed with a .303-inch Lewis light machine gun on a flexible mounting.

The Lewis gun was to be one of the most important aircraft guns of the war, and was an excellent weapon for its time. It had been designed by Colonel Isaac Lewis, an American, just after the turn of the century, and was a light air-cooled weapon. It was fed by a 47–90-round drum magazine mounted on top of the receiver. With its barrel jacket removed, its light weight and handiness made it an excellent aircraft gun. Three other guns were very widely used in aircraft during the First World War.

First there was the gun that became the standard fixed weapon on Allied aircraft, the .303-inch Vickers gun. This was a lightened version of the Vickers machine gun that was standard issue in the British army. As the speed of the aircraft was sufficient to cool the gun by air, water was not needed in the barrel jacket, which was retained to strengthen the barrel. Ammunition feed was from a 250-round belt.

On the Central Powers' side, the two guns most frequently used were the 7.92-mm Parabellum as the flexible gun and the 7.92-mm MBO8, often known as the Spandau, as the fixed gun. This latter was, like the Vickers, a modified version of the standard infantry machine gun, altered to lighten it for aircraft use. Not only was the water omitted, but the barrel jacket also had large holes cut in it to reduce its weight yet further. Both the Parabellum and the Spandau were belt fed.

The first F.B. 5 landed in France on February 5, 1915, and the first British squadron, No. 11, to be fully equipped with this aircraft arrived for service on July 25, 1915. But at the time that the first of these fighters arrived in France in February, an event of much greater impact was about to take place.

Garros—the first 'ace'

Serving in the French air force at the time was Roland Garros, a celebrated pre-war aerobatic pilot. He was anxious to take a more aggressive part in the war, but the aircraft of the time did not allow this. He realised that the future of fighter aircraft lay with the fixed machine gun firing along the axis of the aircraft. He also remembered that a friend of his, Raymond Saulnier, the aircraft manufacturer, had conducted experiments before the war with an interrupter system. This was intended to allow a machine gun to fire through the disc swept by the propeller by halting the firing of the gun by mechanical means whenever a propeller blade was in front of the machine gun's muzzle. The French authorities were impressed by the idea and lent Saulnier a Hotchkiss machine gun with which to conduct his trials.

All went well except for the problem of hang-fire rounds. These resulted from the inconsistent manufacture of rounds, and meant that some rounds were fired very

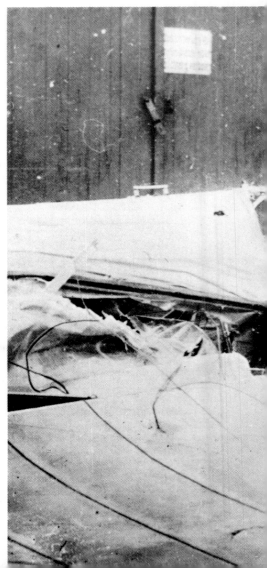

Above: A Voisin LA (Type 3) bomber. The LA was the mainstay of the French bombing force in the early part of the war and one of the main targets for the German fighters over the Western Front. An LA scored the first French air victory on October 5, 1914.

Above right: A prime fighter target. A German observation balloon is moved into position behind the front.

Above far right: Recognition roundels. An RFC groundcrew at work. During the first months of the war identification of friend from foe proved very troublesome, and it was only by a slow process of trial and error that satisfactory markings were found by both sides.

Right: Boelcke's brightest rival. Max Immelmann stands beside the wreckage of his seventh victory.

Far right: The ultimate in *Eindeckers*. Immelmann's three-gun E.IV, which did not prove at all successful.

shortly after they were meant to, with the result that the propeller's other blade might have arrived in front of the muzzle in the interim. So Saulnier fitted wedge-shaped steel deflectors behind the blade to ward off any such rounds. Although similar experiments conducted by Franz Schneider of the German LVG firm were also fairly successful, both sets of experiments were discontinued as a result of the problems with hang-fire rounds.

Early in 1915, Garros went to Saulnier and requested that his aircraft be fitted with the interrupter gear. After much discussion, however, it was decided to omit the interrupter gear and rely on the deflector plates on the propeller blades to ward off any rounds that might otherwise hit them. It was a short-term and very dangerous measure, as the impact of the bullets hitting the blades would inevitably impose asymetric strains on the engine and cause it to fail.

Nevertheless, Garros had his **Morane-Saulnier Type L** (not N as is often quoted) parasol monoplane fitted out and waited eagerly to get into action. His chance came on April 1, 1915, when he approached an **Albatros** two-seater head-on and sent it crashing down. In less than three weeks he disposed of another four German aircraft in the same way, and so became the first fighter 'ace'. This was a term introduced by the French to signify a pilot who had shot down five or more aircraft.

Fokker engineers a change

On April 18, however, Garros' brief career as an ace came to an end. Flying over the German lines his engine was hit and stopped, and the wind carried Garros down over the German lines, where he was captured. As his brief but successful career had received considerable coverage in the French press, the Germans were well aware of the value of their prisoner. More importantly, Garros had not been able to destroy the most important part of his aircraft, the system of deflector plates.

The German authorities immediately sent the forward part of the fuselage to the Dutch designer Anthony Fokker, who was working for the Germans, with instructions to copy it. Fokker's engineers quickly came up with a proper interrupter gear, however, and Fokker persuaded the authorities to allow him to try out an experimental version on his **M.5k** tractor monoplane, using a Parabellum machine gun. These trials were successful, and an improved version of the type, to be known as the **Eindecker** (Monoplane) **I** was ordered into production. The interrupter gear itself was the model of simplicity: a cam at the end of a mechanical linkage was struck by a spur on the propeller just before a blade passed in front of the gun's muzzle. The cam's movement was trans-

mitted via the linkage to the gun's action, which was blocked until the cam returned to its original position once the blade had passed.

The Germans wished Fokker to give a front line demonstration of the new fighter himself, but he refused to do so on the grounds that he was a neutral, and so service

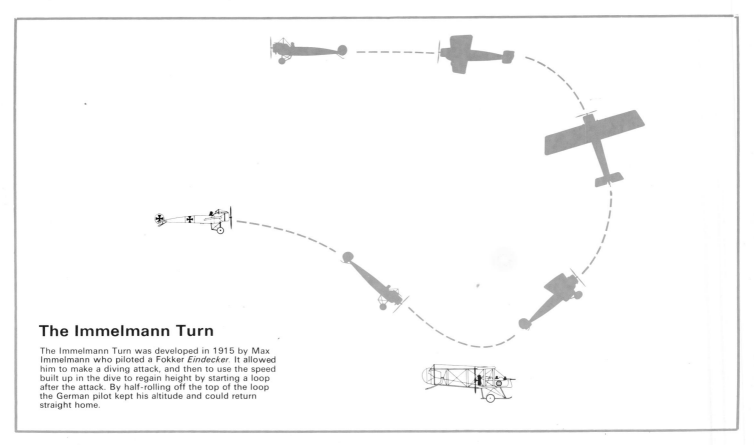

The Immelmann Turn

The Immelmann Turn was developed in 1915 by Max Immelmann who piloted a Fokker *Eindecker*. It allowed him to make a diving attack, and then to use the speed built up in the dive to regain height by starting a loop after the attack. By half-rolling off the top of the loop the German pilot kept his altitude and could return straight home.

Above left: A Fokker Eindecker. An Eindekker begins its dive down onto an Allied aircraft. Although not a good fighter in itself, it had the very considerable advantage of a fixed gun capable of firing through the disc swept by the propeller.

Above: Nieuport 11 *Bébé* fighters. On this French counter to the Fokker the problem of a fixed gun without an interrupter gear was solved by fitting it to the top wing to fire over the propeller of the nimble little fighter.

Right: Fighting trio. Albatros D.III and V biplane, and Fokker Dr.I triplane fighters line a German airfield.

Below: A miscellany of Allied types. From front to back these are: Morane-Saulnier P, S.E.5, D.H.5, F.E.2, and possibly an S.E.5a. The rapid development of aircraft meant a profusion of types in service at all times.

pilots tested the new weapon in action. The EI was underpowered when it appeared with an 80-hp rotary in the summer of 1915, so an improved model, the **EII**, became the first production model to be built in any quantity. This had a 100-hp rotary, and entered service in September 1915. Early examples had a single Parabellum gun, but a further development, the **EIII**, had one, and later two, Spandau guns. Not being built as an intentionally agile fighter, the E series was inevitably a stopgap, whose only real advantage lay in the possession of a fixed machine gun. However, this new weapon soon came into the hands of one of the most influential and able figures in the history of air warfare, *Hauptmann* (Captain) Oswald Boelcke, who had made something of an impression in Germany by his aggressive attitude towards Allied aircraft. In November 1915 he was ordered to visit the Fokker works at Schwerin, where he saw one of the first **EIV**'s, the last version of the Eindecker, with a 160-hp rotary engine. After some initial disappointments as a result of engine failures, Boelcke claimed his first victim with an EIV on January 5, 1916. Previously he had flown the EI which Fokker had used in demonstration flights, and later an EII.

It is with Boelcke, and his great rival *Leutnant* (Lieutenant) Max Immelmann, that the history of air fighting really begins. Up to the end of 1915 air combats had been spasmodic, unplanned affairs. This was all to change now. Boelcke realised the importance of carefully planned tactics and concerted action by a number of pilots, and was soon placed in a position in which he could implement his ideas. The era of the 'Fokker Scourge' was about to break on the unprepared Allies, and with it a period of total dominance of the air by the Germans.

The Germans at the same time had devoted considerable thought to the sort of aircraft that would be needed to carry on the air war in the future. The most important type decided upon was the general purpose C category, which specified an armed two-seater tractor biplane, powered by an engine of more than 150-hp. The specification was carefully thought out, and resulted

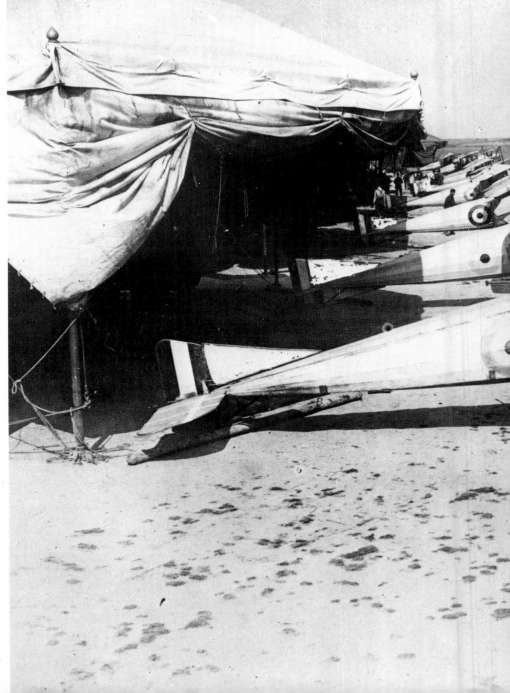

Bottom left: A Fokker Dr.I in 1918. Although this was after the heyday of the type, it was still used by pilots of elite units such as *Jasta* 12, as was the machine illustrated.

Left: Morane-Saulnier parasols of an RFC unit. Such types, with their excellent field of vision downwards, proved to be admirably suited to the photographic reconnaissance role.

Above left: The Albatros D.XI. This ultimate in German rotary-engined fighters was produced in 1918, but was inferior to most of its rivals, its one outstanding feature being its rate of climb: 16,400 feet in 15 minutes.

Above: The Fokker D.VII. This was the best German fighter of the war. The one shown here was evaluated by the RAF after the war. The D.VII was fast, agile and had a superlative performance at high altitudes making it a formidable opponent even in unskilled hands.

in a series of C class aircraft that were to stand Germany in good stead for the rest of the war. As a result of the issue of this specification in the spring of 1915, types such as the **Albatros CI** began to appear in the early summer of 1915. The type was a development of the earlier **BII**, but with the positions of the pilot and observer reversed to put the latter in the rear seat where he had a better field of fire for his flexible machine gun. This was a practice that came to Allied types far too late. The CI was powered by engines ranging from 150 to 180 hp, had a top speed of 90 miles an hour and an endurance of 2½ hours.

At the same time the Allies had largely to make do with sterling but obsolescent types such as the Royal Aircraft Factory **B.E. 2c** and **F.E. 2b**, the **Caudron GIII** and **GIV**, the **Nieuport 10**, and the **Voisin Type 3**. These were aircraft that had been designed before the war. But whereas the Germans suffered from much the same problem, they at least had taken more thought for the future as well as trying to update the aircraft they already had and to provide adequate tactics for them.

BOMBING PATTERNS FOR DISASTER

In August 1914 a handful of French Voisins made the war's first bombing attack. The other powers soon followed suit and from the build-up came the first reprisal raids against civilian targets. Tactics and counter-tactics were developed until the Italians were able to mount a 200-plane attack on Pola in 1918. In those four years were laid the patterns for later celebrated heroics and notorious catastrophies.

Bombing operations in the First World War fell very naturally into two distinct classes: tactical and what the pundits of the day tried to call strategic. Tactical bombing was the logical descendant of the battlefield reconnaissance that had been going on since the earliest days of the war—if one can detect enemy concentrations or bottlenecks, why not attempt to destroy them with bombing? What was called strategic bombing (psychological bombing to break the will of civilians might be a better term) was a later development, and was based on two distinct types of weapon—the airship, in the form of the Zeppelin, and the 'heavy' bomber. The Zeppelin did have a considerable psychological effect when it first went into action over Great Britain, but as fighter defences were strengthened, the losses to the Zeppelin fleet became unacceptable, and the Germans joined the other major powers in concentrating their efforts on heavy bombers. There are very few instances of strategic raids that had any significant results, but these First World War operations did open the way for future developments.

Bombing operations started very early in the war. Equipment was crude, and results poor, but it is clear that at least two nations, France and Russia, had realised the value that might be obtained from a concentrated effort in the way of bombing. By the end of 1914 the French had begun to assemble a a force of **Voisin** bombers to attack targets on the east bank of the Rhine, and the Russians were stepping up their efforts to get a fleet of **Ilya Mouromets** bombers into action bombing German targets in East Prussia. In fact it was the French who made the first bombing attack of the war on August 14, 1914, when several Voisins attacked the German Zeppelin sheds near Metz, from which army Zeppelins had been carrying out reconnaissance missions over Verdun. The day before the Germans had

sent a **Taube** to bomb Paris, but only with propaganda leaflets.

The importance of **Zeppelins** for scouting purposes was fully realised by the British, for the Zeppelins operated by the German navy posed a very considerable threat to the ship-to-ship superiority of the Royal Navy over the Imperial German Navy. With the help of Zeppelin reconnaissance, it might be possible for the Germans to avoid a major encounter with the British, but still be able to pick off elements detached from the Grand Fleet. Therefore early in the war it was decided to try to eliminate the Zeppelins at their bases in Germany.

As it was a matter of naval concern, the raids were carried out by the RNAS. The first went in on September 22, 1914, when four aircraft attacked the Zeppelin sheds at Cologne and Düsseldorf. Only one pilot got through to his target, and the one bomb that exploded missed the sheds. Another raid was sent in on October 6, when two **Sopwith Tabloids**, fitted with 20-lb bombs, again attacked the Düsseldorf sheds, destroying the German army's LZ IX.

The navy felt that better results might be obtained by bombing the Zeppelin works at Friedrichshafen on the Swiss frontier, and three **Avro 504's** were dispatched to this target on November 21. The aircraft penetrated over a hundred miles into Germany, no mean feat in itself, but the Zeppelin works escaped with only minor damage. The Swiss authorities claimed that the British aircraft had violated their neutrality, however, and it was decided to abandon any further ideas about attacks on Friedrichshafen.

The first aircraft carriers

The last raid of this campaign took place on December 25, 1914, when seven seaplanes were launched against the sheds at Cuxhaven. These had been ferried to a

The versatile R.E.8. This was the standard British general-purpose aircraft of 1917–18. It was used in reconnaissance roles, for artillery spotting, even on escort duties, in addition to its use as a light bomber.

point off the German coast in converted cross-Channel steamers, which thus became the world's first aircraft-carriers. Unfortunately for the British, none of the seaplanes found its target.

This was the end of the naval campaign against the Zeppelin until 1918. On July 19 of that year, two **Sopwith Camels** from the new carrier *Furious* attacked the sheds at Tondern. This time 50-lb bombs were used, and the two Zeppelins L 54 and 60 were destroyed in an attack that had taken the Germans completely by surprise.

Although there was a three-and-a-half year gap on the navy operations against the Zeppelin, the RNAS did not give up the idea of bombing entirely. Indeed it was this service that ordered into production the first British heavy bomber, the **Handley Page O/100**, 'The Bloody Paralyser'. The first of these large two-engined biplanes flew at the end of 1915, and deliveries to the RNAS started in September 1916, operations from France starting in November. The O/100 was powered by two 250-hp Rolls Royce Eagle engines, had a speed of 85 miles an hour, a range of 700 miles, and a bomb-load of up to 2,000 lbs. The type was succeeded in production by the O/400, which served from mid-1918 with the Royal Air Force—the new independent service that resulted from the amalgamation of the Royal Flying Corps and the Royal Naval Air Service on April 1, 1918. The O/400 was basically similar to the O/100, but had more powerful 360-hp engines and generally better performance. It was with these two types of heavy bombers that the newly formed RAF undertook most of their long-range attacks into Germany.

Purely tactical bombing along the front lines continued with increasing severity and results throughout the war. It was not a spectacular campaign, but played a very real part in the course of the war. More emphasis was placed on this side of air warfare by the Allies at first, and they were the ones to introduce the specialised light day bomber in the form of the **Sopwith 1½-Strutter**. This was one of the most important aircraft of the war, and was the first British aircraft to be fitted with a fixed forward-firing gun.

Triple-threat 1½-Strutter!

The 1½-Strutter entered service early in 1916, and was immediately successful as a fighter (as which it carried a gunner in the rear cockpit with a flexible Lewis gun), a bomber (as a single-seater), and as a two-seater reconnaissance machine. With the arrival of newer German fighters in the late summer of 1916, the 1½-Strutter was relegated to bombing and reconnaissance operations. Power was supplied by a 110-hp Clerget rotary, and performance figures included a speed of 106 miles an hour, a ceiling of 15,000 feet, and an endurance of 4½ hours. It was a delightful aircraft to fly, and such were its merits that the French built 4,200 of the type under licence.

Although officially a two-seater, its bomb-load with a crew of two was only 130 lbs, so the RNAS pioneered the version as a single-seat bomber carrying 224 lbs of bombs. The 1½-Strutter was obsolescent by the spring of 1917, but it had showed the Allies what might be achieved by a carefully designed tactical bomber.

The 1½-Strutter was succeeded in service as a day bomber by the **Airco D.H. 4** designed by Geoffrey de Havilland, who had designed the **B.E. 2** series. The D.H. 4 was a fast, sturdy and well armed machine, and entered service in the middle of 1917. Power was supplied by a 375-hp Rolls Royce Eagle VII inline, and speed was 143 miles an hour, which was more than most German, or for that matter Allied, fighters could achieve even by the end of the war. The D.H. 4 was produced in large numbers for the British air forces and also for the Americans, who entered the war on April 16, 1917.

Armament comprised one or two fixed Vickers guns and one or two flexible Lewis guns, and a bomb-load of up to 460 lbs. The only failing of the D.H. 4 as a tactical aircraft was the length of fuselage between the pilot and the gunner, which made

Above right: Personal delivery. This was the style of the first 18 months of the war. Throughout the period 1914–1918, lack of accuracy was the main worry of bombing crews and the advocates of strategic bombing.

PERFORMANCE OF PRINCIPAL BOMBERS IN SERVICE 1916

Type	Engine	Max. Speed	Ceiling	Endurance	Load/ armament	Function
Sopwith 1½-Strutter British	Clerget rotary, 110-hp	106 mph at sea level	17,000 ft	4¼ hours	One Lewis and one Vickers machine gun and 12 small bombs	Two-seat Fighter Light bomber
Handley Page O/100 British	Two Rolls Royce Eagle II inlines, 250-hp each	85 mph at sea level	circ. 8,500 ft	700 miles	Up to four Lewis machine guns and 1,800 lbs of bombs	Bomber
Gotha GIII German	Two Mercedes DIVa inlines, 260-hp each	92½ mph at 13,120 ft	20,500 ft	500 miles	Two Parabellum machine guns and up to 1,100 lbs of bombs	Bomber
AEG GIV German	Two Mercedes DIVa inlines, 260-hp each	103 mph at sea level	14,760 ft	4–5 hours	Two Parabellum machine guns and up to 880 lbs of bombs	Bomber
Voisin Type 3 French	Canton-Unné water-cooled radial, 120-hp	70 mph at sea level	11,000 ft	125 miles	One Hotchkiss machine gun and up to 124 lbs of bombs	Bomber
Caproni Ca33 Italian	Three Isotta-Fraschini V4B inlines, 150-hp each	85 mph at sea level	13,400 ft	3½ hours	Up to four Revelli machine guns and up to 1,000 lbs of bombs	Bomber
Sikorsky RBVZ Ilya Mouromets IM-V Russian	Four RBVZ inlines, 150-hp each	80 mph at sea level	11,500 ft	5½ hours	Three machine guns and up to 1,870 lbs of bombs	Heavy bomber/ Recce.

Bombers of 1917

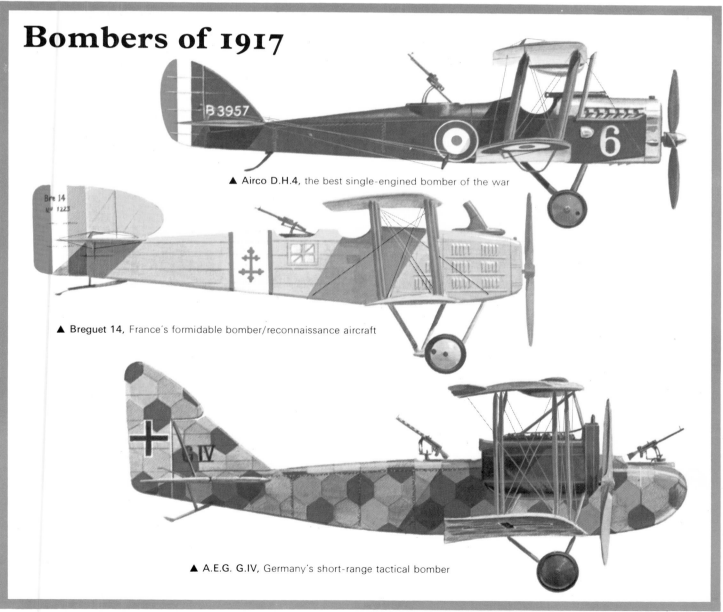

▲ **Airco D.H.4,** the best single-engined bomber of the war

▲ **Breguet 14,** France's formidable bomber/reconnaissance aircraft

▲ **A.E.G. G.IV,** Germany's short-range tactical bomber

communication between the two all but impossible. This fault was rectified on the **D.H. 9,** which entered service late in 1917, but lack of suitable engine meant that the new machine was in all other respects inferior to the earlier D.H. 4. This failing with the engine was in turn rectified in the **D.H. 9A,** which entered service in September 1918. Speed was still lower than the D.H. 4's at 123 miles an hour, but the bomb-load was increased to 660 lbs and the continuous cockpits of the D.H. 9 were retained.

Other British aircraft, such as the **Armstrong Whitworth F.K. 8,** the **Royal Aircraft Factory F.E. 2** and **R.E. 8,** and the **Martinsyde Elephant** were also used as bombers, but their primary roles were more in the way of reconnaissance and fighter operations. Fighters also carried bombs, 20-pounders, and these were used to keep the enemy's heads down and then support advancing troops with machine gun fire. The last operations went under the name of contact patrols, and were instituted during the 1st Battle of the Somme on July 1916. The High Command had found, in those days before the arrival of the 'walkie-talkie', that it was impossible to ascertain the position of front line troops exactly, and so it sometimes happened that conflicting orders were given, or an artillery barrage called down on friendly troops. So aircraft were ordered to patrol the front line and

Above left: The D.H.9A. It was a worthy successor to the D.H.4 and the less successful D.H.9.
Left: The Handley-Page 0/400. This was Britain's main heavy bomber of the war. The aircraft illustrated was one of No. 207 (Bomber) Squadron's complement of aircraft.

ZEPPELIN PERFORMANCE FIGURES

Type	Engine	Max. Speed	Cubic capacity	Useful lift*
Zeppelin Type m (6 built)	Three Maybach C-X inlines, 210-hp each	52 mph	794,500 cubic ft	20,250 lbs
Zeppelin Type p (10 built)	Four Maybach C-X inlines, 201-hp each	60 mph	1,126,400 cubic ft	34,000 lbs
Zeppelin Type q (5 built)	Four Maybach HSLu inlines, 240-hp each	57½ mph	1,264,100 cubic ft	39,000 lbs
Zeppelin Type r (15 built)	Six Maybach HSLu inlines, 240-hp each	64 mph	1,949,600 cubic ft	68,000 lbs
Zeppelin Type v (10 built)	Five Maybach HSLu inlines, 240-hp each	66 mph	1,977,360 cubic ft	85,000 lbs
Zeppelin Type w (2 built)	Five Maybach HSLu inlines, 240-hp each	64 mph	2,418,700 cubic ft	114,500 lbs

*The weight (including crew, fuel and armament) that could be lifted after the weight of the ship has been subtracted.

report back to H.Q. the position of front line elements. Over the front line at low altitudes, these fighters were in the perfect position to take immediate action to help their own ground forces. It was a dangerous and wearying type of flying, but proved of great importance both to the troops at the front and the High Command behind them.

The French aircraft most commonly used for this type of tactical bombing was the excellent **Breguet 14** two-seater, which began to enter service in September 1917. It was powered by a 220-hp (later 300-hp) Renault inline, had a top speed of 121 miles an hour, a ceiling of 19,000 feet, and an endurance of nearly three hours. Armament comprised up to four machine guns and 520 lbs of bombs.

The Germans did not at first develop a specialised battlefield bomber, but preferred to concentrate on the longer-range types, leaving the battlefield to the general purpose C types. These soon proliferated into such successful aircraft as the **Albatros C. VII** and **X,** the latter of which could carry a small bomb-load, the **DFW C V,** the **Hannover CL II,** the **LVG C V** (which could carry up to 250 lbs of bombs), and the **Rumpler C IV** and **VII,** which could carry up to 220 lbs of bombs.

Italy had entered the war on May 24, 1915 on the side of the Allies, and she was a keen exponent of the virtues of tactical bombing, producing such notable designs as the

SIA & B, which was capable of 124 miles an hour and carried a bomb-load of 550 lbs, and the **Ansaldo SVA 5**. However, her greatest part in the development of air power in the First World War lay in the field of strategic heavy bombing.

Outcry against reprisal raids

The start of long-range heavy bomber attacks came in 1915 when the French, who had been building up their bomber force since the German attacks on Paris in September 1914, started to penetrate into Germany. The force was led by *Capitaine Happe*, and was made up of clumsy-looking Voisins. On June 13 a raid was launched against Karlsruhe, and one machine reached Munich on November 17. At first all such raids were directed against purely military targets such as marshalling yards and munitions factories, but after several German raids had hit towns that the French had declared open, the French started a deliberate policy of reprisal raids on civilian centres in towns such as Karlsruhe. Later, in 1915, came the first Zeppelin raids on London. On September 8, the LZ 13 dropped several bombs, killing 13 people and wounding 87.

The outcry was enormous, although at the same time many thousands a day were being lost on the Western Front with far less notice being taken. Aerial defences for

the British capital were immediately strengthened, although, initially, this did not slow down the increasing frequency of German raids. However, as the defences were improved, losses to the Zeppelin, which were by the standards of the day enormously expensive weapons, increased to the point of diminishing returns. It was clear that a more rational way of striking at London would have to be found—in the form of aeroplanes.

The first of these to bomb London had been an **LVG C II** on November 28, 1916, but soon a superior type was made available in some numbers. This was the twin-engined **Gotha G IV**, which began to operate over British soil in June 1917. This bomber was powered by two 260-hp Mercedes inlines, and had a top speed of 90 miles an hour. Ceiling was over 21,000 feet and range more than 300 miles, and a bomb-load of 1,100 lbs could be carried. More importantly, perhaps, the bombers could fly in formation and provide covering fire for each other with their two pivoted Parabellum machine guns. This was impossible for the Zeppelins. Although raids by the latter continued into 1918, the brunt of the offensive was from now on borne by bombers, initially the Gothas, but later the huge **Zeppelin-Staaken R VI**. This four-engined giant had a wing-span of 138 feet 6 inches, and was capable of lifting 2,200 lbs of bombs for a raid over London.

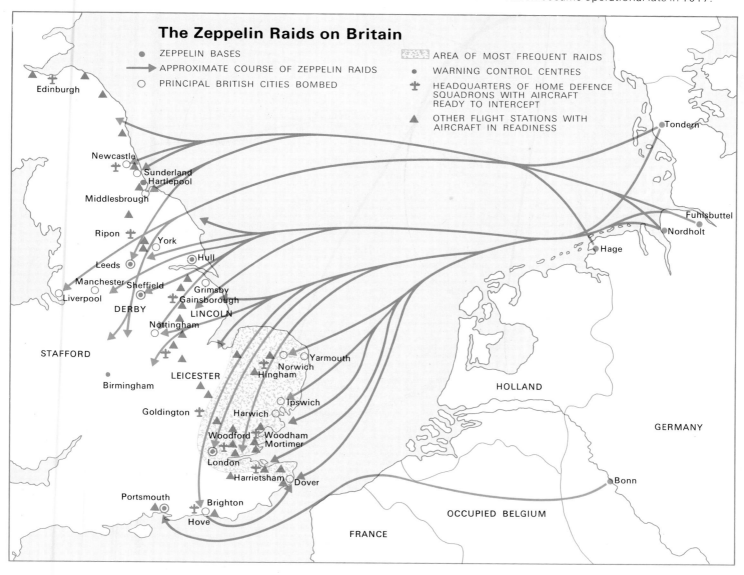

British Bombing Raids on Germany 1917–1918

TOWNS BOMBED BY BRITISH, OCTOBER 1917 OCTOBER 1918

THE WESTERN FRONT

HOLLAND
Essen
Dusseldorf
RUHR
Cologne
Duren
Aachen
BELGIUM
Coblenz
GERMANY
Luxemburg
Trier
Saarburg
Dillingen
Zweibrucken
Heidelberg
Diedenhofen
Falkenberg
Pirmasens
Metz
Saarbrucken
Karlsruhe
Verdun
Courcelles
Bensdorf
Hagenau
Morhange
Stuttgart
Nancy
Saarburg
Strassburg
Epinal
FRANCE
Rhine

The bombing targets. The Zeppelin raids caused massive outcry when they began in 1915 and they were in no small measure responsible for the formation of the RAF and the creation of a retaliatory force which became operational late in 1917.

The Zeppelin Raids on Britain

- ZEPPELIN BASES
- APPROXIMATE COURSE OF ZEPPELIN RAIDS
- PRINCIPAL BRITISH CITIES BOMBED
- AREA OF MOST FREQUENT RAIDS
- WARNING CONTROL CENTRES
- HEADQUARTERS OF HOME DEFENCE SQUADRONS WITH AIRCRAFT READY TO INTERCEPT
- OTHER FLIGHT STATIONS WITH AIRCRAFT IN READINESS

Edinburgh
Tondern
Newcastle
Sunderland
Hartlepool
Middlesbrough
Fuhlsbuttel
Ripon
Nordholt
York
Leeds
Hull
Hage
Manchester
Sheffield
Grimsby
Liverpool
Gainsborough
DERBY
LINCOLN
Nottingham
STAFFORD
Yarmouth
LEICESTER
Norwich
Hingham
Birmingham
HOLLAND
Ipswich
Goldington
Harwich
Woodford
Woodham
Mortimer
GERMANY
London
Harrietsham
Dover
Bonn
Portsmouth
Brighton
OCCUPIED BELGIUM
Hove
FRANCE

Speed was adequate at 84 miles an hour, and the defensive armament of four flexible Parabellum machine guns ensured a good measure of protection against British fighters.

A committee creates the RAF

Ever since the first raids, the public outcry in Britain had increased, and several squadrons of fighters had been recalled from France to try to deal with the raiders. But in the days before ground-to-air radio that an independent air force, under its own ministry, be set up. The result was the Royal Air Force, which came into being on April 1, 1918. It should not be imagined, however, that the German raids on London were the only reason for the committee's recommendation. They were merely the catalyst that brought about the final reaction against many more fundamental errors in the administration of the flying services.

In all, there were 51 airship and 52 aeroplane raids on Great Britain in the First World War. A total of 9,000 bombs was dropped, and their 280 tons killed 1,413 people and wounded another 3,408. Damage totalling £3,000,000 was caused, but the dislocation of resources from the front, and the wasted time of industrial workers forced to take shelter had a far greater impact. Combined with this there was the emotional shock resulting from raids such as that of January 28, 1918, when an exploding bomb caused a press to fall through the floor of Odhams printing

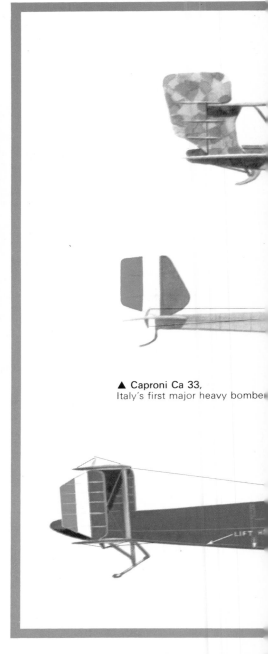

▲ Caproni Ca 33,
Italy's first major heavy bomber

and radar, by the time the raiders had been spotted and the fighters scrambled, the chances of an interception at over 15,000 feet were minimal. The one significant aspect of the whole situation was, however, that it led to demands for means of improving the efficiency of the flying services.

A committee under General Jan Smuts was appointed to look into the matter, and, after much deliberation, this recommended

Above: Handley-Page O/400 bombers operating from Dunkirk. Forty O/400 aircraft were sent on the largest raid of the war in September 1918, against targets in the Saar. Like its predecessor, the O/100, the O/400 could carry Britain's largest bomb of the war, a massive 1,650-pounder. The O/100 carried its fuel in the rear of its nacelles, the O/400 more conventionally and successfully, in its fuselage.

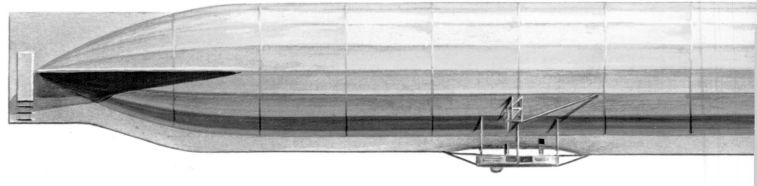

works on to people sheltering below, killing 38 of them and wounding 85 more.

The public demanded that a force to retaliate against Germany be set up, and this began to form in 1917. One wing was operational by October 1917, and by May 1918 four squadrons were in action. On June 6 this force was officially christened the Independent Air Force, under the Command of Major-General Sir Hugh Trenchard. Although the force never grew to the proportions originally intended, the IAF was able to bomb targets in Germany with increasing frequency from its bases in the area around Nancy.

The Russians made some notable contributions to the development of bombing tactics, forming the first real long-range heavy bomber unit. It became operational as a bomber group in mid-1915 and introduced daylight group formation flights of 2–4 Ilya Mouromets later in the same year.

Improved German fighter defences led to another innovation—escort fighters, usually 3 or 4 to cover 2–4 bombers but sometimes as many as 16 escorts.

Italy's mass bomber raids

The other major power interested in strategic bombing was Italy, which had the aircraft necessary in the form of a whole series of large **Caproni** bombers. Nine months after Italy's entry into the war, the first major raid was launched against the town of Ljubljana on February 18, 1916. Further raids on Austrian headquarters behind the front line followed, and then a series of raids was flown against the Austro-Hungarian naval base at Pola in August and September 1917. The series culminated, on October 2, with a raid by 148 Caproni bombers and 11 flying boats. Just over a year later, on October 22, 1918, 56 Capronis and 142 flying boats made the last major raid of the war against Pola.

The Italians were the only ones to make truly strategic raids during the First World War, by massing large numbers of aircraft against a single military target such as Pola or army headquarters. All the other nations undertook raids that were nothing more than a means of raising morale at home and causing minimal damage to the enemy by striking back, no matter what the target was. However, it was impossible for any of the combatants to achieve worthwhile strategic results with the bombers of the time, which were capable neither of carrying a sufficient bomb-load, nor of attaining the necessary bombing accuracy, to 'take out' a target of true strategic value.

The most effective use of bombing in the First World War took place not, as might be imagined, over the Western Front, but in Palestine. There, towards the end of the war, British forces under General Allenby were chasing the Turks north towards Turkey itself. In September, Allenby's offensive was greatly aided by the destruction of the Turkish telephone exchange by the RAF, and Turkish headquarters were kept off-balance by the continual presence of British fighters overhead. Then, as the Turks retreated, two Turkish divisions were spotted moving through a narrow pass. On the 19th the RAF blocked the northern end of the pass then flew fighter and bomber missions against the trapped Tutks. Both divisions were destroyed as fighting entities, and the equivalent of a division was wiped out. This was, of course, the type of success that depends on the physical circumstances, such as terrain, but it showed what could be achieved by the intelligent use of air power alone.

Strategic Bombers

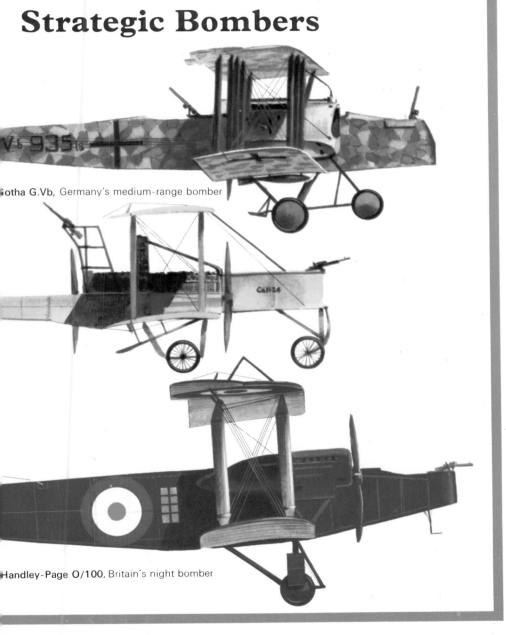

Gotha G.Vb, Germany's medium-range bomber

Handley-Page O/100, Britain's night bomber

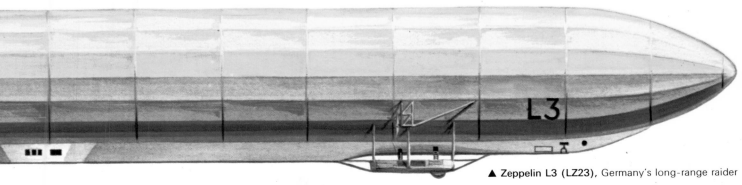

▲ Zeppelin L3 (LZ23), Germany's long-range raider

The ACES

The air war, fought above the mud of the battlefields, wrongly acquired a romantic aura never attributed to the more obvious carnage of the trenches. Nowhere is this false notion more obvious than in the system of 'aces', itself a term derived from the French word for a sporting star. These men were undeniably brave and skilled at the new art of aerial warfare, yes, but every victory that made them famous was a 'kill'—usually in the more tragically literal sense than pilots' jargon.

The origin of the term 'ace' is French, '*as*' being a vogue word for a sporting star at the turn of the century. And the first pilot to whom this accolade could fairly be given was again a Frenchman, Roland Garros, who shot down five German aircraft before being forced down himself in April 1915. There then followed a brief interval while the Germans developed their interrupter gear, inspired by the Saulnier system on Garros' **Morane-Saulnier Type L,** and got the first few examples of the **Fokker Eindecker** to the front.

Anthony Fokker refused to test fly his fighter in combat as technically he was neutral, being a Dutch citizen. But among those chosen to prove the new weapon was Oswald Boelcke. This was the man who was destined to develop the fighter tactics that are still used today.

Above: The fate of the unskilled or unlucky. Lieutenant Roosevelt, an American pilot, lies in the wreckage of his shot-down aircraft.
Far left: One of the greats. The Canadian ace William 'Billy' Bishop, VC, who scored 72 victories.
Centre left: The French ace Charles Nungesser.
Left: The father of air fighting. The redoubtable German ace Oswald Boelcke who was killed in an accident after scoring 40 victories.

Boelcke had already made a name for himself by his aggressive attitude towards air combat, and had won two victories before he was given an Eindecker to fly. This, however, was the aircraft for which he had been waiting. With it he could make air combat a skill rather than a haphazard affair only infrequently likely to be crowned by success. Flying his third sortie in a Fokker, Boelcke claimed his third victory.

His companion and rival at this time was the young Max Immelmann, destined to win almost as great a fame as Boelcke. Whereas Immelmann was a tactician, Boelcke was more—he was also a strategist. Immelmann, popularly known as the 'Eagle of Lille', scored his first victory on August 1, 1915, and was killed, with 15 victories to his credit, on June 28, 1916. The Germans claim that his death resulted from a structural failure in his aircraft, but the British say that he was shot down by the gunner of an **F.E. 2**, Corporal John Waller.

Although Immelmann lacked the genius of Boelcke, he was not without a certain tactical flair, however. A methodical man, he worked out the best way in which to attack Allied types without the latter being able to retaliate, the most famous of these tactics becoming known as the 'Immelmann turn'. This consisted of a diving attack followed by a swift zoom climb with a half-roll off the top, putting the attacker back in position for another attack.

Boelcke's hunting packs

Boelcke's genius, though, was of a much higher level. He realised that despite the fact that pilots were on their own once combat had been joined, the chances of overall success lay in hunting in packs. Thus small numbers of Allied aircraft could be surprised by greater numbers of German aircraft and disposed of with relatively little difficulty, while larger formations of Allied aircraft could be avoided.

Boelcke, because of the results of his individual success, had the ear of Major Thomsen, and he persuaded the latter that what was needed to utilise the potential of the fighter to the full were specialist units of fighters. Thomsen agreed, and so came into existence the *Jagdstaffeln* (Hunting Squadrons), usually abbreviated to *Jasta*. Boelcke himself was appointed to command Jasta 2. With his normal efficiency he set about turning this into a highly trained and efficient unit. The squadron formed on August 27, 1916, but before it had a chance to achieve significant results in combat, Boelcke was killed—not by an Allied airman, but as the result of a flying accident

Above: **Manfred von Richthofen.** The top scorer recuperating from the head wound he received in July 1917.
Below left: Richthofen's funeral. The full military honours were provided by No. 3 Squadron, Australian Flying Corps, which flew in the Somme area.
Below: Richthofen comes in to land in his famous red *Dreidecker*.

with one of his own pilots, Erwin Boehme. On October 28, 1916, during combat with a British aircraft, the wingtips of the aircraft flown by the two friends clashed, and Boelcke came off worst. The fabric began to peel away from the wooden structure supporting the top wing, and the great commander plunged down to the ground and his death.

It is impossible to overestimate the importance of Boelcke in the history of air fighting. Apart from his impressive tally of 40 victories and the award of Germany's highest decoration, the *Pour le Merite*, Boelcke must also be credited with formulating the rules of air fighting, and devising the right sort of unit to put them into action.

The tide turns against Germany

However, by the time of Boelcke's death, the tide of air superiority was swinging against Germany. The 'Fokker Scourge' had amazed Allied leaders when at its height over Verdun in the spring of 1916, and at last Allied air leaders realised the magnitude of their lack of foresight. Here was a prewar design closely based on a French model and not even intended for combat, destroying the best that the Allies had

THE TOP GERMAN ACES	
Name and Rank	'Kills'
Rittm. Manfred Frhr. von Richthofen	80
Oberleutnant Ernst Udet	62
Oberleutnant Erich Loewenhardt	53
Leutnant Werner Voss	48
Leutnant Fritz Rumey	45
Hauptmann Rudolph Berthold	44
Leutnant Paul Baumer	43
Leutnant Josef Jacobs	41
Hauptmann Bruno Loerzer	41
Hauptmann Oswald Boelcke	40
Leutnant Franz Buchner	40
Oblt. Lothar Frhr. von Richthofen	40

Warplanes of the German Aces

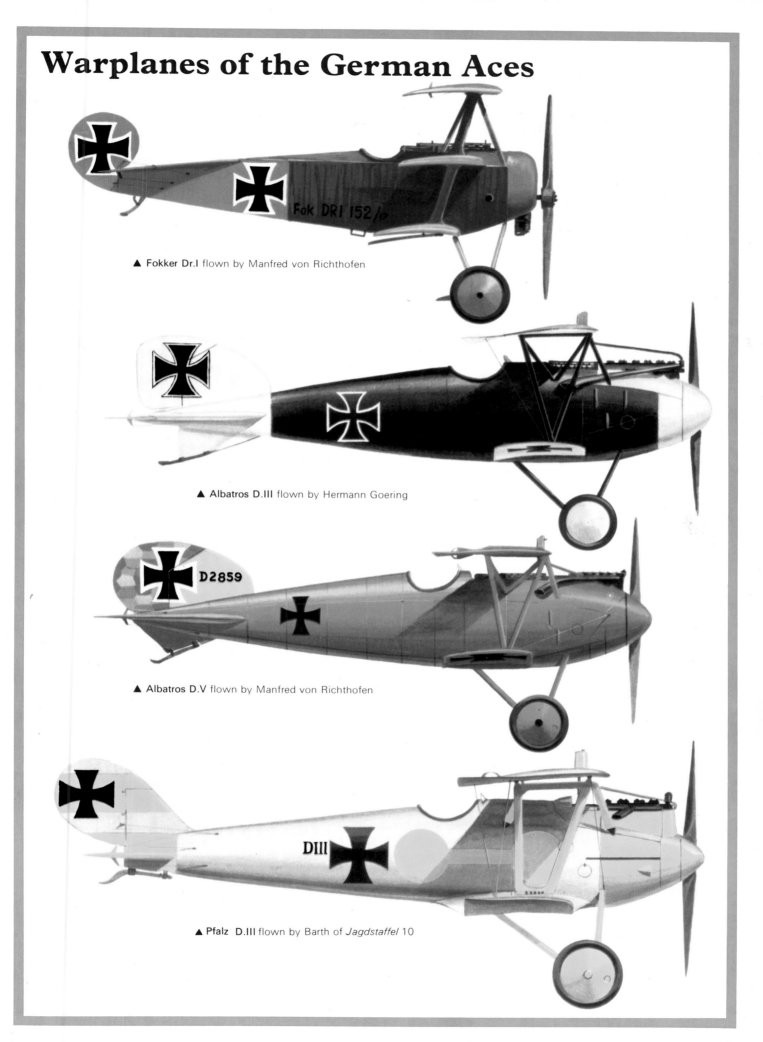

▲ **Fokker Dr.I** flown by Manfred von Richthofen

▲ **Albatros D.III** flown by Hermann Goering

▲ **Albatros D.V** flown by Manfred von Richthofen

▲ **Pfalz D.III** flown by Barth of *Jagdstaffel* 10

merely because it had a machine gun capable of firing through the rotating airscrew. The remedy was clear—the Allies also had to have such equipment. Eventually an excellent design by an expatriate Rumanian, Giurgiu Constantinescu, and the British Major George Colley, known as the C.C. gear, was introduced, but in the short term other countermeasures had to be found.

The answer was a pair of interim types. The French got over the problem of a forward-firing gun by placing it above the top wing to fire over the propeller in the **Nieuport 11 Bébé,** a delightful and docile little tractor sesquiplane, and the British by producing the **Airco de Havilland 2.** This was a small pusher biplane, with the machine gun mounted in front of the pilot. Both these types were in most respects better than the Eindecker, and with their arrival the tide began to turn against Germany. The completion of this reversal came in March 1916, when the superior **Nieuport 17** entered service. This was fitted with a synchronised Vickers machine gun, and was in every way superior to the Eindecker. The Fokker Scourge was over, and the Allies could take the air war to the Germans.

Above: The German ace Buddecke. He flew with the Turks but at his throat is the coveted German *Pour la Mérite.*

The tactics of the period were as yet fluid, and this gave great scope to the individualists on both sides, particularly the Allies. Although the term 'ace' was never recognised officially by the British, the popular press did lionise heroes such as Major Lanoe G. Hawker, a D.H. 2 pilot, who was later shot down by Rittmeister Manfred von Richthofen.

Another name that came to the public's attention was that of Albert Ball, one of the great exponents of the art of freelance air fighting. Initially a dare-devil pilot who would take on any odds, Ball in the last few months of his life became possibly the greatest adept in the art of stalking an enemy aircraft that the world has seen.

Although his squadron had by this time been equipped with the fast, sturdy **Royal Aircraft Factory S.E. 5,** Ball would set off in the morning and evening in his personal Nieuport 17 to stalk unsuspecting 'Huns'. Patiently he would close in on his victim, always flying in the crew's blind spot underneath the fuselage, until he could send a close-range burst into the aircraft. It was a nerve-racking experience that only men with loner instincts like Ball could stand. As with Immelmann, the exact circumstances of Ball's death are uncertain. On May 7, 1917 he dived into a cloud in pursuit of a German aircraft and was never seen again. The Germans claimed that he was shot down by Lothar von Richthofen, Manfred's brother, but this seems unlikely. He had scored 44 victories.

France's legendary loner

Another loner, but one with a completely different temperament, was the legendary French ace Georges Guynemer. A frail-looking boy, he was at first rejected when he tried to join up. But eventually his perseverance was rewarded, and he was sent for flying training. He joined his first squadron on June 8, 1915, and quickly appreciated that he was serving with the cream of the French air service. Guynemer's first victory came on July 19, and from then to the end of his life Guynemer's days were filled with eventful occurrences. He was shot down for the first of seven times in September 1915 but this did not deter him. He continued to fly with his customary disregard for odds or safety, and began to amass a large score of victories. He was lionised by the French press, and while acknowledging that he might be an important morale factor, consistently refused the high command's requests to give up front line flying. The toll on his frail physique exacted by his furious method of combat was enormous, and inevitably he was killed. Again the circumstances are obscure, as Guynemer's aircraft just disappeared over Poelcapelle in Belgium, and the Germans did not until several days later claim that one of their pilots had shot him down. At the time of his death on September 11, 1917 he had scored 54 victories.

Unlike the British, the French and Germans believed in sorting out their best fighter pilots into elite units. Boelcke's Jasta 2, which became Jasta 'Boelcke' after its leader's death, was one such, and Jasta 11, commanded by Manfred von Richthofen, was another. As the Jasta was superseded by the *Jagdgeschwader*, or Hunting Wing, as the size of the various air forces and air units increased, so elite Jagdgeschwader were formed. The most famous of these 'Flying Circuses', as they were dubbed by the British, was Richthofen's Jagdgeschwader No. 1, formed in June 1917. These 'circuses' were intended to be mobile units that could be switched to any sector over which air superiority was needed. With their brightly-coloured **Albatros D I, II, III,** and **V** fighters, which became the standard German fighters from the beginning of 1917, this aim could be readily achieved. But it was only at the price of denuding other units of the leader-

Above: Capitaine René Fonck. The Allied ace of aces, with 75 victories, practices with a carbine on his airfield. He was one of the war's supreme aerial marksmen.
Above right: France's favourite ace. Georges Guynemer, poses in front of his Spad, named *Vieux Charles.* The circumstances of his disappearance in the air have never been explained. The deaths of many of the aces are shrouded in mystery.

THE TOP FRENCH ACES	
Name and Rank	'Kills'
Capitaine René Paul Fonck	75
Capitaine Georges Guynemer	54
Lieutenant Charles Nungesser	45
Capitaine Georges Madon	41
Lieutenant Maurice Boyau	35
Lieutenant Michel Coiffard	34
Lieutenant Jean Pierre Bourjade	28
Capitaine Armand Pinsard	27
Sous-Lieutenant Rene Dorme	23
Lieutenant Gabriel Guerin	23
Sous-Lieutenant Claude Haegelen	23
Sous-Lieutenant Pierre Marinovitch	22
Capitaine Alfred Heurtaux	21
Capitaine Albert Deullin	20

The French No 3

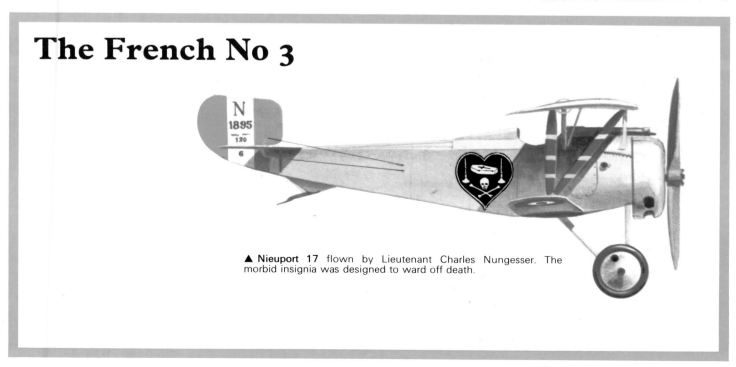

▲ Nieuport 17 flown by Lieutenant Charles Nungesser. The morbid insignia was designed to ward off death.

ship and example that might have improved them. These other units, therefore, were of a much lower overall standard than the British squadrons facing them.

The French elite squadrons

The French too believed in elite units, the most celebrated of which went under the generic term of *Les Cicognes*, or The Storks. Starting with **Morane-Saulnier Type N's,** then moving onto Nieuport 11's and 17's, and finally onto **Spad 7's and 13's,** they embodied the finest pilots of the French air service from 1916 to the end of the war. Units of Les Cicognes could be recognised by the flying stork emblem usually painted along the fuselage.

The British, however, did not believe in grouping the best pilots together in special units, but rather divided them between all front line squadrons. Although this meant that no units scored phenomenally high victory tallies, the overall standard in British squadrons was higher than in French or German ones. The skills of the better pilots could be explained to or picked up by newer and less experienced pilots. Veterans were also there in combat to help and shield newcomers until they could manage on their own. This was, of course, the general run of events in British

Above: 'Billy' Bishop. Bishop is testing the Lewis gun of his Nieuport scout.

THE TOP BRITISH ACES

Name and Rank	'Kills'
Major E. Mannock	73
Lieutenant-Colonel W. A. Bishop	72
Lieutenant-Colonel R. Collishaw	60
Major J. T. B. McCudden	57
Captain A. W. Beauchamp-Proctor	54
Major D. R. MacLaren	54
Major W. G. Barker	53
Captain R. A. Little	47
Captain P. F. Fullard	46
Captain G. E. H. McElroy	46
Captain A. Ball	44
Captain J. Gillmore	44
Major T. F. Hazell	41
Captain J. I. T. Jones	40

squadrons, but there were exceptions. In 'Bloody April' 1917, when the impact of the new twin-gun Albatros fighters made its heaviest impression, pilots with little or no training were sent straight to the front to try to stem the German flood, and it was impossible for the experienced pilots to aid them, so hard pressed were they themselves. This was the worst period for the Royal Flying Corps throughout the war and the average life expectancy of RFC subalterns arriving in France could be measured in days.

Enter von Richthofen

By the autumn of 1916 the Allies had the Nieuport 17, **Sopwith 1½-Strutter, Sopwith Pup,** and several lesser types fitted with a synchronised machine gun in service, and these finished the discomfiture of the Germans started by the D.H. 2 and **Nieuport 11 and 16.** But the arrival of the shark-like Albatros D I and D II series of fighters altered all that late in 1916. These were the first fighters to be fitted with two forward-firing machine guns, and various models were flown by the most successful ace of the war, Manfred von Richthofen. Richthofen was not a natural pilot, but had turned himself into a good one by dint of considerable effort. His real skill lay in his shooting, for he was a natural huntsman.

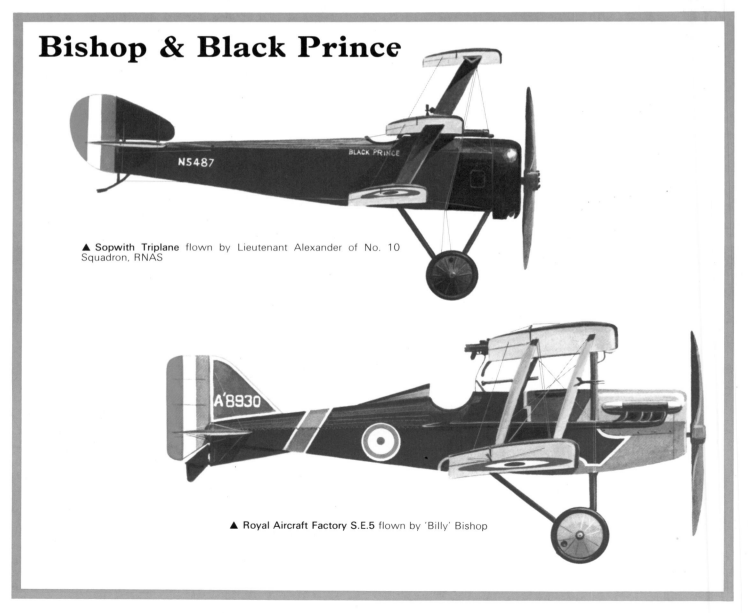

Bishop & Black Prince

▲ Sopwith Triplane flown by Lieutenant Alexander of No. 10 Squadron, RNAS

N5487

BLACK PRINCE

A'8930

▲ Royal Aircraft Factory S.E.5 flown by 'Billy' Bishop

Richthofen was thus able to position himself well in relation to his intended prey, and then close in to finish him off with an accurate burst of fire. A winner of the *Pour le Merite* by the end of 1917, Richthofen became one of the most celebrated people in Germany. His victories mounted steadily, but as with many other aces of the First World War, he was destined to meet a disputed end.

As the result of the success of the **Sopwith Triplane** in 1917 (the triple disposition of the wings gave the type excellent rate of climb and manoeuvrability), Fokker had been asked to produce a similar type for the German air service. But by the time it appeared in the summer of 1917 the concept was obsolescent. Nevertheless, the **Fokker Dreidecker** (Triplane) found favour with some German pilots as a result of its manoeuvrability. Although the Dreidecker was considerably slower than con-

temporary British fighters such as the **S.E. 5a** and **Sopwith Camel**, as long as it could operate defensively over the German lines this was less of a disability than might be imagined. The **Fokker Dr. I** was liked by Richthofen, who was flying one when he was killed, after scoring 80 victories, on April 21, 1918 over the Somme. There is still doubt as to the exact nature of his death—some claim that he was shot down by a Camel flown by Canadian Captain A. R. Brown, some that he was shot down from the ground by the Australian machine gunner R. H. Barron.

Britain's top ace

The most successful British ace of the war was Major Edward 'Mick' Mannock. He was in Turkey when that country entered the war and was thus interned. But the Turks repatriated him on the grounds of his poor health and bad eye-sight. Despite

THE TOP ITALIAN ACES	
Name and Rank	'Kills'
Maggiore Francesco Baracca	34
Tenehte Silvio Scaroni	26
Tenente-Colonello Pier Piccio	24
Tenente Flavio Baracchini	21
Capitano Fulco di Calabria	20

THE TOP RUSSIAN ACES	
Name and Rank	'Kills'
Staff-Captain A. A. Kazakov	17
Captain P. V. d'Argueeff	15
Lieutenant Commander A. P. Seversky	13
Lieutenant I. V. Smirnoff	12
Lieutenant M. Safonov	11
Captain B. Sergeivsky	11
Ensign E. M. Tomson	11

Above left: The highest-scoring Briton. Despite being partially blind 'Mick' Mannock made 73 confirmed 'kills'.
Left: The shy loner, Albert Ball. Both Mannock and Ball were awarded Victoria Crosses for their air activities.

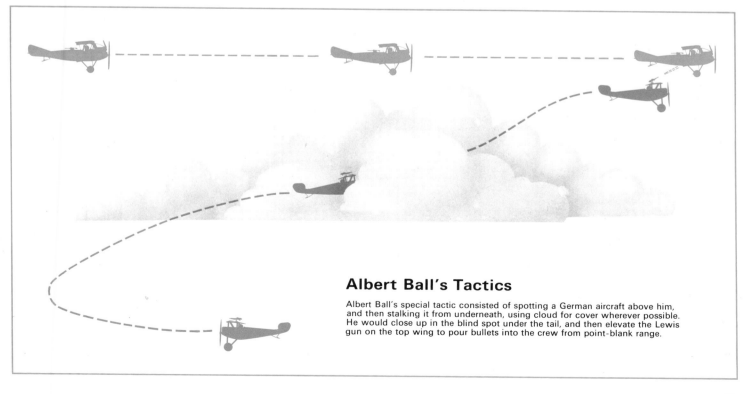

Albert Ball's Tactics

Albert Ball's special tactic consisted of spotting a German aircraft above him, and then stalking it from underneath, using cloud for cover wherever possible. He would close up in the blind spot under the tail, and then elevate the Lewis gun on the top wing to pour bullets into the crew from point-blank range.

being astygmatic in his left eye, he managed to enter the RFC in 1916. He flew his first combat mission on April 7, 1917 and scored his first victory a month later. Success followed success, and soon Mannock had a considerable reputation within the RFC. But apart from being a successful ace in his own right, Mannock was also a great teacher, often lining up victories for novices and leaving the latter to finish off the enemy. It was in the course of such an action that he was killed on July 26, 1918 after scoring 73 victories. As the novice was finishing off the German two-seater that Mannock had lined up, a bullet from the ground pierced Mannock's petrol tank and he was burned alive.

The greatest of all Allied aces was a Frenchman, Rene Fonck. He was a cold, aloof man, more admired than liked by his men. He joined his first unit, an artillery spotting squadron, in the early summer of 1915. His aggressiveness with this unit led to a transfer to a Cicognes squadron on April 15, 1917. He scored his first victory with his new outfit on May 3, and soon acquired a formidable reputation for his shooting. This factor characterised his career throughout the war. Fonck, unusually for the top aces of the First World War, survived the conflict. He scored his last

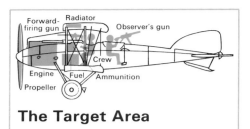

The Target Area

Below left: America's Number Three. Major Raoul Lufbery, 17 'kills', who served with both the French and Americans.
Below: Captain Eddie Rickenbacker. His 26 'kills' made him the top American ace and the man who symbolised for Americans the heroism of the lone fighter pilot.

victory on November 1, 1918 to bring his total up to 75, two more than Mannock. There are grounds, however, for believing that Mannock's total may have been higher, and that he credited some of his victories to novices to start their score. Fonck claimed 30 unconfirmed victories.

America's Rickenbacker

The top American ace, after the United States entered the war in April 1917, was Captain Eddie Rickenbacker. He joined his first combat squadron, the 94th Aero Squadron, on March 4, 1918, and on the 19th of that month made the first patrol flight over the front by an American squadron. Rickenbacker's first victory followed on April 29, and a month later he was an ace with five victories. He ended the war with 26 German aircraft to his credit and as commander of the 94th Aero Squadron.

The other combatant nations also produced aces, but it was over the Western Front that the greatest ones operated. The British system, by which aces were not banded into special units, proved ultimately superior. The British shot down more aircraft than any other nation. And the top 20 British aces shot down more aircraft than the top 20 of any other nation.

America's Master

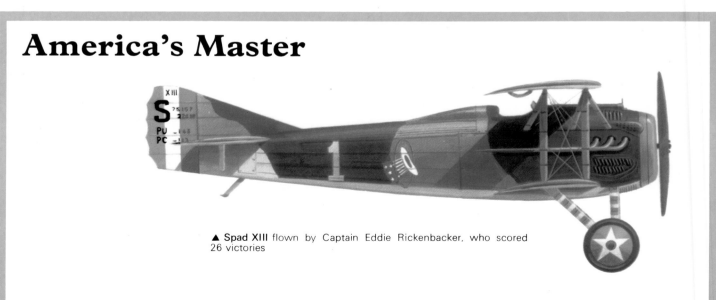

▲ **Spad XIII** flown by Captain Eddie Rickenbacker, who scored 26 victories

Regalia of the Air War

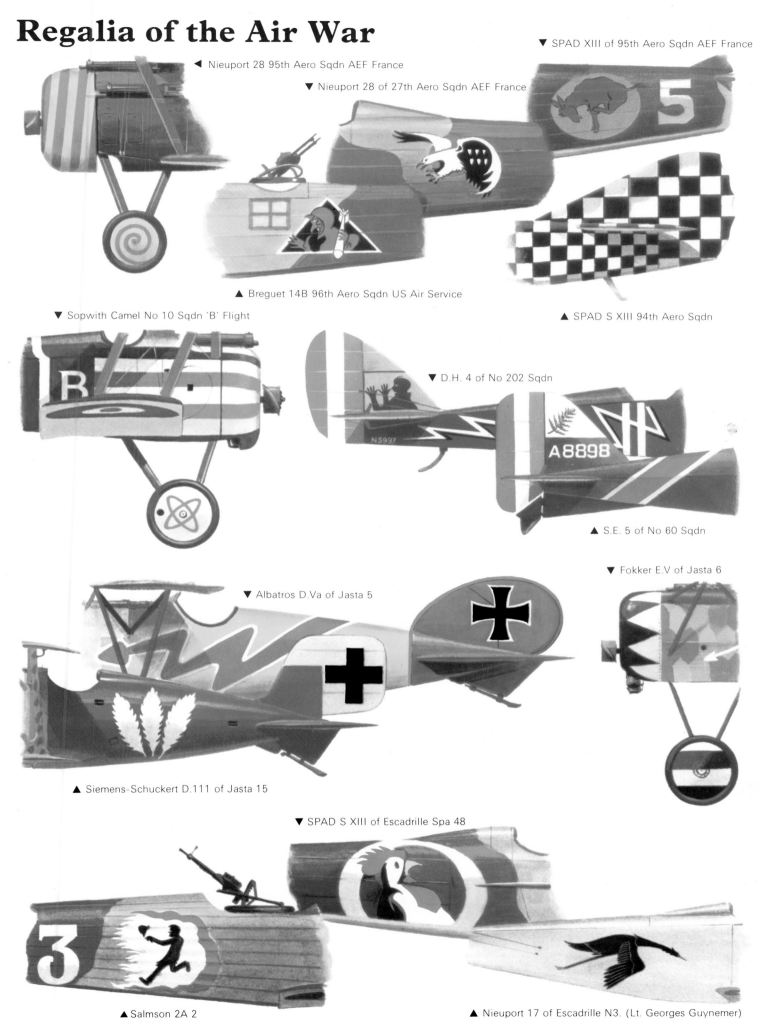

◀ Nieuport 28 95th Aero Sqdn AEF France

▼ SPAD XIII of 95th Aero Sqdn AEF France

▼ Nieuport 28 of 27th Aero Sqdn AEF France

▲ Breguet 14B 96th Aero Sqdn US Air Service

▼ Sopwith Camel No 10 Sqdn 'B' Flight

▲ SPAD S XIII 94th Aero Sqdn

▼ D.H. 4 of No 202 Sqdn

▲ S.E. 5 of No 60 Sqdn

▼ Albatros D.Va of Jasta 5

▼ Fokker E.V of Jasta 6

▲ Siemens-Schuckert D.111 of Jasta 15

▼ SPAD S XIII of Escadrille Spa 48

▲ Salmson 2A 2

▲ Nieuport 17 of Escadrille N3. (Lt. Georges Guynemer)

43

ALLIED DOMINATION

'Bloody April' had ensured that 1917 would be a particularly bad year for the Allies in the air. But by its end new aircraft types and improved organisation were beginning to turn the tide and in 1918, for the first and prophetic time, the effectiveness of American air power was felt in the world. These decisive changes gave the Allies control of the skies in almost all sectors until the war was brought to an end.

The year 1917 had been desperately hard for the Allies. The whittling away of their air superiority from the autumn of 1917 had culminated in 'Bloody April' 1917, in which the Germans achieved total air supremacy. The Germans also led in the field of army co-operation now, and as the year progressed, the C-class general purpose types were joined by the armoured J-class (ground attack) and in 1918 the light CL-class (ground attack and escort) machines. Thus when the Germans launched their final offensives in March 1918, the troops were well-supported by aircraft designed for the role. The tide was beginning to run against the Germans again, however. The latest Allied types, such as the **S.E. 5a,** the **Sopwith Camel,** and the **Spad 13,** were more than a match for the **Albatros D V,** and the Germans' counter-weapon, the **Fokker D VII,** was able to prove its merits only in the closing months of the war, when it was too late to alter the course of events. The story of 1918 is, with the exception of the period of their great offensives in the spring when the Germans won command of the air for the last time, one of Allied domination.

By January 1918, the Allies were in control of the situation in the air above the Western Front. The superiority of fighters such as the Royal Aircraft Factory's S.E. 5a, with its two machine guns, sturdy construction and good performance; the Sopwith Camel, again with two machine guns and good performance plus superb agility; and the French Spad 13, with its two guns, structural integrity and excellent turn of speed, ensured that the German **Albatros** D V and **Va** were not able to cover the now ageing C-class machines in their vital duties.

These machines, with the newer J-class, were now being used more and more for what the Allies called infantry contact patrols. The J-class comprised armoured two seaters for this dangerous low-level work, but their size and lack of manoeuvrability made them relatively easy prey for Allied fighters, and so they had to be escorted. This resulted in a demand for a new type, its requirements being to escort C- and J-class machines of the *Flieger-abteilungen-Infanterie*. The result was the CL-class, designed to the basic specification of the C-class, but with a considerably lighter weight to enable the aircraft of this class to operate with the *Schutzstaffeln* (Protection Squadrons).

The best known of the J-class was the **Junkers J I,** a big, metal-covered biplane, with a wing span of over 52 feet. It was capable of only 96 miles an hour, but could take a large amount of damage and still fly. The aircraft of the newer CL-class are best exemplified by the **Halberstadt CL II** and **IV** (103 miles an hour and three machine guns), and the **Hannover CL II** and **IIIa** (103 miles an hour and two machine guns). Perhaps the most important of these machines was the **Junkers J10** (or **CL. I**) an all-metal cantilever low-wing monoplane. One of the few really advanced designs to emerge from the war it was used as a close-support assault aircraft. Although the Schutzstaffeln did good work in their protective capacity, they had a more important part to play.

Realising that the war was lost unless they managed to achieve a startling military coup against the Allies, the German High Command laid plans for a series of all-out linked offensives, five in number, to be launched from March 1918 onwards. Infantry tactics were altered for these offensives: instead of the massive pre-attack artillery barrage, followed by waves of slow-moving infantry, the 1918 offensives were based on the use of a short, sharp barrage followed up swiftly by light armed infantry led by 'shock troops' who were to push on through the Allied lines, leaving points of resistance to be mopped up by conventional troops.

The essence of the new tactics lay in speed, surprise and flexibility. And to

Below: Sopwith F.1 Camels. They were Britain's most successful fighters. Overhead is a Bristol F.2B two-seater.

provide adequate front line air support and also relay precise information back to headquarters, an advanced type of infantry contact patrol was needed. The ideal aircraft were those of the CL-class, serving with the Schutzstaffeln. These were re-trained for their new tasks and renamed *Schlachtstaffeln* or Battle Squadrons. As the importance and size of these units grew they were banded together to form *Schlacht-geschwader*, or Battle Wings.

The first of the Schlachtstaffeln, or *Schlastas* as they were normally abbreviated, was tested in the Battle of Cambrai in November 1917, and proved its worth.

Eliminate the British!

The strategic thought underlying the five-fold German offensive was to eliminate the British first, and then turn on the French, pushing through their armies to take Paris. The weight of the first stage of the offensive is clearly shown by the numbers of German

AIRFRAME AND ENGINE PRODUCTION 1914–18		
Country	Airframes manufactured	Engines manufactured
Great Britain	55,093	41,034
France	67,982	85,317
America (21 months)	15,000*	41,000*
Germany	47,637	40,449
Italy	20,000*	38,000*
*Approximate figures.		

AIR STRENGTHS, NOVEMBER 1918

Britain: 3,300 aircraft

France: 4,511 aircraft

Germany: 2,390 aircraft

Below: S.E.5a-equipped No 85 Sqdn, RAF. A latecomer to the conflict, the unit moved to the Western Front in May 1918 and flew fighter patrols until the end of the war.

Germany's Ultimate Warplanes

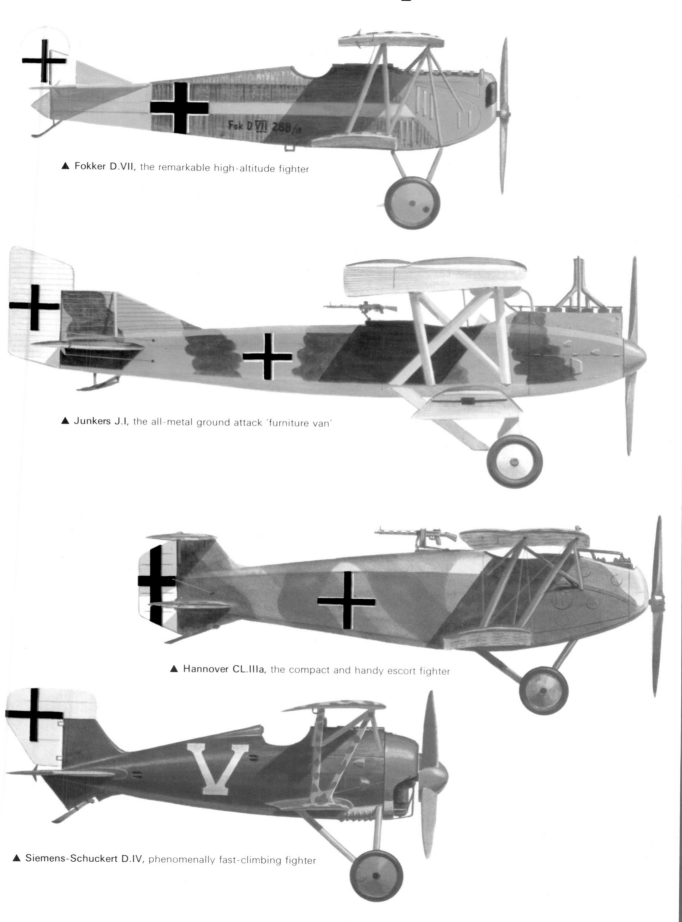

▲ Fokker D.VII, the remarkable high-altitude fighter

▲ Junkers J.I, the all-metal ground attack 'furniture van'

▲ Hannover CL.IIIa, the compact and handy escort fighter

▲ Siemens-Schuckert D.IV, phenomenally fast-climbing fighter

aircraft facing the British and French at the end of March: 1,680 against the former and 367 against the latter.

The first stage of the offensive started on March 20, and was initially very successful, not least due to the efforts of the Schlastas. Aircraft flew in groups of between four and six, the largest tactical formation that could be controlled by one man before the advent of air-to-air radio, with constant replacements moving up to the front line to take over from the flights running low on fuel and ammunition.

The British suffered very heavily at first, but the determination of the ground forces and the constant harassment by British fighters at last managed to halt the Germans. The other four offensives were launched in their turn, but the lessons learned by the Allies in this first one stood them in good stead, and the Germans were held.

This was the only time in 1918 when the Germans were able to gain air superiority over a point of main effort. But from June to the end of the war the Allies had everything their own way. Artillery observation and reconnaissance machines were able to operate efficiently, light bombers flew missions against German concentrations and dumps behind the lines, and fighters harassed German aircraft and attacked troops in their trenches with bombs and machine gun fire.

An important role was played during this period by the best two-seater developed in the First World War, the **Bristol F.2B.** This started life as a general-purpose two-seater, but after a totally inauspicious start it was discovered that the type's speed, armament and manoeuvrability made it an excellent fighter, with the added advantage of a 'sting in the tail'.

The best fighter of the war

The Germans made determined efforts to regain air superiority in the autumn of 1918 with the introduction of the superlative Fokker D VII, which may fairly be claimed to have been the best fighter of the war. (The most successful was the British Sopwith Camel, by which 1,294 enemy aircraft were shot down during the 16 months it was in action.) The Fokker D VII was quite fast at 124 miles an hour, but had excellent performance at high altitude. It could climb to nearly 23,000 feet, and had the amazing ability to 'hang' on its propeller at altitudes where Allied fighters stalled and lost height. This ability proved a very considerable advantage in combat. Deliveries of the type to the squadrons began in April 1918, but only 412 had been handed over by the time of the Armistice.

1918 was the year in which American air power at last began to play an important part in the war. Although the United States had entered the war in April 1917, their air force was in a worse state even than those of the European powers had been in 1914. But by 1918 American energy and drive had worked wonders. Admittedly, no American aircraft had seen action, all of the aircraft with which the American Expeditionary Force's air arm was equipped being derived from French and British sources. However, the magnificent Liberty engine had been designed and was now in production, and plans for a huge expansion of the American aircraft industry were about to bear fruit.

But what the Americans had done was

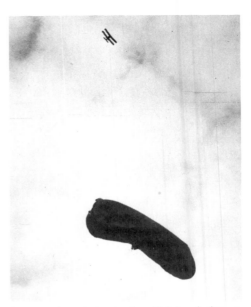

Observation halted. An S.E.5 circles a Caquot balloon hit by an enemy fighter.

build up a comprehensive base and training system in France, so that when their squadrons entered combat they were well prepared and able to replace their losses quickly. American air squadrons first went into action on the Chateau Thierry sector, but their greatest test and success came in the Battle of St Mihiel. Here the American commander, General William 'Billy' Mitchell, had amassed over 1,500 aircraft for the American push in August 1918. By the time of the Armistice there were 45 American squadrons at the front, a remarkable achievement in 18 months from a scratch start.

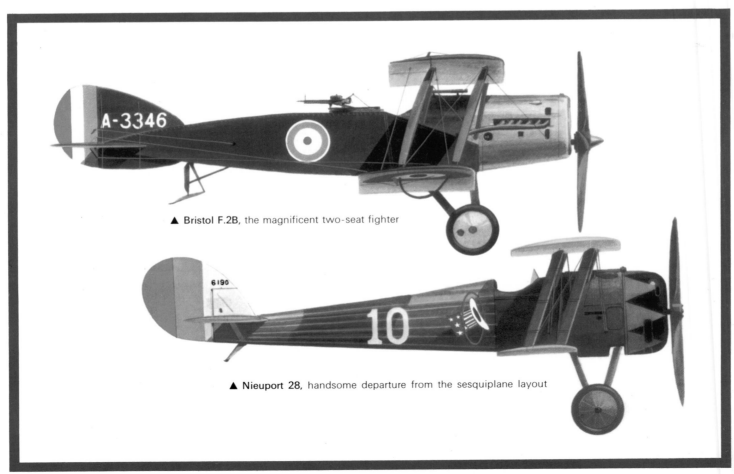

▲ Bristol F.2B, the magnificent two-seat fighter

▲ Nieuport 28, handsome departure from the sesquiplane layout

Sopwith Fighters, 1916-1918

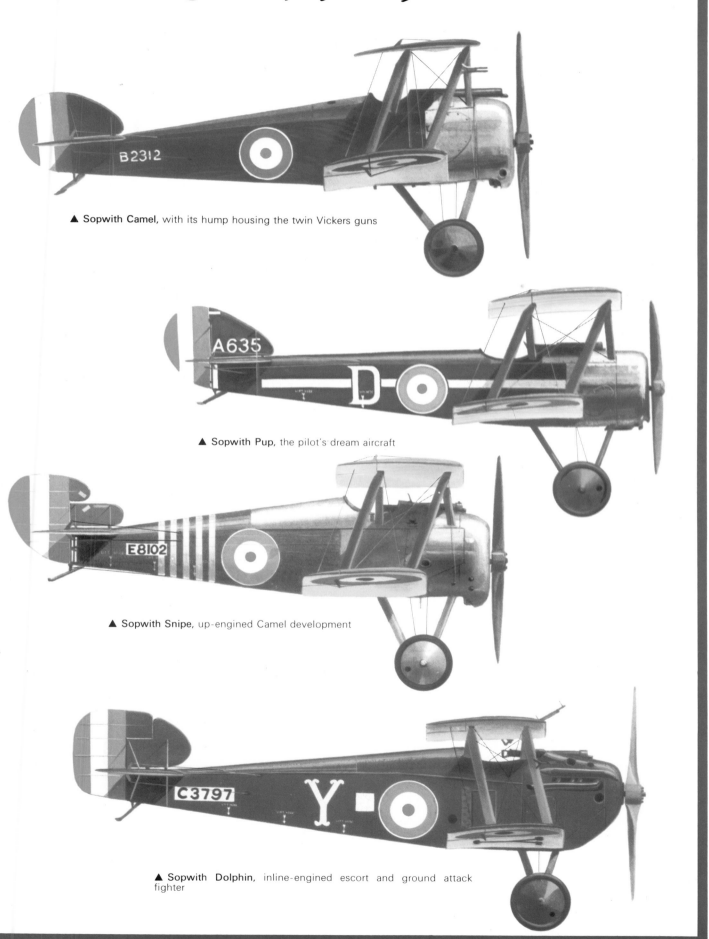

▲ **Sopwith Camel,** with its hump housing the twin Vickers guns

▲ **Sopwith Pup,** the pilot's dream aircraft

▲ **Sopwith Snipe,** up-engined Camel development

▲ **Sopwith Dolphin,** inline-engined escort and ground attack fighter

RACING TO WAR

With the end of World War I public interest in aviation became focused on record-breaking flights and prestige air races. Lindbergh flew the Atlantic, Kingsford-Smith flew the Pacific, and the world's air-speed record was pushed beyond 300 miles an hour. Then Hitler's plans for the Luftwaffe were revealed and efforts were once again concentrated on military aircraft. The B-17 prototype appeared, the Me 109, the Spitfire—the race to World War II was well and truly on.

The First World War left Germany with no air force at all, and the victorious Allies with massive forces equipped with the very latest types and with even better machines already under construction in the experimental shops of the larger aircraft concerns. Air power had proved itself in the First World War, and the future of the aircraft industries of Great Britain, France, and America looked bright. But the 1920's brought a retrenchment, and governments, sensing that their electorates were heartily disenchanted with taxes spent on weapons, decided that the armed forces would have to make do with the weapons they had inherited from the First World War. The aircraft industry was particularly hard hit as the expected civil market had failed to materialise. With little money available for expensive research and development programmes, therefore, military aircraft reflected the growth of the aeronautical art only slowly; the major advances in aero-

dynamics and flying techniques resulted from the increasing number of record flights and prestige races held in the later 1920's and early 1930's. The situation improved for manufacturers in the middle 30's, especially after the announcement of German rearmament, and the lessons of the previous ten years were soon apparent in a new crop of military aircraft. The race to the Second World War was on.

But the world returned to peace in 1919, still counting the cost of the war in men and money, flying tried to pick up from the point it had reached in 1914 when the war interrupted things. The great barrier separating the two major English-speaking nations was the Atlantic, and soon efforts to fly across it were being made.

One notable attempt was that of Harry Hawker, who had played so important a part in the design of early Sopwith machines, in May, but his Sopwith single-engined aircraft was forced to ditch in the Atlantic.

The two-man crew was picked up by a Danish ship. Later in the same month, the first successful crossing was made between the 16th and the 27th, when a **Curtiss NC-4** flying boat, piloted by Lieutenant-Commander A. C. Read of the United States Navy, flew from Newfoundland to Lisbon with stops in the Azores. Two similar aircraft had not managed to get across.

The Atlantic non-stop

Of considerably greater importance, both from the point of view of flying and of raising public interest in record-breaking flights, was the first non-stop crossing of the Atlantic, when Captain J. Alcock and Lieutenant A. Whitten-Brown flew from Newfoundland to a crash-landing in County Galway in Ireland on June 14–15, 1919. Their aircraft was an adapted **Vickers Vimy** twin-engined bomber from the First World

War, and their flight of 1,950 miles was achieved in 16 hours 27 minutes.

While these, the first of many record-breaking flights in the 1920's and 1930's were going on, aircraft designers were trying to take stock of the lessons of the First World War and apply their findings to the few aircraft that the poor financial state of the world would allow. Although it played only a small part in First World War aircraft, it was clear that the material that would play the greatest part in future aircraft designs was metal. A fair amount of metal had been used in the 1917 **Junkers J I,** and in 1918 Junkers introduced the world's first operational all-metal plane, the **CL. I (J10)** ground support aircraft. Both these designs were notable for their use of the thick-section cantilever wing, covered by the characteristic Junkers skinning of metal with corrugation, running chord-wise across the wing, to provide extra stiffening. This thick section cantilever wing, with

either metal construction (Junkers) or wooden construction (Fokker, although designed by Reinhold Platz for the Fokker fighters of the First World War), was destined to play a great part in the aircraft of the inter-war years. Such wings, used either in biplanes or monoplanes, allowed much of the otherwise necessary rigging to be eliminated, with a consequent improvement in performance.

The main disadvantage of the Junkers corrugated skinning was that it had a high drag factor. Realising this, another German, Adolf Rohrbach, started work on smooth-skinned wings in which the metal itself took some of the load. This was the origin of the 'stressed skin' construction in universal use today. An early example of Rohrbach's thinking was his **E.4/2** four-engined airliner of 1920, designed for Zeppelin-Staaken. Rohrbach's work was carried on and improved upon by his American collaborator, H. A. Wagner.

Another design feature which was to enjoy increasing popularity in the 1920's was the monocoque fuselage. This had been invented before the First World War, but only came into its own with the increasing use of metal. In this system, the fuselage skinning was designed as part of the structure, and could thus be made to bear loads. This meant that the basic fuselage structure itself could be simplified and lightened. An early example of a monocoque fuselage was the **Deperdussin Monocoque** of 1912. An interesting post-war example was the all-metal **Short Silver Streak** of 1920.

The military fall behind

Other major developments of the immediate post-war years included the Handley-Page-invented slotted wing of 1920, which gave much more improved low speed handling characteristics, and the first successful examples of a retractable undercarriage. In 1920 there appeared the **Dayton-Wright R.B.** racer, a high-wing monoplane in which the undercarriage retracted into the fuselage. Two years later another American monoplane racer, the **Verville-Sperry Racer,** introduced the type of undercarriage that retracts into the lower surface of the wing. As the decade advanced, flaps became more common as a method of increasing lift at low speeds, thus enabling landing speeds to be kept reasonably low; metal propellers became relatively widespread, especially in the United States; and considerable work was done to improve engine efficiency, and produce more power with the aid of various types of supercharger.

Although civil air transport got off to a slow start after the war, contrary to the expectations of most, as the 1920's progressed civil aircraft began to assume an ever more important part in the aircraft field, particularly in exploiting the most up to date developments in the designer's art. Most military authorities were still content to let others pay for the privilege of blazing the trail, being content themselves to accept the new developments at second hand. Thus military aircraft, with a few exceptions, lagged behind civilian types by a generation of about four years.

The first airliners were converted military types such as the **D.H. 4,** the **Vickers Vimy,** the French **Goliath** and the **Junkers F 13,** developed from the J 10 close support aircraft of late 1918. The lead in producing a new type was taken early on by Fokker, now back in his native Holland. Utilising the thick-section Platz wing, mounted on top of the fuselage, Fokker developed a series of small airliners and long-range aircraft such as the **F II,** which had very good

commercial success for the time. Important from the military point of view was the fact that civil types had to fly many more hours than their military counterparts, and this helped prove materials, improve the reliability of engines, and explore the techniques of long-distance navigation and flight in bad weather and at night.

Although Fokker's designs were sound, practical flying machines, they were unadventurous aerodynamically with their high-drag slab-sided fuselages, and in 1927 the Americans began to succeed Fokker in the forefront of civil aircraft design with the **Lockheed Vega.** This had completely unbraced wings, a well-streamlined monocoque fuselage, and with a 425-hp engine was capable of 135 miles an hour and a range of 900 miles. From this time onwards the American have kept a little-challenged lead in the design of passenger aircraft.

The error of British ways

Just at this time when civilian operators were forging ahead with braced or unbraced monoplane airliners, the standard military machines continued to be little more than updated versions of First World War aircraft. Admittedly, the compact biplane configuration still offered the highest manoeuvrability, which was considered to be of paramount importance in fighters, but little thought was given to the possibilities of high performance monoplane bombers. If such a bomber had been developed, the limitations of the biplane fighter would have been quickly made apparent—for the bomber would have been able to outrun the fighter. As it was, it was not until the middle 1930's and the introduction of the monoplane **Bristol Blenheim** bomber in the era of the **Gloster Gladiator** biplane

fighter, that the British fully realised the error of their ways. The Americans had seen this earlier, in 1932, when the **Martin B-10** first appeared.

But in the 1920's, British military aircraft continued to be types such as the **Gloster Gamecock, Fairey Firefly, Bristol Bulldog,** and at the end of the decade the **Hawker Fury,** the first military aircraft to be capable of more than 200 miles an hour in level flight when it was introduced in 1929. Britain found more use for light bombers such as the **Fairey Fox** than 'heavy' types, but the Americans, thanks to the prodding of General 'Billy' Mitchell, who had sacrificed his career to his belief in the importance of strategic bombing, kept in the forefront of bomber development with aircraft such as the **Martin NBS-1** and **Curtiss B-2.**

Contemporary American fighters comprised a whole series of Curtiss and Boeing biplanes, most of them fitted with high-powered radials, which the Americans greatly favoured for their light weight and lack of mechanical complexity. The Europeans, with a more sophisticated approach to the designer's art, favoured inline engines for military types, as these lent themselves to better streamlining, and therefore the possibility of higher performance.

The most celebrated event in the history of aviation, and one whose importance it would be difficult to exaggerate, was the Schneider Trophy. In the lean years between the wars, the effort devoted to preparing engines and aircraft for the races pushed the state of the aeronautical art along where otherwise it might have stagnated. The races were for seaplanes, the winners of one year's race staging the next event. The first country to win three consecutive races was to keep the trophy in perpetuity.

Speed records fall

The race's greatest era began in 1925 when an American **Curtiss R3C-2** piloted by Jimmy Doolittle won at an average speed of 232.5 miles an hour. This was the last time that the race was won by a biplane. In 1926 the Schneider Trophy was won by an Italian Macchi floatplane, but the next year Britain won with a **Supermarine S.5** at an average speed of 281.65 miles an hour. The S.5 was the precursor of the series of floatplanes designed by Reginald J. Mitchell, whose designing career culminated in the **Supermarine Spitfire** fighter. The S.5 was a low-wing monoplane powered by a Napier Lion 800-hp inline. In 1929, an S.6 won, powered by a Rolls-Royce inline. This started the association between the Rolls-Royce engine concern and Supermarine that was perpetuated in the Spitfire. The S.6 won at an average speed of 328.63 miles an hour and later set up a world speed record of 357.7 miles an hour. The last race in the series occurred in 1931, when a **Supermarine S.6B** won the trophy outright for Britain at an average speed of 340.6 miles an hour and later raised the world speed record to 407 miles an hour.

Throughout the ten years after the war, a succession of great long distance flights had begun to open up the world to civil aviation,

BOMBER DEVELOPMENT, 1934–39				
Country	Type	Introduced (lbs)	Bombload (lbs)	Range (miles)
France	Amiot 143	1935	1,984	807
	Amiot 351	1940	2,645	1,550
	Bloch 210	1937	4,350	683
	Lioré et Olivier 451	1939	3,085	1,040
Germany	Dornier 17E-1	1937	1,760	990
	Heinkel 111E-1	1938	4,410	1,100
	Junkers 86E-1	1936	2,200	1,243
	Junkers 87A-1	1937	1,100	620
Great Britain	Armstrong-Whitworth Whitley I	1937	7,000	1,250
	Boulton-Paul Overstrand	1934	1,600	545
	Bristol Blenheim I	1937	1,000	1,125
	Fairey Hendon II	1936	1,660	1,360
	Handley-Page Hampden I	1938	4,000	1,200
	Vickers Wellington I	1936	4,500	2,550
Holland	Fokker T-V	1937	2,200	1,012
Italy	Fiat BR20M	1939	3,528	1,710
	Savoia-Marchetti 81	1935	2,205	932
	Savoia-Marchetti 79-I	1938	2,205	1,180
Japan	Kawasaki Ki-48-I	1939	792	1,491
	Mitsubishi G3M	1938	1,765	2,900
	Mitsubishi Ki-21	1937	1,650	1,678
Poland	PZL P-23b	1936	1,543	932
United States	Boeing B-17B	1939	10,500	2,400
	Douglas DB-7	1939	1,764	630
	Martin B-10B	1934	2,260	1,240
	Martin Maryland	1939	1,800	750
USSR	Ilyushin DB-3	1937	5,500	2,485
	Tupolev SB-2	1936	1,320	745

Fighter development between the Wars

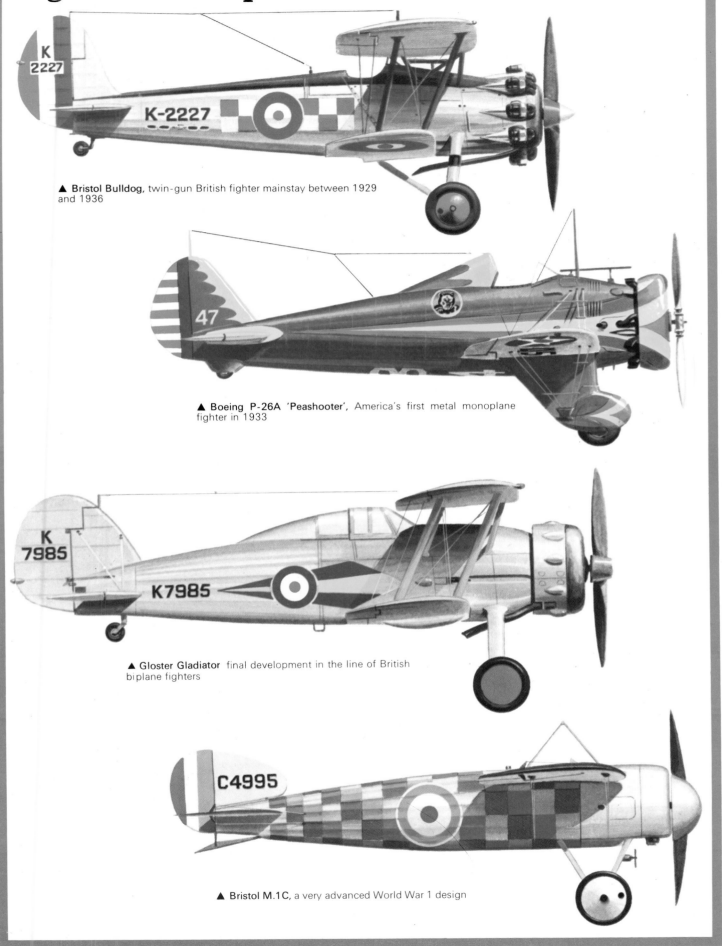

▲ **Bristol Bulldog**, twin-gun British fighter mainstay between 1929 and 1936

▲ **Boeing P-26A 'Peashooter'**, America's first metal monoplane fighter in 1933

▲ **Gloster Gladiator** final development in the line of British biplane fighters

▲ **Bristol M.1C**, a very advanced World War 1 design

Date	Aeroplane	Engine	Place	Pilot	Country	Speed mph
7/2/20	Nieuport-Delage 29	300 hp Hispano-Suiza	Chicago	S. Lecointe	F	171.05
28/2/20	Spad 27	300 hp Hispano-Suiza	Chicago	J. Casale	F	176.15
9/10/20	Spad S.20 bis.	300 hp Hispano-Suiza	Buc	Comte de Romanet	F	181.87
10/10/20	Nieuport-Delage 29	300 hp Hispano-Suiza	Buc	S. Lecointe	F	184.36
20/10/20	Nieuport-Delage 29	300 hp Hispano-Suiza	Villacoublay	S. Lecointe	F	187.99
4/11/20	Spad S.20 bis.	300 hp Hispano-Suiza	Buc	Comte de Romanet	F	192.02
12/12/20	Nieuport-Delage 29	300 hp Hispano-Suiza	Buc	S. Lecointe	F	194.53
26/9/21	Nieuport-Delage 29	300 hp Hispano-Suiza	Villesauvage	S. Lecointe	F	205.23
21/9/22	Nieuport-Delage 29	300 hp Hispano-Suiza	Villesauvage	S. Lecointe	F	211.91
13/10/22	Curtiss Army Racer	375 hp Curtiss D.12	Detroit	W. G. Mitchell	A	222.98
15/2/23	Nieuport-Delage 29	400 hp Hispano-Suiza	Istres	S. Lecointe	F	233.03
29/3/23	Curtiss R-6	465 hp Curtiss D.12	Dayton	R. L. Maughan	A	240.78
2/11/23	Curtiss R2C-1	600 hp Curtiss D.12	Mineola	A. Brow	A	259.16
4/11/23	Curtiss R2C-1	600 hp Curtiss D.12	Mineola	A. J. Williams	A	266.60
11/12/24	S. I. M. B. Bernard Ferbois V.2	450 hp Hispano-Suiza	Istres	A. Bonnet	F	278.50
4/11/27	Macchi M.52	800 hp Fiat A.S.3	Venice	M. di Bernardi	I	297.83
30/3/28	Macchi M.52 bis.	800 hp Fiat A.S.3	Venice	M. di Bernardi	I	318.64
12/9/29	Supermarine S.6	1,900 hp Rolls-Royce R.	Calshot	A. H. Orlebar	GB	357.75
29/9/31	Supermarine S.6B	2,600 hp Rolls-Royce R.	Lee-on-Solent	G. H. Stainforth	GB	407.00
10/4/33	Macchi-Castoldi M.C.72	2,500 hp Fiat A.S.6	Desenzano	F. Agello	I	423.88
23/10/34	Macchi-Castoldi M.C.72	3,100 hp Fiat A.S.6	Desenzano	F. Agello	I	440.69
26/4/39	Messerschmitt Bf 209V1	2,300 hp Daimler-Benz DB 601R	Augsburg	Fritz Wendel	G	469.22

A = America; GB = Great Britain; F = France; I = Italy; G = Germany.

and prove the techniques of such flights. In November and December 1919, a Vimy flown by Ross Smith had managed the 11,000 miles from Great Britain to Australia in 28 days; in May 1923 Lieutenants Macready and Kelly flew a Fokker monoplane across the USA non-stop in 27 hours; between April and September 1924 two American Douglas biplanes made the first flight round the world, a distance of over 27,000 miles in 15½ days' flying time: in November 1925 Alan Cobham made the first of his many solo long-distance flights when he flew from London to Cairo in a **de Havilland 50;** the next year he flew the same machine to India, to South Africa, and to Australia.

Flight of the decade

The most celebrated flight of the decade occurred between May 20 and 21, 1927, when Charles Lindbergh flew his **Ryan 'Spirit of St. Louis'** the 3,600 miles from New York to Paris in the first solo non-stop west to east crossing of the Atlantic in 33 hours 39 minutes. In April the following year (April 12 and 13, 1928) a **Junkers W.33** monoplane flew across the Atlantic from east to west for the first time in 37 hours, and

later that year, in May and June, Sir Charles Kingsford-Smith made the first crossing of the Pacific, in a Fokker monoplane, from California to Australia, via Hawaii and Fiji. In the same year a Savoia flying boat was flown by two Italians non-stop from Rome to Brazil.

Racing and record-breaking continued into the 1930's to give impetus to the machines that would fight the next war. In 1932, the year after the S.6B's world record, the American **Gee Bee 7-11 Super Sportster** set up a landplane speed record of 294.4 mph, and two years later, in the last of the great long-distance races, a **de Havilland Comet** twin-engined monoplane flew from England to Melbourne in Australia in just under three days at an average speed of 180 miles an hour.

Throughout the 1920's advances in high-strength, low-weight steel, aluminium, and magnesium alloys, had continued apace. The time was now ripe for these advances to be turned into practical hardware. The Americans led the way, with a new generation of airliners. The last of the old generation had been the corrugated-skin **Junkers Ju 52/3m** of 1931, but in February 1933 the **Boeing 247** arrived. This was a clean, stressed-skin twin-engined low-wing

Above left: The Short Silver Streak. Britain's first all-metal stressed-skin aircraft appeared just after the end of World War I.

Above: The Supermarine S.6. This float-plane racer won the Schneider Trophy race of 1929, and then raised the world air speed record to 357.75 mph on 12 September 1929. The S.6's successor, the S.6B, was to win the Schneider Trophy outright in 1931 and raise the speed record to over 400 mph for the first time—407 mph.

monoplane with a retractable undercarriage, with variable pitch propellers and flaps. The Boeing 247 was soon followed by the **Douglas DC-1** in July 1933 and the **Lockheed Electra** in February 1934. The slightly larger **DC-2** flew in May 1934, followed by the definitive airliner of the period, the **DC-3,** in December 1935. These aircraft set the seal on American superiority in such machines.

The Germans tried to compete with types such as the **Heinkel 70 'Blitz',** a streamlined low wing monoplane intended for fast internal air routes, the **Heinkel 111,** basically an enlarged twin-engined version of the 70 developed as an airliner and as a

Top left: The Atlantic non-stop. The Ryan Spirit of St. Louis, in which Charles Lindbergh became the first man to make a solo, non-stop west–east transatlantic flight, in 1927.

Top right: Across America non-stop. Lt. John Macready and Lt. Oakley Kelly, the pilots of a non-stop flight from San Diego to Fort Harrison, New York, in 1923.

Above right: Doolittle's Curtiss R3C-2. The architect of the Tokyo Raid won the Schneider Trophy race in 1925.

medium bomber, and the **Junkers Ju 86** which had some small success as an airliner. In 1936-37 the Germans brought out the **Junkers Ju 89** and **Dornier 19** prototypes for heavy bombers intended for operations over vast land areas but these projects were abandoned after the death of General Wever, their principal advocate. By 1938–39 the **Focke-Wulf FW 200 Condor** and the **Ju 90,** both four-engined airliners rather advanced for their time, had appeared and established several new records. But significantly the Germans had no heavy bomber, a field in which the Americans again led the world. Although the French had built the **Bordelaise A.B. 20** and the

Russians the **Tupolev ANT-6,** four-engined heavy bombers earlier, it was the Americans who led the field with the **Boeing Model 299** of 1935, which eventually emerged as the **Boeing B-17** 'Flying Fortress' heavy bomber. At the same time the equipment of American fighter (or pursuit) squadrons was principally the **Boeing P-26,** a low-wing monoplane, which had, however, a fixed undercarriage. More advanced types, such as the **Curtiss P-36** and **Republic P-35,** both of which had fully retractable undercarriages, were in process of design.

German rearmament revealed

The military side of the European aviation industry had also sprung into action again, spurred on by the revelation of rearmament in Germany. Germany had been forbidden from having an air force by the Treaty of Versailles in 1919, but Hitler's ambitions would brook no such restriction, and the existence of the Luftwaffe was revealed in 1935.

For many years the Germans had been training clandestinely and their designers working in secret or abroad so it was not long before several new, advanced types appeared. Among these was the **Messer-**schmitt Me 109 monoplane fighter, the **Junkers Ju 87 Stuka** dive-bomber, in which the Germans placed great hopes, and the **Heinkel He 111** and **Dornier Do 17** medium bombers.

Britain, too, had started to rearm, and her obsolete bombers, such as the **Handley-Page Heyford,** and obsolescent fighters, such as the **Gloster Gauntlet** and later **Gladiator,** were about to be phased out in favour of a new generation of monoplane fighters armed with eight instead of two or four machine guns, such as the **Hawker Hurricane** and Supermarine Spitfire and light and medium bombers such as the **Bristol Blenheim, Vickers Wellington, Handley Page Hampden, and Armstrong Whitworth Whitley.**

Further east, the Russians had been making determined efforts to catch up with the West, and led the world in fighter design in the mid-1930's with the **Polikarpov I-16** the world's first low-wing monoplane fighter equipped with a fully retractable undercarriage. It was first flown in 1933 and was years ahead of its time. More importantly, new fighters and bombers were beginning to take shape on the boards of Russian designers for service in the decade starting in 1940.

WARS
Between Wars

In the 1920s, unrest in the British and French colonies led to the use of air forces in a new role—economical and effective policing operations. But the major developments came in the late 1930s in the Spanish Civil War, which allowed the Germans to try out new aircraft and to perfect aerial tactics, and the Sino-Japanese War, which acted as a proving ground for Japanese men and machines. The experience gained by these powers in these wars between wars had a significant effect on the course of the global conflict that followed.

After the First World War there was a lull in the technical development of military aircraft. Money was in short supply, and governments demanded that their air forces use the types in existence at the war's end. Such resources as were made available were devoted principally to the design and production of new fighters. So the world's air forces sat back to digest the lessons of the First World War while consolidating their position as independent or semi-independent arms on their own. There was little chance for actual combat testing of ideas in the first decade after the war, for the only actions that were fought after the First World War were in the Russian Civil War, and in the British and French policing wars in their colonies. This was altered, however, in three wars fought in the 1930's: The Italian invasion of Ethiopia, the Spanish Civil War, and the Sino-Japanese war. In these three, and especially the last two, much that was later to be confirmed in the Second World War was learned.

As the First World War ended, the Civil War in Russia that had been going on since the revolution of November 1917 was reaching its height. The communist revolutionaries (Reds) were hemmed in on three sides by the counter-revolutionaries (Whites) and on the fourth by the new Polish state. But the Whites were disorganised and lacked any form of central command, and so the Reds were able to hang on.

Neither side possessed many aircraft, let alone a body that might be called an air force, so it was not until the arrival of British, American, French, and Italian troops to support the Whites and to safeguard Allied supply dumps from the war, that air power became a factor of any importance. Even so, the aircraft available were few, and opposition negligible, with the result that the interventionist forces, as they were called, were able to roam over the Red lines at will. The British, operating in north Russia, deployed the most aircraft, but little of importance or significance was achieved up to the time that the Allies realised that the Whites' cause was hopeless and pulled out.

Airborne troubleshooters

The colonial powers, especially Britain and France, had always had trouble with dissident elements along the frontiers of their remoter colonies, and it was a considerable drain on national coffers to police these areas with conventional ground forces. But in the years after the First World War, the leaders of the Royal Air Force, which was struggling to maintain its independence, persuaded the government that in the aeroplane they had the perfect policing weapon—even obsolete types left over from the war could be based in the centre of a tribal dispute and still be able to fly swiftly out to any point from which trouble was reported, and there intimidate the aggressive faction or destroy its villages by bombing. The policy worked with some success along the North-West Frontier in India, in Iraq and the Aden Protectorate, and in East Africa. The French also conducted similar operations in the hinterland of their North African possessions.

These policing operations were cheap and economical in manpower, and went a considerable way to ensuring that the RAF, in particular, survived as an independent arm. But these operations were a diversion from the main stream of the development of flying as a military art, although they did lead to some interesting aircraft. For the need to supply air bases in remote areas resulted in the development of aircraft capable of both the bomber and transport roles, so that men and equipment could be flown out to remote areas, where

the transport aircraft could then be used as a bomber. Examples of this concept were the **Vickers Valentia** and **Bristol Bombay.**

With the introduction of more advanced designs in the 1930's, a new generation of aircraft untried in combat arrived. And when the Italians invaded Ethiopia in 1935, students of air warfare waited to find out how modern aircraft would fare in combat. The war itself was over in eight months, but in that time the Italian air force had played a not inconsiderable part in the overcoming of the ill-trained Ethiopian forces. The very latest in equipment, such as the **Fiat CR 32** fighter and the **Caproni Ca 133** bomber/transport, was used, the fighters to harass the opposing ground forces, and the bombers to ferry in supplies, as well as bomb Ethiopian towns and troops. But there was no air opposition, and so few true conclusions could be drawn.

Italians anger the world

The Italians, to the anger of world opinion, had also dropped poison gas from the air, but this had not been very successful. Apart from everything else the nature of the terrain and the irregular type of warfare being waged meant that air power was of reduced capability. The Italians' greatest achievement was in the consistent and regular use of their bomber/transport aircraft fleet to ferry men and equipment around, thereby improving the techniques of long-distance flight over inhospitable and little-known country.

The two wars that did play a major part in the development of air forces as they were at the beginning of the Second World War were the Spanish Civil War and the Sino-Japanese War. The latter has never received adequate attention from the Western powers.

The Japanese had been slow to start building up their air force, relying almost exclusively on aircraft imported from other countries, or built under licence. But while doing so they learned the technology of the Western powers, and fully analysed the particular merits and failings of each type, carefully building up a fund of experience and knowledge with which to start producing their own aircraft types. One of the starting points of the war about to erupt in the Far East was the Manchurian incident in 1931, and in this Japanese-designed aircraft made their first appearance. Incident followed incident in the next six years, and by the time war proper broke out between China and Japan in 1937, the Japanese had built up their army and navy air forces into formidably armed and trained weapons. The Chinese found themselves in a hopeless position—most of their pilots were Western mercenaries of dubious abilities, and their aircraft were a motley array of obsolete and obsolescent Western types.

At first the Japanese had everything their own way, with their fighters opening up the way for the long-range bombers,

Left: A Heinkel IIIB-2. This medium bomber of the Condor Legion unloads over Valencia during the Spanish Civil War. Here the Germans gained much valuable combat experience.

Warplanes of the Sino-Japanese War

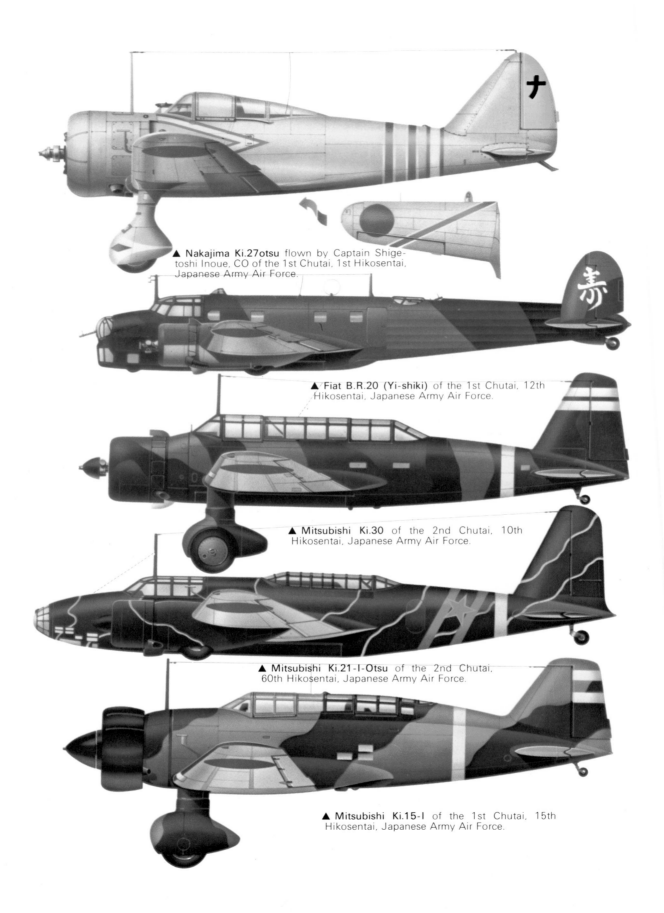

▲ Nakajima Ki.27otsu flown by Captain Shige-
toshi Inoue, CO of the 1st Chutai, 1st Hikosentai,
Japanese Army Air Force.

▲ Fiat B.R.20 (Yi-shiki) of the 1st Chutai, 12th
Hikosentai, Japanese Army Air Force.

▲ Mitsubishi Ki.30 of the 2nd Chutai, 10th
Hikosentai, Japanese Army Air Force.

▲ Mitsubishi Ki.21-I-Otsu of the 2nd Chutai,
60th Hikosentai, Japanese Army Air Force.

▲ Mitsubishi Ki.15-I of the 1st Chutai, 15th
Hikosentai, Japanese Army Air Force.

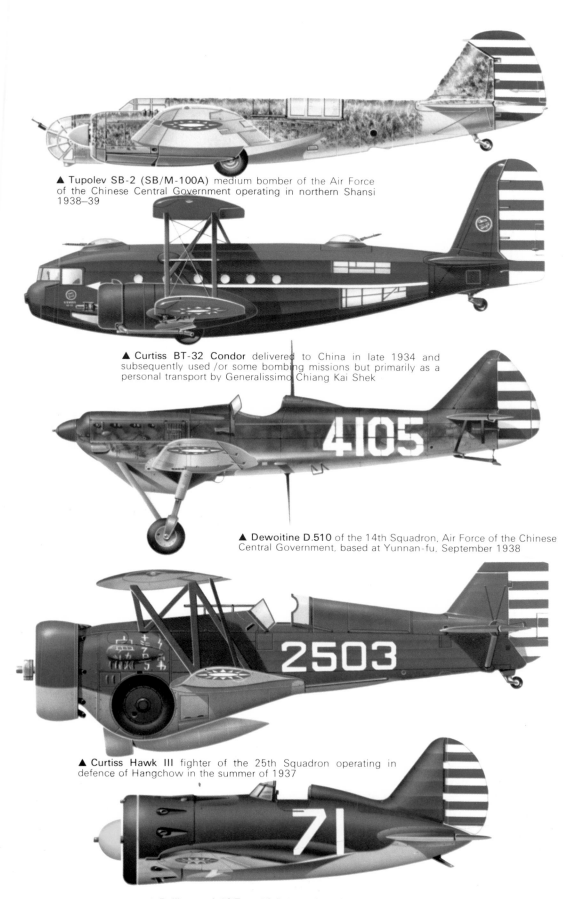

▲ Tupolev SB-2 (SB/M-100A) medium bomber of the Air Force of the Chinese Central Government operating in northern Shansi 1938–39

▲ Curtiss BT-32 Condor delivered to China in late 1934 and subsequently used /or some bombing missions but primarily as a personal transport by Generalissimo Chiang Kai Shek

▲ Dewoitine D.510 of the 14th Squadron, Air Force of the Chinese Central Government, based at Yunnan-fu, September 1938

▲ Curtiss Hawk III fighter of the 25th Squadron operating in defence of Hangchow in the summer of 1937

▲ Polikarpov I-16 Type 10 fighter of the 4th Fighter Wing operating from Changkiakow in the northern Shansi early in 1938

which were thus able to launch strategic attacks on most of the major Chinese targets. Success was not always achieved, however. Growing overconfident of their abilities, the Japanese left over 200 aircraft parked in neat rows on an airfield late in 1937; the Chinese launched a surprise air strike and succeeded in destroying nearly all of them. On another occasion a force of **Aichi D3A** dive-bombers was left without escort, and Chinese fighters destroyed all but one of the Japanese aircraft.

The forgotten war

The Japanese were engaged in another war, undeclared and largely ignored by press and historians, known as the Nomonhan Incident and fought out over the 129-day period between 11 May and 16 September, 1939, along the ill-defined Manchukuoan-Mongolian border. On the ground, where the young Soviet general Grigori Zhukov first showed his abilities, the Soviets were superior but in the air the Japanese machines and pilots proved themselves superior to such modern Soviet aircraft as the fast **SB-2** bombers and **I-153** and **I-16** fighters. The Soviets used rocket-armed aircraft for the first time in the conflict and claimed 320 victories in the air. The Japanese claimed 1,162 destroyed in the air and 98 on the ground.

The real Japanese losses totalled 162 aircraft while the Soviets lost 400, but perhaps the most significant thing to emerge from this inconclusive war was that the Japanese machines were excellent and their pilots well trained. Facts that the Americans ignored to their cost.

The mainstay of the Japanese bomber forces at this time were the Navy's **Mitsubishi G3M** and the Army's **Mitsubishi Ki-21,** supported by **Mitsubishi A5M** and **Nakajima Ki-27** low-wing monoplane fighters. The two last were advanced types for their time of design, in the early 1930's, but their spatted undercarriages were proving a severe hindrance in operations.

The Chinese had by now pulled their airbases back beyond the range of Japanese fighters, and the attacking bombers were beginning to suffer heavy casualties when operating beyond the range of their own fighters. The Japanese therefore set up advanced refuelling bases from which fighters could escort the bombers the whole way to their targets. This was only an interim solution, however, the real answer lying in the adoption of a long-range escort fighter. This was the **Mitsubishi A6M Zero-Sen** which first appeared over China in late Autumn 1940, and fitted with a droppable long-range tank, was capable of escorting bombers on deep penetration raids. The Zero-Sen was a naval fighter, and was the first such aircraft capable of besting its land-based opponents under most combat conditions.

The two most noteworthy aspects of the Sino-Japanese War were the appearance of the Japanese as an independent air power, and the emergence of naval aircraft as the equals, if not superiors, of their land-based counterparts. The chief air adviser to the Chinese, Claire Chennault, an American, warned his American superiors of the capabilities of the Japanese, but he

was disbelieved, the Western powers being firmly convinced that Japanese aircraft design was limited to copying western designs, and that Japanese aircrew were racially inferior. The lesson of this western bigotry was to be dearly paid for at Pearl Harbor and over the Malayan peninsula.

Ominous Japanese leadership

The Japanese, as a result of their island location, were forced to develop their forces along maritime lines, even in aircraft. The Japanese were early protagonists of the aircraft-carrier, and when they began to develop their own aircraft, they soon began to produce advanced types. While the Western powers were content to produce carrier aircraft that were inferior to land-based machines, the Japanese decided that as their naval aircraft would also operate from land bases, they must be the equal of any possible opponent. In the Zero-Sen they found the right answer.

Of more immediate consequences for the Western powers was the Spanish Civil War, which started in 1936 when General Francisco Franco crossed from Spanish Morocco to fight the Republican (communist) government. Italy and Germany saw this as a heaven-sent opportunity to test their new weapons, at the same time as aiding the Falangist (fascist) party under Franco. Soviet Russia, naturally went to the aid of the Republicans and tried out her operational hardware. Thus the scene was set for a major conflict in Spain, with Soviet Russia, Germany, and Italy using that unfortunate country to try out their new aircraft, weapons and tactics.

Franco received quick aid from his allies when German **Junkers 52/3** and Italian **Savoia-Marchetti 81** transport aircraft operated a shuttle service across the Strait of Gibraltar to reinforce the rebel forces in southern Spain. Soviet Russia riposted by sending out large numbers of aircrew and aircraft, together with the necessary spares and groundcrews, to support the Republicans. In all the Russians sent about 1,500 aircraft both complete and in parts to be assembled in Spain, 300–350 of which might be serviceable at any one time. These consisted mostly of **Polikarpov I-15** biplane and **I-16** monoplane fighters, and Tupolev SB-2 monoplane bombers. The Italian contribution was made up mostly of **Fiat CR 32** biplane fighters and **Savoia-Marchetti SM 79** and 81 monoplane bombers. Germany's Condor Legion was equipped at first with **Heinkel 51** biplane fighters and Junkers 52/3 transport/bomber monoplanes.

New planes tip the balance

Initially the opposing forces were relatively evenly balanced, the Italian and Russian bombers being almost immune to the biplane fighters. But with the arrival of the I-16 fighter the balance swung in favour of the Republicans, both the CR 32 and Heinkel 51 being easy meat for the Soviet aircraft. The Nationalist air arm was hard pressed until mid-1938 when their fighter units received the first **Messerschmitt Me 109** (and later some **Fiat G.50**) monoplanes. These proved to be more than

a match for the Republican I-16s and the balance continued to swing against the Republicans with arrival of the new German bombers, the **Dornier 17** and **Heinkel 111.** The Germans also took the opportunity to combat test their new dive-bomber, the **Junkers 87,** at least three flights of which were sent to Spain. With these types

---

Right: A captured Polikarpov I-16. This one was captured by the Nationalists and repainted in their own colours. The Russian-designed fighter proved very successful in Spain.
Below: Fiat B.R.20 bombers, of the Italian Legion's 35th Autonomous Group, on a mission over Spain.
Bottom right: Scramble! Pilots of Messerschmitt Bf 109E fighters of the Condor Legion sprint to their machines for a combat sortie.
Bottom left: After the war. A line-up of Nationalist aircraft. Nearest the camera are two Junkers 52 transports, with S.M. 79 and S.M. 81 bombers behind them.

Germany was able, once the tactical bugs had been eliminated, to secure the skies for Franco's forces. The Germans, having been banned from possessing an air force by the Treaty of Versailles, had forgotten the tactical lessons of the First World War and, instead of flying in loose formations that gave the maximum tactical flexibility, they had reverted to rigid formations that were impossible to handle in the air. Successful Soviet-led air operations made them realise their errors and, largely as a result of the efforts of the great German fighter leader and tactician Werner Moelders, they introduced the loose 'finger-four' formation that could quickly divide into the optimum tactical unit of leader and wingman. However, the Russians, hampered by rigid 'political liability' controls from Moscow, did not manage to assimilate these lessons, which was to cost them dear only a few years later. The non-involved powers also failed to appreciate German developments, and so suffered in World War II until combat had taught them the hard way.

The Luftwaffe myth

As World War II approached, Soviet Russia, Italy, and Germany pulled out of Spain, leaving the Spaniards to fight the war to a finish themselves. But what had the 'interventionists' learned? It appears that Italy and Soviet Russia learned little, Italy remaining content with slow but very manoeuvrable biplane fighters and medium bombers, Russia remaining totally inflexible in her tactical approach. Germany had learned more, particularly in the field of tactics. But she had failed to see the strategic lessons. Her bombing of ports, intended purely as a military measure, had had a far greater economic than military success, and her tactical achievements, particularly close ground support and the use of dive bombers as 'heavy artillery' could only be realised under conditions of air superiority such as those that prevailed during the later stages of fighting in Spain. Thus Germany came to rely too heavily on the power of her air force in aiding ground troops, forgetting the importance of longer-range penetrations. Although the techniques were improved in the period up to the beginning of World War II, the Luftwaffe never became the war-winning weapon its leader, Hermann Goering, imagined, but merely a tactical adjunct of the army. The whole nature of strategic air power had been entirely neglected.

Finally, mention must be made of Guernica, where on April 25, 1937, German fighters and bombers first straffed, then bombed with high explosive and then incendiaries, this small town in northern Spain. About 1,600 of the population of 10,000 were killed. Not unnaturally, the world press seized upon the event and turned it into an example of German ruthlessness and the efficiency of air attack against civilians. This press campaign went far in creating the attitude so prevalent at the beginning of World War II, that bombing was the ultimate strategic weapon. Yet bomb-loads were far too light, and accuracy far too low, for it to be anything of the kind.

The War over Spain

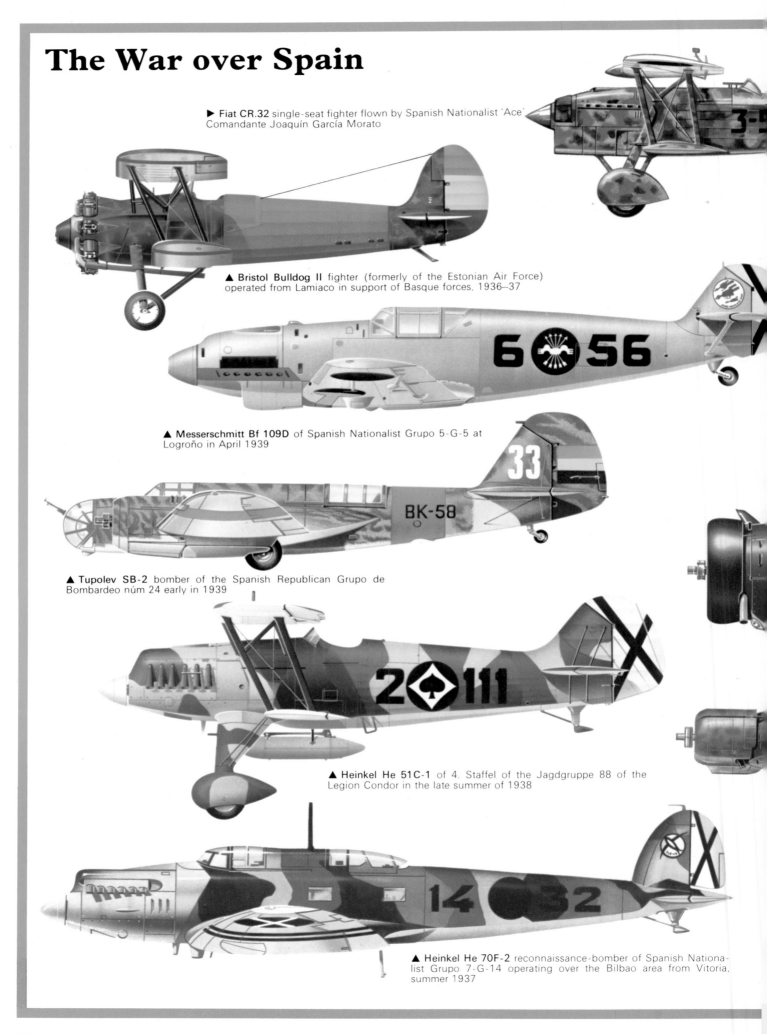

▶ Fiat CR.32 single-seat fighter flown by Spanish Nationalist 'Ace' Comandante Joaquín García Morato

▲ Bristol Bulldog II fighter (formerly of the Estonian Air Force) operated from Lamiaco in support of Basque forces, 1936–37

▲ Messerschmitt Bf 109D of Spanish Nationalist Grupo 5-G-5 at Logroño in April 1939

▲ Tupolev SB-2 bomber of the Spanish Republican Grupo de Bombardeo núm 24 early in 1939

▲ Heinkel He 51C-1 of 4. Staffel of the Jagdgruppe 88 of the Legion Condor in the late summer of 1938

▲ Heinkel He 70F-2 reconnaissance-bomber of Spanish Nationalist Grupo 7-G-14 operating over the Bilbao area from Vitoria, summer 1937

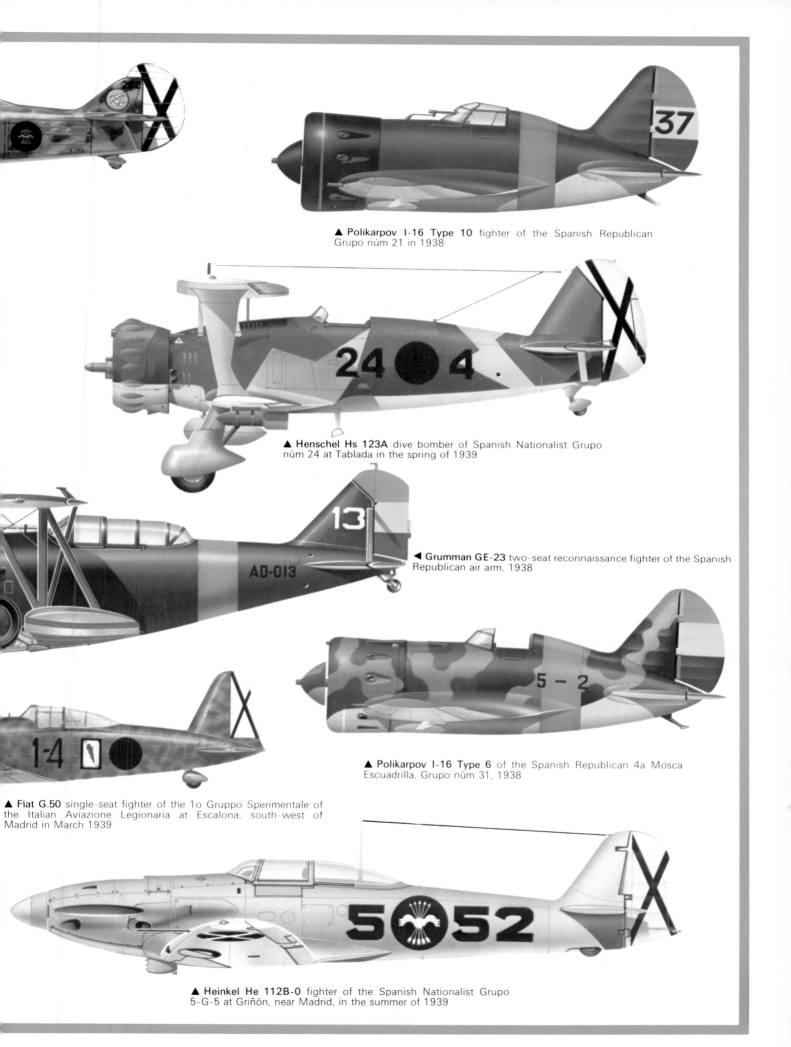

▲ Polikarpov I-16 Type 10 fighter of the Spanish Republican Grupo núm 21 in 1938

▲ Henschel Hs 123A dive bomber of Spanish Nationalist Grupo núm 24 at Tablada in the spring of 1939

◄ Grumman GE-23 two-seat reconnaissance fighter of the Spanish Republican air arm, 1938

▲ Polikarpov I-16 Type 6 of the Spanish Republican 4a Mosca Escuadrilla, Grupo núm 31, 1938

▲ Fiat G.50 single-seat fighter of the 1o Gruppo Sperimentale of the Italian Aviazione Legionaria at Escalona, south-west of Madrid in March 1939

▲ Heinkel He 112B-0 fighter of the Spanish Nationalist Grupo 5-G-5 at Griñón, near Madrid, in the summer of 1939

63

FROM FIRST SEAPLANE TO ZERO

In 1910 Eugene Ely flew a Curtiss biplane off an improvised platform on an American cruiser. Two months later he made the first successful landing on a ship. At about the same time the world's first practical seaplane was making its maiden flight. Naval air power became an established reality during World War I and 1918 saw the completion of the first aircraft carrier. By the end of the 1930s America led the world in carrier design but the Japanese, with their superlative Mitsubishi Zero, were the leaders in carrier aircraft. These were the years of pioneering and development in a branch of air warfare that was to have a shattering significance in the decade of world-wide conflict that lay ahead.

Naval aircraft fall into two basic categories: those that operate from the sea itself, and those that take-off and land on wheeled undercarriages, and are therefore based on land or aircraft-carriers. The first practical example of the former class was the **Curtiss seaplane A.1** of 1911. This was basically a standard landplane fitted with a central supporting float under the fuselage and two balancing floats under the wings. The idea was similar to that of the machine on which the Frenchman Henri Fabre had made tentative hops on March 28, 1910. The Curtiss machine flew for the first time on January 26, 1911 off San Diego in California, and was soon followed by a succession of Curtiss seaplanes.

Seaplanes themselves fall into two major categories: floatplanes, in which the aircraft is supported above the surface of the water on one or two boatlike floats connected to the aircraft by struts; and flying boats, in which the fuselage of the aircraft itself has a boat-shaped bottom, allowing it to float on the water.

The first example of the second basic type of naval aircraft was also American. On November 14, 1910, Eugene Ely flew a Curtiss biplane off an 83-foot platform built over the forecastle of the cruiser *Birmingham*. A little later, on January 18, 1911, Ely flew from San Francisco out to sea and landed on board another cruiser, the *Pennsylvania*. Before the First World War, however, little more was done to develop the potential of aircraft as sea-borne weapons. Although naval air arms were organised, the major part of their effort was devoted to the improvement of seaplanes as scouting weapons. Typical of the designs of the period were the **Curtiss H.4** in the United States, the **Short S.27**, a modified version of which became the first British aircraft to take off from a moving ship, and the **Sopwith Bat Boat** in Great Britain, the **FBA** in France, the Russian **Grigorovich M-5** and the **Hansa-Brandenburg W** in Germany. In Germany however, more thought was given to **Zeppelins** than to seaplanes as the navy's chief scouting weapon.

As a result of the efforts of Churchill and the First Sea Lord, Fisher, the British Royal Naval Air Service was well-equipped and had formulated a clear idea of its role by the beginning of the war, with most of its strength being devoted to patrol work around the shores of Britain herself and over her fleets, but an important portion being dispatched to northern France to guard against German efforts along the Channel coast, which would threaten Britain's ability to reinforce and resupply her military forces in France. In this sector the naval air forces continued to play an important and often overlooked part throughout the war, even after their amalgamation with the Royal Flying Corps on April 1, 1918.

As the war progressed, and the importance of the submarine as a commerce raider became increasingly apparent, so the importance as defensive weapons of the patrol flying boat and the non-rigid airship increased. The best flying boat of the war, the **Felixstowe F.2A**, was a direct result of this need to keep watch for Germany's U-boats as they sortied out across the North Sea towards the Atlantic and the best hunting grounds. In the United States, the **Curtiss H.12** had replaced the H.4 in production in 1916, and many of these were bought by the British.

Airborne submarine destroyer

The naval air station at Felixstowe was at the time commanded by Squadron-Commander J. C. Porte, who had in 1915 discovered that the major failings of the H.4 were its poor powerplants and badly-designed hull. Porte designed a new hull and fitted Hispano-Suiza engines to his improved version of the H.4, which thus became the **Felixstowe F.1**. Similar work on the H.12, but with Rolls-Royce engines, produced the **F.2** and **F.2A**. These had a speed of 95 miles an hour, an endurance of six hours, and an armament of up to seven Lewis guns and 460 lbs of bombs. The slightly larger **F.3**

Above: Landing-on. A Sopwith 1½ Strutter prepares to touch down on an early aircraft-carrier's flight-deck.
Far left: Macchi M.5. This fighter flying-boat taxies out for take-off.
Left: Attack! A Short 184 seaplane releases its torpedo. An aircraft of this type was responsible for the first success with an air-dropped torpedo, when a Turkish merchantman was sunk on 12 August 1915.

had a similar performance, but could carry 920 lbs of bombs. The first submarine to be destroyed by an aircraft was *UC-36*, which was sunk by an F.2A on May 20, 1917.

Obviously the most likely place to spot a submarine was around the convoy it was going to attack, and the British Admiralty realised that there was clearly a need for some sort of aerial escort for convoys. An aircraft would not have the necessary slow speed to accompany convoys, nor the endurance, so the British turned to the SS type of non-rigid airship. This was essentially a large gas bag with the fuselage of an obsolete **B.E. 2** aircraft slung below it on wires. This combination could stay over a convoy in coastal waters for some six hours, and pose a considerable threat to submarines with its 160 lbs of bombs. More importantly, perhaps, was the fact that the SS airships carried radio and could summon up destroyers to deal with underwater intruders. By the end of the war the concept of such 'blimps', as they came to be called, had been developed to produce airships that could stay in the air for almost two days. The great failing of airships, however, was that their capabilities declined as wind speed increased. This was more important to the Germans than the British or French, as their airships were designed to accompany a fast fleet rather than a slow convoy.

Of more significance for future operations, however, was the development of the aircraft carrier. An American pioneered the taking-off and landing of aircraft on a ship, a technique that was still so limited by the beginning of the First World War, that recourse was made to seaplane tenders. These were pioneered by the British, and consisted of converted ferries, with a complement of some four to six seaplanes, which were hoisted out onto the sea for take-off, and recovered after alighting near the tender, by crane. This had decided disadvantages, though, in that the ship had to be stationary during both parts of the operation, and was therefore very vulnerable. What was needed was a method of launching and recovering aircraft from a moving ship. Nevertheless, some successes were achieved by aircraft tenders.

One first scored by an aircraft from a tender was the first torpedo sinking of a ship by an aircraft. This occurred on August 12, 1915, when a **Short 184** from the *Ben-my-Chree* sank a Turkish merchantman. The torpedo was destined to become one of the most potent weapons used by naval aircraft, but its successes in the First World War were not great—aircraft performance, particularly in the field of load-carrying, meant that torpedoes could not be carried by many types. The best torpedo-bomber of the war was the **Sopwith Cuckoo**, which however did not become operational until October, 1918.

Ditch or make for land

The problem of launching an aircraft from a moving ship was partially solved in 1915, when a platform was fitted in the bows of the tender *Vindex*. Flight-Lieutenant H. F. Towler flew a **Bristol Scout** from this on November 3. But there was no way of landing on again. The pilot had either to ditch near his ship or make for land. It

was as yet an unsatisfactory system. An improvement was the fitting of a longer flight deck to the tender *Campania* in 1916. Specially adapted **Fairey Campania** seaplanes could be launched from a wheeled trolley on this, and could land alongside to be recovered.

The problem of landing on a moving ship was solved by Squadron-Commander E. H. Dunning. On August 2, 1917 Dunning landed his **Sopwith Pup** fighter on the 284-foot take-off deck of the aircraft-carrier *Furious*. A few days later he was killed trying to repeat his success. The basic difficulty remaining was how to stop the aircraft after it had landed. At first longitudinal arrester wires were fitted, but as aircraft landing speeds and weights increased, it was found necessary to substitute transverse arrester wires. *Furious* was a converted light battle-cruiser, with a flying-off deck over her forecastle, but as landing

on this deck meant that the pilot had to sideslip in before the superstructure and funnel, a landing-on deck was built over the quarterdeck. It was discovered, however, that the air turbulence set up by the above-mentioned obstacles made it all but impossible to land on it.

The answer lay in a totally unobstructed flight deck. The first ship to have such a deck was the *Argus*, completed in 1918. *Argus* can therefore be considered as the world's first true aircraft-carrier, except for the fact that she was a conversion, rather than a ship built *ab initio* as a carrier. The first real carrier was the Japanese *Hosho*, laid down as such in 1919 and commissioned in 1923. Finally, as far as carriers are concerned, mention must be made of aircraft-launching catapults. The Americans had experimented with these before the First World War, but again it was the British who made the idea practic-

AIRCRAFT CARRIER DEVELOPMENT 1914–39						
Ship	Nationality	Completed	Displacement	Aircraft	Crew	Speed (knots)
Ben-My-Chree	British	1914*	2,651	—	250	24
Campania	British	1915*	18,000	10	600	22
Furious	British	1918*	22,000	20	737	32½
Argus	British	1918*	15,775	20	495	20½
Langley	American	1922*	12,700	55	400	15
Hosho	Japanese	1922	7,470	21	550	25
Eagle	British	1924*	22,600	21	790	24
Akagi	Japanese	1925	26,900	60	2,000	31
Lexington	American	1925*	33,000	90	3,300	34
Hermes	British	1924	10,850	15	720	25
Kaga	Japanese	1928	26,900	60	2,019	27
Ranger	American	1934	14,500	86	2,000	29½
Ark Royal	British	1938	22,000	72	1,575	31
Yorktown	American	1938	19,900	100	2,200	29½
Hiryu	Japanese	1939	17,300	73	1,101	34½

*Converted.

CARRIER AIRCRAFT 1919–39						
Type	Purpose	Country	Date	Armament	Speed mph	Range miles
Loire-Nieuport 41	db	France	1937	496-lb bomb and 3×7.5-mm mg	162	745
Aichi D1A	db	Japan	1934	682-lb bomb and 2×7.7-mm mg	174	659
Aichi D3A	db	Japan	1938	814-lb bomb and 3×7.7-mm mg	242	1,131
Mitsubishi B1M	tb	Japan	1923	18-in torpedo or 1,070 lb of bombs and 2×7.7-mm mg	127	230
Mitsubishi A5M2	f	Japan	1937	2×7.7-mm mg	265	460
Mitsubishi A6M2	f	Japan	1939	2×20-mm cannon and 2×7.7-mm mg	316	1,165
Nakajima B5N2	tb	Japan	1937/9	18-in torpedo or 1,765 lbs of bombs and 4×7.7-mm mg	235	609
Blackburn Baffin	tb	UK	1934	1,765-lb torpedo or 2,000 lbs of bombs and 2×.303-in mg	136	450
Blackburn Skua	db	UK	1938	500-lb bomb and 4×.303-in mg	225	760
Fairey Fly-catcher	f	UK	1923	2×.303-in mg	133	311
Fairey IIIF	r	UK	1928	2×.303-in mg and 500 lbs of bombs	120	450
Fairey Swordfish	tb	UK	1936	1,610-lb torpedo or 1,500 lbs of bombs and 2×.303-in mg	139	1,030
Gloster Sea Gladiator	f	UK	1937	4×.303-in mg	245	425
Boeing FB-1	f	US	1925	1×.5-in and 1×.3-in mg	167	509
Boeing F3B	f	US	1927	1×.5-in and 1×.3-in mg	156	500
Boeing F4B	f	US	1929	1×.5-in and 1×.3-in mg	187	401
Brewster F2A	f	US	1939	1×.5-in and 1×.3-in mg	301	1,095
Curtiss TS-1	f	US	1922	1×.3-in mg	125	482
Curtiss F6C	f	US	1925	2×.3-in mg	155	361
Curtiss F11C	f & b	US	1933	474 lbs of bombs and 2×.3-in mg	205	560
Curtiss SBC-3	db	US	1937	500-lb bomb and 2×.3-in mg	220	635
Douglas TBD	tb	US	1937	21-in torpedo or 1,000 lbs of bombs and 1×.3-in and 1×.5-in mg	206	435
Grumman F3F	f	US	1935	2×.3-in mg	264	980
Vought SB2U	b	US	1937	1,000 lbs of bombs and 2×.3-in mg	250	635

Above: A Sopwith 1½ Strutter, fitted with a skid landing-gear, takes off from a carrier.
Right: HMS Furious. Once a light battle-cruiser, she first had a flight-deck laid over the bows, then another over the stern, and was finally converted to proper aircraft-carrier configuration.
Below: Sopwith 2F.1s. These shipboard Camels are on the forward flight-deck of HMS *Furious*. The paling was intended to prevent the wind from blowing the aircraft around on the deck or over the side.

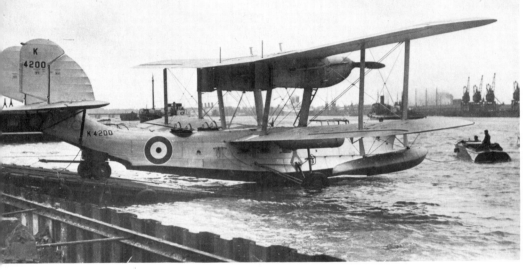

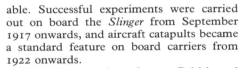

able. Successful experiments were carried out on board the *Slinger* from September 1917 onwards, and aircraft catapults became a standard feature on board carriers from 1922 onwards.

With the exception of some British and Italian raids, naval aircraft were used for tactical rather than strategic purposes, with convoy and escort and fleet scouting being the principal tasks. The best aircraft of the war, as far as strictly naval flying is concerned, was the Curtiss H.12/Felix-stowe F.2A, with some Italian, French and Russian flying boats also performing creditably. These were the Italian **Macchi M.5** flying boat fighter and **M.8** patrol flying boat, the Russian **Grigorovich M-9** and the French **FBA** (Franco-British Aviation) **Type H.** The Germans concentrated on floatplanes rather than flying boats, with the emphasis on defensive fighters, and produced a series of excellent Hansa-Brandenburg aircraft. The best of these were the **KDW, W.12** and **W.29,** the last of which was a formidable mono-plane two-seater, armed with two fixed Spandau guns and one Parabellum gun for pilot and gunner respectively.

America and Japan forge on

Some of the land-based aircraft used by the Royal Naval Air Service from its bases in northern France also made some interesting contributions. The RNAS was largely responsible for the introduction of heavy bombers into the British air forces, and its first two aircraft of this category were the **Handley-Page O/100** and **O/400.** The RNAS also had first claim on Sopwith types in the early part of the war, and was responsible for the introduction of the **1½-Strutter** and the **Triplane,** which in turn led to the celebrated **Fokker Dreidecker.**

Although Great Britain had emerged from the First World War as the leading exponent of naval air power, this lead was soon frittered away in the internecine squabble that resulted from the establishment of the Royal Air Force. The Navy wished to have its own independent air arm, but the RAF refused. So the Navy's aircraft were decided upon by the RAF, and their pilots provided by that service as well. It was not until 1937 that the Royal Navy reacquired its own air force, by which time the United States and Japan had emerged as the two major contestants for the leadership in the realm of naval air power.

The United States' naval air arm had got off to a slow start, but after the First World War it forged ahead. It stayed out of the government's way, and its great leader from 1921 to 1933, Rear-Admiral W. A. Moffett, concentrated on laying the foundations for the great air arm the US Navy was to have in World War II. The full efforts of press publicity were used, and whereas 'Billy' Mitchell and the United States Army Air Corps came in for considerable opposition,

Top left: Fairey Barracuda. This torpedo-bomber was the final expression of Britain's adherence to the multi-seat torpedo aircraft. On 3 April 1944, Barracudas crippled the German battleship *Tirpitz*.
Above left: Vickers Supermarine Scapa. This flying-boat was typical of the patrol boats built by Britain between the wars.
Above: HMS Argus. She was Britain's first true purpose-built aircraft-carrier heralding a complete change in naval tactical thinking.
Above right: Felixstowe F.2A. This flying boat, one of the best of its type in World War I, was based on the Curtiss America series of boats with a new hull designed by Commander J. Porte.

the Navy's air arm grew surely and steadily. Admiral W. S. Sims, America's great capital ship protagonist, had become a staunch advocate of the aircraft-carrier in 1922, and by 1929 the US Navy had one old and two new aircraft-carriers. Much still needed to be learned about carrier operations, but the Americans went to their task with a will.

On the other side of the Pacific, Japan had got off to a good start in developing a naval air arm with the commissioning of the *Hosho* in 1923. Greatly aided by ex-RNAS airmen who did not wish to serve with the RAF, the Japanese were soon making considerable strides in the development of techniques such as night and poor-weather

flying, long distance navigation and extended over-water flights.

Both the Japanese and the Americans at first had difficulty in devising the right way to use their new weapons. To most naval thinkers, the battleship still reigned supreme, although Mitchell's well-publicised demonstration attacks on surrendered German dreadnoughts had shown their vulnerability to air attack. So the carrier was at first considered merely as an adjunct of the battle-line. Carrier aircraft were intended to strike and cripple the enemy's battleships so that the battle-line could close and finish the job.

Speed and armour

But this ignored the carrier's lack of defensive armour and her high speed. It was only in the 1930's that the Americans, and to a lesser extent the Japanese, realised that carriers should form separate striking groups of their own, in company with fast cruisers and destroyers, using their superior speed to evade more heavily armed, but slower, opponents. Where the Japanese did have an advantage, however, was in the armoured flight decks of their carriers. This they learned from the British; and although it reduced the hangar space available below decks, it did afford vital protection from armour-piercing bombs dropped either by a dive-bomber at low altitude or a level bomber at high altitude.

The British, although they had led the way with aircraft-carriers during and in the first few years after the First World War, had by the beginning of the 1930's lapsed into third place, partly as a result of the inter-service squabbles that had prevented the formation of a coherent tactical doctrine for which carriers could be built, and partly as a result of her meagre defence vote. Though British carriers were tough and sea-worthy, they were slower than contemporary American and Japanese carriers, and had a considerably lower aircraft complement. France's carriers were not up to the standard of the big three's, and the only other country to have a carrier before the beginning of World War II was Germany. Her sole carrier was the *Graf Zeppelin* and, although launched before the outbreak of hostilities, she was never commissioned.

As far as the actual aircraft themselves were concerned, these always lagged behind their land-based contemporaries until the late 1930's. Except in the specialised field of flying boats, in which excellent designs such as those of the British Short Brothers and the German Dornier and Blohm und Voss companies were outstanding, the exigencies of carrier life necessitated that old-fashioned design concepts and structures be retained when they had been abandoned by landplane designers. Biplanes lingered on, retractable undercarriages made a tardy appearance, and the need for folding

wings to fit under low hangar roofs meant clumsy, drag-producing shapes and folding mechanisms.

On the whole the Americans led in the field of carrier aircraft design, and by the second half of the 1930's aircraft with low wings, retractable undercarriages and all metal structure were the rule. Yet because of the extra needs of carrier operation, these aircraft, be they fighters, torpedo-bombers, dive-bombers, or level bombers, were always of a lower performance than their land-based counterparts. This was all to change, however, as a result of the Japanese experience in China.

It had been a tenet of carrier operations ever since the First World War's end that carrier aircraft would fight only other carrier aircraft. Thus all that was essential was that one's own aircraft be superior to any possible enemy's carrier aircraft. But of course the Japanese found out that with the type of modern, amphibious warfare developing in the late 1930's, carrier aircraft would often be called upon to oppose land-based aircraft. Thus it was essential to develop machines in each category that could take on the best land-based aircraft on equal terms. The Americans did not realise this until it was too late. Their fighters and attack aircraft were no match for Japan's superlative **Mitsubishi Zero.** Only after 18 months of harrowing combat would the Americans introduce a type equal, if not superior, to this excellent aircraft.

PROGRAMME For a War

The enormity of the conflict which followed Germany's invasion of Poland in the Autumn of 1939 caught even the Luftwaffe unprepared. But the air forces of all the other countries which were ultimately to become engaged in World War II were even more inadequately equipped. Biplanes were still front-line fighters in both America and Britain, and Germany and Japan led the fighter field in their theatres. But in the end it was the foresight of the Allied Powers, who had not neglected the development of heavy bombers, that was to expose the fatal flaws in the strategic planning of their enemies. Nonetheless there were some strange aircraft types amongst that motley array which lined up on each side in 1939 ready to do battle in the first major war in the air.

When World War II broke out after the German invasion of Poland on September 1, 1939, no power in Europe was prepared for it. The situation was simple. Hitler had briefed his military commanders to prepare for all-out war by the mid-1940s and by 1942 at the earliest. In the meantime he had built up the Greater German Reich by exploiting the unwillingness of Germany's neighbours to bring on another European war. In 1939 he was convinced that he would be able to get away with it again in the case of Poland without having to meet any challenge from France and Britain. The United States had declared itself firmly neutral, while the interests of the Berlin-Rome Axis in the Far East were endorsed by Imperial Japan. Thus when he invaded Poland, Hitler was only thinking of a campaign lasting weeks, followed by another patched-up peace. The Wehrmacht and its Luftwaffe did not have the resources for more. Neither were Britain and France ready for war. Their declaration of war on Germany on September 3 meant that the new European conflict was very different from that of 1914, when all parties had been eager for the fray and confident of its outcome. War, in short, had materialised before its practitioners had equipped themselves with the right tools.

For Germany, war with Britain and France meant that Germany was immediately faced with war on two fronts when she was barely equipped to tackle Poland with 100 per cent hopes of a rapid victory. For Britain and France, their declaration of war in support of Poland meant absolutely nothing unless Poland could hold out long enough to enable the Western Allies to build up sufficient strength to invade western Germany. In the meantime they were trying to localise the conflict. Militarily speaking it was a very gentlemanly war to begin with—apart from the case of the hapless Poles. Neither side wanted to provoke the other past all reasonable grounds, the Western Allies until they were ready, Hitler until he was

finished with Poland and could try for another of his celebrated 'agreements'.

But even if the will for all-out war had existed in 1939 the weapons for waging it did not. This applied to air warfare above every other arm.

The major fallacies besetting the com-

batant air forces in 1939 can best be analysed by examining the reasoning which had supplied both the RAF and the German Luftwaffe with their most important military aircraft.

Prophets embarrassed

In Britain, an excellent case in point was the **Bristol Blenheim**, originally a promising type which had become invested with almost magical powers—and correspondingly impossible tasks—simply 'because it was there'. The Blenheim had sprung from a civilian design with stressed-skin, all-metal construction: the largely privately-financed low-wing monoplane **Bristol Type 142** of 1935. This clean and advanced aircraft outpaced the RAF's front-line fighter, the biplane **Gloster Gauntlet**, by 82 mph on its official trial (the Gauntlet's best speed was 225 mph). Such a performance was acutely embarrassing to those British prophets of disarmament who

claimed that British know-how had given the RAF the best fighters in the world, but it was easy to develop the argument that the new fast bomber would render the best enemy fighters impotent by its speed. This was by no means a purely British conceit, for across the Channel the first monoplane medium bombers for the Luftwaffe—the **Dornier Do 17, Heinkel He 111, and Ju 88**—all adhered to the fallacy that speed negated enemy gun-power.

What mattered in 1939 was that the Luftwaffe had been given numbers of operational aircraft which none of her immediate opponents could hope to match. It did not matter at the time that those numbers had been delivered at the expense of far more important, long-term designs. The Luftwaffe's line-up in September 1939 was perfectly capable of beating the air arms of every single neighbour of Germany and its aircraft had more than enough range for the job. But the watchword for the entire German Wehrmacht had always been 'one target at a time'. Every single international crisis in Hitler's expansionist policy since the occupation of the Rhineland in 1936 had left no reserves to spare, and the same applied to the Polish campaign in 1939. There was not even a central fighter force for the defence of the Reich, although this oversight was as much due to Göring's arrogance as to Hitler's refusal to sanction the earmarking of any resources for purely defensive duties.

Of the Western Allies, France was undoubtedly in the worst state as far as her air arm was concerned. Her bomber force suffered from the inability to find an adequate

Top: Ju 88, Germany's best bomber. First flown in 1936, some 15,000 Ju 88s were built between 1939 and 1945, over 9,000 of them bombers.
Centre: The dreaded Ju 87 Stuka. At first this dive-bomber demoralised opposition; but when it met RAF fighters its vulnerability was decisively exposed.
Bottom: Boeing P-26A pursuit ships. This wire-braced monoplane was typical of mid-'30s fighters. By 1939 it was obsolete and outclassed by Japanese fighters.
Far left: The biplane Gladiator. The belief that manoeuvrability would prevail over the speed and firepower of the new monoplanes was soon proved wrong.

replacement for the obsolete **Bloch 210**, production of which had ceased in 1936. The Bloch 210 was still in service in 1939, even though it was considered unsuitable for day bombing missions. Although three promising types had emerged, only vestigial numbers of them had been ordered by the time war broke out. None of the three looked further ahead than the twin-engined, medium bomber concept. They were the **Lioré et Olivier LeO 451**, the **Bloch MB 131**, and the **Amiot 340**. The main French fighter in September 1939 was the **Morane-Saulnier M.S. 406**. Outclassed by Germany's **Me 109** fighter on all counts, it was at least sturdy and manoeuvrable. A superior French fighter had been ordered, the **Dewoitine D.520**, with stressed metal construction and an in-line engine, maximum speed 320 mph, armed with one 20-mm cannon and four wing machine guns, but it had only just started to come off the production lines in September.

Exaggerated confidence

In the creaky, improvised scaffolding which constituted the Allied war plan in September 1939, the French placed a wildly exaggerated confidence in the capacity of the RAF to launch heavy bombing attacks on Germany. The trio of bombers with which RAF Bomber Command went to war in September 1939 consisted of the **Handley Page Hampden**, the **Armstrong Whitworth Whitley**, and the **Vickers Wellington**. The latter was by far the best machine, with a maximum range of 1,600 miles and maximum bomb-load of 4,500 lbs. Its best virtue, however, was the incredible toughness of its lattice-work 'geodetic' construction, the brain-child of Vickers' brilliant designer Barnes Wallis. It was Wallis who had produced the single-engined **Wellesley** bomber of 1937, which had shattered the World Long Distance Record by flying from Ismailia, Egypt, to Darwin in Australia—a non-stop distance of 7,157 miles—in November 1938.

Much more important, however, was the fact that the British Air Ministry specifications of 1936 had already led to the design of the RAF's first four-engine heavy bombers, the **Short Stirling** and **Handley Page Halifax**. The prototypes of both had flown by the end of October 1939 and as a result both eventually entered service in late 1940.

British bombing policy was embryonic in September 1939. Official policy regarded the prospect of inflicting damage on German civilian property—let alone inflicting civilian casualties—as anathema. No firm pattern of vital German industrial targets had been drawn up—targets which the bombers actually in service could attack with a fair chance of success. Bad-weather navigation and bomb-aiming were problems whose solution lay in the future. The man who was to become Bomber Command's most famous pilot, Guy Gibson, later recorded the apprehension with which he and his comrades faced the prospect of taking off for the first time in a Hampden with a full bomb-load— 'None of us had ever done it before and we did not even know whether our Hampdens would unstick with 2,000 pounds of bombs'. And in the first weeks of World War II only one target was regarded as legitimate by RAF Bomber Command and the Luftwaffe. This was the warship—provided only that it could be attacked with no danger to civilians, either at sea or in an open harbour.

Fatal weaknesses hidden

Although the Luftwaffe of September 1939 was more than a match for the Allied opposition, it too had much to learn. The dive-bombing units—later to contribute one of the most dreaded words of the war, 'Stuka' (from *Sturzkampfflugzeug,* dive-bomber) had yet to be tried in action in close collaboration with mobile ground troops. The obsolescent **Henschel HS 123**, a biplane, was still in service as a ground-attack aircraft. The most serious weakness in the fighter arm still lay concealed: the concept of the 'destroyer' fighter. The **Messerschmitt Me 110** twin-engined heavy fighter was cast in the destroyer role, carving through the enemy fighters to let the bombers through. Not until it came up against adequate fighter opposition would its fatal weaknesses be revealed. The best weapon by far in the Luftwaffe's armoury was the **Messerschmitt Me 109E** fighter: 357 mph maximum speed, two 7.9-mm machine guns and two 20-mm cannons.

As far as modern monoplane fighters were concerned the RAF's main fighter in September 1939 was the **Hawker Hurricane,** with the **Supermarine Spitfire** following it into service. At the beginning of hostilities fourteen Hurricane squadrons were classed as fully operational, while only nine Fighter Command squadrons had been equipped with Spitfires. The biplane **Gladiator** was still in service, and the **Boulton Paul Defiant,** a fighter with a rear turret, still awaited exposure as the death-trap it was against the Me 109.

In September 1939, Germany's hapless partner in the 'Pact of Steel' was clinging firmly to her policy of 'non-belligerence'. Of all the countries of Europe, Mussolini's Italy was perhaps the least ready for war in any shape or form. Her air force, the *Regia Aeronautica,* lacked any fighter of the calibre of the Me 109 or Spitfire. Low power engines and weak armament were the main bugbears of Italian fighter design. The best Italian aircraft was probably the hunchbacked, tri-motor **Savoia-Marchetti S.M.79**—a good bomber which could also carry a brace of torpedoes. Italy also had produced the flying prototype of a fourengined bomber, the **Piaggio P.108**; she was in fact the only Axis power to employ such an aircraft, although it did not enter service with the Regia Aeronautica until 1942.

Out of date innovator

The other major pro-Axis neutral in September 1939 was Soviet Russia. Barely six months had passed since Soviet aircraft had been fighting German and Italian types in the Spanish Civil War, but the signing of the Soviet-German Non-Aggression Pact of August 1939 had totally reversed Soviet Russia's position *vis-à-vis* the Axis bloc. In September 1939 Soviet Russia's standard fighter was still the **Polikarpov I-16,** the tubby **Rata**— once an all-round innovator with its retractable undercarriage, four-gun armament, and cantilever wings, but now far gone in obsolescence.

The backbone of the Soviet bomber force was made up of two basic types: the **Tupolev SB-2** and **Ilyushin DB-3F** (later renamed **Il-4**). In many respects the SB-2 was a parallel to the German Dornier 17: it was designed as a medium-range 'fast' bomber, carried only three machine guns for self-protection, went into series-production in 1936, and was immediately battle-tested in Spain where (together with the earlier **SB-1**) it gained the nickname 'Katyusha', and where its high speed performance led the Soviet air force command—like their German counterpart—to draw some wrong conclusions regarding its capabilities. As a result large numbers of these bombers were in first-line service until late 1942 and provided easy meat for German fighters.

The DB-3F (Il-4), a long-range medium bomber developed from the **DB-3 (TsKB-26)** of 1936, was built in large series until mid-1944 and, together with the fourengined **TB-7** (later **Pe-8**), was the mainstay of the Soviet ADD (Long-Range Aviation). A number of DB-3Fs came under the Soviet naval command and some of these naval bombers were to gain the distinction of being the first Soviet aircraft to drop bombs on Berlin (August 1941). Used in large numbers throughout the war years, the Il-4 was also to give good service as a naval torpedo bomber.

Apart from these standard types the Soviet air force could also field a very large number of older machines ranging from single-engined biplanes to four-engined bomber-transports, and there were some very promising new types in the pipeline.

Japan, the third member of the Axis bloc in September 1939, had been involved in all-out war with China for over two years. This was no polite war, respecting civilian lives and property, but the full, brutal experience. By September 1939, Japanese military aircraft had been well and truly blooded. One striking feature was Japan's rapid development of long-range twin-engined bombers for her Army and Navy air forces. The first of these was the **Mitsubishi G3M** ('Nell'), with a bomb-load of 2,200 lbs and a range of 2,900 miles. 'Nell' was a Navy bomber, entering service in 1937; her Army counterpart was the **Mitsubishi K.21** ('Sally'), with a performance similar to that of the British Handley Page Hampden. By 1939 these Japanese bombers (particularly 'Nell'), had given a clear enough warning of

the shape of things to come in the Far East by their impressive operations against Chinese coastal cities, flying from southern Japan and Formosa. At the time Europe went to war Japan's standard Navy fighter was the **Mitsubishi A5M** ('Claude')—a fixed-undercarriage, low-wing monoplane with two fuselage machine guns and a top speed of 273 mph. The Army equivalent was the **Nakajima Ki.27** ('Nate') which had a slightly superior performance to that of the 'Claude'.

US Hawks for export

The United States' front-line fighters in September 1939 were soon to enter the fray in the Atlantic theatre as many of them were exported before and after the outbreak of hostilities. These aircraft included the **Curtiss P-36,** known as the **Hawk 75A** (aircooled radial engine, 300 mph) and the **Curtiss P-40 Warhawk** (liquid-cooled inline, 350 mph). France promptly ordered 100 P-36s the year they appeared (1938) and all surviving French P-36s were taken over by the RAF in 1940, in which service they soldiered on as the **Mohawk**. The P-40 was America's first mass-produced fighter and it was also exported to Britain, France, Soviet Russia (after the German invasion of 1941) and China (the French order being ultimately taken over by the RAF). Export P-40s were known as **Tomahawks** in the RAF; the **P-40E-N** were named **Kittyhawk.** The P-40's armament consisted of six .50-inch machine guns. In performance and hitting-power the P-40 was somewhat inferior to the leading European fighters; the preference of American designers for heavy machine guns rather than cannon was to last right through World War II into the jet age, with the favourite standardised calibre being the big .50.

As far as naval aviation was concerned in September 1939 the top three powers were Japan, Britain, and America. The Japanese carrier fighter in 1939 was still the Mitsubishi Claude, but design work was well advanced on the superb **Mitsubishi A6M Zero-Sen** which appeared the following

PRINCIPAL BOMBERS IN SERVICE 1939						
Country	Type	First ordered	Engine(s)	Max. loaded range	Crew	Number built
Great Britain	Armstrong Whitworth Whitley	1936	Two Armstrong-Siddeley Tiger VIIIs, 860 hp	1,500 miles	5	1,824
	Bristol Blenheim I	1936	Two Bristol Mercury VIIIs, 840 hp	1,090 miles	3	6,260
	Handley-Page Hampden	1936	Two Bristol Pegasus XVIIIs, 1,000 hp	1,460 miles	4	1,430
	Vickers Wellington I	1936	Two Bristol Pegasus XVIIIs, 1,000 hp	1,600 miles	6	11,461
Italy	Savoia-Marchetti SM-79 *Sparviero*	1936	Three Alfa-Romeo 126 RC 34s, 780 hp	1,000 miles	4–5	1,200 approx.
	Fiat BR-20 Cicogna	1936	Two Fiat A80R C-41s, 1,030 hp (Take off)	1,150 miles	6	600 approx.
Germany	Heinkel He 111H	1936	Two Junkers Jumo 211Fs, 1,140 hp	1,311 miles	5	7,450
	Dornier Do 17Z	1936	Two Bramo 323, 1,000 hp	745 miles	4–5	522
	Junkers Ju 88A	1937	Two Junkers Jumo 211 B1s, 1,210 hp	2,546 miles	4	14,980
	Junkers Ju 87B	1936	One Junkers Jumo 211D 1,100 hp	342 miles	2	5,709
Japan	Mitsubishi Navy 96 G3M 'Nell'	1936	Two Mitsubishi Kinsei 42s, 1,000 hp (Take off)	2,900 miles	7	1,048
	Mitsubishi Ki-21 Army 'Sally'	1936	Two Nakajima Ha-5 Kais, 1,900 hp	1,670 miles	7	1,880
France	Amiot 143 Bn4/5	1934	Two Gnome-Rhone 14 Kjrs, 870 hp	640 miles	5–7	153
	Liore-et-Olivier Le0-451	1937	Two Gnome-Rhone 14N48/48s	1,530 miles	4	600
Soviet Russia	Ilyushin DB-3	1937	Two M-88Bs, 1,100 hp	1,620 miles	3–4	5,000 +
	Tupolev SB-2	1934	Two M-103s, 990 hp	1,430 miles	3	6,000 +
United States	Boeing B-17C 'Flying Fortress'	1935	Four Wright Cyclone R 1820-65s, 1,200 hp	2,000 miles	6–8	12,677
	Douglas B-18 Bolo	1937	Two Wright Cyclone R 1820-53s, 1,000 hp	1,100 miles	6	350

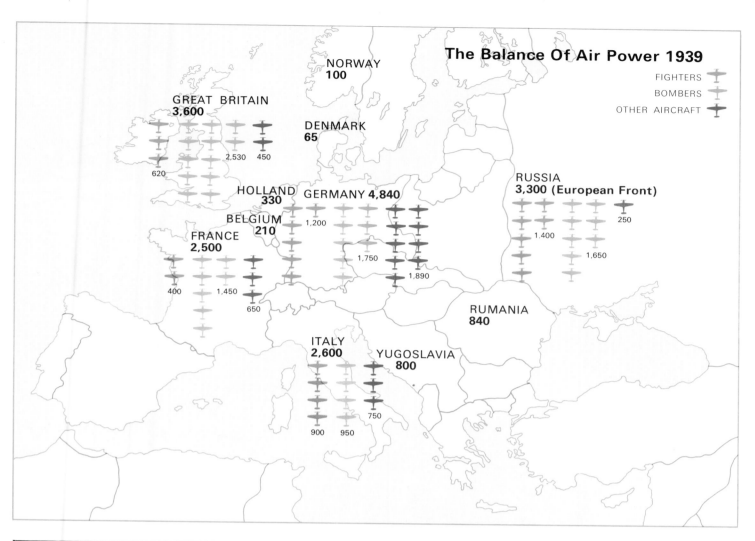

The Balance Of Air Power 1939

FIGHTERS
BOMBERS
OTHER AIRCRAFT

NORWAY **100**

GREAT BRITAIN **3,600**
2,530 450
620

DENMARK **65**

HOLLAND **330**
GERMANY **4,840**
1,200
1,750
1,890

BELGIUM **210**

FRANCE **2,500**
400 1,450
650

RUSSIA **3,300** (European Front)
250
1,400
1,650

RUMANIA **840**

ITALY **2,600**
YUGOSLAVIA **800**
750
900 950

NEW AIRCRAFT TYPES 1939-40

Country	Type	Engines	Max. speed	Max. loaded range	Rate of climb	Ceiling	Crew	Number ordered
Great Britain	Bristol Beaufighter	Two Bristol Hercules III = 1,425 hp	321 mph	1,470 miles	5.8 mins to 10,000 ft	26,500 ft	2	5,962
	Handley Page Halifax	Four Rolls-Royce Merlin Xs = 1,145 hp	281 mph	1,860 miles	45 mins to 20,000 ft	20,000 ft	7	6,177
	Short Stirling	Four Bristol Hercules XIs = 1,590 hp	270 mph	1,930 miles	30 mins to 15,000 ft	17,000 ft	7	1,759
United States	Grumman F4F	Pratt & Whitney R-1830-76 Twin Wasp = 1,200 hp	330 mph	1,150 miles	2,265 ft per min	29,000 ft	1	7,898
	Bell P-39 Airacobra	Allison V-1710-85 = 1,200 hp	355 mph	675 miles	2,040 ft per min	29,000 ft	1	9,558
	North American B-25 Mitchell	Two Wright Cyclone 2600-29s = 1,850 hp	275 mph	1,350 miles	19 mins to 15,000 ft	24,200 ft	1	9,817
Japan	Mitsubishi A6M2 'Zeke'	Nakajima Sakae = 925 hp	316 mph	1,265 miles	7 mins to 19,865 ft	33,785 ft	1	10,611
	Mitsubishi G4M 'Betty'	Two Mitsubishi Kasei 25s =1,850 hp	271 mph	2,262 miles	13.21 mins to 16,400 ft	29,365 ft	7	2,479

PRINCIPAL FIGHTERS IN SERVICE 1939

Country	Type	First ordered	Engine(s)	Max. speed	Max. loaded range	Crew	Number built (all versions)
Great Britain	Supermarine Spitfire I	1936	Rolls-Royce Merlin II = 1,030 hp	365 mph	395 miles	1	Over 20,000 produced
	Hawker Hurricane I	1936	Rolls-Royce Merlin II = 1,030 hp	324 mph	525 miles	1	14,553 produced
	Boulton Paul Defiant	1937	Rolls-Royce Merlin III = 1,440 hp	304 mph	460 miles	2	1,060 produced
	Gloster Gladiator I	1935	Bristol Mercury IX = 856 hp	253 mph	254 miles	1	527
Germany	Messerschmitt Bf109E	1938	Daimler-Benz DB 601A = 1,100 hp	354 mph	412 miles	1	1,540
	Messerschmitt Bf 110	1938	Two Daimler-Benz DB 601 As = 1,100 hp	349 mph	565 miles	2	6,140
Italy	Fiat CR-42	1939	One Fiat A-74 RC 38 radial = 840 hp	244 mph	480 miles	1	1,781
	Fiat G-50	1938	One Fiat A-74 RC 38 radial = 840 hp	293 mph	420 miles	1	708
France	Dewoitine D-520	1939	One Hispano-Suiza 12Y = 1,000 hp	329 mph	620 miles	1	740
	Morane-Saulnier MS-406	1936	One Hispano-Suiza 12Y-31 = 860 hp	302 mph	497 miles	1	2,260
	Bloch MB-150/151	1938	One Gnome-Rhone 14N-25 = 1,080 hp	301 mph	373 miles	1	825
Japan	Mitsubishi A5M 'Claude'	1936	One Nakajima Kotobuki Model 3 = 640 hp	280 mph	746 miles	1	1,094
	Nakajima Ki-27 'Nate'	1936	One Nakajima Ha-1b = 710 hp	292 mph	340 miles	1	3,399
Soviet Russia	Polikarpov I-16	1934	One M-62 = 850 hp approx.	326 mph	500 miles	1	7,000
United States	Grumman F2F	1934	One Pratt & Whitney Twin Wasp Jr = 650 hp	233 mph	535 miles	1	55
	Curtiss P-36	1936	One Wright Cyclone GR-1820-G205A = 1,200 hp	239 mph	960 miles	1	210

Warplanes of the 1930s

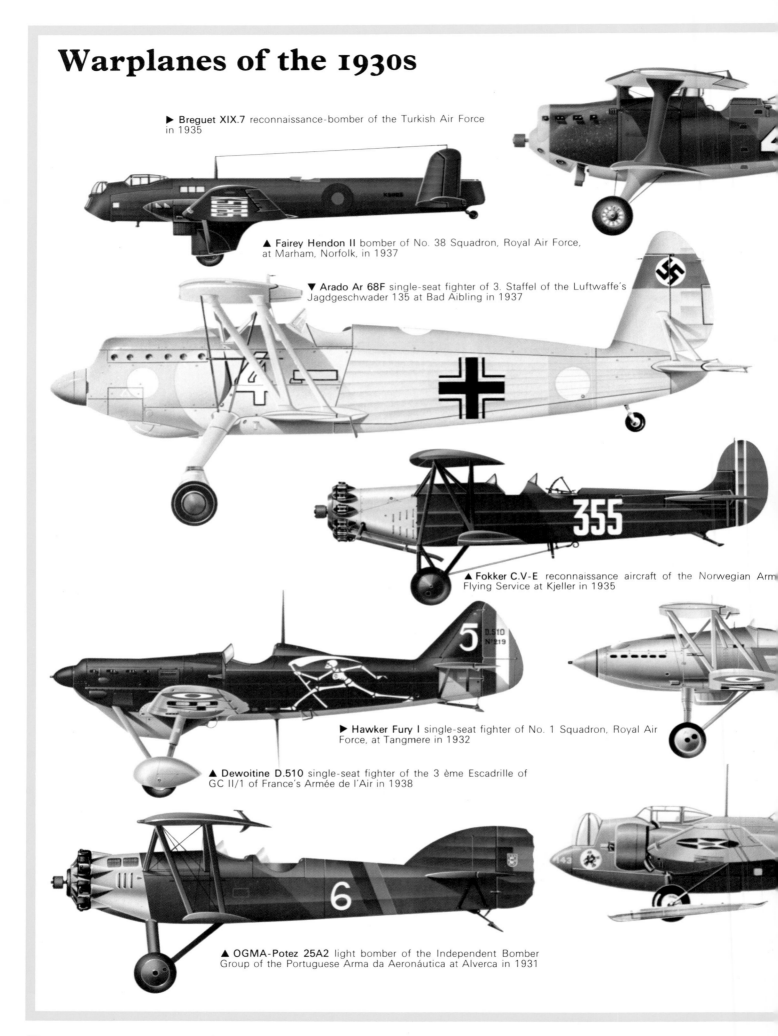

▶ Breguet XIX.7 reconnaissance-bomber of the Turkish Air Force in 1935

▲ Fairey Hendon II bomber of No. 38 Squadron, Royal Air Force, at Marham, Norfolk, in 1937

▼ Arado Ar 68F single-seat fighter of 3. Staffel of the Luftwaffe's Jagdgeschwader 135 at Bad Aibling in 1937

▲ Fokker C.V-E reconnaissance aircraft of the Norwegian Army Flying Service at Kjeller in 1935

▶ Hawker Fury I single-seat fighter of No. 1 Squadron, Royal Air Force, at Tangmere in 1932

▲ Dewoitine D.510 single-seat fighter of the 3 ème Escadrille of GC II/1 of France's Armée de l'Air in 1938

▲ OGMA-Potez 25A2 light bomber of the Independent Bomber Group of the Portuguese Arma da Aeronáutica at Alverca in 1931

▲ Curtiss BF2C-1 fighter/dive bomber of the US Navy's VB-5 aboard USS Ranger in 1935

▲ Caproni Ca 133 of the Bombergeschwader of the Austrian Air Force's Fliegerregiment 2 at Zeltweg, 1937

▲ Heinkel He 70F-1 reconnaissance-bomber of 3. Staffel of the Luftwaffe's Aufklarungsgruppe (Reconnaissance Wing) (F)/123 in 1936

▲ PZL P.11c single-seat fighter flown by the squadron commander of the Polish Air Force's No. 113 Squadron, 1st Air Regiment, at Warsaw-Okecie in 1938

▲ Martin B-12A bomber of the 11th Bombardment Squadron, US Army Air Corps, at Hamilton Field, California, circa 1935

▲ Handley Page Heyford I bomber of No. 99 Squadron, Royal Air Force, at Upper Heyford, Oxon, 1934

year. Britain's main carrier aircraft at the outbreak of war were the **Blackburn Skua** fighter/dive bomber and its 4-gun 'turret' fighter version, **Roc,** the Fleet Air Arm counterpart of the RAF's Defiant. Its best strike aircraft was easily the biplane **Fairey Swordfish.**

American carrier-borne fighters were still the dumpy **Grumman F2F** and **F3F** 1930s-vintage biplanes with retractable under-carriages, but, like the Japanese, American designers were working on an advanced and modern monoplane fighter, the **F4F,** which entered service in 1940. Japanese carrier air groups were equipped with the formidable **Aichi D3A2** ('Val') dive-bomber and the **Nakajima B5N2** ('Kate') torpedo-bomber. The American torpedo-bomber in 1939 was the lumbering **Douglas TBD-1 Devastator.** A really effective American naval dive-bomber did not appear until the **Douglas SBD Dauntless.**

There is now no doubt over what was America's best airborne asset in September 1939: the **Boeing B-17,** the 'Flying Fortress', which would become one of the key weapons in the Allied air offensive against Germany. The first prototype had flown in July 1935 and had made such an impression on the Army Air Corps that 65 production models were ordered that year. The Air Corps order was firmly cut down to only 39 of the original total because of their unprecedented cost, and controversy raged as to the value of the fledgeling B-17. Experiments in the United States in the 1930s had come up with improved bomb-sights, aircrew oxygen supply, and superchargers to boost high-altitude performance, and by 1940 selection of the .50-inch machine gun as the mainstay of its defensive armament had produced most of the familiar features with which the B-17 was to go to war in the Philippines in December 1941.

B-17 leads the world

The existence of the B-17 meant that the United States was the only power in the world which had produced a modern bomber for strategic air operations by September 1939. (The few dozen Tupolev/Petlyakov TB-7 'heavies' of the Soviet Air Force in existence at that time were still beset by technical problems and, in the event, never became a serious contender in this field.) The Japanese had hedged the problem with their long-range lightweights in their war with China. Germany, concentrating on large numbers for the Luftwaffe's overall strength, had not tackled it at all. Britain's insular geographical position had led to the

initiation of a heavy bomber development programme, which meant that she would be the first European power with a truly strategic bomber force. But France, the major partner in the European anti-German alliance of September 1939, had the weakest bomber force of all.

Germany had the best operational fighter in September 1939, the Messerschmitt Me 109, but mounting deliveries of the British Hurricanes and Spitfires would soon redress that balance. France had only one comparable fighter—the Dewoitine D.520—and that got into volume production just too late. Both RAF Fighter Command and the Luftwaffe had 'jokers in the pack' as far as fighters were concerned; the Boulton-Paul Defiant in the RAF, and the Me 110 in the Luftwaffe.

In ground-attack aircraft Germany was supreme, although the experience of the Polish campaign would be needed to give German strike air-crews vital combat experience. Another strong German advantage was the lavish provision of mobile anti-aircraft guns for the ground forces, which would make nearly every Allied tactical air strike a

suicidal operation in the campaign of 1940. No other army in the world in 1939 had such amenities. Indeed, the terrifying intensity of German anti-aircraft fire (the Allies soon adopted the German military abbreviation 'flak' from *Fliegerabwehrkanone*) remained a nightmare to Allied pilots right down to the last day of hostilities in Europe.

There were certainly long-term strategic flaws in the Luftwaffe's make-up in September 1939—flaws which time would prove to be fatal. But for the moment there were more than enough compensating factors. Apart from numbers and the anti-aircraft superiority already mentioned, the Wehrmacht's superb supply machine functioned magnificently until the battle of Moscow in December 1941. This meant that the Luftwaffe enjoyed another facility which was denied to the Allies until the RAF met the Luftwaffe in the Battle of Britain—the first time in World War II that Allied and German fighters met on anything like equal logistical terms. The campaigns in Norway, the Low Countries, and France in 1940 saw the handfuls of Allied pilots thrown into the battle from makeshift airfields and forced to

Upper left: Boeing's giant XB-15. Even bigger than the B-17, this lumbering bomber of 1937 was designed to fly 5,000 miles but proved too slow and vulnerable.
Lower left: An early B-17. Though deficient in firepower, armour and self-sealing tanks, the pre-war US Army Air Corps B-17 Fortresses were to lead to one of the great aircraft of World War 2.
Upper right: A veteran B-17F. 'Hell's Angels' typifies the thousands of 8th Air Force Fortresses that fought their way in daylight across Hitler's Europe.
Lower right: Curtiss A-18 An interesting US attack bomber tested before the war.

make do with a dwindling stock of fuel and spares—the ground crews performed near-miracles to keep aircraft flying.

The vital fuel factor

Apart from these immediate factors, the vital long-term problem was that of fuel to keep the aircraft flying, and here the scales were bound to tip against the Axis powers. It seemed inconceivable that Germany would be able to wage a war on all fronts, although it was known that she had been trying out experimental fuels. As it turned out the genius of Albert Speer created an almost incredible output of synthetic aviation fuel in the latter years of the war; but in 1939 and 1940 the Allies were totally unable to mount any kind of efficient bombing offensive against the main sources of German oil supply. Fuel problems were even greater where Italy and Japan were concerned—indeed, America's economic cold-shouldering of Japan in 1940/1941 was the factor that determined Japanese strategists to make an all-out bid to seize and hold the oil-producing regions of the Pacific before it was too late. The situation at the end

of the war—both in the European theatre and in the Pacific—proved this to the hilt, with German and Japanese aircraft constantly grounded (and training of replacement aircrews drastically cut) for lack of fuel.

Another problem confronting the major air forces of the world on the threshold of global conflict was the natural tendency of all air ministries to deploy their most obsolete combat aircraft to the apparently quieter theatres to 'put them out to grass', as it were. The speed with which World War II developed proved time and again that such deployment—the inevitable result of insufficient military expenditure—simply did not pay. Thus the initial defence of the island of Malta, the focal point of the Mediterranean war, depended on the makeshift use of a dozen or so crated Sea Gladiators which just happened to be there at the right time. One of the first British air raids against Italian positions in North Africa was made by a **Vickers Valentia**—a bulbous biplane of World War I appearance—buzzing an Italian airfield at rooftop height with the crew frantically pulling the pins out of hand grenades and lobbing them out through the

door. The pick of Japan's Zero aces, hastily sent to Rabaul for the formation of an élite fighter wing, found that the only aircraft for them to fly were antiquated 'Claudes'. When the British invaded Ethiopia in 1941 to throw the Italians out, they used pre-war Wellesley bombers for air support. Such instances happened time and again, revealing the essentially casual and unprepared way in which war was waged between 1939 and 1941.

From formality to horror

One of the nastiest aspects of World War II is the comparison between the horrors that attended its close and the stilted, traditional formality which announced it. Until the first Luftwaffe strikes savaged Polish air forces on the ground simultaneously with the crossing of the frontier by German ground troops it had not been accepted that war did not necessarily come with formal ultimatums and declarations of a state of hostility as of old, but with the devastating, rabbit-punch attack to seize and hold the initiative from the start and eliminate as much potential enemy resistance as possible in the opening hours of the campaign. Thus the careful timing of the German attack on Poland in September 1939 was brought to full perfection with 'Operation Barbarossa', Germany's attack on her erstwhile ally Soviet Russia, in June 1941, and by the Japanese carrier strike at the US Pacific Fleet in Pearl Harbor in December of the same year. It was ironic that only the examination of German and Japanese ruins by Allied strategic bombing surveys finally brought home the realisation that war was now a total affair. It had been that way ever since Guernica in the Spanish Civil War.

Thus the side which was bidding for a snap victory was only to be expected to use surprise attacks to gain the initiative, and this was an integral part of the German plan for the destruction of Poland in 1939.

Poland's air force consisted of a front-line fighter which looked hopelessly antiquated beside the German Messerschmitts, but which nevertheless belied its looks. This was the **PZL P-11,** with a maximum speed of 243 mph and an armament of four 7.7-mm machine guns. An ugly-looking but agile machine, the PZL P-11 had the advantage of manoeuvrability conferred by lower speed, but that was all. The best bomber in the Polish armoury was the twin-engined **PZL P-37 Los** (Elk), but only 36 of them were in service in September 1939. But Poland's main trouble in 1939 was numbers as much as types. Total operational aircraft numbered 397, with another 348 in the training schools and on reserve. Against this total the Luftwaffe deployed for the attack had 897 bombers, dive-bombers, and ground-attack aircraft and 210 single- and twin-engined fighters, and a huge force of 474 reconnaissance aircraft and transports.

For the German and Polish nations at dawn on September 1, 1939, this was the only balance of power that mattered. All the other factors affecting the international balance of air power would need time to show themselves—in months for some, in years for others. In the tiny theatre in which the 1939 Polish campaign was fought—the first major engagement of World War II—it would be virtually settled in seven days.

In September 1939 a new word entered the languages of the world—Blitzkrieg. Its meaning was 'lightning war'. War carried out with a frightening and deadly efficiency combining fast-moving ground attacks with a furious air assault. This first campaign of World War II resulted in the conquest and occupation of half Europe and the creation of a spectacular, yet not entirely deserved, reputation for the Luftwaffe that was to have enormous repercussions in the ensuing conflict.

The first *Blitzkrieg* ('lightning war') campaign of World War II saw the destruction of Poland's armed forces by the German Wehrmacht in four weeks (September 1–28, 1939). The Polish campaign seemed to prove that the German Panzer divisions were invincible on the ground and that the Luftwaffe was invincible in the air. Neither

was true.

The Panzers had no direct opposition worthy of the name in Poland. Nor was control of the skies over Poland gained automatically. As for the legendary co-operation between the Luftwaffe and the ground forces, supposedly rehearsed in the Spanish Civil War, it was a technique still

in process of evolution during the Polish campaign and much still had to be learned. Poland, the Luftwaffe's first victory, did look impressive. But the long-term defects in the German air force were concealed by the success in Poland and by the subsequent campaigns in Scandinavia, the Low Countries and France.

BLITZKRIEG!

Geography favoured Germany in her invasion of Poland: the frontier of the Reich curved round western Poland like an open hand poised to snatch. The two German army groups entrusted with the invasion took full advantage of this fact and could advance into Poland on converging lines. Each army group had the air cover and support of a Luftwaffe air fleet or *Luftflotte*—Luftflotte 1, under Kesselring, in the north and Luftflotte 4, under Löhr, in the south-west. The Luftwaffe's deployment was based on the gamble that the French would not attack in the West in support of Poland. Germany would have been totally unable to fight an all-out, two-front war in

In Poland the Luftwaffe enjoyed an emphatic superiority in numbers. It had more bombers, and more fighters to protect them. The German level bombers—**He 111s** and **Do 17s**—were medium bombers with adequate ranges for the missions they would have to fly; their weaknesses in defensive armament would not be revealed as long as the fighters gave them proper protection. The dive-bombers—*Sturzkampfflugzeuge* or **Stukas**—and ground-attack aircraft (**Ju 87s** and **Hs 123s**) proved capable of great accuracy in pinpoint attacks in support of the ground forces. Poland's best fighter was the obsolescent **PZL P. 11** with its open cockpit and high, strutted wing. Against

Upper left: Arming an Me 110. Planned as a long-range fighter, the twin-engined Me 110 was heavily armed with two 20 mm cannon and five machine guns.
Upper right: Start of a Ju 88 sortie. Carrying 500 kg bombs on its external racks, a Ju 88A warms up at dispersal. Though fitted with dive brakes it usually bombed in level flight.
Lower left: Architect of Blitzkrieg. Hitler watches the final assault on Warsaw through a binocular periscope.
Below: Me 110 over the White Cliffs. When it met RAF fighters the 110 proved a disappointment, being deficient in speed and manoeuvrability.

troyer' formations of long-range, two-seater **Me 110** heavy fighters, could hold their own with ease; the PZLs were totally outclassed by the **Me 109** fighter.

The Luftwaffe's initial brief was to gain undisputed control of the air as soon as possible. But this went awry at the outset of the campaign, and a week of improvisation was needed before it became clear that large-scale Polish bomber reprisals were not going to materialise.

Fog, failure and anti-climax

Fog on the morning of September 1 forced the cancellation of Operation 'Seaside'— Göring's plan for a massed initial strike against Warsaw. The first day was one of failure and anti-climax for the Luftwaffe. Ju 87 Stukas should have prevented the Poles from blowing the vital Vistula bridge at Dirschau, in the 'Polish Corridor' between Pomerania and East Prussia: their target was the demolition-point, which had been carefully marked down by reconnaissance. The Stukas hit their target but the Poles still managed to blow the bridge.

Half the Stuka *Gruppen* (Wings) in Löhr's air fleet were assigned to bombing airfields far behind the Polish lines, and the only effective ground-support mission flown on the southern sector on September 1 was by one Gruppe of Hs 123 biplanes armed with two machine guns and lightweight incendiary bombs. Kesselring's bombers hammered the known Polish airfields but created no holocaust of Polish aircraft. The Luftwaffe's failure to wipe out the Polish air force was the biggest paradox of all. There was no large-scale air battle in the opening days of the campaign. Instead, the Polish fighter pilots and bomber crews were thrown hopelessly off balance by the speed of the German advance on land, which overran the forward Polish airfields. And it was the Stukas which contributed most to the speed of that advance.

As soon as concentrations of Polish troops were spotted they were broken up by Stuka attacks. As the shaken Poles conceded defeat in the western provinces of the country and began to pull back to the Vistula for a rally in the east, Stukas pounded road and rail keypoints in the track of the retreat. There were mistakes, most notably at the expense of forward troops who were bombed by their own side in the confusion of battle—a tragic by-product of modern war which has never been eliminated since.

Another example of how close air/ground liaison could get too close occurred on September 8, when Stukas took out bridges across the Vistula at Gora Kalwarja. They were trying to block the Polish line of retreat across the river, but instead they destroyed the bridges before the 1st Panzer Division could dash across and thus were instrumental in causing a halt in the advance until sappers could throw a new bridge across.

The Poles recoil

For the Ju 87s and Hs 123s, their finest hour came during the crisis of the campaign: the 'Battle of the Bzura'. Battered, disintegrating, but still formidable in numbers, the Polish 'Poznan Army' was falling back on Warsaw when General Kutrzeba seized the chance of launching it across the River Bzura, at the flank of the German 8th Army, on the night of September 9–10. The German thrust at Warsaw was thrown out of gear by this menace. The German 8th and 10th Armies were forced to wheel to their left to contain the harassing Polish attacks and the Luftwaffe was called in to strike at the Polish bridgeheads across the Bzura. Both Stukas and Henschels were used.

The Henschels tackled the Piatek Bielawy bridgehead, their main weapons being four small 110-lb bombs apiece and two machine guns, mounted to fire through the engine cowling. The Stukas struck at Lowicz and Sochaczew while the level bombers joined in. After a 48-hour crisis the Poles recoiled across the Bzura in the face of these incessant Luftwaffe attacks. The troops of

Polish and German Air Strengths, 1939			
Poland	Fighters:	P-11	108
		P-7	30
	Total		138
	Bombers:	P-23	118
		P-37	36
	Total		154
Germany	Fighters:	Me 109 } Me 110	210
	Bombers:	Ju 87, Hs 123,	249
		Do 17, He 111	648
		Ju 86	
	Total		897

Aircraft Losses in Polish Campaign, 1939		
Poland: Combined Fighters and Bombers 333 (inc. 116 interned in Rumania)		
Germany:	Fighters	79
	Bombers	109
		188*
(*Plus 97 of all types counted as lost to strength by damage.)		

8th Army then reinforced their left flank, sealing the Poles into a massive pocket around Kutno where they held out until September 19.

Once the crisis on the Bzura had been weathered the Germans sealed off Warsaw and drove their 'outer pincers' into eastern Poland to sweep up the surviving Polish forces in the field. Five more days passed before the Polish High Command realised that the campaign was lost.

On the 17th, under the terms secretly agreed at the time of the German-Soviet Non-Aggression Pact of August 23, 1939, the Red Army rolled into eastern Poland. On that day the surviving Polish aircrews were ordered to fly their machines across the frontier and seek asylum in Rumania; a number also managed to escape to be interned in Latvia. Up until the 16th the Poles had continued to throw sporadic bombing attacks against the advancing Germans, but the Russian invasion was the end. Once Red Army and Wehrmacht forces made contact in the Brest Litovsk area the last bastions of Polish resistance were the trapped pockets to the west and in Warsaw, the capital, determined to hold out to the last.

What happened at Warsaw was a result of this determination. Warsaw was not an 'open city' as understood by international law: it contained troops and guns, an armed garrison which refused to surrender and barricaded and fortified all approaches. The intensive air bombardment of September 25 was ordered by Hitler. It was not carried out by the full strength of Luftwaffe strike aircraft because the great redeployment for the expected campaign in the West had already begun. On the 25th, however, Warsaw was savaged by 400 bombers, dive-bombers, and ground-attack aircraft, all making repeated sorties. Large areas of the city were reduced to blazing ruins and the garrison commander opened surrender negotiations on the following day. With the formal capitulation of the shattered capital on the 28th, the Polish campaign came to its end.

The Polish air force had lost 333 aircraft in the campaign, 82 of them bombers. Some 116 aircraft of all types got out to Rumania before the final collapse, and they were interned in that country. But they had drawn blood on the Luftwaffe with a vengeance. Total German aircraft losses (all types) came to 285 machines, including 67 single-engined fighters, 12 twin-engined fighters, 108 bombers and 97 other types. In addition, the Luftwaffe had to strike 279 severely damaged aircraft from its strength, making a total loss of 564 aircraft in 28 days.

Scandinavia's turn

The German occupation of Denmark and Norway in April 1940 revealed another potent weapon in the Luftwaffe's armoury: airborn forces. It also proved the deadliness of the Ju 87 Stuka against shipping, and the suicidal results of sending warships into waters dominated by enemy aircraft when it was impossible to give the ships air cover of their own.

Denmark would be tackled by the German army pouncing across the frontier with no declaration of war, with paratroops securing key airfields and bridges. Norway was a more complex problem. The Navy would land troops at Narvik, Trondheim, Bergen, Kristiansand, and Oslo, while airborne troops would take the vital airfields at Stavanger and Fornebu.

All the initial landings went well on the morning of April 9, 1940, apart from the attempt to seize Oslo and Fornebu airfield. In the Drobak Narrows of Oslo Fjord the Norwegians ashore were not taken in as the German warships came steaming up the fjord and opened fire, sinking the new German cruiser *Blücher* and forcing the other warships and transports to retire. The lumbering **Ju 52** transports heading for Fornebu with airborne troops had to turn back because of bad weather.

The Norwegians in the Oslo/Fornebu region were thoroughly alerted; their handful of obsolescent **Gloster Gladiator** biplane fighters had time to take to the air and engage the Me 110s sent to patrol over Fornebu. In fact it was a Me 110 squadron— 1./ZG 76—which finally tipped the scales at Fornebu. Its commander, Lieutenant Hansen, hung on over Fornebu, waiting for the Ju 52s and coping easily with the gallant attacks of the Norwegian Gladiator pilots, until his Me 110s were down to

Air weapons of the Blitzkrieg

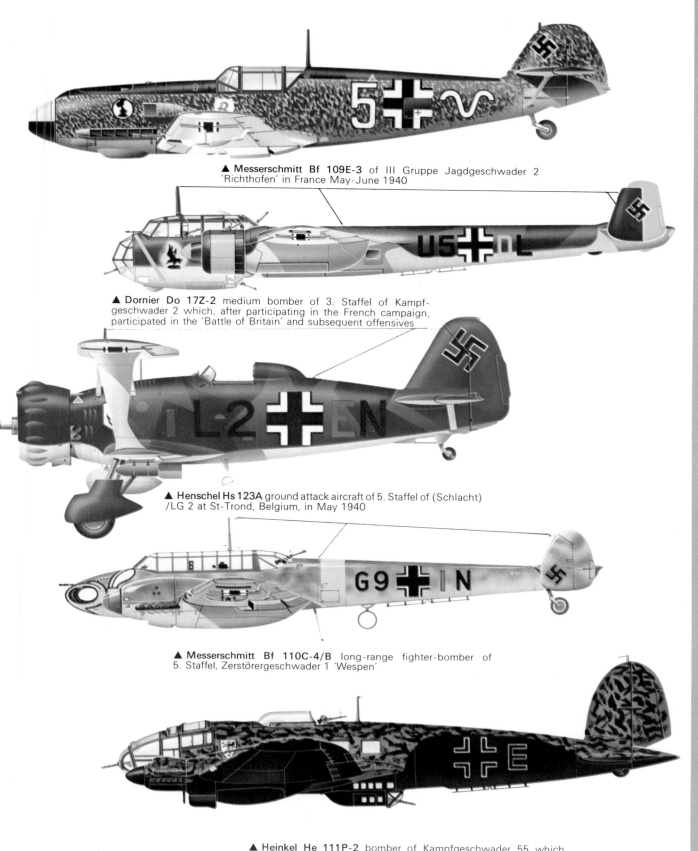

▲ Messerschmitt Bf 109E-3 of III Gruppe Jagdgeschwader 2 'Richthofen' in France May-June 1940

▲ Dornier Do 17Z-2 medium bomber of 3. Staffel of Kampfgeschwader 2 which, after participating in the French campaign, participated in the 'Battle of Britain' and subsequent offensives

▲ Henschel Hs 123A ground attack aircraft of 5. Staffel of (Schlacht) /LG 2 at St-Trond, Belgium, in May 1940

▲ Messerschmitt Bf 110C-4/B long-range fighter-bomber of 5. Staffel, Zerstörergeschwader 1 'Wespen'

▲ Heinkel He 111P-2 bomber of Kampfgeschwader 55 which, after termination of the French campaign, operated against the United Kingdom from Dreux, Chartres and Villacoublay

The Defenders against the German Invasion

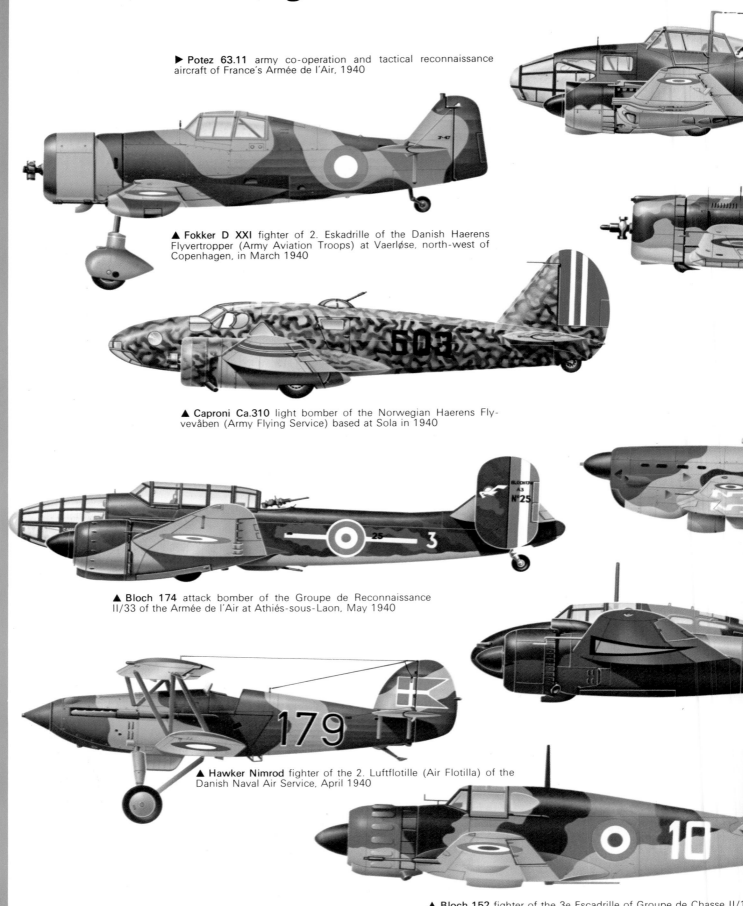

▶ **Potez 63.11** army co-operation and tactical reconnaissance aircraft of France's Armée de l'Air, 1940

▲ **Fokker D XXI** fighter of 2. Eskadrille of the Danish Haerens Flyvertropper (Army Aviation Troops) at Vaerløse, north-west of Copenhagen, in March 1940

▲ **Caproni Ca.310** light bomber of the Norwegian Haerens Flyvevåben (Army Flying Service) based at Sola in 1940

▲ **Bloch 174** attack bomber of the Groupe de Reconnaissance II/33 of the Armée de l'Air at Athiés-sous-Laon, May 1940

▲ **Hawker Nimrod** fighter of the 2. Luftflotille (Air Flotilla) of the Danish Naval Air Service, April 1940

▲ **Bloch 152** fighter of the 3e Escadrille of Groupe de Chasse II/1 of the Armée de l'Air at Etampes, May 1940

▼ Curtiss Hawk 75A-1 fighter of the 1e Escadrille of the Groupe de Chasse II/5 of the Armée de l'Air, winter 1939–40

▲ Fokker D XXI fighter of the 1e Jachtvliegtuigafdeling (Fighter Group) of the Dutch Luchtvaartafdeling at De Kooy on 10 May 1940

▲ Hawker Hurricane I of the 2e Escadrille 'Le Chardon', Groupe I, of the 2e Regiment of the Belgian Aéronautique Militaire at Diest, 1940

Morane-Saulnier MS 406 fighter of the 1e Escadrille the Groupe de Chasse I/2 of the mée de l'Air at Nimes, July 1940

▲ Gloster Gladiator II of the Jageravdeling (Fighter Flight) of the Norwegian Army Flying Service at Fornebu, April 1940

▲ Fokker G Ib fighter of the 4e Jachtvliegtuigafdeling (Fighter Group) of the Dutch Luchtvaartafdeling at Schiphol, May 1940

▲ Fairey Battle I light bomber of the 5e Escadrille, Group III, of the 3e Regiment of the Belgian Aéronautique Militaire at Evère-Bruxelles, May 1940

their last dregs of fuel. He then made the audacious decision to land his fighters on Fornebu and try to gain a foothold. Five Me 110s landed on his orders and managed to 'hold' the field until the Ju 52s returned—a piece of military cheek which retrieved a near-disastrous situation for the Germans. The five surviving Norwegian Gladiators were ordered to land on frozen lakes to the north and west of Oslo. Only one managed to land intact, leaving the Luftwaffe with total air superiority over southern Norway by the second day of the campaign.

Air superiority is decisive

This air superiority enabled the German expeditionary force in Norway to consolidate its hold on the south of the country and begin its drive to the north to join up with the forces landed by sea. When the British finally landed in Norway at Namsos and Aandalsnes to try to restore the situation, they had to do so in the teeth of Luftwaffe air power which smashed remorselessly at their bases and supply-ships and harried the movements of their troops ashore.

The Allies pushed down the Gudbrandsdal Valley as far as Lillehammer before falling back on Aandalsnes, and by April 26 the situation had become so hopeless in the two burning bases that the decision was made to withdraw from central Norway and concentrate on taking and holding Narvik, the one sector where the Allied countermeasures had met with success. Desperate efforts on the part of the Luftwaffe reinforced General Dietl's mountain troops after they had been pushed out of Narvik, but the Allies continued to advance and it seemed that Dietl's men must either surrender or cross into Sweden and accept internment. But this small Allied success was more than cancelled out by the fiasco in Belgium and the evacuation from Dunkirk. The French and British troops had to pull out from Narvik in the first week of June.

The Norwegian campaign saw the first successful airborne invasion and airlift of supplies in military history. It was an easy battle for the Luftwaffe; the worst threat to the German fighters were the Norwegian Gladiators, eliminated in the first 48 hours. In the constant strikes against the Allied bases and shipping at Namsos and Aandalsnes showed the Stuka to be a deadly anti-shipping weapon.

Sweep into the Low Countries

In 1914 the German master-plan for the defeat of France had respected Dutch neutrality and had accepted the risk that the German violation of Belgian neutrality might provoke Allied countermoves. The result had been four years of static trench warfare in the West. Twenty-five years later Hitler resolved to reduce Holland and Belgium as the prelude to the decisive Battle of France. Speed was of the essence. Holland and Belgium were to be the first victims but the decisive victory could not be won there. In view of the ease with which the Low Countries could be converted into morasses of water obstacles, they must be defeated quickly and the Luftwaffe

was the key to the speedy conduct of operations.

Denmark and Norway had been the first to feel the impact of German airborne troops. Holland and Belgium were the first theatres of World War II where airborne forces won decisive victories.

The killer punch against Holland would be spearheaded by paratroops taking the airfields of The Hague and rounding up the Queen and the Dutch Government. Airborne forces would seize the Maas bridges at Rotterdam and hold them until the ground forces, driving north-west from Breda, could join up.

Kesselring's Luftflotte 2 covered the operations of Army Group 'B' (Bock) in Holland and Belgium; Sperrle's Luftflotte 3 supported von Rundstedt's Army Group 'A' on the central sector. Between them the two Luftflotten numbered 1,120 level bombers (Do 17s, He 111s, and **Ju 88s**), 358 dive-bombers (nearly all Ju 87s), 1,264 fighters (Me 109s and Me 110s), and 648 reconnaissance aircraft (**Fieseler Fi 156s, Hs 126s,** and **He 46s**). In addition there were 475 Ju 52 transports and 45 gliders. The knock-out blow against Holland had as its priority the capture of all airfields which might otherwise be used as advanced bases by the Allied air forces, and airborne forces had a vital role to play.

Holland's air force, by comparison with the might of Luftflotte 2, was negligible. The Dutch had nine **Fokker T. V** medium bombers and ten single-engine **Fokker C. X** reconnaissance bombers. Their best fighter, the **Fokker D. XXI,** was no match for the German Me 109—and there were only 29 of them operational. In addition there were 23 modern **Fokker G. I** twin-boom heavy fighters/ground attack machines, and the Dutch navy could contribute 11 **Fokker T. VIII-W** reconnaissance and torpedo-bomber float planes. This pitiful weakness in air power was the direct result of four decades of determined neutrality.

Fiascos and forced-landings

Thus the Luftwaffe encountered little or no resistance in the air during the attack on Holland, but it ran into plenty on the ground. The attack on the airfields around The Hague—Ypenburg, Ockenburg, and Valkenburg—was a fiasco, worse even than the initial setback at Oslo during the Norwegian campaign. Spirited resistance flung the German airborne troops off the Hague airfields. The German transports were generally foiled by the volume of Dutch flak sent up from the airfields and by the ground obstacles strewing the most obvious landing approaches; the Ju 52s were forced to use the Hague motorway or crash-land on the coastal dunes.

At Rotterdam, the Germans managed to capture the vital Willems bridge across the Maas with troops flown in by 12 **Heinkel He 59** seaplanes. Paratroops meanwhile had taken Rotterdam's Waalhaven airfield in the teeth of desperate resistance by the Dutch Queen's Grenadiers. But prompt Dutch countermeasures sealed off the tenuous German hold on the Maas crossing through which they hoped to break the resistance of Rotterdam. The German foothold in the city was reduced to

a small bridgehead under constant attack.

The result was the German plan to blow out the Dutch hold on the northern bank of the Maas by a massed bombing attack—an attack which went on while Rotterdam's surrender was still being negotiated due to the tragic failure to contact most of the bombers and call it off. Some 57 He 111s of *Kampfgeschwader* (bombing group) 54 dropped 97 tons of high-explosive bombs into the designated triangular target area on the north bank of the Maas. Resulting fires gutted the heart of Old Rotterdam. It was a tragic accident which nevertheless finally cracked the Dutch will to resist. Holland surrendered on May 15.

Holland had fallen in five days and once again the Luftwaffe's airborne forces had been in the forefront of the battle—but they had taken a severe mauling. Out of the total of 430 Ju 52 transports allotted to the Dutch landings, two-thirds were destroyed or damaged beyond repair. The going had been hardest around The Hague, where German losses stood at 90 per cent. It has often been pointed out that the losses suffered by the German navy during the Norwegian campaign were a decisive factor on limiting German hopes for an invasion of Britain. No less important were the losses of the German airborne arm in Holland—losses which could not be made good in a mere three to four months.

Upper left: Ju 88 taxies out. The four men in the 88 were crowded together for good morale. The single rear gun later gave way to four separate hand-held guns.

Upper right: M.S.406 and Battle. The only numerous fighter of the Armée de l'Air and the day bomber of the RAF Advanced Air Striking Force were both hacked down in quantity by Me 109s and flak.

Above: Ju 87R over Norway. This Stuka variant carried long-range tanks and made many long missions to attack shipping.

Epic at Eben-Emael

In May 1940 the best anti-tank obstacle in Western Europe was believed to be Belgium's Albert Canal — steep-sided, studded with pill-box defences, and 'pegged' by Fort Eban Emael, as tough a proposition to standard attack as anything the much-vaunted Maginot Line had to offer. The Germans took Eben-Emael in a day in a daring, glider-borne attack which wrote a new chapter in the brief history of airborne warfare.

Eben-Emael was in fact only one of four targets earmarked by the Germans for the surprise cracking of the Albert Canal line. Four 'special attack detachments', all of them glider-borne, had trained under conditions of the strictest secrecy for the mission, the other three being assigned

bridges over the Canal at Vroenhaven, Verdzewelt, and Kanne. But it was the Eben-Emael attack in May 1940 which won the attention of the world.

The fighting at Verdun in World War I had proved that the most sophisticated forts in existence could not eliminate enemy forces which managed to get right on top of them.

The German glider force delivered specially-equipped assault pioneers to the outer carapace of the fort—men equipped with hollow-charge blocks of explosive for cracking armoured cupolas and blinding observation-domes. Acting with energy and daring these 55 men reduced the Belgian garrison to the state of a helpless tortoise cowering in its shell in just over 10 minutes. It was the first successful use of glider-borne troops in World War II. Once again 'Auntie Ju', as the Germans called the faithful Junkers Ju 52 transport, proved its worth, delivering the 41 **DFS 230A** gliders (each of which could take up to ten soldiers) to their targets. They cracked the main Belgian defence-line along the Albert Canal, and they opened the way to Brussels, at the very heart of Belgium, for the orthodox ground forces.

Outnumbered and out-thought

But the main German assault was the central drive of Army Group 'A' through Belgium and Luxembourg to the Meuse, breaking through the Allied line at Sedan and driving westward to reach the Channel in ten days. Here the Luftwaffe showed its virtuosity as a tactical arm, while the Allied air forces suffered from outnumbered and inferior aircraft—and the permanent loss of the initiative in the first 24 hours of the campaign.

The French contributed the majority of the Allied fighters: 278 **Morane-Saulnier M.S. 406**, 36 **Dewoitine D. 520s** (a modern design which had just begun to arrive at the front), 140 Bloch fighters (**MB 151s and 152s**), and 98 **Curtiss Hawk 75s** (the latter purchased from the United States before the war). Britain fielded some 40 **Hurricanes** and 20 Gladiators (the two British Gladiator squadrons were on the point of receiving their new Hurricanes when the offensive opened). The Belgian air force also operated a handful of Hurricanes.

In bombers the Allies were hopelessly outclassed. The best of the modern French bombers (**LeO 451s, Breguet 693 AB-2s,** and **Amiot 350s**) had only just begun to arrive and were flung into the battle in driblets. Of the British bomber squadrons in France, the **Fairey Battle** light bomber was a death trap when faced by modern fighters and the excellent German flak; the **Bristol Blenheim** was an infinitely better machine but still needed fighter protection. At least one Blenheim squadron (No. 114) was wiped out on the ground by a Do 17 strike on the morning of the 11th, before it had managed to fly a single mission.

From the outset of the campaign the Allied bombers were frittered away on fruitless missions which were carried out with great gallantry but at an appalling cost. The deadliest targets of the first ten days were the German-held bridges across

the Albert Canal. Here the first British bomber pilots of World War II won their Victoria Crosses—posthumously. German fighter opposition was not the only headache of the Allied pilots. The dense anti-aircraft fire put up by the German mobile flak, which could be in position within minutes, accounted for most of the victims shot down while attacking the Albert Canal bridges.

Nor were the Allies given the opportunity to operate from secure bases. The scorching pace of the German advance kept the Allied squadrons retreating from airfield to hastily-improvised airfield. Once again, the Ju 87 Stukas were key weapons in the German offensive. The all-important crossing of the Meuse on May 13 was spearheaded by a Stuka strike at the French-held bank, which was so minutely timed that the first German troops across landed while clods of earth thrown up by the Stuka bombs were still falling.

Setback for the Luftwaffe

Once the great Allied retreat had begun the German fighters and Stukas took on another role: keeping the roads to the front clogged with terror-stricken floods of refugees. Do 17 reconnaissance aircraft spied out Allied troop concentrations as soon as they were formed. But the Luftwaffe's successes in this initial, fluid stage of the battle for the West were noticeably curtailed when the advance on the ground ran out of steam. On May 24, von Rundstedt's need to rest the Panzer units approaching Dunkirk along the coast was endorsed by Hitler, the motive being that the German tank forces must be conserved for the decisive attack on central and southern France. The mobile phase was over; and in the last act at Dunkirk the lion's share of the action was passed to the Luftwaffe, which undertook an impossible task with very mixed results.

Göring assured Hitler that the Luftwaffe could easily cope with the smashing of the Dunkirk pocket. Not for the first time in World War II his subordinates knew perfectly well that they had been given a job beyond their resources but were powerless in the face of Göring's lofty status in the Nazi hierarchy.

Adverse weather and dense smoke over the target area meant that during the nine days of the Dunkirk evacuation—May 26 to June 4—the Luftwaffe was only able to launch effective attacks over a period of $2\frac{1}{2}$ days. German bombers—particularly the Ju 87s—managed to sink seven French destroyers and torpedo-boats and six British destroyers. They also accounted for five large passenger ships and a quarter of the myriad 'little ships' flung into the evacuation by the British. But the Luftwaffe failed to prevent 338,226 British and French soldiers from getting away to England and spirited patrolling by the British fighter squadrons in southern England cost the Luftwaffe 156 aircraft. This was 50 more than the RAF's own losses during the fight and the most punishing 'round' fought by the Luftwaffe since the opening of the offensive on May 10. To take one example: on May 27, the day of the first heavy Luftwaffe attack on Dunkirk, II *Fliegerkorps* lost 23 aircraft—exceeding the combined total of the last ten days.

BATTLE of Britain

Winston Churchill's oratory has immortalised the famous 'Few' who in 1940 defended Britain, then holding out alone and ill-prepared against the German juggernaut that had successfully rolled across most of Europe. They, against enormous odds, were the victors in the first air battle fought independently of a ground offensive and, significantly, they inflicted the first defeat upon the Nazis and gained vital time to re-group and re-arm. But it was touch and go, and the RAF only just managed to pull off one of the greatest feats in military history.

The Battle of Britain was not the first encounter for which the Wehrmacht had never planned: Denmark and Norway claim that honour. But the Wehrmacht had certainly never been given the right tools for the job of conquering Britain. It did not have an invasion fleet; it had no long-range heavy bombers. It did have a nucleus battle fleet of excellent modern warships and a nucleus airborne army—both of which had suffered heavy losses in April and May. Hitler did not want to *have* to invade Britain, but when Britain refused to be 'reasonable' and give up he found himself with no other choice.

After France capitulated a whole month went by until Directive 16 ('Sea Lion'), ordering preparations for an invasion to begin, was signed on July 16. From the start the onus was placed on the Luftwaffe. The German army was ready to go; the German navy could not protect an invasion fleet from determined British attacks; the Luftwaffe must therefore destroy all opposition from the air and guarantee the total command of the skies during—and after—the crossing. And this meant destroying RAF Fighter Command by forcing a battle on German terms.

Air Chief Marshal Dowding had managed to keep Fighter Command alive by refusing to fritter away his fighter squadrons in the Battle of France. He knew that his No. 11 Group, in the south-east—'invasion corner'—must bear the brunt of the fighting. The chain of radar stations along the south coast would give invaluable advance information of approaching German air formations. His vestigial reserves in the north and west must be doled out to 11 Group as sparingly as possible. Fighter production from the factories was increasing encouragingly—but the RAF was dwarfed by the Luftwaffe's numbers and incessant attacks on the southern fighter bases and the radar chain could, he knew, destroy

Fighter Command within a week.

In a long-term battle of attrition the RAF's chances of victory were negligible but the British had an immense advantage —they were fighting on their home ground. If their pilots got shot down they would not be captured but could be flying again within hours. The British also had the obvious advantage in endurance, whereas the best weapon in the Luftwaffe's armoury —the **Messerschmitt Me 109** fighter— had an operational endurance over southern England of 20–30 minutes at best.

Luftwaffe objectives

Moreover, the Battle of Britain was the first large-scale air battle of World War II. Dowding's objective was simple: to maintain Fighter Command as an active threat. The Luftwaffe commanders—Kesselring (Luftflotte 2), Sperrle (Luftflotte 3), and Stumpff (Luftflotte 5)—had a fuzzy multitude of objectives which prevented them from marking down the destruction of Fighter Command as the crux of the battle. These objectives included the interdiction of British shipping traffic in the Channel, the bombing of radar and fighter stations, and—due to Hitler's interference—the bombing of London. The capital was bombed to crack the British will to resist, but was ostensibly a 'response' to a small-scale British raid on Berlin—itself a clever psychological move by Churchill to divert German attention from more important targets.

Channel attacks proved how vulnerable the **Ju 87s** and **Me 110s** really were when faced with modern fighter opposition. The switch to raids on London lost the Luftwaffe the battle by taking the pressure off Fighter Command when the RAF was nearing the end of its tether and, incidentally, exposing the German bombers by pushing them beyond the range of effective fighter escort.

The month of July opened the Battle of

Britain in earnest, with the three Luftflotten attacking coastal convoys, ports, and fighter bases in the south-east. These attacks were met head-on and were roughly handled, but the pressure on Fighter Command was intense from the start and never let up. As early as July 10, to take one example, No. 54 Squadron (**Spitfires**), based at Hornchurch, could only put up eight aircraft and 13 pilots—a loss of ten aircraft in 48 hours. Only the constant rotation of battle-weary squadrons by Dowding and Air Vice Marshal Park (commander of the all-important No. 11 Group), plus the heightened production of aircraft under the dynamic impetus of Lord Beaverbrook, Churchill's Minister of Aircraft Production, enabled Fighter Command to continue the

battle without bleeding to death.

In August the three Luftflotten at last put out their full strength. Göring had ordered that the offensive should be heralded by a smashing, concentrated blow—code-named *Adlertag* or 'Day of the Eagles'. But it took over a fortnight to materialise. The first ten days of August saw increasingly scaled-up repetitions of the July attacks, which proved that the British radar was even more efficient when picking up large German air formations.

Adlertag was finally scheduled for August 13; pinpoint raids on the 12th were to 'blind' the British radar stations. Some radar stations were in fact put off the air on that day, but only for a few hours. Aldertag itself proved a sorry anti-climax. It went off at half-cock in the morning; co-ordination between the German fighters and bombers was bad and the afternoon raids failed to saturate the British defences. The greatest flaw in the German plan lay in faulty intelligence: even if every identified airfield had been attacked according to plan, none of them was in fact vital to Fighter Command's deployment pattern.

August 15 was the first and only time that the three Luftflotten attacked together. It was also the heaviest single day's fighting of the entire battle, with the Luftwaffe flying over 2,000 sorties and the RAF 974. Luftflotte 5, having the longest way to fly, came off worst, suffering losses of just under 20 per cent; it took no further large-scale part in the battle. Luftflotten 2 and 3 kept up the pressure in the days which followed the battles of the 15th. August 18 in particular stands out as a definite landmark in the defeat of the dreaded Stuka. The eight Stuka Gruppen had lost 39 out of 281 aircraft in the first two weeks of August; on the 18th alone they lost 17 more, and had to be pulled out of the battle.

Göring intervened in the battle on the

which Hitler himself was still insisting— scattered over London's dockland. Churchill immediately ordered the bombing of Berlin in retaliation, to which Hitler responded by vowing to raze Britain's cities, starting with London.

Mass raids broken up

Like the German invasion itself, all turned on the survival of RAF Fighter Command— and while the target was London the vital airfields could operate again. By September 14, Fighter Command was back on its feet with a vengeance. The mass daylight raids on London on Sunday, September 15, were broken up by the British fighter attacks—with interceptions by over 300

military significance. Britain's survival in 1940 was secured in the critical days of September.

Fighter Command's ordeal in the first fortnight of September is conclusive proof that the Luftwaffe should have won the Battle of Britain. August was a month which the Germans squandered, and as far as the invasion of Britain was concerned they could not afford to do so. Bad intelligence was partly to blame: it took until the end of August before Fighter Command's defences were sounded out. The Luftwaffe's commanders completely underestimated the British rate of fighter production—in 1940 it was twice as high as that of Germany. And Göring and his subordinates were hopelessly off the mark in failing to use a

19th, appointing new (and younger) fighter commanders—Galland, Trautloft, Mölders, Lützow—all operational airmen and proven aces. He insisted that the Me 109s must stick closer to the bombers—which only restricted the German fighters still more. Göring also refused to accept the proven weaknesses of the Me 110 and Ju 87, not to mention those of the much-vaunted 'wonder bomber', the **Ju 88**. The Ju 88's main asset had been considered its speed, but that (and its weak defensive armament) could not stand up to the much faster 8-gun Spitfire. A four-day comparative lull ensued—and then the crisis of the battle opened for RAF Fighter Command, with massive attacks concentrating, at last, on the vital airfields of Kent, Surrey, and Sussex. By September 7, Fighter Command was on the brink of defeat when it was saved by the commencement of mass daylight attacks on London.

London's delineation as a major target dated back to the night of August 24/25, when some German bombs intended for the Thameshaven oil tanks—a 'correct' military target according to the conventions upon

Spitfires and **Hurricanes** in 20 minutes. The speed with which the formations were broken up on the 15th also proved that the morale of the German bomber pilots, not unnaturally, was faltering.

The Luftwaffe, in switching from the airfields to London, had squandered another week, but it could still have won the battle. What mattered by nightfall on September 15 was that Fighter Command was still very much alive—with only Dowding, Churchill and a few of their closest collaborators knowing how near breaking point the RAF Fighter Command in fact was. However, the equally exhausted Germans felt they were making no progress and this, together with the impressive damage being done by RAF Bomber Command to the German invasion barges across the Channel, caused Hitler to postpone 'Sea Lion' indefinitely on September 17 and to order the dispersal of the invasion fleet. The bombing of London and other major British cities—the 'Blitz'—was approaching the close of its second week and would rage on throughout the winter of 1940/41. But the 'Blitz' raids were largely devoid of

Far left and above: The Heinkel 111. Dubbed 'The Spade' by its crews, the He 111 was numerically the predominant bomber of the Luftwaffe from 1937 until near the end of World War 2. It carried bombs tail-down in vertical cells in the fuselage, and later had external racks for large bombs or torpedoes. Wherever the opposition was ineffectual the 111 did a formidable job.

This page, left: Spitfire I squadron. These early Spitfires of No. 610 Squadron, Auxiliary Air Force, based at Acklington, were photographed during the height of the battle. Though the Hurricane was by far the most numerous of Britain's fighters, the Spitfire was a superior machine and a match for the Me 109.

systematic approach to their problem; they constantly changed the main objectives to be attacked. All these failures worked to the advantage of the British.

Fighter Command's mainstay in the Battle of Britain was the Hurricane as far as numbers were concerned, but it was slightly inferior to the Me 109 and soon

The Aircraft that fought the Battle of Britain

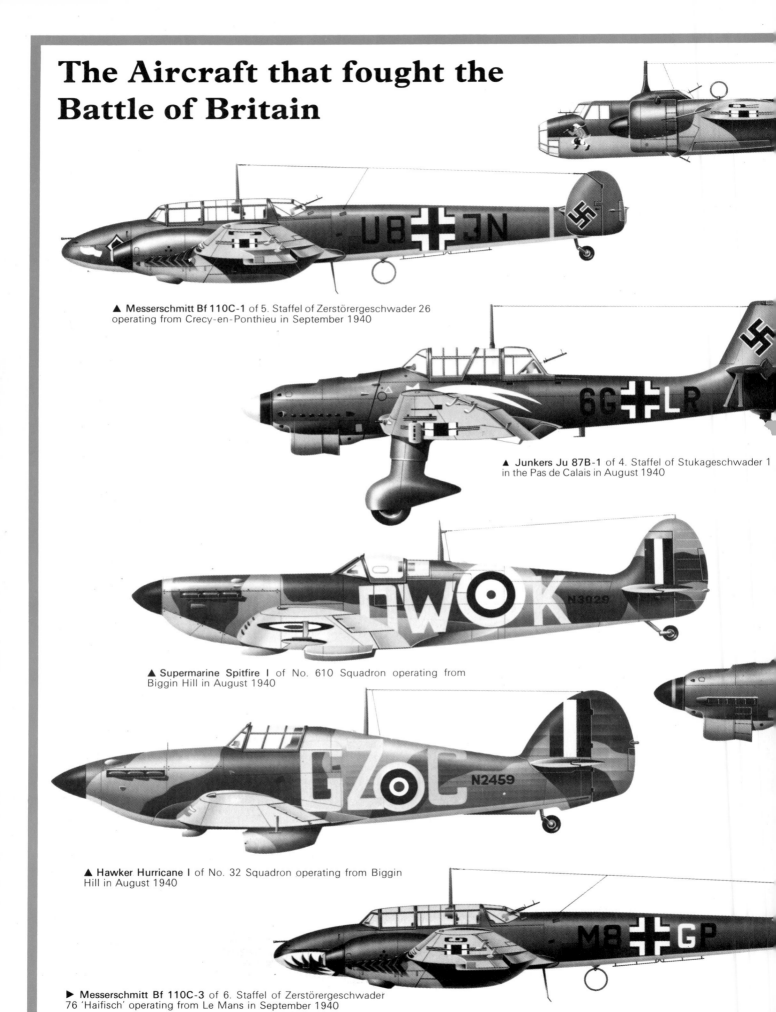

▲ **Messerschmitt Bf 110C-1** of 5. Staffel of Zerstörergeschwader 26 operating from Crecy-en-Ponthieu in September 1940

▲ **Junkers Ju 87B-1** of 4. Staffel of Stukageschwader 1 in the Pas de Calais in August 1940

▲ **Supermarine Spitfire I** of No. 610 Squadron operating from Biggin Hill in August 1940

▲ **Hawker Hurricane I** of No. 32 Squadron operating from Biggin Hill in August 1940

▶ **Messerschmitt Bf 110C-3** of 6. Staffel of Zerstörergeschwader 76 'Haifisch' operating from Le Mans in September 1940

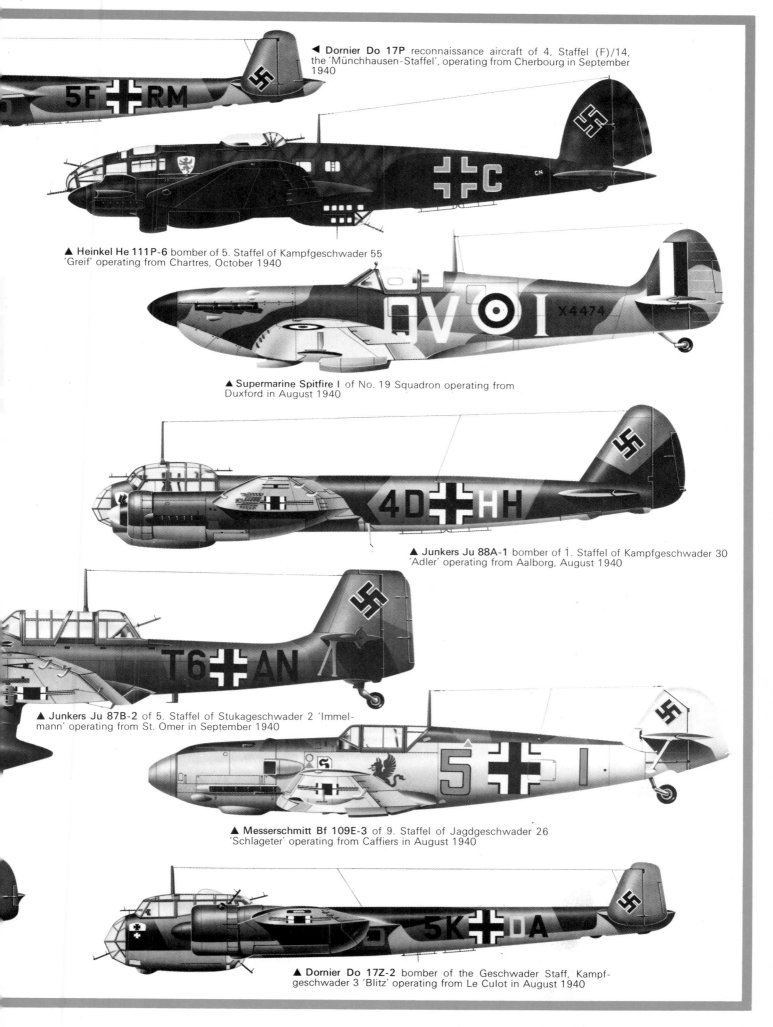

◄ **Dornier Do 17P** reconnaissance aircraft of 4, Staffel (F)/14, the 'Münchhausen-Staffel', operating from Cherbourg in September 1940

▲ **Heinkel He 111P-6** bomber of 5. Staffel of Kampfgeschwader 55 'Greif' operating from Chartres, October 1940

▲ **Supermarine Spitfire I** of No. 19 Squadron operating from Duxford in August 1940

▲ **Junkers Ju 88A-1** bomber of 1. Staffel of Kampfgeschwader 30 'Adler' operating from Aalborg, August 1940

▲ **Junkers Ju 87B-2** of 5. Staffel of Stukageschwader 2 'Immelmann' operating from St. Omer in September 1940

▲ **Messerschmitt Bf 109E-3** of 9. Staffel of Jagdgeschwader 26 'Schlageter' operating from Caffiers in August 1940

▲ **Dornier Do 17Z-2** bomber of the Geschwader Staff, Kampfgeschwader 3 'Blitz' operating from Le Culot in August 1940 came to be earmarked for attacks on the bomber streams. The German fighters—including the Me 110 'destroyers'—had the benefit of cannon armament, enabling their pilots to land damaging hits at longer ranges than were available to the Spitfires and Hurricanes with their octuple batteries of machine guns. However, crippled by their endurance limitation and by the close-support tactics forced on them by Göring, the Me 109s could not defend the bombers, all of which had revealed grave deficiencies in their defensive armament.

Defiant too easily defied

But RAF Fighter Command was also found to have a weak card in its hand: the **Boulton-Paul Defiant**, a two-seat fighter with a rear turret which had promised well during the skirmishing over Dunkirk. Easy meat for the Luftwaffe's fighters during the Battle of Britain, the Defiant was withdrawn from the fight at the end of August after the almost complete destruction of No. 264 Squadron. Like the German Me 110, the Defiant was the product of fallacious thinking between the wars. Whereas the German machine was too large and slow for a day fighter, the smaller British two-seater had no forward firing armament.

Matched against the Spitfire, the Me 109 showed that it was the slower machine. The superior German system of fuel injection also enabled Me 109 pilots to get out of trouble by half-rolling into a steep dive. The Rolls-Royce Merlin which powered the Spitfires and Hurricanes during the battle had a floating carburettor and the 'negative

BATTLE OF BRITAIN: British and German Air Strengths	
RAF Fighter Command (as of August 8)	
Hawker Hurricane	527
Supermarine Spitfire	306
Bristol Blenheim	82
Boulton-Paul Defiant	26
	941
Luftwaffe (as of August 13)	
Me 109	734
Me 110	268
Ju 87	336
Ju 88, He 111, Do 17	949
	2,287
LOSSES: Aug. 8–Sept. 15, 1940	
RAF Fighter Command:	800
Luftwaffe: (fighters)	663
Luftwaffe: (bombers)	691
	2,154

G' caused by a sudden dive caused the engine to cut. Flipping the aircraft onto its back to counter this gave the Me 109 a long enough start to get away in a plummetting dive.

When the British were able to make their first evaluation tests on a captured Me 109 another advantage of the German machine was revealed: the rudder pedals were placed some 6 inches higher in the Me 109, making

Below: Me109Es cross the Channel. This was the only Luftwaffe aircraft not outclassed by RAF day fighters.
Top right: Mass attacks on London begin — giving the RAF vital time to recover.
Bottom right: Hurricanes in France. The wisdom of Dowding's decision not to waste precious fighters in the defence of France is borne out by the fate of these machines of 87 Squadron. Most were lost.

it harder for the blood to sink to the pilot's feet during a sharp pull-out, and therefore harder for him to 'black out' because of the centrifugal drain of blood from the brain. On the other hand, the clumsier cockpit construction of the Me 109 meant that it gave its pilots inferior visibility to that enjoyed by the RAF pilots. The Me 109 was even smaller than the trim Spitfire and its cockpit was found to be uncomfortably cramped when examined by the British.

As far as tactics were concerned the Germans had the advantage of experience when the Battle of Britain opened. The more far-sighted British fighter leaders were quick to abandon the neat, geometrical patrolling formations and attack patterns laid down in pre-war years and adopt the more flexible method of the Germans. This became known as the 'finger-four': a basic unit of four aircraft, with each leader protected by his wing-man. A major controversy was caused by the 'wing theory': the co-ordinated use of entire squadrons in combat which the British tried with indifferent results during the battle. Championed by the commander of No. 12 Group, Air Vice Marshal Leigh-Mallory, and by the forthright legless pilot Douglas Bader, the idea was tried with Bader's Duxford Wing of five squadrons. There was no head-hunting in the Luftwaffe after the battle but in Britain Dowding and Park, the real victors, were shabbily treated and removed to unimportant commands. On the other hand, Leigh-Mallory eclipsed Dowding and eventually rose to the command of the Allied Expeditionary Force in 1944.

The Bombing OFFENSIVE

Expensive lessons on the limitations and vulnerability of bombers had to be painfully learned in the early weeks of the war, but it was only after a year that the established conventions of war were totally abandoned and strategic bombing began in earnest. Both sides pursued their indiscriminate assault on civilian and military targets and only later, in a war of fascinating offensive and defensive gadgetry, were bombing techniques so tellingly improved that selected targets could be attacked with any real expectancy of success.

Caution and restraint were the watchwords when the bombers' war opened in September 1939. While the Wehrmacht was engaged in smashing Poland, neither the Allies nor Hitler wanted to escalate the war by opening an all-out bombing offensive. The Allies wanted to localise and confine the conflict; Hitler hoped that a settlement could be reached with the Allies once Poland was out of the way. Thus the bombing war was run for nearly a full year under what can best be described as strict military decorum. But there were technical reasons as well.

For 20 years, fear of the bomber had been a nightmare. The dread of mass raids showering poison gas and high explosive on civilian populations had created a 'gas phobia' which events were to prove unfounded. At the same time, political pressures had made their mark on strategic thinking and had put a brake on the evolution of the bomber. In Germany, the desire to mass-produce tested and proved twin-engined bomber aircraft types edged out the development of a long-range heavy bomber. Vicious financial limitations on military and aircraft development in Britain and France had similar effects.

It was not the fault of the experts. Germany's General Wever, Luftwaffe Chief-of-Staff until his death in an air crash in 1936, had championed the cause of a long-range heavy bomber programme. He had been blocked by the Luftwaffe's Quartermaster-General, General Udet, by the Secretary of State for Air, General Milch, and by Göring himself. In Britain the brilliant designer Barnes Wallis, the brains behind the R-100 airship and the **Wellesley** and **Wellington** bombers, had in 1939 presented his plan for a 'Victory Bomber' which could carry a 10-ton bomb against strategic targets, but his idea was pooh-poohed as science fiction. In 1939 neither Germany nor the Allies were equipped to wage a strategic bomber offensive; the very idea was anathema to the politicians; military targets were the only

A formation of Lancasters. This bomber was the backbone of the RAF bombing effort and featured in two notable raids, the sinking of Tirpitz and the Dams Raid.

objectives considered, but there was the greatest confusion as to what they might be.

For both sides, one target was clear-cut right from the start—warships and their bases. Even so, British and German bomber crews were under the strictest orders not to bomb naval bases unless the enemy ships were there for fear of inflicting civilian loss of life and provoking reprisals.

The aircraft of RAF Bomber Command in 1939 consisted of the **Handley Page Hampden**, the **Bristol Blenheim**, the **Vickers Wellington**, and the **Armstrong-Whitworth Whitley**—all of them twin-engined, with bomb loads up to 4,500 lbs apart from the Whitley with its maximum of 7,000 lbs, and all with inadequate defensive armament. Their average maximum range with light bomb loads was approximately 1,340 miles. Considerable confusion was caused to AA gunners by the fact that the Hampden and Blenheim both bore some superficial resemblances to the **Do 17** and **Ju 88** respectively.

A lesson in destruction

The Blenheims and Hampdens opened Bomber Command's war with strikes against German battleships in the Schillig Roads, the pocket-battleship *Admiral Scheer* being the main target. It was an innocuous debut. The British were learning from

RAF Bomber Sorties and Losses, 1939–45	
Night sorties —	297,663
Losses —	7,449
Day sorties —	66,851
Losses —	876

British and American Bomber Offensive against Germany, 1939-45

Year	RAF Bomber Command	US 8th Air Force
1939	31 tons	—
1940	13,033 tons	—
1941	31,504 tons	—
1942	45,561 tons	1,561 tons
1943	157,457 tons	44,165 tons
1944	525,518 tons	389,119 tons
1945	191,540 tons	188,573 tons

Americans by day—B-17s and B-24s. The mighty US Army 8th Air Force was the primary Allied instrument of retribution against the Germans by day, dropping more than 600,000 tons of bombs between 1942 and 1945. More than half its bomb groups were equipped with the Boeing B-17 Fortress, pictured marshalling before take-off, at point of bomb release, and as a sad wreck undergoing German inspection in a Dutch field. The fourth picture shows the B-17's partner, the B-24 Liberator. Flak claimed this one from the 15th Air Force in Italy. In spite of tight formations losses were high.

scratch—everything from taking off with a full bomb load to finding the target in bad weather and coping with enemy flak.

The dearest lesson they had to absorb came on December 18 when a close formation of 22 Wellingtons flew over Wilhelmshaven and the Heligoland Bight in perfect, cloudless fighter weather without fighter protection. The belief that the mass firepower of Wellingtons in formation could keep off fighter opposition was shattered by the Wellington's vulnerability to beam attacks. Ten Wellingtons were shot down during the sweep and another three were written off on crash-landing in Britain. The losses suffered by this daytime 'Battle of Heligoland Bight' were instrumental in Bomber Command's switch to night operations, on which it concentrated for the rest of the war.

In this early, cautious period of mutual anti-shipping strikes the Luftwaffe did no better than the RAF. Prime targets for the Germans were the capital ships of the British Home Fleet, most notably the battleships *Rodney* and *Nelson*, the world-famous battle-cruiser *Hood*, and the aircraft-carrier *Ark Royal*. On September 26 the Home Fleet was sighted on a North Sea sweep. Nine **He 111s** and four Ju 88s were sent out to attack. *Hood* was hit by a dud; *Ark Royal* was narrowly missed by a dive-bombing Ju 88 whose pilot claimed a

The American Bomber Force

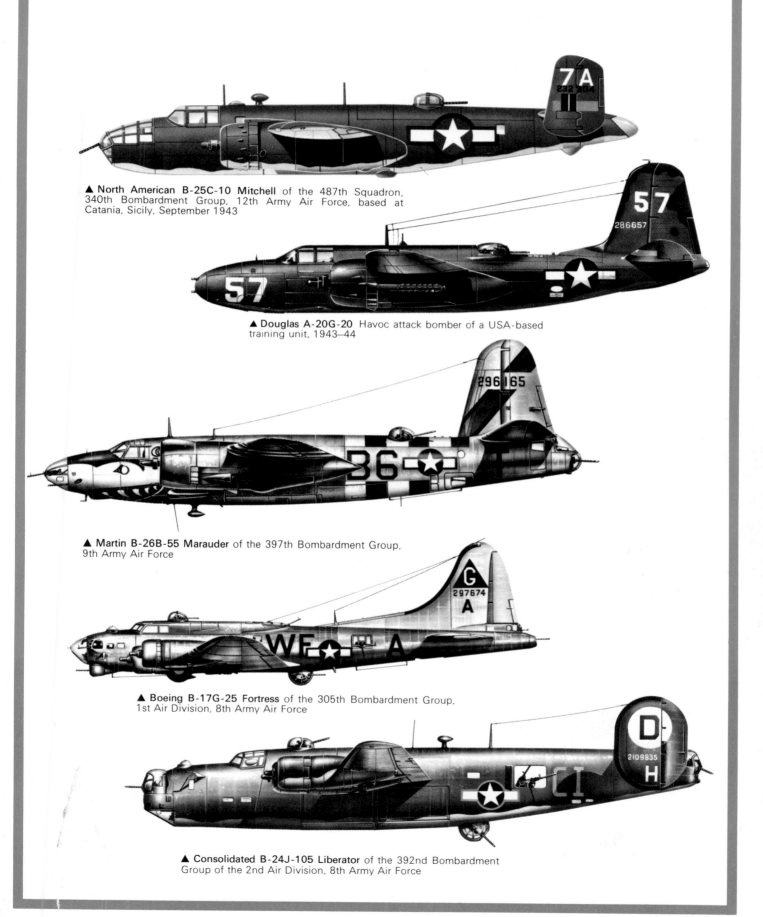

▲ North American B-25C-10 Mitchell of the 487th Squadron, 340th Bombardment Group, 12th Army Air Force, based at Catania, Sicily, September 1943

▲ Douglas A-20G-20 Havoc attack bomber of a USA-based training unit, 1943—44

▲ Martin B-26B-55 Marauder of the 397th Bombardment Group, 9th Army Air Force

▲ Boeing B-17G-25 Fortress of the 305th Bombardment Group, 1st Air Division, 8th Army Air Force

▲ Consolidated B-24J-105 Liberator of the 392nd Bombardment Group of the 2nd Air Division, 8th Army Air Force

Bombers of the RAF

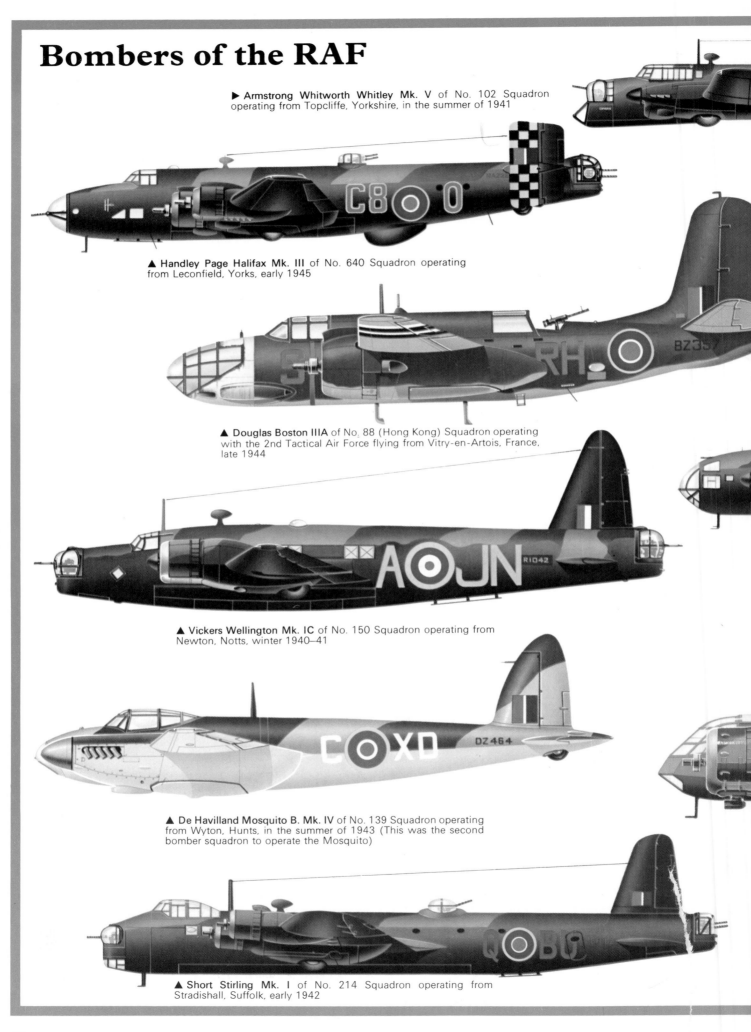

▶ Armstrong Whitworth Whitley Mk. V of No. 102 Squadron operating from Topcliffe, Yorkshire, in the summer of 1941

▲ Handley Page Halifax Mk. III of No. 640 Squadron operating from Leconfield, Yorks, early 1945

▲ Douglas Boston IIIA of No. 88 (Hong Kong) Squadron operating with the 2nd Tactical Air Force flying from Vitry-en-Artois, France, late 1944

▲ Vickers Wellington Mk. IC of No. 150 Squadron operating from Newton, Notts, winter 1940–41

▲ De Havilland Mosquito B. Mk. IV of No. 139 Squadron operating from Wyton, Hunts, in the summer of 1943 (This was the second bomber squadron to operate the Mosquito)

▲ Short Stirling Mk. I of No. 214 Squadron operating from Stradishall, Suffolk, early 1942

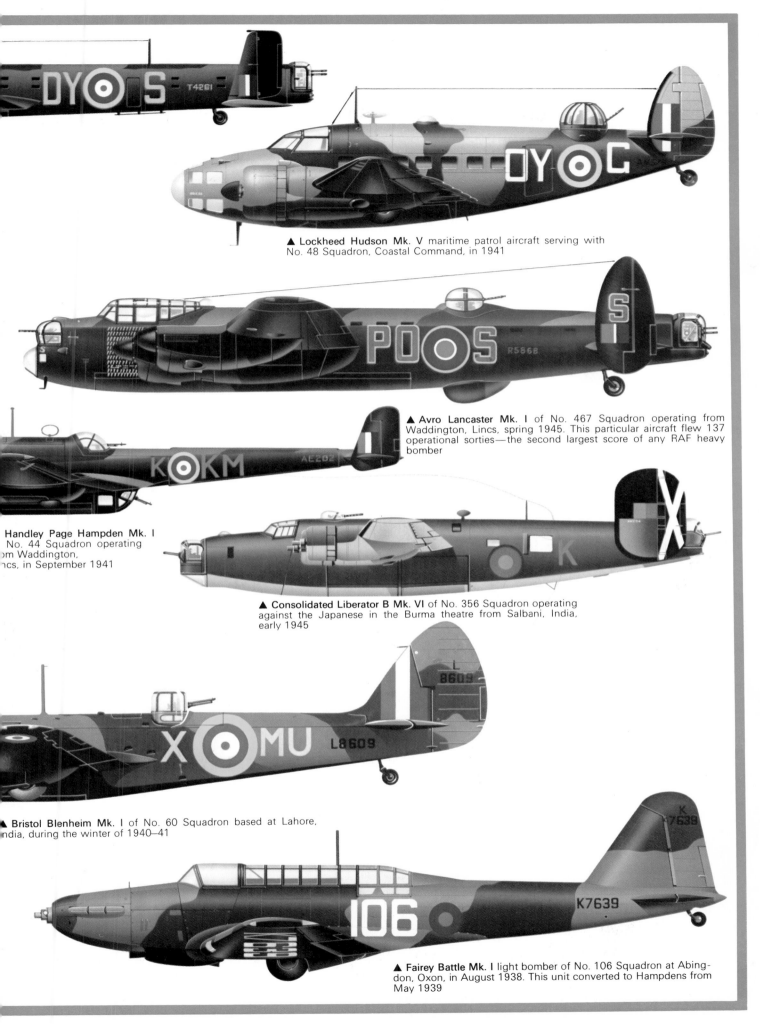

▲ Lockheed Hudson Mk. V maritime patrol aircraft serving with No. 48 Squadron, Coastal Command, in 1941

▲ Avro Lancaster Mk. I of No. 467 Squadron operating from Waddington, Lincs, spring 1945. This particular aircraft flew 137 operational sorties—the second largest score of any RAF heavy bomber

Handley Page Hampden Mk. I No. 44 Squadron operating om Waddington, ncs, in September 1941

▲ Consolidated Liberator B Mk. VI of No. 356 Squadron operating against the Japanese in the Burma theatre from Salbani, India, early 1945

Bristol Blenheim Mk. I of No. 60 Squadron based at Lahore, ndia, during the winter of 1940—41

▲ Fairey Battle Mk. I light bomber of No. 106 Squadron at Abingdon, Oxon, in August 1938. This unit converted to Hampdens from May 1939

possible hit. The German propaganda machine claimed that *Ark Royal* had been sunk and the subsequent embarrassment drove the guiltless German pilot, Corporal Francke, to the verge of suicide.

Later, on October 16, the Luftwaffe attacked the Home Fleet base at Rosyth in the Firth of Forth. The *Hood* was there but was not attacked, according to previous orders, as she was entering dock; the cruisers *Edinburgh* and *Southampton* were lightly damaged. The following day Scapa Flow, the great British naval anchorage in the Orkneys, was attacked by four Ju 88s, but they only managed to damage the old training depot battleship *Iron Duke*, a thoroughly redundant veteran of Jutland.

Bomber myths dispelled

Thus the opening weeks of World War II dispelled many pre-war myths about the potency of the bomber. Anti-shipping attacks needed pinpoint accuracy and special techniques; low-level bombing was not the answer, and both sides found that far too many of their bombs were failing to explode. (This was also the period when the German U-boats were having trouble with dud torpedoes.) In the Norwegian campaign of April 1940, Ju 87 attacks on shipping proved for the first time how deadly the dive-bomber could be in attacks on warships.

But the story of strategic bombing in World War II really begins in the summer of 1940, when concern for civilian life and property was abandoned by both sides. The Luftwaffe found that the heaviest raids could not bring about the total destruction of 'military targets', the most obvious examples being port installations, aircraft factories, radar stations, and fighter airfields in the Battle of Britain. And the commanders of the Luftwaffe and of Bomber Command entered a new phase in their history, trying to create an offensive strategy out of the deliberate bombing of civilian populations.

Throughout most of 1940 Bomber Command's objectives were constantly changing. In April the British bombers were set to mining the canals of Denmark and the waters of the Kattegat to cut off the German footholds in Norway—a technique which naturally proved ineffective against the German air-lift. During the Battle of France they raided the Ruhr and oil tanks at Hamburg, and made 'billiard-shot' attacks—placing delayed action bombs into railway tunnels—in attempts to slow up the German advance.

Berlin is bombed

Then came Churchill's order to bomb Berlin in retaliation for the German bombs that fell on London. The long distance to Berlin inevitably reduced bomb-loads to the lightest, but the initial morale effect was striking: Göring had promised that no British bomber could ever get to Berlin. But the mood of the Berliners soon turned to hatred and desire for vengeance. The loathing of the cowardly Allied *terrorflieger*, once implanted by Goebbels' propaganda, was never quenched throughout the war; and the German civilian population held as firm as did the British under the bombing.

At the same time as the first raids on Berlin, Bomber Command was playing a vital role in the Battle of Britain by pressing home repeated attacks against the German invasion barges massing in the Channel ports.

Hitler's reaction was to order the razing of every major British city, but this was not so easy. Anyone could find and hit London —it was huge and it had England's biggest river coiling right through it. For targets deeper inland electronic devices had to be used: overlapping *Lorenz* radio beams which told the pilot when he was on course, and the intersecting *Knickebein* and *X-Gerät* beams, which crossed over the target and signalled an automatic bomb release as the bomber hit the intersection point. The specially-trained *Kampfgruppe* 100 used the X-Gerät guidance system on the night of November 14, 1940, when 449 bombers from *Luftflotten* 2 and 3 savaged Coventry. But the rapid British discovery that both these German systems could be jammed or distorted did much to negate the threat for the time being. The escalating 'radar war' had begun, with both sides seeking to develop new 'black boxes' which the enemy could not jam.

The British had to swallow even more unpalatable home truths in 1941. The great German invasion of Soviet Russia in

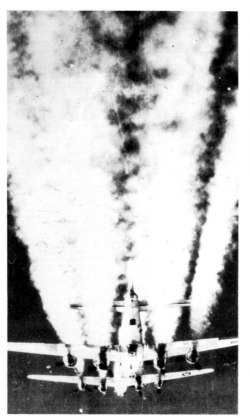

RAF Bomber Command Targets and Tonnage for Period for January 1-September 1, 1943		
Hamburg	—	11,000 tons
Essen	—	8,000 tons
Duisburg	—	6,000 tons
Berlin	—	6,000 tons
Dusseldorf	—	5,000 tons
Nuremberg	—	5,000 tons

Top left: Mosquito attack. The versatile Mosquito was used in almost every role from long-range bomber to night fighter. These Mk VIs hit this ship at Sandshaven with bombs, rockets and guns.
Left and above: Fortress formation. Despite Severe losses the 8th AF B-17 and B-24 Bomb Groups persisted in proving the viability of the close formation attack by day. What finally turned the scales was all-the-way escort by P-51 Mustangs equipped with drop tanks—in the picture on the left one is visible in the distance escorting the B-17Gs of the 381st BG.

June 1941 proved that Germany's industrial war potential had been totally under-estimated and that all the Bomber Command raids carried out against German industrial targets had been useless. Further investigations showed that the bomber crews, for all their bravery, were simply not hitting their targets. Attempts to cripple the communications system of the Ruhr valley failed completely. Moreover, Luftwaffe General Kammhuber's night fighter network, controlled by radar, was beginning to make itself felt. There was a brighter side: the big new bombers had entered service—the **Short Stirling** and **Handley Page Halifax,** with maximum bomb loads of

14,000 lbs and 13,000 lbs respectively. The twin-engined **Avro Manchester** gave repeated engine trouble, but it led to the four-engined **Lancaster,** the most successful British bomber of the war, developed from the basic Manchester concept as an experiment. But the course of the war still produced weakening distractions and the greatest of these in 1941 was the threat posed by the presence of the German battle-cruisers *Scharnhorst* and *Gneisenau* in Brest, which got the lion's share of British bombs in 1941.

Harris's war on will

1942 was an important turning-point for Bomber Command. On February 22, Air Marshal Harris took over as its commander. He thought—although he was never able to prove it—that bombing could win the war by destroying Germany's ability to wage war and her will to do so. Churchill backed him enthusiastically.

At the same time Harris had absorbed the lesson that greater accuracy was needed and that electronic aids were the answer. Three new British devices were eventually found to answer satisfactorily—Gee, which gave navigators the benefit of a radio grid for pinpointing their position, Oboe which gave an exact pinpoint guide for bombing or target marking accurately, and H2S which provided a radar map of the ground over which the aircraft was passing. These devices enabled bombers to fly in denser formations—'bomber streams'—and considerably reduce their time over the target area. But time was also needed to acquire experience in using them. Another process which Harris backed was target marking: the birth of the 'Pathfinder' force, which flew ahead of the main bomber stream and marked the target with coloured flares. Here again tragic mistakes were made, most notably when target markers missed Saarbrücken and illuminated the small town of Saarlouis instead, resulting in its elimination.

Nevertheless, Harris' obsession with the psychological effect of mass raiding had caused the first 'thousand-bomber raid' of 30–31 May 1942, when a total of 1,046 aircraft headed for Cologne. It rendered 45,000 German citizens homeless and killed 469 of them, but it did not bring about the abrupt termination of the war, as Harris had hoped, and did not even eliminate Cologne's industrial output. The raid had called for the total strength of Bomber Command plus all suitable bombers from Coastal Command and even 367 aircraft from training and conversion units and the loss for the night was 43—3.6 per cent. Nor did the 'thousand raid' disrupt the German fighter defences. The Cologne raid proved yet again that Bomber Command could not deliver knock-out blows. True, it was an ominous warning of what the Germans could expect in the future. But that could not win the war either.

Throughout 1942 the RAF also made repeated experiments with daytime raids on specially-selected targets. Down to October of that year as many as 45 daytime raids were launched. Favourite targets for the Lancasters in these raids were the U-boat yards at Lübeck, Danzig, and

Gdynia along the Baltic coast—most of them at ranges impossible to cover before the advent of the Lancaster. One of the most notorious raids (as far as British losses were concerned) was the low-level precision raid of April 17, 1942 on the M.A.N. works at Augsburg, where U-boat engines were manufactured. The raid was made by 12 unescorted Lancasters of Nos. 44 and 97 Squadrons. The M.A.N. works, badly damaged, did not resume its full output for six months but seven of the Lancasters were lost.

But Harris had set his face against concentrated strikes of this nature, whether by day or night. British technicians could produce specialised weapons for specialised targets, as was abundantly proved by the 'Dams Raid' of May 17, 1943, when the Möhne and Eder dams were breached in the Ruhr. But Harris was later to state, in unequivocal terms, 'the destruction of factories, which was nevertheless on an enormous scale, could be regarded as a bonus. The aiming points were usually right in the centre of the town'.

Thus the accuracy of the Dams Raid was followed within months by the fire-storm raid on Hamburg with the destruction of what, by any standards, were military and strategic targets simply a 'bonus'.

One of the greatest nuisance weapons with which the RAF plagued the Luftwaffe was the **de Havilland Mosquito.** Starting life as a low-cost private experiment ignored by RAF top brass the Mosquito achieved a unique service record. Powered by twin Merlins, it had a maximum speed of nearly 400 mph. Armed with four 20 mm cannon and four machine guns it was a formidable fighter. In its unarmed bomber version the Mosquito could eventually carry up to 4,000 lb of bombs. It was the ideal intruder for daytime reconnaissance, easily outpacing intercepting fighters. And, when fitted with the 'Oboe' navigation pin-pointer, it was used to put down the initial marker flares for the incoming night bomber streams.

The Lancaster itself became Bomber Command's best heavy bomber. With a crew of seven it had a maximum range of 1,660 miles and usually carried 14,000 lb of bombs. Specially modified Lancasters carried the spinning 'bouncing bomb' (actually a sophisticated depth-charge) against the Ruhr dams. In 1944 and 1945 the massive 'Tallboy' (12,000 lb) and 'Grand Slam' (22,000 lb) bombs appeared and were dropped by Lancasters. Outsize, streamlined darts that passed the speed of sound as they dropped, 'Tallboy' and 'Grand Slam' were designed to drill deep below the surface on impact and destroy their target by the 'earthquake effect'. Barnes Wallis, designer of the bombs, had promised that with them near-misses would be as good as direct hits. The shattered span of the Bielefeld Viaduct proved him right in 1945. The bombs shattered formerly impregnable U-boat pens and, much more important, flying-bomb sites and Hitler's V.3 secret weapon. The latter was a giant, multi-barrelled 'jet' gun with its vitals deep underground. Wallis' bombs wrecked it before completion.

CAPABILITIES OF PRINCIP	
Country	**Type**
Germany	Heinkel He 111
	Dornier Do 217
	Ju 88A-6
	Heinkel He 177
	Focke-Wulf FW-20
Great Britain	Vickers Wellington
	Short Stirling
	Handley-Page Halif
	Avro Lancaster
	D.H. Mosquito
United States	Boeing B-17G
	Boeing B-29
	North American B-
	Mitchell
	Consolidated B-24
	Liberator
Soviet Union	Petlyakov Pe-2
	Ilyushin Il-4
	Tupolev SB-2
Italy	Savoia-Marchetti
	SM-79
	Fiat BR-20
	Piaggio P-108B

Bombers of the Soviet Air Force

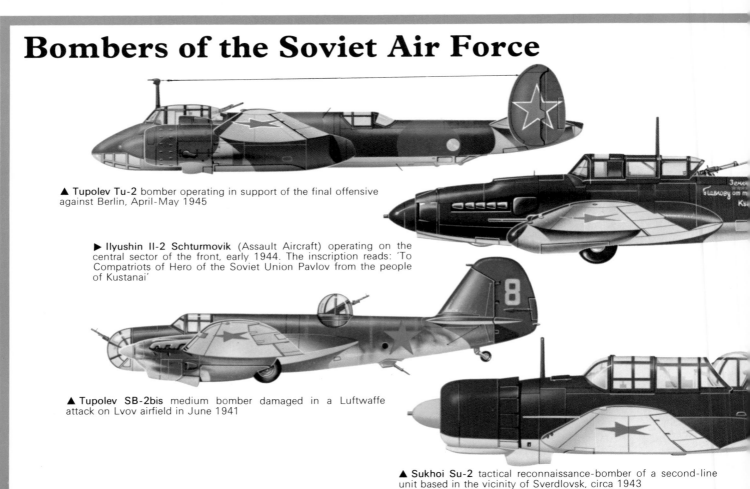

▲ **Tupolev Tu-2** bomber operating in support of the final offensive against Berlin, April-May 1945

▶ **Ilyushin Il-2 Schturmovik** (Assault Aircraft) operating on the central sector of the front, early 1944. The inscription reads: 'To Compatriots of Hero of the Soviet Union Pavlov from the people of Kustanai'

▲ **Tupolev SB-2bis** medium bomber damaged in a Luftwaffe attack on Lvov airfield in June 1941

▲ **Sukhoi Su-2** tactical reconnaissance-bomber of a second-line unit based in the vicinity of Sverdlovsk, circa 1943

...MBERS 1939–45

Max. load	Max. range
5,510 lbs	1,740 miles
8,818 lbs	1,500 miles
5,720 lbs	1,696 miles
14,400 lbs	2,795 miles
4,626 lbs	2,760 miles
6,000 lbs	1,325 miles
14,000 lbs	1,930 miles
13,000 lbs	1,030 miles
22,000 lbs	1,660 miles
4,000 lbs	1,370 miles
17,600 lbs	1,850 miles
12,000 lbs	3,250 miles
4,000 lbs	1,275 miles
5,000 lbs	1,700 miles
2,200 lbs	1,200 miles
4,400 lbs	2,500 miles
1,320 lbs	1,430 miles
2,750 lbs	1,243 miles
3,520 lbs	1,860 miles
7,716 lbs	1,550 miles

The end of the Tirpitz

Like the 'bouncing bomb', however, these weapons were for the specialised use of No. 617 Squadron, which added to its laurels with the sinking of the battleship *Tirpitz* on November 12, 1944. The bulk of Bomber Command was reserved for the Battle of Germany. Guided to its target by the coloured flares of the preceding Mosquitoes and other 'Pathfinder' aircraft, RAF Bomber Command's aircraft carried the war home to Germany with clusters of incendiaries and 4,000 lb high explosive bombs—the proportion of the incendiaries depending on the estimated inflammable nature of the town to be attacked.

The American **B-17** designed from the outset for daylight missions, concentrated much more on defensive armament than did the Lancaster, carrying up to 13 heavy .5-inch machine guns. It had a crew of ten and a maximum range of 1,850 miles. When massed in formation the B-17s were confidently expected to be able to put up an impenetrable barrage of defensive fire. This was proved disastrously fallacious on August 17, 1943, when Schweinfurt and Regensburg were attacked. The target was a vital one—the heart of the German ball-bearing industry. But the day was a disaster for the B-17s. Total American losses for the day came to 60 shot down plus over 100 damaged out of the 363 B-17s which set out. Of these 363 only 315 arrived at the targets. The total loss rate worked out at 19 per cent of the raiding force—an unprecedented score. Nor was this first

raid on Schweinfurt unique. Between October 8 and October 14, 1943, Bremen, Marienburg, Danzig, Münster, and Schweinfurt, were attacked in daytime for an overall loss of 148 aircraft.

Fighters were the main reason. In the first Schweinfurt raid the Luftwaffe sent up approximately 300 fighters during the day. The only fighter escort which the Allies could provide covered a shallow arc barely extending to the Paris-Cologne area. These deep-penetration raids were doomed to murderous losses until the long-range **P-47 Thunderbolt** and **P-51 Mustang** escort fighters came into operational service in sufficient numbers in 1944.

The Allied reaction was to switch the focal point of the bombing offensive to the German aircraft industry which had some effect, but in the winter of 1943–44 the German war industry, under the brilliant leadership of Reichminister Albert Speer, was effectively dispersed. Superhuman efforts on the production lines shot German fighter production to record levels. In February 1944, 905 **Me 109s** were turned out; the June figure was 1,603. Comparable figures for the **Focke-Wulf 190** were 209 for February and 689 for June 1944. Despite 'Big Week'—the Allied blitz against the Luftwaffe—total fighter production for 1944 reached 25,285 fighters: the best figure for any year of the war. But there was another side to the coin. Between January and April 1944 the Luftwaffe lost over 1,000 pilots—items which no production line could synthesise. Men, not machines, were the Luftwaffe's problem by the summer

Top: **Bielefeld viaduct**. Hundreds of water-filled craters testify to the RAF's efforts to sever this vital rail link. What finally did it was Barnes Wallis's 22,000 lb 'earthquake' bomb (biggest craters) which shook it until the spans fell.

The bombing of Europe. Germany's invasion of Russia in 1941 proved that the estimates of damage inflicted by Bomber Command were greatly exaggerated and the effort was stepped up, the USAAF bombing by day and RAF by night.

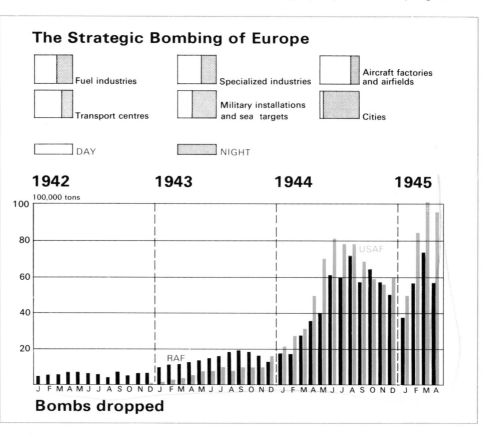

The Strategic Bombing of Europe

Fuel industries — Specialized industries — Aircraft factories and airfields
Transport centres — Military installations and sea targets — Cities

DAY   NIGHT

1942   1943   1944   1945

100,000 tons

USAF

RAF

J F M A M J J A S O N D J F M A M J J A S O N D J F M A M J J A S O N D J F M A

Bombs dropped

The Axis Bomber Force

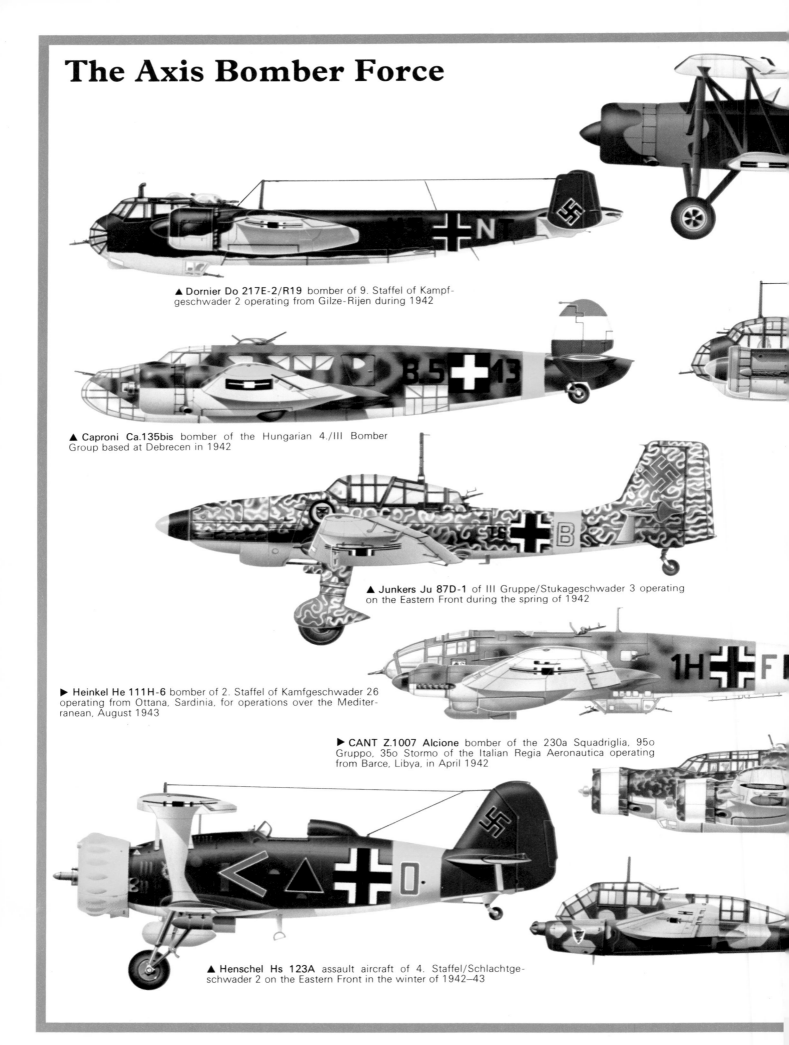

▲ **Dornier Do 217E-2/R19** bomber of 9. Staffel of Kampf-geschwader 2 operating from Gilze-Rijen during 1942

▲ **Caproni Ca.135bis** bomber of the Hungarian 4./III Bomber Group based at Debrecen in 1942

▲ **Junkers Ju 87D-1** of III Gruppe/Stukageschwader 3 operating on the Eastern Front during the spring of 1942

▶ **Heinkel He 111H-6** bomber of 2. Staffel of Kamfgeschwader 26 operating from Ottana, Sardinia, for operations over the Mediterranean, August 1943

▶ **CANT Z.1007 Alcione** bomber of the 230a Squadriglia, 95o Gruppo, 35o Stormo of the Italian Regia Aeronautica operating from Barce, Libya, in April 1942

▲ **Henschel Hs 123A** assault aircraft of 4. Staffel/Schlachtge-schwader 2 on the Eastern Front in the winter of 1942–43

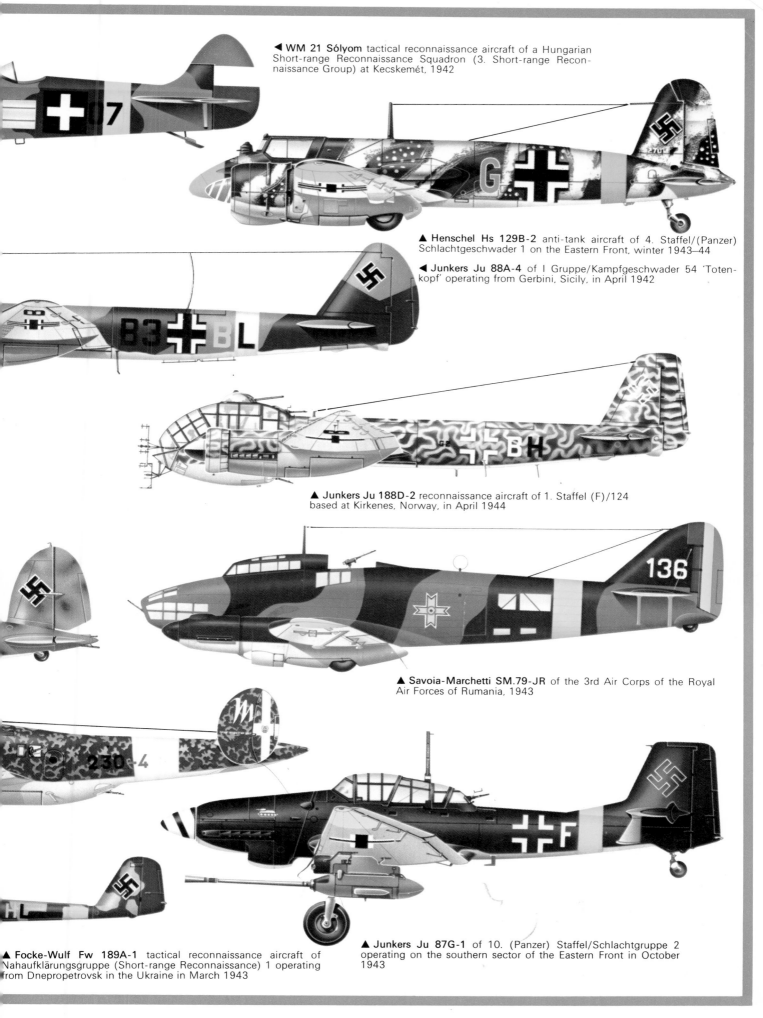

◄ **WM 21 Sólyom** tactical reconnaissance aircraft of a Hungarian Short-range Reconnaissance Squadron (3. Short-range Reconnaissance Group) at Kecskemét, 1942

▲ **Henschel Hs 129B-2** anti-tank aircraft of 4. Staffel/(Panzer) Schlachtgeschwader 1 on the Eastern Front, winter 1943–44

◄ **Junkers Ju 88A-4** of I Gruppe/Kampfgeschwader 54 'Totenkopf' operating from Gerbini, Sicily, in April 1942

▲ **Junkers Ju 188D-2** reconnaissance aircraft of 1. Staffel (F)/124 based at Kirkenes, Norway, in April 1944

▲ **Savoia-Marchetti SM.79-JR** of the 3rd Air Corps of the Royal Air Forces of Rumania, 1943

▲ **Focke-Wulf Fw 189A-1** tactical reconnaissance aircraft of Nahaufklärungsgruppe (Short-range Reconnaissance) 1 operating from Dnepropetrovsk in the Ukraine in March 1943

▲ **Junkers Ju 87G-1** of 10. (Panzer) Staffel/Schlachtgruppe 2 operating on the southern sector of the Eastern Front in October 1943

of 1944, and soon another would be added—fuel.

Insolent Channel dash

The Allies had been forced to switch the objectives of their bombing offensive constantly ever since its inception in the spring of 1940. By the spring of 1944, a few isolated tactical successes had been won but the overall balance showed very little practical reward for the thousands of tons of bombs which had been dropped. The Battle of the Atlantic had brought about the bombing of U-boat factories and pens. The unwelcome presence of *Scharnhorst* and *Gneisenau* in Brest had concentrated Bomber Command's attentions upon that port for nearly a year, and still the ships had been able to steam almost insolently home to Germany through the Channel. Harris's carpet bombing of German cities had by no means caused German morale to shatter. Renewed mass attacks on strategic targets—in daylight for accuracy—had been hideously mauled by the Luftwaffe, and subsequent attempts to destroy the Luftwaffe had also failed.

But beginning in May 1944 the vital fuel stocks of the Reich were singled out for destruction. Targets long planned were now hit again and again: synthetic oil and petrol plants in Germany at Brüx, Böhlen, Leuna, and Zwickau; the great Rumanian oil wells at Ploesti—the latter hammered 20 times in six weeks. At the end of May, Pölitz, with its former monthly output of 47,000 tons, was put out of business for two months. Luftwaffe fuel reserves, so painfully amassed, vanished. By September 1944 the Luftwaffe was down to one-fifth of its minimum requirements: 30,000 tons. And it was at this point that the collapse of German industry, so long averted by Speer's efforts, began in earnest.

Long before the catastrophic effects of the Allied fuel offensive were felt in depth by the Luftwaffe, the bombing offensive in the West had become integrated with the invasion of Europe. Pre-invasion bombing was vitally important. The idea was to seal off the whole area behind the Normandy battlefield by wrecking the road and rail centres through which the Wehrmacht could rush reinforcements to the invasion sector, and this was effectively done. But the whole vexed question of tactical bombing raises the constant problem of air/ground liaison. This had already been shown at Monte Cassino in January 1944, when the generals insisted that the Abbey be destroyed. This the bombers emphatically achieved but at a sad cost to the front-line troops in the area. The same happened in Normandy in July, when American bombers laid down an 'explosive carpet' along the break-out line. It must be concluded that the most effective work done on the Western Front between D-Day and the end of the war was that of the fighter-bombers and the rockets, not the level-bombing formations.

As the front crawled eastward to the frontier of the Reich and finally closed up to the Rhine, the British and American strategic bombing programme continued to hammer at the German cities. On the night of February 13 the catastrophic area

bombing of Dresden began—the most deadly raid of the war in the West. Casualties are still impossible to compute. The raid added nothing whatever to the Allied advance, either in the East or West. And still Berlin remained a top-priority target. The raids went on without respite until the morning of April 21, 1945, when the US 8th Air Force launched the 363rd Berlin raid of the war—the very morning that the first Russian shells fell in the German capital.

Was it all worth it?

What did the Allied bombing achieve? For years it was the only way in which the war could be carried home to the German people, and this undoubtedly was of the highest importance to Allied morale. It failed to ruin that of the Germans. By the time that the bombing finally managed to grind German war production to a standstill, the Eastern and Western Fronts were closing in on the German homeland anyway. With special weapons and training, immense damage was done to special targets—the *Tirpitz*, the dams, the U-boat pens—but never on a large scale. But it is certain that the continuation of the mass raids was instrumental in whittling down the Luftwaffe's reserve of trained pilots. It is equally certain that had the German aircraft industry been able to deliver jets such as the Me 262 earlier, the Luftwaffe might have caused the Allies to severely restrict the bomber offensive.

Another effect of the bombing war was the immense progress made in radar and navigational aids. By 1944 bombers were relying almost exclusively on instruments to get to their targets by night—so much so that one Luftwaffe officer advocated the suspension of the Berlin black-out in order to illuminate the bombers more clearly! As the tank man's war was governed by the race to find a bigger gun to beat the enemy's thicker armour, so the bomber's war depended on the need to develop interference-proof electronic devices and continue to jam those of the enemy.

Hamstrung by the rejection of a heavy bomber construction programme, the Luftwaffe's bomber arm dwindled rapidly after 1943, but it still showed that it was fully capable of mounting a devastating strike. In June 1944, American bombers flew to Soviet Russia to operate from Poltava and Mogilev airfields on their first 'shuttle bombing' raids against Germany. Tracked to its destination by a **Heinkel He 177**, the American bomber force was attacked on its airfields by 200 German bombers on the night of June 22. A flight of 600 miles was involved and total surprise was achieved. Not a German aircraft was lost, but 43 B-17s and 15 Mustangs were destroyed on the ground, plus 300,000 gallons of fuel. It was a daring and effective raid; but its effects were immediately swamped by the great Soviet summer offensive which opened the following day and eventually drove the Wehrmacht back to the Vistula. If one seeks to compare the comparative effects of air and ground warfare, a cynic might well use this example as a symbol. Bombs can destroy. But only troops can occupy ground.

The bombing of Germany. In the spring of 1940 the RAF made its first major air raid of the war, but it was not until the American 8th Air Force efforts got into their stride in late 1943 that the strategic bombing offensive really began. The success of early raids is debatable but the concentration of effort late in the war against transport systems, vital components factories and oil production centres did shorten the war. RAF Bomber Command concentrated on the night bombing of cities mounting the first 1,000 bomber raid, against Cologne, in May 1942, the first major raid against Berlin in November 1943. The Americans, bombing by day, suffered heavily until long range fighter escort in 1944 gave protection on deep penetration raids.

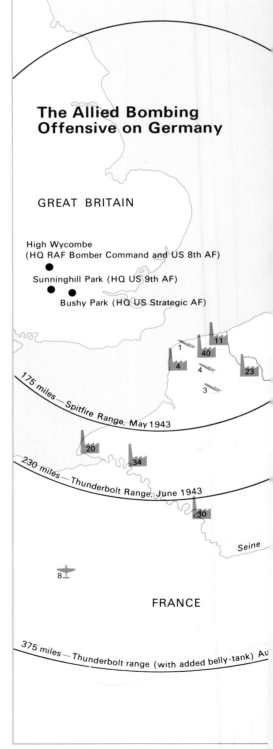

The Allied Bombing Offensive on Germany

GREAT BRITAIN

High Wycombe
(HQ RAF Bomber Command and US 8th AF)

Sunninghill Park (HQ US 9th AF)

Bushy Park (HQ US Strategic AF)

175 miles—Spitfire Range, May 1943

230 miles—Thunderbolt Range, June 1943

375 miles—Thunderbolt range (with added belly-tank)

Seine

FRANCE

Aircraft
1 Amsterdam
2 Augsburg
3 Bremen
4 Brussels
5 Dessau
6 Gotha
7 Kassel
8 Le Mans
9 Oschersleben
10 Regensburg
11 Wiener Neustadt

V Bombs
1 Mimovecques
2 Peenemunde
3 Siracourt
4 Wizernes

U-Boats
1 Emden
2 Flensburg
3 Kiel
4 Wilhelmshaven

5 Vegesack

Dams
1 Eder Dam
2 Mohne Dam
3 Sorpe Dam

Industrial
1 Berlin
2 Bochum
3 Bonn
4 Boulogne
5 Brunswick
6 Chemnitz
7 Cologne
8 Dortmund
9 Dresden
10 Duisburg
11 Dunkirk
12 Dusseldorf
13 Erfurt
14 Essen
15 Friedrichshafen
16 Furth

17 Hamburg
18 Hannover
19 Karlsruhe
20 Le Havre
21 Leipzig
22 Liegnitz
23 Lille
24 Lubeck
25 Ludwigshafen
26 Magdeburg
27 Metz
28 Munich
29 Nuremberg
30 Paris
31 Prague
32 Rostock
33 Rotterdam
34 Rouen
35 Saarbrucken
36 Schweinfurt
37 Stettin
38 Stuttgart
39 Ulm
40 Watten

41 Wuppertal

Oil
1 Bohlen
2 Brux
3 Derben
4 Dollbergen
5 Dulmen
6 Farge
7 Floridsdorf
8 Freiham
9 Gelsenkirchen
10 Heide
11 Hitzacker
12 Korneuburg
13 Leuna
14 Linz
15 Lobau
16 Lutzkendorf
17 Molbis
18 Moosbierbaum
19 Neuburg
20 Nienburg
21 Ploesti

22 Politz
23 Reisholz
24 Rositz
25 Ruhland
26 Salzbergen
27 Salzgitter
28 Schwechat
29 Wesseling
30 Zeitz

Railways
1 Altenbacken
  Neuenbecken
2 Aschaffenburg
3 Bebra
4 Bielefeld
5 Bingen
6 Breslau
7 Darmstadt
8 Frankfurt
9 Freiburg
10 Gera
11 Giessen
12 Halle

13 Hameln
14 Hamm
15 Hanau
16 Heilbronn
17 Karlsruhe
18 Koblenz
19 Lehrte
20 Lohne
21 Mainz
22 Mannheim
23 Minden
24 Mulhouse
25 Munich
26 Munster
27 Oberlahnstein
28 Offenburg
29 Osnabruck
30 Paderborn
31 Pasing
32 Rastatt
33 Rheine
34 Rosenheim
35 Salzburg
36 Schwerte

37 Seelze
38 Siegen
39 Soest
40 Stendal
41 Strasshof
42 Treuchtlingen
43 Vienna
44 Wurzburg

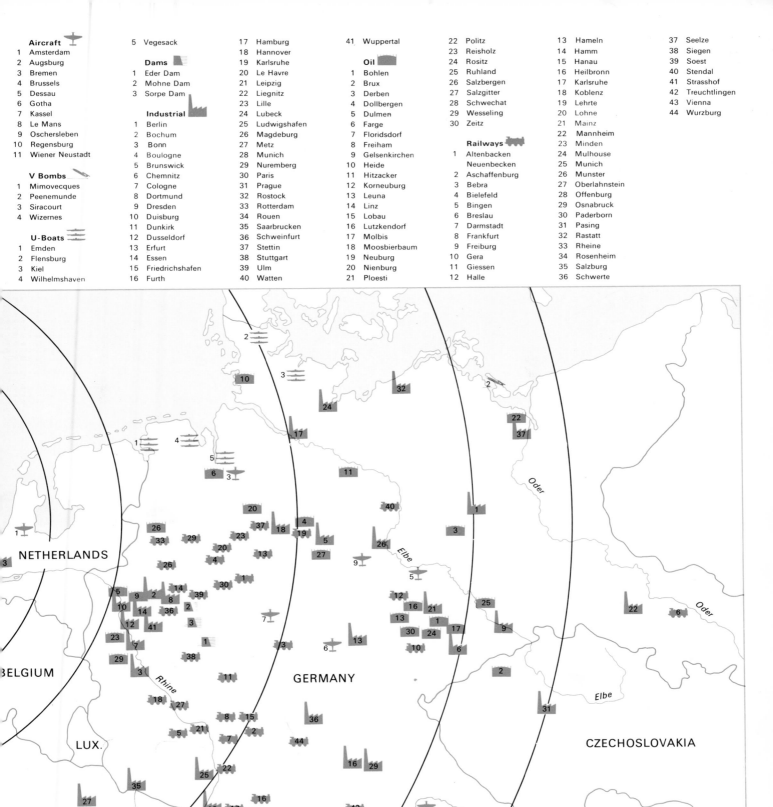

105

FIGHTERS' WAR

The command of the skies over Europe depended on fighter power. Britain's superb fighters saved her in the desperate days of 1940. The German Navy's daring 'Channel Dash' of 1942 proved the effectiveness of a fighter umbrella, but by the end of that year Germany's abundant fighters were on the defensive attempting to halt the round-the-clock stream of Allied bombers. Ingenious electronic devices and the first jet fighters were brought into the fray in vain and America's superlative long-range fighters finally made the task impossible. But regardless of their ultimate success or failure, fighters—famous, infamous and obscure—played a vital and colourful role in all the diverse theatres of the air war.

After the Luftwaffe's failure to break RAF Fighter Command in the Battle of Britain (September 1940) and the German invasion of Soviet Russia (June 1941), the Luftwaffe in the West assumed the strategic defensive for the remainder of the war. The fighter war in the European Theatre of Operations (ETO) now became an inevitable extension of the Allied bombing offensive. The British, and later American, attempts to break Germany's ability to make war turned on whether or not the German fighter arm could inflict unacceptable losses on the Allied day and night bomber streams. It was a defensive battle which the Luftwaffe had to win. It could certainly have done so and, in fact, came within an ace of victory. But although the Luftwaffe had superb fighters and a generous cross-section of the best fighter pilots in the world, it also had Hitler and Göring. Their ignorant meddling in the work of their professional subordinates effectively prevented the Luftwaffe from retaining command of the skies over western and central Europe.

Göring publicly ridiculed the figures of American bomber production as faked. As soon as the big Allied raids started hitting the cities of the Reich, Hitler reacted by ordering more bombers for retaliation—not more fighters to shoot down the Allied bombers. General Adolf Galland, the fighter ace promoted to the command of the German fighter arm, had fought in the Battle of Britain and to him and the other seasoned Luftwaffe fighter commanders, it

was a nightmare to know that the reasons for the German defeat over Britain had not been learned where it mattered—at the top—and that they were bidding fair to lose the Battle of Germany for the same reasons. Galland called the Luftwaffe's deployment in Soviet Russia, the Reich, the West, the Mediterranean and North Africa, a blanket that was not big enough— stretching it here would only tear it there. But to Hitler fighters were defensive weapons; and in Hitler's personal brand of military philosophy the fighting of defensive battles—let alone winning them—was not to be considered.

In 1941 the German fighter arm was given a powerful shot in the arm with the entry into service of the improved Messerschmitt fighter—the **Me 109F**—and the new **Focke-Wulf 190**. The Me 109F was more streamlined than the **109E**, faster, and its cannon had a higher rate of fire. The Fw 190 was even more hard-hitting: four 20-mm cannon and two machine guns. Its maximum speed of 395 mph at 17,000 feet was complemented by superb manoeuvrability. The Fw 190 gave its British opposite number, the **Spitfire V**, very hard times indeed in 1941, and only the hurried introduction of the **Spitfire IX** began to even the scales. Indeed the appearance of the Fw 190 may be compared to the World War I 'Fokker Scourge' of 1915.

Galland's fighter umbrella

The Me 109F and the Fw 190 were the mainstays of one of the greatest tactical victories won by the Luftwaffe in World War II: the escape of the *Scharnhorst, Gneisenau,* and *Prinz Eugen* from Brest to Germany through the English Channel in February 1942. Galland commanded the air side of the operation, on which everything turned. He called up every available fighter along the Atlantic coastline for the job of guaranteeing constant, orbiting air cover at all levels. Whirling air battles on February 12 enabled the battle squadron to run the Dover Narrows and enter home waters in safety. Thanks to Galland's air umbrella, not a bomb nor a torpedo hit the ships, and although *Scharnhorst* and *Gneisenau* both ran onto mines they reached port free of molestation by the RAF. So fast were the Fw 190s that their pilots had to lower wheels and flaps to get their speed down in order to attack the lumbering **Swordfish** biplanes which tried to torpedo the ships, causing some Swordfish crewmen to look incredulously for a German aircraft-carrier.

But such successes were peripheral. The worst threat remained the Allied bombing offensive, which gathered momentum in 1942 with the first American **B-17** raids from British bases. As the latter got into their stride it became clear that Germany could expect nothing less than round-the-clock bombing—the Americans by day and the British by night. By the summer of 1941, General Kammhuber's night-fighters had proved that the chain of radar stations, each

controlling the interception of a single fighter, was able to cope with isolated raiders. The German night-fighters were not new types. The Messerschmitt **Me 110** had come into its own as a night-fighter, and the ubiquitous **Ju 88** also proved tractable in the role. Fitted with *Lichtenstein* contact radar from August 1941 the fighters increased their scores and night-fighter aces began to emerge—Streib, Lent, Schnaufer, the Prince of Lippe-Weissenfeld, and others.

But Kammhuber's system was severely tested by the first mass raids of 1942. The problem was the restriction of the fighter to its ground-control radar zone instead of the freedom of operating in the bomber stream itself. But the beginning of the end was signalled in the last week of July 1943 with the repeated fire raids on Hamburg, the first 'firestorm' raids of the war. The British blinded the German radar by dropping clusters of foil strips—'Window'— which cluttered the screens with false contacts. The shock of Hamburg triggered off frantic orders for more fighters. Tactically, it led to the experiment of *Wilde Sau*—'Wild Boar'. This was born of the Allied radar jamming and it involved single-engined fighters roving at will without radar, intercepting by visual contact. By special arrangement, the German AA fire would be kept below a certain level. Once the raiders dropped their target markers the action would start. Initial successes with Wilde Sau were soon reversed by heavy and mounting losses and the technique was dropped by order in March 1944.

Beaufighter at Malta. By May 1941 the long-range 'Beaus' had begun to defend the beleaguered island. Soon they took the offensive; this one has under-wing bomb racks, while retaining all its guns.

Deadly 'slanting music'

Another peak of German night successes was due to the improved Lichtenstein SN-2 radar and the use of *Schräge Musik*—'Slanting music'. The latter consisted of two cannon mounted inside the fighter's fuselage, firing obliquely upwards, and enabling fighters to attack by closing in from behind and below. The SN-2/Schräge Musik combination inflicted startling new losses on Bomber Command during the winter of 1943–44. It set back Harris's plan to 'wreck Berlin from end to end'; it hacked down 78 out of 823 bombers during the attack on Leipzig on the night of February 19–20, 1944; and on the night of March 30–31, in the biggest night battle of the war, over Nuremberg, it destroyed 95 out of 795 RAF Lancasters and Halifaxes, 12 crashed in England and another 59 were badly damaged.

But the dominant problem was the mass Flying Fortress formations which came by day. It was not merely a question of putting up enough fighters to cope with the massed fire-power of the B-17 formations but of the fire-power needed to knock down the giant bombers. The Luftwaffe tried head-on attacks. It tried dive-bombing. It tried rocket attacks with 21-cm missiles and—on Hitler's orders—experiments were made with armoured-car size 5-cm cannon mounted on the **Me 410** heavy fighter. (The Me 410 itself was a sad story: a failure developed from a failure introduced to redress the balance of a failure). The Me 410 was the improved variant of the **Me 210,** which had been designed to replace the Me 110 as a twin-engined 'destroyer' fighter. Neither the Me 210 nor the Me 410 lived up to expectations. And the pulverising recoil of the 5-cm gun led to the abandonment of the project. The latter experiment, however, was not completely hare-brained: it was part of the search for a 'stand-off' missile for use against massed bomber formations. Such a missile did eventually emerge in the form of 5-cm R4M rockets, carried in broadsides of 24. These rockets proved devastatingly successful—but too late. They were, in fact, part and parcel of the sad story of the **Messerschmitt Me 262**: the revolutionary jet fighter that could and should have denied the Allies the control of the skies over Europe in 1943.

The first jet fighter

Experiments with jet-propelled aircraft were not a German preserve: they were arrived at virtually simultaneously by the British and the Germans. But the first successful prototype of a combat jet was certainly the German Me 262, first flown in July 1942. With its, initially, orthodox tailwheel undercarriage a swift tramp on the brakes was needed to bring the tail up and enable the aircraft to gain take-off speed. Galland flew the Me 262 in May 1943, but Hitler did not see it fly until November 1943. And when he did he threw it away by insisting that 'here at last is our Blitz bomber!'—and refusing to allow the Me 262 to be developed as a fighter until far too late. The final variant of the Me 262, with a tricycle undercarriage and salvoes of R4M rockets, was indeed a deadly operational reality by the end of the war—almost two years too late.

Other desperate Luftwaffe fighter attempts to beat the swarms of Allied bombers included the **Me 163,** the only rocket-powered fighter in history to see service. Armed with cannon and rocket missiles it could climb to 39,370 feet in 3 minutes 25 seconds—but its powered endurance was only about 8 minutes. An even more desperate venture was the so-called 'People's Fighter': the **Heinkel He 162 Salamander.** Designed for mass operations by Hitler Youth pilots, the He 162 was constructed of lightweight non-strategic materials. Its dorsally-mounted turbojet gave a maximum speed of 522 miles per hour at 19,680 feet and it was armed with two cannon. The trouble with the 'People's Fighter' was that it was so tricky that the most experienced pilots were needed to fly it and in 1945, when the aircraft was declared 'operational', experienced Luftwaffe pilots were very few indeed.

Those who had survived—justly deemed *Experten*—were flying the latest marks of the time-tested Me 109 the **109G** and the **109K**. The superb Focke-Wulf 190 had been evolved into the still more superb **Ta 152,** the 'long nose' Focke-Wulf with a maximum speed of 468 miles per hour at 34,500 feet and an armament of one 30-mm and four 20-mm cannon. These were Germany's best operational piston-engined day fighters at the close of World War II. The best piston-engined night fighter was

---

FIGHTER DEVELOPMENT 1939–45

Country	Type	First ordered	Max. Speed	Max. loaded range	Rate of climb	Ceiling	Number built	Basic armament
Germany	Focke-Wulf FW 190A	1940	395 mph	380 miles	4.75 mins to 16,500 ft	37,000 ft	20,000+	Two 7.9-mm machine-guns four 20-mm cannon; one 550-lb bomb
	Focke-Wulf Ta 152	1944	468 mph	565 miles	5.6 mins to 26,250 ft	42,650 ft	67	One 30-mm cannon, four 20-mm cannon
	Me 109G	1941	387 mph	450 miles	6 mins to 19,000 ft	38,500 ft	21,600	Two 13-mm machine-guns, three 20-mm cannon
Great Britain	Supermarine Spitfire IX	1941	415 mph	434 miles	8.05 mins to 30,000 ft	41,000 ft	5,600+	Two 20-mm cannon, four .303-in machine-guns
	Hawker Tempest V	1942	435 mph	1,530 miles	14 mins to 30,000 ft	36,500 ft	805	Four 20-mm cannon, 2,000 lbs of bombs or eight 60-lb rockets
	De Havilland Mosquito	1940	378 mph	1,830 miles	12.85 mins to 20,000 ft	34,500	7,781	Four 20-mm cannon, four .303-in machine-guns
United States	Lockheed P-38 Lightning	1940	414 mph	2,260 miles	12 mins to 25,000 ft	39,000 ft	9,923	One 20-mm cannon, four .50-in machine-guns
	Republic P-47 Thunderbolt	1941	429 mph	925 miles	13 mins to 20,000 ft	36,100 ft	15,329	Six or eight .50-in machine-guns; two 1,000-lb bombs or ten 5-in rockets
	North American P-51 Mustang	1940	443 mph	2,080 miles	7.5 mins to 20,000 ft	41,900 ft	14,686	Four or six .50-in machine-guns; two 1,000-lb bombs or ten 5-in rockets
Soviet Union	Lavochkin La-5	1941	341 mph	400 miles	5 mins to 16,400 ft	34,490 ft	8,000+	Two 20-mm cannon; 330 lbs of bombs
Italy	Macchi C202	1940	360 mph	373 miles	6.5 mins to 18,000 ft	36,100 ft	1,518	Two 12.7-mm, two 7.7-mm machine-guns
	Reggiane R2001	1941	337 mph	646 miles	6 mins 20 secs to 16,400 ft	39,200 ft	252	Two 12.7-mm, two 7.7-mm machine-guns; four 220-lb bombs

The Soviet Fighters

▲ Polikarpov I-16 Type 24 fighter with the inscription 'For Stalin!' operating on the central sector of the front in the summer of 1941

▲ Yakovlev Yak-3 fighter flown by Hero of Soviet Union Sergei Luganskii on the central sector of the front during 1944

▲ LaGG-3 fighter operating in the Ukraine, summer 1942

▲ Mikoyan-Gurevich MiG-3 of the 34th Fighter Aviation Regiment operating from Vnukovo in the winter of 1941-42 as part of the Western Sector, Moscow Corps Command IA-PVO. The legend beneath the cockpit reads 'For the Fatherland'

▲ Lavochkin La-7 fighter of the 18th Guards Fighter Regiment on the northern sector of the front, 1944

The RAF Fighters

▲ Westland Whirlwind fighter of No. 263 Squadron based at Exeter, January-April 1941

▲ North American Mustang Mk. III of No. 315 Squadron operating from Brenzett, summer 1944 (this particular aircraft was flown by S/Ldr. Horbaczewski, the symbols beneath the cockpit indicating four V-1 'kills')

▲ Supermarine Spitfire Mk. II of No. 41 Squadron based at Hornchurch in December 1940. This particular aircraft was flown by the CO, S/Ldr. D. O. Finlay, D.F.C.

▲ Hawker Typhoon Mk. IB fighter-bomber of No. 198 Squadron based at Martragny, France, in the summer of 1944

▲ Douglas Havoc Mk. I night fighter of No. 23 Squadron operating in the intruder role from Ford, summer 1941

▲ Bristol Beaufighter Mk. IF of No. 25 Squadron based at Northolt, October 1940

▲ Boulton Paul Defiant II of No. 125 Squadron operating from Colerne in February 1942

▲ Curtiss Tomahawk IIA of No. 349 Squadron (the second Belgian squadron in the RAF) based at Ikeja, West Africa, spring 1943

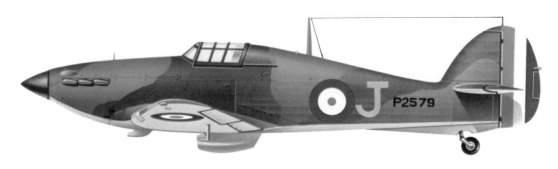

▲ Hawker Hurricane I of No. 73 Squadron at Rouvres, France, in March 1940

▲ Curtiss Kittyhawk III of No. 250 Squadron operating in southern Italy in the autumn of 1943

the **Heinkel He 219 Uhu,** but only 294 of this type were produced before capitulation.

Teardrops and tank-busters

In RAF Fighter Command, the Spitfire remained in frontline service throughout the war, like its opposite number the Me 109. Subsequent marks included the Mk V (1941–42), the Mk IX (which appeared in 1942 and remained first-line squadron equipment until the end of the war), the belated **Mk VIII** (appearing in 1943 and mostly sent overseas to the Mediterranean and Burma fronts), the **Mk XIV** (appearing in 1944 with the new Rolls-Royce Griffon engine, final examples of this series also had the advantages of the cut-down rear fuselage and 'teardrop' cockpit hood), and finally the **Mk 21** and **Mk 22,** the last Spitfire variants, too late to see war service. Several versions of a naval variant, the **Seafire,** were produced for carrier service with the Fleet Air Arm.

the specialised Hispano Mk V cannon, four of which were carried in the **Tempest V.** The Tempest's speed (432 miles per hour at 18,400 feet) and hitting-power enabled it to take on the best of the 1944–45 German fighters, even the Me 262.

The Americans were swift to push ahead with long-range fighters. The first of these to see service was the **Lockheed P-38 Lightning,** a distinctive twin-engined, twin-boomed aircraft which was proved to be prone to technical troubles in the air over Europe but which served with distinction in the Pacific theatre. The massive **Republic P-47 Thunderbolt** (with a span of 40 feet 9 inches and a loaded weight of 13,360 lbs) was the first successful long-range fighter to escort the B-17s. With a 200-gallon drop-tank the Thunderbolt's range was extended to 1,125 miles. But the best American fighter of the war was undoubtedly the North American **P-51 Mustang,** the result of close co-operation between Britain and the USA. The excellent

Other American fighters also did invaluable service in the European theatre. The **Curtiss P-36** was exported to France and quantities passed to the RAF where they served as the **Mohawk IV** in the Mediterranean and Far East. The **Curtiss P-40,** America's land-based fighter mainstay in 1940–41, also served with the British Desert Air Force as the **Tomahawk** and the **P-40E** as the **Kittyhawk.** The RAF also experimented with the **Bell P-39 Airacobra** (remarkable in that its engine was positioned behind the cockpit, driving the airscrew by a 10-foot shaft passing beneath the pilot's legs). The Airacobra was particularly welcomed by the Soviet Air Force and 4,773 of them were sent to Russia.

The Soviet Air Force needed time to recover from the terrible first weeks of the German invasion of June 1941, which virtually wiped out the front-line strength of the Red Air Force. The principal Soviet fighter in 1941 was still the stubby little **I-16,** which had earned the nickname

The **Hurricane,** too, lived on. It became a major item of British Lend Lease and served with the Soviet Air Force. The **Mk IIB** had 12 wing machine-guns; the **IIC** had four 20-mm cannon. The **IID** was a modification carrying a pair of 40-mm cannon and did sterling service as a 'tank-buster' in Africa, proving once more what a splendid gun platform the Hurricane was.

Unlike the Luftwaffe, the RAF did not get itself hamstrung in its fighter development. Early experiments with heavy, twin-engined fighters produced the splendid **Bristol Beaufighter,** with its murderous armament of four 20-mm cannon and six wing machine guns and a maximum speed of 321 miles per hour. The Beaufighter was successfully developed into an anti-shipping strike aircraft, carrying rockets or a torpedo. From the Hawker stable a new concept of of heavy, single-seat interceptor fighter emerged. First came the **Typhoon,** dogged by engine trouble, but finally superb in the low-level, ground-attack role, and then the **Tempest,** fitted with the specially designed 'Hawker High Speed Wing'. The latter was sharp and thin, necessitating the design of

Left, Spitfires, Western Desert. Though it cut their performance, these Mk VCs needed the prominent filter under the nose to keep sand out of the engine.
Upper right: Lightning in Italy. The twin-boom P-38—this is an F-5 photo-reconnaissance type—had the range that was so lacking in RAF single-seaters.
Lower right: Yak-9s, Eastern Front. Like other Soviet fighters the Yak-9D was small and highly manoeuvrable.

Mustang airframe married to the Rolls-Royce Merlin engine produced, at last, a fighter which could escort bombers deep into Germany and as far as Berlin itself.

Learning the hard way

Fighter escort tactics had to be learned the hard way. At first the German fighters were swift to benefit from the Allied tendency to stick too close to the bombers, thus restricting their manoeuvrability, but later the escorts learned to effectively engage German interceptors away from their charges.

Rata in the Spanish Civil War. But new fighters were already in the pipeline and the first of these was the **Yakovlev Yak-1,** rushed into large-scale service at the end of 1939. The Yak-1 vaguely resembled the British Hurricane, but had an armament of one 20-mm cannon and two 12.7-mm machine guns. In the following year the Yak-1 was supplemented by the **LaGG-3** and **Mikoyan-Gurevich MiG-3,** then from 1943 onwards the **Yak-9,** the **La-5, Yak-3** and the **La-7.** The main emphasis until 1943 was on mass-production. None of the early 'second generation' fighters was the equal of the best German fighters on the Eastern front but their numbers dwarfed the Luftwaffe in the East from then onwards. The odds were as heavily stacked against the German pilots in Russia as against those tackling the Flying Fortress bomber streams in the West—frequently with ten German fighters pitted against 300 Soviet. However, the later versions of Soviet fighters—especially the La-7 and Yak-3—were equal to, if not better than, the best the Germans had in line and from then on the Soviets did not look back.

The American Fighters

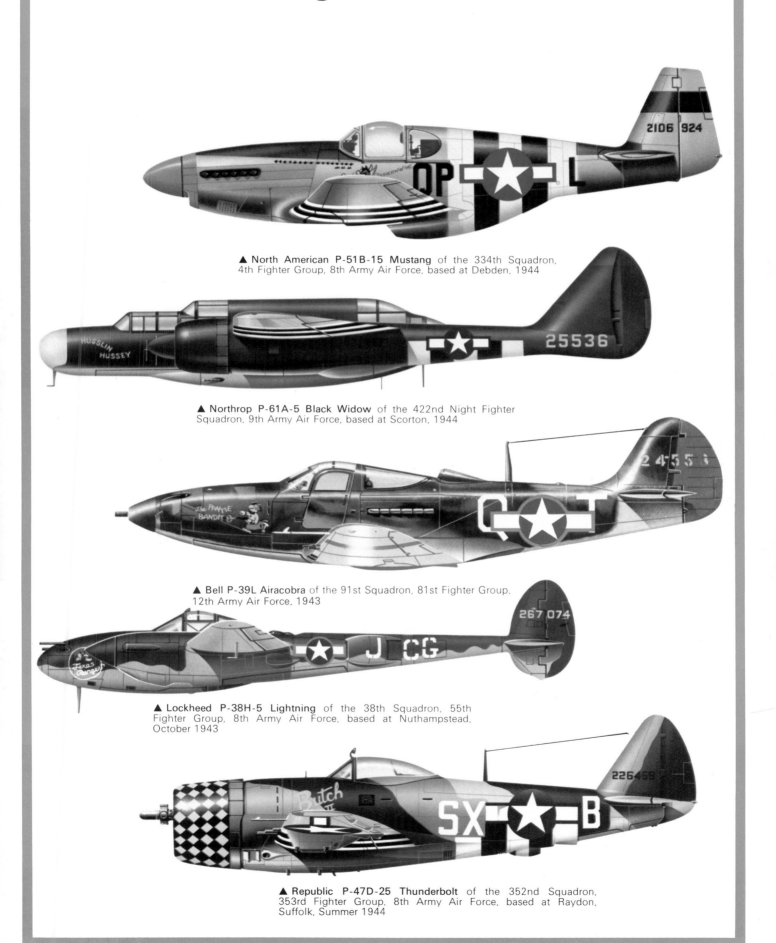

▲ North American P-51B-15 Mustang of the 334th Squadron, 4th Fighter Group, 8th Army Air Force, based at Debden, 1944

▲ Northrop P-61A-5 Black Widow of the 422nd Night Fighter Squadron, 9th Army Air Force, based at Scorton, 1944

▲ Bell P-39L Airacobra of the 91st Squadron, 81st Fighter Group, 12th Army Air Force, 1943

▲ Lockheed P-38H-5 Lightning of the 38th Squadron, 55th Fighter Group, 8th Army Air Force, based at Nuthampstead, October 1943

▲ Republic P-47D-25 Thunderbolt of the 352nd Squadron, 353rd Fighter Group, 8th Army Air Force, based at Raydon, Suffolk, Summer 1944

The Fighters of Germany and her Allies

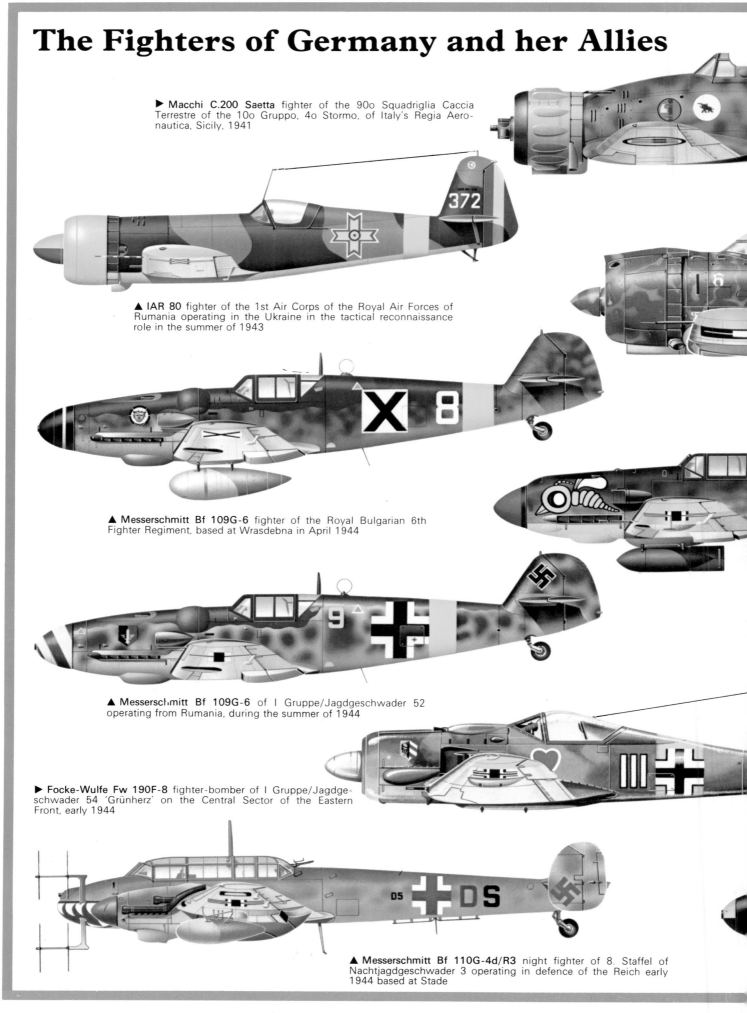

▶ Macchi C.200 Saetta fighter of the 90o Squadriglia Caccia Terrestre of the 10o Gruppo, 4o Stormo, of Italy's Regia Aeronautica, Sicily, 1941

▲ IAR 80 fighter of the 1st Air Corps of the Royal Air Forces of Rumania operating in the Ukraine in the tactical reconnaissance role in the summer of 1943

▲ Messerschmitt Bf 109G-6 fighter of the Royal Bulgarian 6th Fighter Regiment, based at Wrasdebna in April 1944

▲ Messerschmitt Bf 109G-6 of I Gruppe/Jagdgeschwader 52 operating from Rumania, during the summer of 1944

▶ Focke-Wulfe Fw 190F-8 fighter-bomber of I Gruppe/Jagdgeschwader 54 'Grünherz' on the Central Sector of the Eastern Front, early 1944

▲ Messerschmitt Bf 110G-4d/R3 night fighter of 8. Staffel of Nachtjagdgeschwader 3 operating in defence of the Reich early 1944 based at Stade

▲ Fiat CR.42 Falco fighter of the 95a Squadriglia, 18o Gruppo Caccia Terrestre of the Italian Regia Aeronautica based at Eechloo, Belgium, in November 1940

▲ Reggiane Re.2000 'Héja' fighter of the Hungarian 1./1 Fighter Squadron, summer 1942

▲ Avia B.534-IV fighter of the Slovakian Air Force operating from Zitomir-Kiev, Ukraine, in the summer of 1941

▲ Messerschmitt Bf 109E-7B of the Gruppe Staff, III Gruppe/ SKG 210 operating over the Central Sector of the Eastern Front in the autumn of 1941

▲ Reggiane Re.2001 Ariete fighter of the 359a Squadriglia Autonome (Autonomous Squadron) of the Italian Regia Aeronautica's 22o Gruppo operating from Sicily and Sardinia in 1942

▲ Messerschmitt Bf 109G-10/U4 fighter of the Croatian Jagdstaffel based at Eichwalde in November 1944

▲ Messerschmitt Bf 109F-2 of III Gruppe/Jagdgeschwader 54 'Grünherz' operating on the Leningrad Front during the winter of 1941—42

For want of a cannon

From the high-speed seaplane racers held between the wars for the Schneider Trophy the Spitfire had evolved in Britain. Italy too had been a top contender but, unlike the British designer of the Spitfire, R. J. Mitchell, Italy's Mario Castoldi was hampered by the lack of development of high-power engines in his country. His **Macchi C.200,** designed in 1937, was the best Italian fighter at the outbreak of war but it had only a medium-powered Fiat radial engine. In addition its armament, two 12.7-mm machine guns in the fuselage, was extremely light. The **Fiat G.50** and the **Reggiane Re 2000** which followed had excellent manoeuvrability, falling off abruptly above 15,000 feet, and light armament.

By far the best Italian fighter of the war was the **Macchi C.202 Folgore,** which appeared in 1942. This was given the advantage of a well-developed engine, the Daimler-Benz DB 601, which was built under licence by Alfa Romeo. But again the C.202 was impaired by its light machine gun armament. Better Italian designs were in the pipeline by the time Italy dropped out of the war in 1943, most notably the **Regianne Re 2001,** the **Re 2005,** and the **Macchi C.205 Veltro.** These were hampered by dwindling supplies of engines from Germany and by the belated acceptance that cannon fire-power was indispensable to modern fighter design.

The obvious reason was the vastly superior hitting-power of the cannon over that of the machine gun. In the RAF stormy debates were the prelude to the introduction of cannon as a modification of the original eight-gun batteries of wing-mounted machine guns, but once introduced the cannon proved its worth a hundred times over. The cannon gave the fighter an additional role: that of a ground-strafer with explosive shells. For the German fighter arm, cannon-fire and later rockets were indispensable in attacking the Allied bombers. The massed cones of .5-inch machine gun fire thrown out by the B-17 formations were justly dreaded. The smaller calibre of the British .303-inch Browning machine guns gave much less trouble to the Me 110s and Ju 88s of the German night-fighter arm. Side by side with hitting-power went the other indispensable attributes that nagged the fighter designers of World War II—constant improvements in range, protection and manoeuvrability.

Cab ranks and suicide

In the last resort any aircraft can carry bombs and the concept of the fighter-bomber enjoyed a chequered history in World War II. Hitler's obsession with retaliatory bombing imposed impossible tasks on the German fighters operating over Britain. On the other hand, Leutnant Heinz Knocke's experiments with dive-bombing attacks on Flying Fortress formations initially paid handsome dividends. Britain's all-purpose 'wonder plane', the **de Havilland Mosquito,** was a natural in the fighter-bomber role. So was the **Hurricane II,** which earned the nickname of the 'Hurribomber', and the Bristol Beaufighter. The advent of the air-to-ground rocket added more punch to the fighter-bomber. A salvo of rockets from a Beaufighter could blow a ship out of the water and, in the bloody fighting for Normandy which culminated in the slaughter of the Falaise Gap in August 1944, the rocket-firing Typhoons became in the Wehrmacht's book the most feared aircraft. 'Cab ranks' of fighter bombers, stacked up over the Normandy battlefield, made it virtual suicide for any German vehicle to move by day in good flying weather.

Top left, Me 109Es, Western Desert. Tropical versions of the ubiquitous 109 played both a defensive and offensive role; this pair is from I/JG. 27.
Top right, Kittyhawks, Western Desert. Over 3,000 served Commonwealth squadrons in North Africa and Italy.
Bottom left: Petlyakov Pe-2, Russia. A versatile three-seater capable of 355 mph.
Bottom right: The supreme Mustang. A P-51B (furthest away) and three P-51Ds.

But the Allies did not have things entirely their own way. On January 1, 1945 the Luftwaffe mounted their last great fighter offensive of the war. On that day massed fighter ground-strafing sweeps wiped out whole groups of Allied aircraft—nearly 300 in all. For a week, the RAF's 122 Wing had to carry on the fighter war in North-West Europe virtually single-handed. Nor was Hitler's insistence that the Me 262 must operate as a bomber totally misguided. Low-level attacks by bomb-carrying Me 262s remained a headache on the Western Front right down to the end of the war. Travelling fast and low, they made it almost impossible for Allied radar screens to pick them up. The Tempest pilots evolved a technique called 'rat-catching' to cope with the nuisance of the Me 262s, sending a brace of Tempests to known Me 262 bases to catch the German jets as they landed. Limited successes were won, but the dense flak which screened every German airfield used by jets made these forays very dangerous and unprofitable. By May 1945 the aircraft operating in the ETO enjoyed speed and hitting-power which would have been inconceivable five years before, but it was still found that the fastest and most heavily-armed fighter was still not immune to well-directed barrages of defensive fire from the ground.

The Finnish Air War

Twice during the years 1939–44, Finland found herself at war with the Soviet Union and in both conflicts the Finnish air arm distinguished itself. The first Russo-Finnish conflict began on 30 November 1939 when Soviet forces invaded Finland following the infamous 'Mainila Incident'. A Finnish force of 116 aircraft of all types, many of them obsolescent, fought an opposing Soviet force of between 900 and 1,000 aircraft virtually to a standstill, but by February 1940, the Soviet Air Forces were deploying an estimated 2,200 aircraft against Finland and, despite valiant resistance, the Finnish government was forced to accept Soviet surrender terms on 13 March 1940, bringing to an end the so-called 'Winter War'.

Fighting between Finnish and Soviet forces was resumed on 22 June 1941, the new conflict being known as the 'Continuation War' and the Finnish air arm now possessing 559 aircraft of which 307 were combat types. As the bulk of the Soviet Air Forces was engaged in Central Russia, the Finns established air superiority and rapidly regained territory lost as a result of the Winter War. Towards the end of 1942, however, there was a noticeable improvement in quality and increase in quantity of Soviet aircraft deployed against Finland, and by the time that the Finns had been forced to engage in violent defensive battles on the Karelian Isthmus in the summer of 1944, the Finnish air arm once again found itself confronted with the overwhelming air superiority that it had experienced during the closing phase of the Winter War. On 4 September 1944, the Finnish government was again compelled to accept surrender terms. During the course of the Continuation War, the Finnish air arm had lost 536 aircraft (only 209 of these on operations) but claimed the destruction of 1,567 Soviet aircraft in combat.

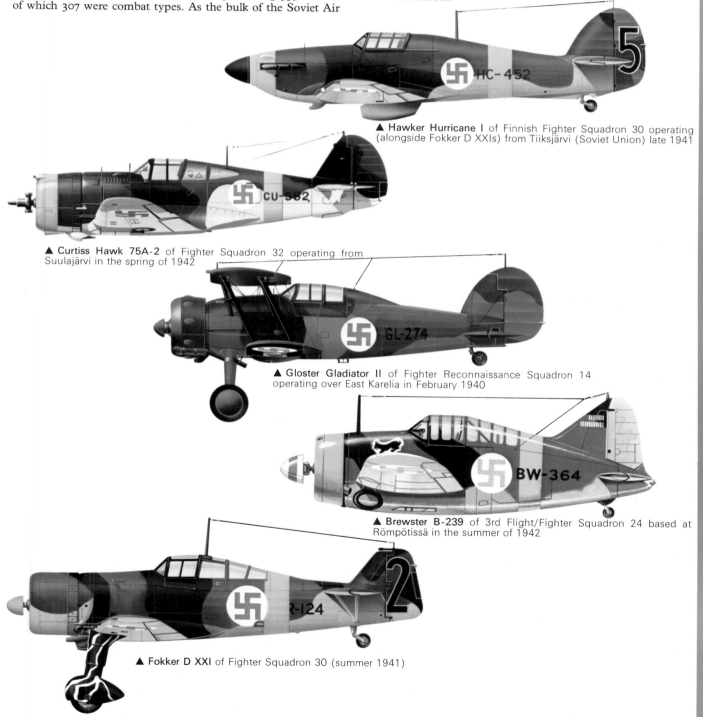

▲ Hawker Hurricane I of Finnish Fighter Squadron 30 operating (alongside Fokker D XXIs) from Tiiksjärvi (Soviet Union) late 1941

▲ Curtiss Hawk 75A-2 of Fighter Squadron 32 operating from Suulajärvi in the spring of 1942

▲ Gloster Gladiator II of Fighter Reconnaissance Squadron 14 operating over East Karelia in February 1940

▲ Brewster B-239 of 3rd Flight/Fighter Squadron 24 based at Römpötissä in the summer of 1942

▲ Fokker D XXI of Fighter Squadron 30 (summer 1941)

AERIAL COMMAND OF THE SEAS

The deadly effectiveness of the Swordfish sortie against Italian battleships in Taranto, the crippling success of the Japanese strike at Pearl Harbor, and the almost insolent ease with which the German Navy brought off its 'Channel Dash' under an effective fighter umbrella, all offered early and conclusive proof that sea power without air power was no power at all. Each of the combatant major powers learned their lesson and built effective, though sometimes too specialised, maritime aircraft. But the strategic planning and co-ordination of effort of the Allies was superior, and ultimately decisive, in this vital sphere which virtually dictated whether nations could maintain the ability to wage a war which all concerned clearly saw was one of survival.

Once the military aeroplane had been successfully developed naval warfare was never the same again. No longer could the warships roam at will, with only their opposite numbers to worry about. The same applied to the merchant navies. To the danger of enemy surface raider and submarine action was added the threat of the air.

Especially in the European theatre the role of coastal and maritime aviation became of paramount importance in World War II. In her attempts to strangle Britain's supply lifeline across the Atlantic, Germany failed to bring the modern resources of air power even remotely to bear. And one of the main reasons was the *ad hoc* way in which Germany's new military might had been developed, being based largely on personality pressures between the leaders of the Reich. The results of this were serious enough for the bomber arm of the Luftwaffe, but the situation was even more glaring as far as naval/air liaison was concerned.

Despite the splendid new warships built for Germany after Hitler's accession to power in 1933, the need for a powerful modern naval air arm as an adjunct to the activities of the fleet was never accepted. Göring's paranoid obsession with his private empire produced his watchword 'everything that flies belongs to me'. Only once in World War II did the Luftwaffe and the German navy work closely together and that was during the 'Channel Dash' of February 1942—a venture that was pressed forward on Hitler's insistence.

The Luftwaffe's technical experience could have given Admiral Raeder a German fleet air arm by 1939 but for Göring's jealousy and pig-headedness. And a measure of common sense tempered by generosity could have given Admiral Dönitz better long-range reconnaissance for the U-boats in the Atlantic, which would probably have lost the Allies the Battle of the Atlantic. As it was the U-boat packs were often vectored onto their targets by the few far-flying Condors available. More of them would probably have meant much worse Allied shipping losses.

It was not that the Luftwaffe had failed to acquire the machines. There was the **Heinkel He 115** twin-engined floatplane, a sound torpedo-bomber; the **Blohm & Voss Bv 138** with a range of 2,670 miles, and the **Dornier Do 18** and **Do 24** flying boats. The **Ju 87** dive-bomber and the **Ju 88** and **Heinkel He 111** all proved excellent anti-shipping aircraft. But the basic weakness—a long-range bomber—could not be denied. The Luftwaffe sought for a stop-gap in the form of the converted **Focke-Wulf Fw 200 Condor,** an elegant four-engined airliner. Heavily armed with a 20-mm cannon in a dorsal turret plus five machine guns the Condor could carry up to 4,620 lbs of bombs, and had a maximum range of 3,950 miles. A Condor squadron was formed in 1940 for reconnaissance work and strike duties over the British naval approaches and was subsequently raised to *Geschwader*—Group —status. But only 263 Condors of all versions were ever built; their crews had to come and collect them as the machines crawled off the production line.

A special naval command

Condors took part in bombing raids on England in 1940, most notably in the Blitz on Liverpool and Birkenhead in August. Anti-shipping operations got under way slowly but spectacularly with the sinking of the 42,000-ton liner *Empress of Britain* off the north-west coast of Ireland (October 26, 1940). In March 1941 a special naval command—*Fliegerführer Atlantik*—was set up to co-ordinate all anti-shipping work by the Luftwaffe and operations against Britain's Atlantic convoys got under way.

They met with a rapid check with the British adoption of the CAM (Catapult Aircraft Merchantmen) ships, which could launch a **Hurricane** against enemy airborne raiders. Despite the fact that the 'Hurricat' pilot had to leave his aircraft and hope to be picked up after descending by parachute, the CAM ships soon proved their worth and by the autumn of 1941 the Condors were reduced to reconnaissance duties, radioing back information and

leaving the attack to U-boats. In December a Condor homed six U-boats onto Convoy HG-76, but it cost six Condors in all, which were shot down by **Martlets** (British-flown **Grumman F4Fs**) from the new escort-carrier HMS *Audacity*.

The depressing situation in the Atlantic was redeemed when in early 1942 the Germans woke up to the fact that the Allies were sailing convoys to Soviet Russia past the North Cape with what amounted to total immunity. General Stumpff's Luftflotte 5, which had played a very subfuse role since its ignominious defeat in the Battle of Britain, suddenly found itself in the forefront of the battle as the one Luftwaffe unit able to launch heavy air strikes against convoys which had little or no fighter defences.

Luftflotte 5 was hastily reinforced and soon included the only bomber unit which had specialised in torpedo-work: KG 26, the 'Löwen' Geschwader, equipped with torpedo-carrying He 111s. The Russian convoys soon felt the results, starting with Convoy PQ-15 in May 1942. The attacks were preceded by shadowing by Blohm und Voss Bv 138 flying-boats, followed by Ju 88 dive-bombing attacks and torpedo attacks by the He 111s. PQ-16 came in for the same treatment during its passage (May 22–30), but the real slaughter was reserved for PQ-17. This convoy was scattered because the British Admiralty was unable to pinpoint the whereabouts of the German battleship *Tirpitz* and assumed that she had put to sea to attack the convoy. No such danger actually existed, but the scattered ships of the convoy were left totally defenceless. Between them, U-boats and the aircraft of Luftflotte 5 sank 24 out of the 34 ships of the convoy.

Golden Comb bares its teeth

The next convoy, PQ-18, sailed in September and it had an escort-carrier, the *Avenger*. The same pattern was repeated: spotting and shadowing by a Bv 138, followed by torpedo and bombing attacks. This time the German pilots used the 'Golden Comb' technique: a formation

Left: The view of the attacker. This destroyer and merchant ship are hove-to amidst foam from bombs. At first even major naval vessels lacked AA defence.

Above: Grumman F4F Wildcat. This highly manoeuvrable fighter was the first Lend-Lease aircraft for the Royal Navy which called it the Martlet.
Left: Luftwaffe limits. The East Coast and Arctic convoy routes were within range but, crucially most of the Atlantic was not.

approach in line-abreast by 30 Ju 88s and 55 He 111s, each aircraft dropping its two torpedoes simultaneously. Despite the fact that PQ-18 had been given the strongest escort ever provided for a convoy to Soviet Russia, 13 out of its 40 ships were sunk on passage.

These attacks finally convinced the British Admiralty that the PQ convoys could not go on. When the convoys were resumed they were sailed in two parts in order to disrupt the attackers and for the summer of 1943 they were discontinued entirely. When resumed again at the end of 1943, Luftflotte 5 was a shadow of its former self, for the demands of the other fronts since Stalingrad and the loss of Tunis imposed constant demands on the aircraft concentrations in the Far North.

One flicker of hope for the prospects of efficient long-range naval operations reposed in the **Junkers Ju 290,** intended to replace the Condor. It was the nearest the Germans ever got to producing a long-range heavy bomber, apart from the **Heinkel He 177 Greif.** Like the Condor, the Ju 290 was a development of a civil airliner concept. Only a limited number were ever completed and were soon taken off anti-shipping operations, being confined to reconnaissance and patrol duties.

Inter-service rivalry, plus the belated recognition of the strategic meaning of an unanticipated war against Britain in 1939, deprived the Luftwaffe of any major success on the Atlantic sealanes. Its successes against the Russian convoys were different and rank as a definite victory, and were won by the Luftwaffe's orthodox, medium-range aircraft operating in the absence of efficient Allied fighter cover. But mention must be made of the slaughter dealt out to the British Mediterranean Fleet and Malta convoys in 1941 and 1942.

The Battle of the Atlantic

SPITZBERGEN

Summer route

Barent Is.

Banak

Murmansk

Winter route

Archangel

Narvik

GREENLAND

JAN MAYEN

ICELAND

Trondheim

Faroes

Berlin

London

Brest
Paris
Lorient

Bordeaux

1500 MILES

1375 MILES

1095 MILES

560 MILES

Lisbon

Azores

Gibraltar

0 MILES   500   1000

Canary Is.

LIMIT OF LAND-BASED CATALINA PATROLS – – –
ALLIED CONVOY ROUTES
HEINKEL III AND JUNKERS 88
FOCKE-WULF 200
JUNKERS 290 AND BLOHM & VOSS B 222

In May 1941 the battle for Crete was fought. The German invasion of the island was the Luftwaffe's last major airborne offensive of the war, and while the land battle was being fought Admiral Cunningham's Mediterranean Fleet tried desperately to support the army. Apart from the handful of Allied aircraft defending Malta, the Luftwaffe had the skies over the Mediterranean to itself and a formidable concentration had been amassed on the airfields of southern Greece for the campaign: eight bomber and five fighter Gruppen. By June 1, 1941, when the British finally completed the evacuation of Crete and left the island to the decimated German paratroop units, three cruisers and six destroyers had been sunk. Two battleships, the carrier *Formidable,* two cruisers, and two destroyers had been so badly damaged that they could not be repaired in the British Mediterranean dockyards. The Mediterranean Fleet was neutralised.

Malta strikes back

But again the German success was washed out by the demands of other fronts. The invasion of Soviet Russia was launched on June 22 and half the Luftwaffe strength in the Mediterranean was withdrawn for it. The concentration upon Soviet Russia meant that Malta got an inevitable reprieve. The British immediately began to strike back at the Axis convoy routes from Malta, using destroyers, submarines—and coastal command aircraft. These three methods of

attack dealt out such damage that by November 1941 the Axis loss rate on sending supplies to Rommel in North Africa was as high as 63 per cent.

The effectiveness of the British airborne offensive against the Axis depended largely on the up-and-down fortunes of the desert war. When the British held the airfields of Cyrenaica they could throw in **Blenheims, Beaufighters, Douglas Bostons,** and **Wellingtons** against the Axis convoy routes; when Rommel stood on the Egyptian frontier Malta alone had to carry on the offensive. The result of this equation was that in the first quarter of 1942 furious attempts were made to neutralise Malta for good as a prelude to the conquest of the island. By May the Luftwaffe had virtually accomplished this task, flying non-stop raids from the airfields of Sicily, only 60 miles away from Malta. Last-minute deliveries of **Spitfires** retained a vestige of fighter defence on the island which was then given another reprieve, paradoxically enough by Rommel's defeat of the 8th Army at Gazala and his invasion of Egypt. The conquest of Malta was shelved and, when it was finally recognised that Rommel had been fought to a standstill, however temporarily, at Alamein, Malta had again received just enough reinforcements to hold on.

By the end of August 1942 Malta was on the offensive again. The main weapons in the strikes against the Axis convoy routes were **Bristol Beaufort** torpedo-bombers escorted by Beaufighters. The Beaufort, like the Beaufighter itself, owed much to the

basic Blenheim design. It was the standard RAF torpedo-bomber for over four years, entering service in December 1939 and soldiering on until replaced in the torpedo role by the Beaufighter in 1943. These air strikes, through August and September, meant that Rommel had no margin whatever as far as fuel reserves were concerned, and were therefore instrumental in helping Montgomery beat off the last German offensive in Egypt at Alam Halfa at the end of September. It was a Beaufort which torpedoed 'Rommel's last tanker'—the *Proserpina,* which could have delivered the fuel which might possibly have crucially helped Rommel at Alamein.

Failure and a lucky strike

The Beauforts and Beaufighters stationed in the United Kingdom had mixed successes. They failed completely to score even one hit when the *Scharnhorst* and *Gneisenau* sailed through the English Channel in February 1942. Eight months before No. 42 Squadron, flying Beauforts, had been sent out for a night strike against the pocket-battleship *Lützow,* which was returning to Germany down the Norwegian coast. A solitary Beaufort which had got lost (and nearly shot down after blundering over the German airfield at Lister in southern Norway) found its target by accident and launched a lone attack. No AA fire came from the *Lützow;* it was later believed that the Beaufort was mistaken for a Ju 88, whose silhouette vaguely resembled the Blenheim/Beaufort planform. A lucky hit

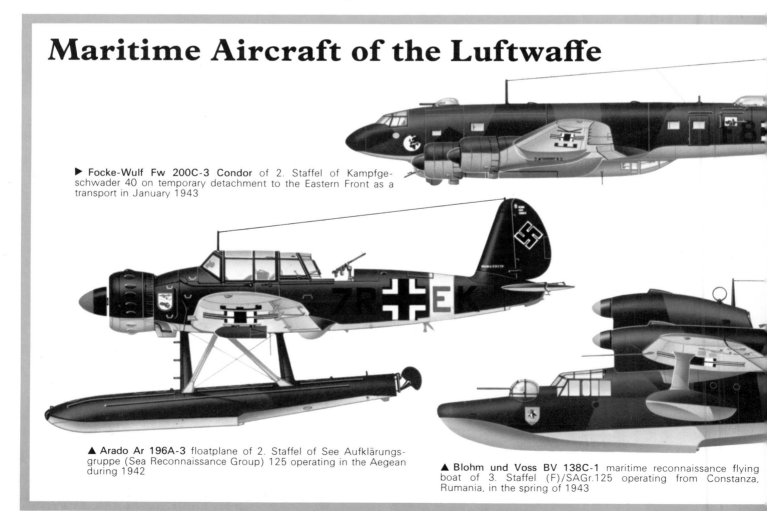

Maritime Aircraft of the Luftwaffe

▶ Focke-Wulf Fw 200C-3 Condor of 2. Staffel of Kampfgeschwader 40 on temporary detachment to the Eastern Front as a transport in January 1943

▲ Arado Ar 196A-3 floatplane of 2. Staffel of See Aufklärungsgruppe (Sea Reconnaissance Group) 125 operating in the Aegean during 1942

▲ Blohm und Voss BV 138C-1 maritime reconnaissance flying boat of 3. Staffel (F)/SAGr.125 operating from Constanza, Rumania, in the spring of 1943

on *Lützow* put her in dry dock at Kiel, but did not knock her out of the war. Individual hunting was tried (known as 'Rover' missions) but losses were heavy.

One of the most daring Beaufort strikes of the war took place in December 1941, after RAF photo-reconnaissance had found that the battle-cruiser *Gneisenau* had been moved out into the open waters of Brest harbour, offering a slim chance of a torpedo attack. Flt-Lt. K. Campbell pressed home his attack and wrecked *Gneisenau's* starboard propeller shaft, but was shot down and killed by the withering flak from the German battle-cruiser and the harbour defences.

As far as the British Fleet Air Arm was concerned the outstanding aircraft of the war was the antiquated **Fairey Swordfish,** a three-seater torpedo bomber with a maximum speed of 138 miles per hour. The Swordfish first distinguished itself on the night of November 11, 1940, in the famous torpedo attack on the Italian battle fleet in Taranto harbour. The Italian battleships *Littorio, Conte di Cavour,* and *Caio Duilio* were all sunk or beached, swinging the naval balance in the Mediterranean decidedly in favour of the British. The Taranto raid made history: it was the first time that aircraft proved decisively that air power had rendered the traditional might of the battle fleet helpless without constant air cover.

Swordfish from the carrier *Victorious* put the first British torpedo into the battleship *Bismarck* in May 1941, while others from *Ark Royal* later succeeded in jamming *Bismarck's* rudder and thus ensured that she would be brought to action by the battleships of the British Home Fleet.

The Swordfish's most tragic operation was the hurried and ill-fated Fleet Air Arm strike against *Scharnhorst* and *Gneisenau* during the 'Channel Dash', when all six aircraft attacking were shot down by the swarming German fighter escorts without scoring a single hit.

But even this failure, however heroic, did not hasten the demise of the Swordfish as an operational aircraft. A successor, the **Fairey Albacore,** was indeed mooted and produced, but the Albacore did not in fact replace the Swordfish which continued to serve with the Fleet Air Arm. The final chapter in the extraordinary story of the Swordfish came in 1943 when it was pressed into service as an anti-submarine weapon, firing salvoes of underwing rockets at U-boats caught on the surface.

Upper right: Beaufighter TF.X. Seen firing a salvo of rockets, the Mk X of Coastal Command was also able to carry a torpedo and was deadly against shipping.

Lower right: Consolidated Catalina. With an endurance of 24 hours, this very reliable sentinel could also be strongly aggressive — as here. The Catalina, of which over 2,000 were built, had a range of over 3,000 miles and was used in all theatres of the war by the British, the Americans and the Russians. It was a Catalina that found and followed the *Bismarck* after she had sunk the *Hood* and thereby denied her escape to the safety of a French port.

Britain's major long-range naval reconnaissance aircraft of World War II was the **Short Sunderland** flying-boat. In the same way as the FW 200 Condor, it was descended from a civilian design, in this case the **Short Empire** passenger flying-boat of the '30s. Much of the Empire configuration was retained by the Sunderland. It was a big machine, with a span of 112 feet and a length of 84 feet, and it had two decks, containing crew's quarters, sleeping berths, officers' wardroom, workshop and galley. Most of these facilities were very welcome on the long ocean patrols the Sunderland flew, its normal range being 2,980 miles. The Sunderland could carry up to 2,000 lbs of bombs or depth-charges and its long range automatically made it a key weapon in the struggle against the U-boats. This flying boat had a crew of 13 and it bristled with defensive armament: two .50-inch and up to 12 .303 machine guns. This defensive capability impressed itself strongly on its Luftwaffe opponents, who dubbed the Sunderland *Fliegendes Stachelschwein*—the 'flying porcupine'. The Sunderland (five marks in all) continued in production up to October 1945, over 700 being built.

The long-range 'Cat'

The other key Allied flying-boat of the war was equally as famous: the American **Consolidated PBY Catalina.** The Catalina's best quality was its enormous range: two Pratt & Whitney Twin Wasp

radial engines gave it the reach of 3,100 miles. The PBY first flew in 1935. A civilian machine—the **Model 28**—was purchased by Britain in 1939 and tests resulted in orders of the military PBY for Britain, which eventually received over 650 of the type. In May 1941 it was a Catalina which located and shadowed the *Bismarck* after the sinking of the *Hood*, without which the German battleship would almost certainly have escaped in safety to France. Catalinas were used in all theatres of the war by the American and British services, most of them serving with the US Navy, which received an overall total of 2,026. A substantial number were also flown by the Soviet Naval Air Arm, most of these machines being a licence-built version known as the **GST**, but 138 improved **PBN-1s** were supplied to Soviet Russia in 1943–44 under Lend-Lease.

Two other British flying-boats deserve mention. The first was the **Saro Lerwick**, which appeared in 1938 and was selected for RAF Coastal Command. A deep-hulled, twin-engined machine it had many problems and only a few sorties were flown with it by a single squadron before it was declared obsolete in 1942 and replaced by the Catalina. And the other came from the same stable as the elegant **Spitfire**. This was the antedeluvian-looking **Supermarine Walrus**: an ungainly-looking biplane with a pusher engine, defended by two Vickers K machine guns and manned by a crew of four.

Enter the Walrus

The Walrus entered service with the Fleet Air Arm in 1936 and it was the first amphibious aircraft to be catapulted from a warship. It became the standard spotter plane carried by British battleships and cruisers and large numbers were also used as air/sea rescue machines. During the PQ-17 fiasco on the Russian run, the British warship escort withdrew so precipitately that a Walrus making a scheduled patrol was left behind. Its crew were rescued, however, and survived the ordeal.

The Japanese produced two magnificent flying-boats which did them stirling service in the Pacific war. The first of these was the **Kawanishi H6K** 'Mavis' with an enormous wing-span of over 131 feet. Powered by

four Mitsubishi Kinsei 46 radials, 'Mavis' had a range as impressive as that of the American PBY: 3,107 miles. It carried a crew of nine and up to 3,527 lbs of bombs. Long-range patrolling was its most usual task and it became a bird of ill omen to the Allies in the early months of 1942, when Japanese swept all before them in the western Pacific. Occasionally, it was also used as a torpedo-bomber.

The Hell-ship is stopped

'Mavis' was succeeded by 'Emily', the **Kawanishi H8K,** which appeared in 1942. By the time it entered service in some numbers in 1943 the inadequacies of Japan's wartime potential were already beginning to bite and only 167 'Emilys' were ever completed, though it was a superb design. The **H8K2** version had a maximum speed of 283 miles per hour and a 4,000-mile range, plus a maximum bomb load of 4,410 lbs. Its crew numbered ten and it bristled with defensive armament: five 20-mm cannon and four 7.7-mm machine guns.

Where maximum range was concerned, 'Mavis', 'Emily', the PBY, the Sunderland, Fw 200C Condor and Liberator reigned supreme in World War II, but in the early stage of the war at sea much valuable work was done by two lesser-known aircraft. The first of these was the **Avro Anson,** the RAF's 'Faithful Annie', which first entered service in 1936 and was not phased out until the 1960s. The Anson was a twin-engined shore-based maritime reconnaissance aircraft, defended by two machine guns, one forward-firing, the other in a dorsal turret. It stayed in first-line service until 1942 and then soldiered on as a trainer. Total British production (which ended in May 1952) reached 8,138 machines (plus an additional 2,882 built in Canada) and the Anson became a familiar sight in the early war years shepherding coastal convoys around the British Isles.

It was incredibly airworthy, as was proved by the case of two Australian Ansons, one of which crashed bodily on top of the other during an airborne collision. The crews baled out, but the pilot of the upper machine found that his controls were still answering and managed to make a

Douglas A-20 Havoc. Called Boston by the RAF, this fast bomber served in all theatres. This one, from the US 5th AF, is skip-bombing a Japanese ship.

belly-landing with the aircraft still locked together.

Another maritime patrol workhorse—and a real boon to the RAF—was the **Lockheed Hudson,** a twin-engined design originally produced to British specifications. Some 800 Hudsons were purchased for the RAF but Lend-Lease added around 1,170 more. It was a Hudson which located the 'hell-ship' *Altmark* in February 1940. *Altmark* had been the supply-ship of the pocket-battleship *Graf Spee* in the South Atlantic and was trying to return to Germany with Merchant Navy POWs taken during *Graf Spee*'s war cruise. The Hudson's report led to *Altmark*'s interception and boarding in neutral Norwegian waters and the triumphant return of the POWs to England. A Coastal Command Hudson was also the first aircraft to sink a U-boat with rockets, in May 1943. The Hudson had a crew of

The Beaufighter of Coastal Command

▲ Bristol Beaufighter TF Mk. X torpedo-fighter serving with No. 455 Squadron as part of the UK-based strike force operating in late 1944

five and a maximum range of 2,800 miles; later versions of it could carry up to 1,400 lbs of bombs. During the later war years the Hudson served on air/sea rescue, training and troop transport duties.

During the latter half of the war the Americans produced some superb naval strike aircraft. Paramount among these was the **Chance Vought F4U Corsair,** adopted by the US and Royal Navies and, at the time of its appearance, the most powerful naval fighter ever built.

By VJ-Day Corsairs had shot down over 2,000 enemy aircraft. The **F4U-4** version had a maximum speed of 446 miles per hour at 26,000 feet and could deliver the same broadside as the **Grumman Hellcat** fighter—six .50-inch Browning machine guns—and it could also carry two 1,000 lb bombs or eight rocket projectiles. The total Corsair production reached 12,681 aircraft and by the end of the war British and American-flown Corsairs were serving together in the Pacific theatre. The Fleet Air Arm began to receive the Corsair in mid-1943 and 19 Royal Navy squadrons were

eventually equipped with it.

Another notable American naval aircraft was the **Curtiss SB2C Helldiver,** a carrier-based dive-bomber armed with two fixed 20-mm cannon and two .50 inch machine guns. The Helldiver could carry up to 1,000 lbs of bombs internally and the same amount under the wings. Although not operational until late 1943, it was to play an important part in the Pacific Island campaigns.

One of the most famed American medium bombers of World War II was the twin-engined **North American B-25 Mitchell,** the aircraft which dropped the first Allied bombs on Tokyo in the 'Doolittle Raid' of April 18, 1942. Apart from its maximum bomb-load of 3,000 lbs, the Mitchell also carried a powerful punch in the shape of its heavy armament. The machine was a superb gun platform and the **B-25H** and **J** versions had eight and 12 forward-firing machine guns while the **G** had two .50s and a massive 75-mm cannon which more than compensated for its slow rate of fire and heavy recoil by its ability to sink small vessels with a single shot.

Mention must also be made of an Italian design which proved to be a magnificent land-based torpedo-bomber during the campaign in the Mediterranean. This was the **Savoia-Marchetti S.M.79 Sparviero.** It hardly looked the part, being a hunch-backed tri-motor design dating back to mid-1930s. By the time of Italy's entry into the war the S.M.79 was the standard bomber of the Regia Aeronautica. The **S.M.79-II** was developed for the torpedo-bombing role and it did much damage to Malta convoys. It had a crew of four, had a maximum speed of 270 mph and a range of 1,243 miles, and could carry up to 2,750 lbs of bombs or two torpedoes.

Allied debt to Hitler

The obvious requirements of coastal and carrier-borne aircraft are range, endurance, hitting-power, and last but not least, a modicum of comfort for the crews committed to hours of weariness over the sea. It was not surprising that the leading naval powers of World War II—Britain, the United States, and Japan—all produced excellent examples. It was also significant

that Germany and Italy, with their basic misconception of naval strategy and neglect of the importance of the aircraft-carrier in modern naval warfare, proved woefully inadequate (with the exception of the Italian S.M.79) in producing such aircraft.

It is almost incredible to reflect on how much the Allies owed to Hitler and Göring. Not only could an adequate long-range German coastal aircraft force have saved the *Bismarck,* it would have transformed the course of the commerce war in the Atlantic.

Moreover, even a limited carrier-building programme could have sent *Scharnhorst, Gneisenau,* and *Bismarck* (let alone the powerful pocket-battleships) out on to the high seas with their own carrier protection, to murder Allied convoys. As it was, only one German carrier—*Graf Zeppelin*—was launched, and the miserable stop-go policy which beset her meant that she was never completed.

Mussolini's navy fared even worse, for excessive reliance was placed on Italy's commanding position in the central Mediterranean. When finally Mussolini ordered the liners *Roma* and *Augustus* to be converted into carriers it was too late. By the time of the Italian armistice in September 1943 the *Roma* (rechristened *Aquila*) was almost ready for her sea trials, but had not received any aircraft, while work on the *Augustus* had only got as far as removal of her liner superstructure.

The way in which the massive American and British task forces cruised off the very coast of Japan in the closing months of the war was ample reward for the policy of taking care to keep the naval air arm up to date and equipped with the best possible machines. Excellent Allied designs 'in the pipeline' by the end of the war against Japan were legion. There was the **Grumman Bearcat,** successor to the Hellcat, with a speed of 447 miles per hour and a 4-gun (heavy machine gun or cannon) wing armament. The British land-based **Tempest** design had been elaborated into the **Sea Fury,** one of the most sophisticated piston-engined fighters every built. Another newcomer was the **Hornet,** twin-engined single-seat successor to the legendary **Mosquito.** A fast US Navy 'twin' was the Grumman F7F Tigercat.

The Swordfish of the Fleet Air Arm

▲ Fairey Swordfish Mk. I torpedo-bomber of No. 824 Squadron aboard HMS Eagle in 1940

FLYING to fight

The military dream of the sudden, surprising and decisive attack was made a reality by the inter-war development of aircraft, parachutes and gliders. This new and daring method of attack was widely used during World War II and, inevitably, lessons had to be learned from the heavy casualties of the early combined operations before any airborne forces could be unleashed against their objectives with any kind of certainty of success. But these early efforts paved the way for some spectacular military operations in which aircraft and aircrew played a key role.

World War II developed three principal methods of airlifting troops into action: by parachute, by direct airlift in transports, and by glider. The evolution of the aircraft between two world wars had seen extensive experimentation with airborne troops by all major powers, which bore fruit between 1939 and 1945.

The first country to use airborne troops in World War II was Germany, during the campaign in Scandinavia in April 1940. The troops concerned were the responsibility of the Luftwaffe, whose workhorse for this type of operations was the time-trusted **Junkers Ju 52/3m**—'Iron Annie', as she was affectionately known by German servicemen. An antiquated looking, tri-motor design, the Ju 52 served throughout the war. It had a basic crew of two or three and could carry up to 18 troops or some 10,000 lbs of cargo. Some 3,000 machines of this basic type were built and used from the cold Arctic to Africa.

German glider-borne troops hit the world's headlines in May 1940 with their amazing assault on Fort Eban-Emael in Belgium. The standard German troop-carrying glider of World War II was the **DFS 230**, which could carry ten fully-armed soldiers. These gliders were also used during the hazardous landing on Crete in May 1941, in North Africa, and in September 1943 during the daring rescue by German airborne commandos of Mus-

until the Soviet invasion of Japanese-held Manchuria—one week after the first nuclear bomb had been dropped on Japan.

The Japanese also used paratroops, both in the invasion of the Dutch East Indies in 1942 and three years later, in attempts to reinforce the Philippines against the American invaders.

But in the overview by far the most extensive use of airborne troops was made by Britain and the United States in the liberation of Europe, between 1943 and 1945, the first large-scale Allied airborne attack taking place during the assault on Sicily—'Operation Husky'—in July 1943.

Sicily was the first bi-national invasion which the Allies attempted, and was shared by the British 8th Army and the American 7th Army. In the British sector the airborne attack was a tragedy. It was made by 134 gliders towed by American-flown **Douglas C-47s** (the Allied counterpart to Germany's Ju 52). On D-Day, July 10, the airborne force (the British 1st Airborne Division) had to contend with strong winds made worse by the faulty navigation of their tugs and as a result the gliders were released too far out. Nearly 50 of them came down in the sea. drowning their troops. Most of the other gliders landed way off target and only 12 of them reached the correct landing-zone. A total force of only 73 officers and men reached their objective: a key bridge on the Syracuse road. By the time the

—in good time for the invasion of France. In the battle for Sicily, and later on in Italy, German airborne troops were encountered. Although after Crete they did not operate in their correct role, these picked men were formidable ground troops, holding on in defensive positions in apparently impossible situations. The battle of Cassino, where a couple of battered German parachute regiments blocked the approaches to Rome against all-comers for over four months, was their finest hour.

For the decisive assault on the Normandy coast in June 1944 the British and Americans used airborne forces to secure the west and east flanks of the beach-head: the American 101st and 82nd Divisions for 'Utah' Beach in the West and the British 6th Airborne Division for 'Sword' Beach in the east. Both airborne assaults used united parachute- and glider-borne troops. The Americans favoured the **Waco CG-4A** glider with its capacity for 15 fully-laden troops, the British the **Airspeed Horsa** and **GA Hamilcar.** The massive Hamilcar, the first Allied glider capable of carrying a light

---

solini from an Italian mountain-top hideaway.

Although Soviet Russia was the first country in the world to possess the potential of airborne and parachute troops, demonstrated to the world on manoeuvres near Kiev in 1937, and was eventually to organise at least eight airborne brigades, these specially trained units were used in the role conceived for them only once, in Autumn 1943. Owing to poor navigation of their transport crews and the unexpected arrival of a German mechanised division, this operation was a bloody fiasco and there were no larger scale Soviet airborne activities

British 5th Division fought its way through to join hands with the airborne troops the latter were down to a strength of 19 men.

Specialists in decisive roles

Nor did the American glider force supporting the 7th Army landing do much better, being scattered widely over south-eastern Sicily. Their main contribution was to add to the demoralisation of the Italian forces on the invasion sector. Apart from everything else, this tragic muddle led to more attention being paid to navigational proficiency training of airborne transport crews

7-ton tank, could also carry two Bren-gun carriers, or two scout cars, or a mobile Bofors gun. Tugs for these gliders ranged from **Stirlings** and **Halifaxes** to C-47s and **Albemarles.**

The D-Day airborne landings were perilous. They were made at night and the Allied air forces commander, Leigh-Mallory, had warned Eisenhower that losses of 80 per cent to tugs and gliders might be expected. Scanty AA fire, excellent radar jamming, and evasive tactics did not produce anything like this loss figure but the drops were far from accurate. Only one-sixth of the US 101st Division was in

position by the dawn of June 6, the result largely of scatter caused by evasive tactics. Nevertheless, the sluggish German response plus the gallantry and dash of the troops going into action, secured the objectives by the time the seaborne assault force arrived.

The next major Allied airborne operation was a brilliant success—but strategically unneccessary. It was the spearhead of the invasion of southern France, originally intended to be synchronised with the Normandy landings, then delayed by the slow pace of the Italian campaign plus the need to concentrate tugs and gliders for the Normandy assault, and finally launched in August 1944 on the insistence of the Americans and Russians. 'Dragoon', as the invasion of southern France was code-named, was largely a paratroop affair, carried out by 396 aircraft in nine relays and preceded by special pathfinders. It was the most successful Allied airborne operation to date, with 60 per cent of the paratroops landing on or nearby their dropping-zones. But it was largely a sledge-hammer to crack a nut, for after the heavy losses suffered in Normandy it was no part of the Wehrmacht's plan to fight for the south of France.

Arnhem—an ominous name

The next major Allied airborne drop will always be associated with one of the most ominous names of World War II: Arnhem. The plan was Montgomery's and it was thrown up by the stiffening of German resistance as the Allied troops neared Germany. After the collapse in Normandy and the runaway Allied advance across France to the western borders of the Reich, Field-Marshal Model managed against all expectations to re-establish a firm front in the West at the moment when the Allies were running out of steam.

To prevent the onset of a battle of attrition in the West, Montgomery proposed Operation 'Market Garden': the opening-up by airborne troops of a narrow corridor along which 21st Army Group could burst into the north German plain, with the vital bridges over the key Dutch waterways captured in advance by the airborne forces. Paratroop and glider forces were to peg out the corridor by digging in at Eindhoven, Veghel, Uden, Nijmegen, and finally between Heelsum and Oosterbeek on the north bank of the Neder Rijn, the latter force—that assigned to the British 1st

Above: Ju 52/3m—Rommel's supply-line. The Afrika Corps relied increasingly on the Luftwaffe for all its needs, and the main load carrier was the Ju 52/3m.
Below: Ju 52/3m over Holland. In May 1940 these aircraft brought the troops that spearheaded the Blitzkrieg. 'Iron Annie' was first flown in 1932 and despite heavy losses continued in production until 1945.

Right: Horsa and Sherman. Though the glider was made of mere plywood, its value was immense. Note the 'invasion stripes' on the rear fuselage.
Right below: B-17s over friends. Soon after D-day these Fortresses of the 94th Bomb Group lowered their landing gear and flew slowly over French partisans dropping supplies.

Airborne Division—entrusted with the vital job of seizing Arnhem bridge and holding it for two to four days until the ground forces joined up.

It was a daring and original plan about which Montgomery has always remained unrepentant. Unfortunately not enough attention was paid to stark reality. For a start the problems in the path of the advancing ground forces were underestimated. It was totally unknown that Field-Marshal Model himself—together with General Student, virtuoso of the German airborne arm and the brains behind the capture of Crete in May 1941—were actually in the Arnhem area, and would not, therefore, have to weigh up confusing reports before deciding on counter-measures. But the most serious failure of Allied Intelligence was the fact that two *Waffen*-SS Panzer divisions were refitting in the Arnhem sector. So it was that the airborne troops at the very tip of the 'Market Garden' spearhead—British 1st Armoured —would immediately face counter-attacks by crack German armoured units and were, in any case, confined to one single passable road leading to their desperately battling paratroop comrades.

Moreover, an accident of war gave the entire Allied plan to the Germans within hours of the first landings at Arnhem. A body found in a wrecked American glider which came down near Student's command post at Vught was found to be carrying a full set of the operational orders—an instant dispersal of the 'fog of war' of which Model and Student took the fullest advantage. Contrary to certain reports there is no truth in the assertion that the whole Arnhem operation was betrayed to the Germans by certain members of the Dutch underground.

No 'lightning breakthrough'

Yet another setback for the Arnhem forces was the dispersal of the troops over the dropping and landing zones and the extremely leisurely pace at which they finally moved in to occupy Arnhem, as well as the tardy drop of desperately needed reinforcements in the shape of the Polish paratroop brigade. The main force failed to take the bridge. They were instantly counter-attacked and forced to dig in way off their original objective. In the end they had to hold on for a murderous week of street fighting before the survivors could be pulled out.

Total failure at Arnhem was countered to some extent by the American success at Eindhoven and Nijmegen, but Montgomery's vision of a lightning breakthrough had vanished. All 'Market Garden' did was to push a salient further into the German front which would later become a useful take-off point for the final assault on the Rhine—and teach the Allies once more to have a healthy respect for the speed of German reactions. Even at this late date, it was clear that the war was far from over. No matter how well trained, no airborne troops could hold out against armour with nothing more hard-hitting than the 2-pounder bombs of the PIAT projector.

Further delays to the decisive Allied assault on the Rhine—the most formidable natural barrier between the Allies and Berlin—were imposed by the totally un-

Combined Bomber Offensive, February 9-June 6, 1944	
Allied aircraft employed:	21,949
Bomb tonnage dropped:	76,200 tons
Selected road and rail targets:	80
Targets destroyed:	51
Targets severely damaged:	25
Targets slightly damaged:	4

expected German offensive in the Ardennes of December 1944. Eisenhower refused to be argued out of his careful, threefold approach to the 'Battle of the Rhine' and the final assault did not go in until the fourth week of March.

On March 23, 1945, Montgomery's army group opened up a smashing bombardment by 3,300 guns along a front of 25 miles. Three firm bridgeheads were pegged out on the east bank of the Rhine by troops crossing in assault boats, and Montgomery threw in two airborne divisions on the 24th which extended his bridge-head to a depth of six miles. The Americans were luckier: they already had a bridge, captured intact at Remagen, which enabled them to launch an immediate land exploitation; and by nightfall on April 1 the Allies had closed an immense ring around the entire area of the Ruhr.

Top: Stirling and Horsa. The Stirling was obsolescent as a bomber by 1944, and with nose and dorsal turrets removed the Mk IV became a premier glider tug. This picture was taken before 'invasion stripes' were painted on just prior to D-day—when losses of up to 80 per cent were forecast. **Left: Horsa on D-day.** British airborne troops hastily couple up an ammunition limber to a Jeep after pulling them out through their Horsa's nose.
Below: The beach on D-day. Avoiding craters left by Allied bombing, amphibious Dukw vehicles and waterproofed trucks swarm ashore from two landing ships. Airborne troops secured the flanks of the beachheads and transport operations were on an immense scale, but the real tonnage for the sustained battle had to come later by sea, including the fuel and munitions for Allied fighters that were based in Normandy.

The most daring operation

There then followed an exhilarating fortnight of non-stop advance to the line of the Elbe, halted only by the pressures of grand strategy and international politics which stopped the American 9th Army from pushing right on to Berlin itself. This decision meant that the most daring airborne operation of the war was never attempted: a *coup de main* which would establish the Allies in Berlin itself.

This was to be the crowning operation of 'Eclipse', the code name for the final defeat of Germany. It was drawn up by General Gavin, whose US 82nd Airborne Division had taken Nijmegen in the Arnhem campaign, and General Taylor, commander of the US 101st Division. The main targets in Berlin were the airfields: Tempelhof for 82nd Division and Gatow for 101st. Desperate resistance was only to be expected and the assault force was huge: the initial plan called for 3,000 fighters for close escort, 1,500 transport aircraft, over 1,000 gliders, and 20,000-odd paratroops—a bigger force than that which had landed in Normandy on the morning of D-Day.

Between Paderborn and Berlin itself, 22 objective lines had been marked out for 9th Army's advance on Berlin. By April 15 the Americans were across the Elbe—Objective 'Gold'—and were building up a bridge-head before pushing on to 'Silver'. Beyond 'Silver' lay 'Silk', 'Satin', 'Daisy', 'Pansy', 'Jug', and then, finally, 'Goal'—the airfields on the outskirts of Berlin. But on April 15, 1945, General Simpson heard to his astonishment and disappointment that he was to go no further than the Elbe. Berlin was to be left to the Russians—and the most sensational airborne attack plan of World War II was returned to the files.

ECLIPSE OF T'

Neither the shattering effect of Pearl Harbor—a classically planned and executed air strike—nor the decided early superiority of Japanese aircraft could deter the Americans in the Pacific. They clung on desperately and struck back, first at Coral Sea and then, tellingly, at Midway to win parity in the air. Then began the long haul back across the Pacific, the development of new aircraft, completed at breakneck speed, and the hard-won superiority in the air. The Superfortresses hit at Japan, the Kamikaze force had its wild, retaliatory fling, but not even that suicidal fanaticism could compete with the power of the shockwaves from the atomic bomb. The conflict in the Pacific theatre was initiated, dictated and decided by the war in the air.

There was a striking similarity between the breakdowns of the American and Japanese air forces at the outbreak of the Pacific war in December 1941. Both sides possessed army and navy air forces. The opposing navy air forces both operated the best fighters, flown by carefully selected and trained pilots, of their respective countries: the army air forces operated long-range bombers and somewhat inferior interceptor fighters. The vital difference, however, was that the Japanese had carefully planned a surprise offensive aimed at seizing the initiative in the air and holding it, while the American forces in the Pacific, with Washington obsessed with the desire not to provoke an all-out war with Japan, were deployed for the defensive. And this tacit yielding of the initiative by the Americans was to have disastrous results for the Allied cause in 1940/41.

For the American Pacific Fleet to play a decisive role in the central Pacific its navy base at Pearl Harbor, Oahu, in the Hawaiian Islands, was vital. That was where the fleet was concentrated when the Japanese struck. But the security of the Hawaiian archipelago was not the sole American concern. In the western Pacific lay the Philippine Islands, a republic under American patronage which the USA was pledged to defend. An American general, MacArthur, commanded in the Philippines; American aircraft were based on Filipino airfields and American troops formed the core of the garrison. In the event of a Japanese attack the American forces in the Philippines were expected to defend themselves until the American Pacific Fleet could come to their aid, force a decisive naval battle on the Japanese Combined Fleet, and spearhead the counter-attack.

Japanese planning had accepted this as obvious and had proceeded to meet it by making the tackling of the US Pacific Fleet

the first priority. With the Pacific Fleet out of the way the garrison of the Philippines would be isolated and defeated where it was. And defeated it had to be, since there could be no question of carrying out attacks on the other vital, oil-bearing islands of the south-west Pacific with a powerful enemy force poised to counter-attack. Admiral Isoroku Yamamoto, commander of the Japanese Combined Fleet, therefore welcomed the plan to knock out the battleships of the US Pacific Fleet at its anchorage with the use of naval air power. And the Imperial Japanese Navy which he had been instrumental in creating was superbly equipped to do so, with the best carrier force in the world.

Nostalgia governs tactics

Naval theory, while accepting that the air-craft-carrier had come to stay, was still beset —both in the USA and Japan—by strategical nostalgia. The big gun of the battleship had always been the key weapon at sea and was still expected to be in 1941. While expanding their carrier force the Japanese had also begun the construction of warships which the carrier had made obsolete: the 18-inch gun super-battleships of the *Yamato* class. Rather as the first tanks were seen as aids for the infantry rather than a weapon in their own right, aircraft-carriers were regarded as service vessels for the battleships. With carriers, a battle fleet could carry its own air umbrella. But it took the first year of the Pacific war for both sides to realise that carrier fleets could not only defend themselves but also destroy their opposite numbers.

Carrier aircraft had evolved into three indispensable types: the fighter, the dive-bomber, and the torpedo-bomber. The Japanese carrier fighter in December 1941 was one of the best warplanes in the world: the **Mitsubishi A6M2 Zero-sen,** code-named 'Zeke' by the Americans. With a flashing maximum speed of 331 mph it could out-manoeuvre anything the Allies could put into the sky for the first two years of the Pacific

war, and was armed with two cannon and two machine guns. The Japanese **Aichi D3A**— 'Val' — dive-bomber had been developed from study of German designs and was the standard Japanese dive-bomber at the out-break of the war, while the torpedo-carrying role was assumed by the **Nakajima B5N2**— 'Kate'. The American **F4F Wildcat** carrier fighter was no match for the Zero. It had in fact been operational for over a year before Pearl Harbor, serving with the British Fleet Air Arm as the **Martlet** and had claimed the honour of being the first British-flown American fighter to shoot down a German bomber. The **Douglas SBD Dauntless,** first ordered in 1939 in SBD-1 form, was a fine dive-bomber and could take heavy punishment—it was in fact the aircraft which scored the lowest loss rate of any American carrier plane. On the other hand the **Douglas TBD-1 Devastator** torpedo-bomber was a death-trap: too slow, and with only two machine guns as defensive armament. Only cast-iron fighter cover could have guaranteed the Devastator success and it seldom had.

In the Philippines the Americans pinned their hopes on three main types. Most important of all was the **Boeing B-17,** the 'Flying Fortress', the world's first opera-tional all-metal four-engined bomber. There were 36 B-17s on the island of Luzon in December 1941 and they were supplemented by long-range reconniassance in the shape of the excellent **PBY Catalina** flying-boats. But the fighter defence was a different story. It depended almost entirely on the **Curtiss P-40F Warhawk**—like the Navy's Wild-cats, outclassed on most points by the Zero.

America's fatal flaw

The overall American defence was geared to accepted 'standards' of warfare: that there would be a formal declaration of war before hostilities were opened. This may have made sense in 1939 but not in December 1941— two years and three months since the Wehrmacht had simply crossed the Polish

Left: A Kamikaze pilot. Most were in-experienced pilots and had to take a special 7-day course before embarking on their 'one plane, one ship' missions.

Japanese Warplanes

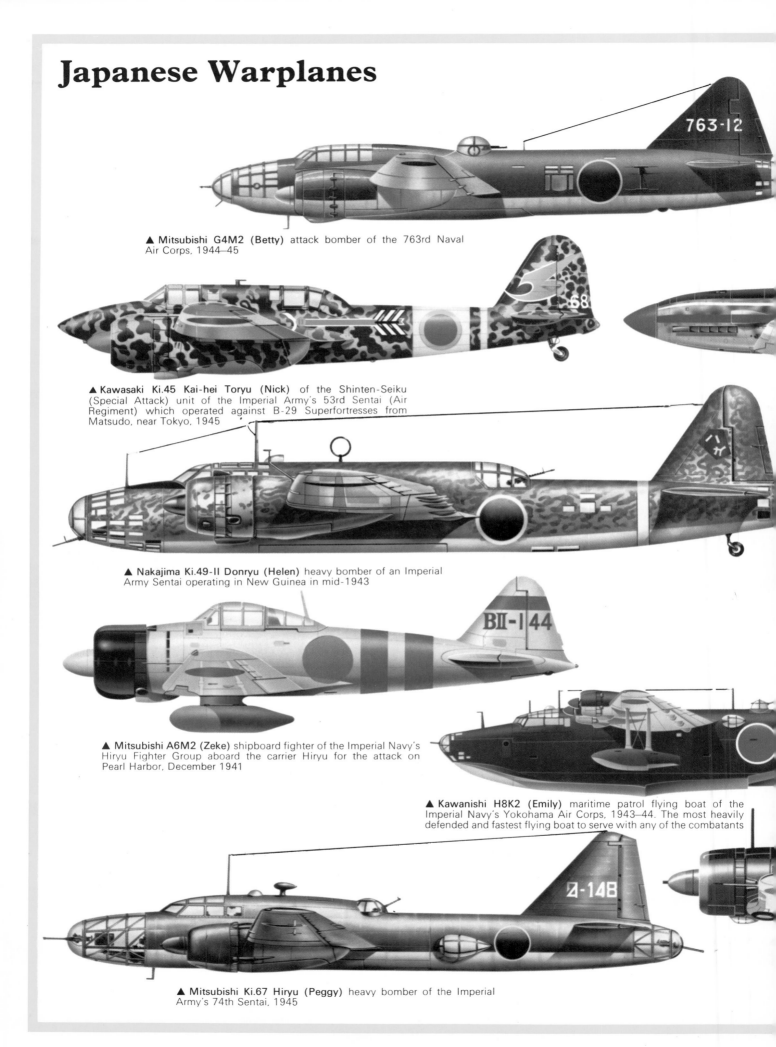

▲ Mitsubishi G4M2 (Betty) attack bomber of the 763rd Naval Air Corps, 1944–45

▲ Kawasaki Ki.45 Kai-hei Toryu (Nick) of the Shinten-Seiku (Special Attack) unit of the Imperial Army's 53rd Sentai (Air Regiment) which operated against B-29 Superfortresses from Matsudo, near Tokyo, 1945

▲ Nakajima Ki.49-II Donryu (Helen) heavy bomber of an Imperial Army Sentai operating in New Guinea in mid-1943

▲ Mitsubishi A6M2 (Zeke) shipboard fighter of the Imperial Navy's Hiryu Fighter Group aboard the carrier Hiryu for the attack on Pearl Harbor, December 1941

▲ Kawanishi H8K2 (Emily) maritime patrol flying boat of the Imperial Navy's Yokohama Air Corps, 1943–44. The most heavily defended and fastest flying boat to serve with any of the combatants

▲ Mitsubishi Ki.67 Hiryu (Peggy) heavy bomber of the Imperial Army's 74th Sentai, 1945

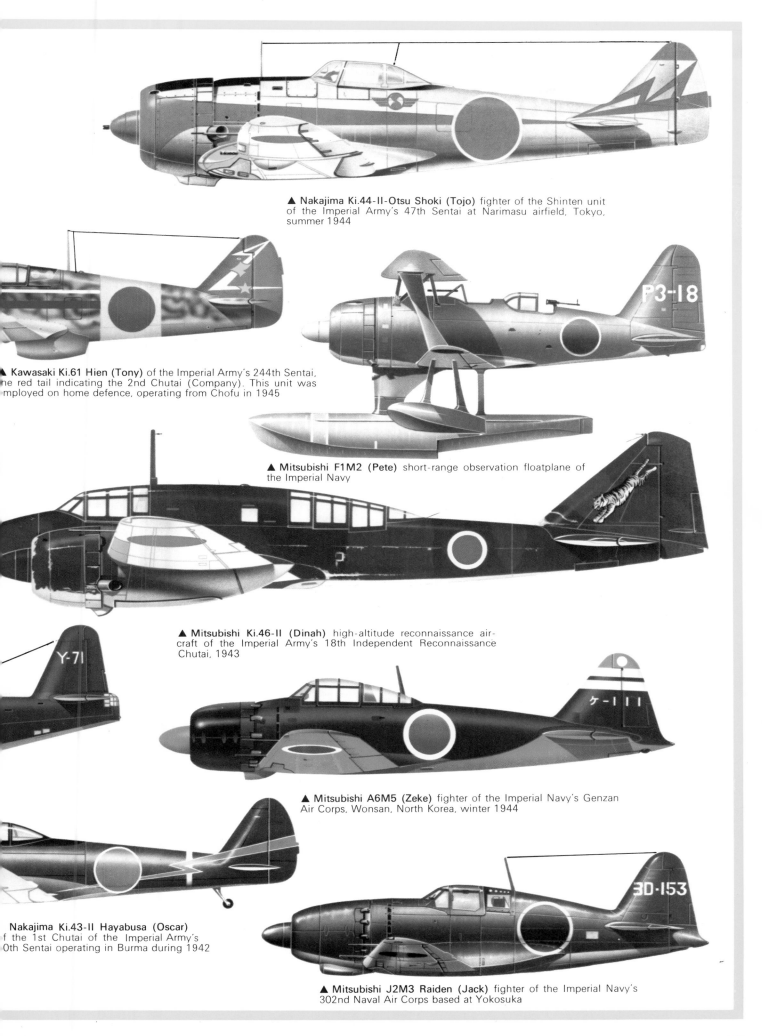

▲ Nakajima Ki.44-II-Otsu Shoki (Tojo) fighter of the Shinten unit of the Imperial Army's 47th Sentai at Narimasu airfield, Tokyo, summer 1944

◀ Kawasaki Ki.61 Hien (Tony) of the Imperial Army's 244th Sentai, the red tail indicating the 2nd Chutai (Company). This unit was employed on home defence, operating from Chofu in 1945

▲ Mitsubishi F1M2 (Pete) short-range observation floatplane of the Imperial Navy

▲ Mitsubishi Ki.46-II (Dinah) high-altitude reconnaissance aircraft of the Imperial Army's 18th Independent Reconnaissance Chutai, 1943

▲ Mitsubishi A6M5 (Zeke) fighter of the Imperial Navy's Genzan Air Corps, Wonsan, North Korea, winter 1944

◀ Nakajima Ki.43-II Hayabusa (Oscar) of the 1st Chutai of the Imperial Army's 50th Sentai operating in Burma during 1942

▲ Mitsubishi J2M3 Raiden (Jack) fighter of the Imperial Navy's 302nd Naval Air Corps based at Yokosuka

133

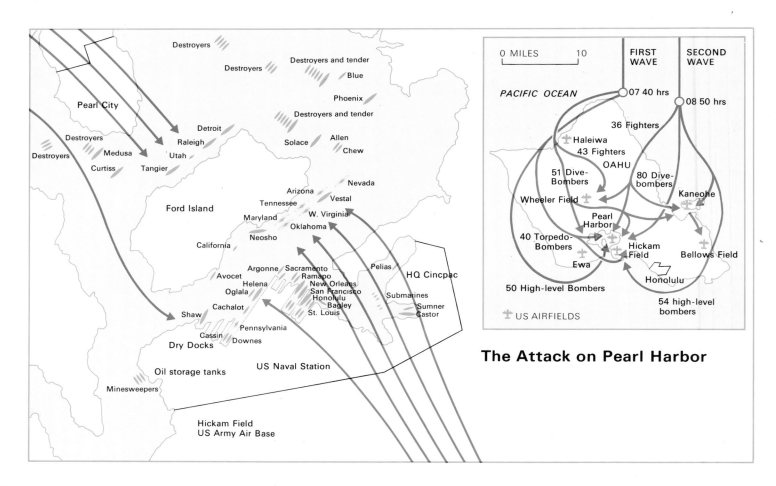

Destroyers

Destroyers

Destroyers and tender

Blue

Phoenix

Destroyers and tender

Pearl City

Detroit

Raleigh

Destroyers

Medusa

Utah

Curtiss

Tangier

Solace

Allen

Chew

Nevada

Arizona

Vestal

Tennessee

Ford Island

W. Virginia

Maryland

Oklahoma

California

Neosho

Argonne Sacramento

Pelias

Avocet

Ramapo

HQ Cincpac

Helena

New Orleans

San Francisco

Oglala

Honolulu

Bagley

Submarines

Cachalot

St. Louis

Shaw

Sumner

Castor

Cassin

Pennsylvania

Dry Docks

Downes

Oil storage tanks

US Naval Station

Minesweepers

Hickam Field
US Army Air Base

0 MILES 10

FIRST WAVE

SECOND WAVE

PACIFIC OCEAN

07 40 hrs

08 50 hrs

36 Fighters

Haleiwa

43 Fighters

OAHU

51 Dive-Bombers

80 Dive-bombers

Kaneohe

Wheeler Field

Pearl Harbor

40 Torpedo-Bombers

Hickam Field

Bellows Field

Ewa

Honolulu

50 High-level Bombers

54 high-level bombers

✈ US AIRFIELDS

The Attack on Pearl Harbor

Left: Blazing battleships. Flame and smoke pour from the stricken giants USS *West Virginia* and *Tennessee* after the Pearl Harbor attack. Firefighting and other emergency services were overwhelmed.

Below left: Discovering the Zero. Although reported to Western intelligence the Mitsubishi Zero-Sen (strictly, the A6M2) was an unpleasant surprise when it appeared as an escort over Pearl Harbor. This was one of nine shot down. Out of 354 aircraft only another 15 'Vals' and five 'Kates' were lost.

Below: An A6M2 takes off for glory. Launched 230 miles from the target, the Zeros needed their long-range tanks.

frontier. The Philippines garrison had its eyes—the PBYs—and the US Pacific Fleet at Pearl Harbor had the equivalent in the form of the aircraft operated by the carriers *Lexington* and *Saratoga*—but both of them depended on some advance warning.

By contrast the Japanese would operate under no such impediment. Their only main worry once the decision to strike had been made was the difficulty in putting a sufficiently strong strike force over the Philippines. All six fleet carriers—*Kaga, Akagi, Hiryu, Soryu, Zuikaku,* and *Shokaku*—were earmarked for the Pearl Harbor strike. This left the Philippines attack force with the smaller carriers *Ryujo, Zuiho,* and *Taiho,* with a combined operational capacity of little more than 50 aircraft—a figure that was halved in windy conditions. The answer was found in falling back on flying skills to extend the range of land-based Zero fighters flying from Formosa. Repeated training gradually extended the mileage which could be squeezed from the Zero's total fuel capacity of 182 gallons until the all-time record for economical consumption was set by the crack pilot Saburo Sakai: he managed to lower his Zero's fuel consumption from 35 gallons per hour to under 17. This meant that the immense distance to be covered—almost 1,200 miles from Formosa to the airfields of Luzon—could be mastered by the Zeros without the need for a carrier force. This transformed the Japanese plan and gave them another surprise advantage over the Americans, who could not believe that the Japanese had any fighters which could hit them direct from land bases. Saburo Sakai and his fellow Zero pilots had a nerve-racking task: cruising at 180 knots at 12,000 feet, barely above stalling speed with engine revolutions hovering between 1,700 and 1,850 revs. per minute. But in the Japanese plan it meant that both Pearl Harbor and the Philippines could be dealt smashing attacks at the same time.

Although the main objective at Pearl Harbor was the Pacific Fleet, and that in the Philippines the American air strength, the two attacks were in fact very much alike. First came surprise, so that the attackers would not find American fighters already in the air waiting for them. Next came the suppression of enemy flying activities: the favoured initial ingredient of Blitzkrieg since the Polish campaign. Finally, pinpoint attacks would exploit the benefits of the first two provisions and eliminate the key strategic targets.

Eight battleships not enough!

Another point working in favour of the Japanese was the fact that the US Pacific Fleet did not operate its carriers in close co-operation with the battle fleet. On the morning of Sunday, December 7, 1941, the two Japanese air strikes were able to make their approaches to Oahu with no opposition whatever from American carrier-borne aircraft. Still less were there any counter-strikes from the American carriers. But the Japanese plan depended on eliminating *all* the capital ships of the US Pacific Fleet. It was left to the discretion of the strike force commander to decide whether or not the warships at anchor in Pearl Harbor justified a strong enough force to be attacked and thus to reveal the Japanese hand. It would have

taken a clairvoyant naval strategist to see that eight battleships, although a superb target, were not enough. Commander Mitsuo Fuchida, the Japanese strike force commander, was thoroughly justified in making his decision to attack. It was his chief, Vice-Admiral Chuichi Nagumo, who made the decision to withdraw his carrier force after the strikes on Pearl Harbor and not finish the job by seeking out and destroying the American carriers.

Nagumo's task force included six aircraft carriers, *Kaga, Akagi, Hiryu, Soryu, Zuikaku,* and *Shokaku,* with a total strength of 493 planes; two battleships; three cruisers; nine destroyers; three submarines and eight tankers to refuel the squadron at sea. The force sailed on November 26 on an easterly course along the 43rd Parallel. On December 2 came confirmation of the order to attack and on December 6 the force turned towards Oahu. The following day, on Sunday, December 7, at 0615, Nagumo despatched the first wave of attackers.

The first of the two Japanese air strikes on Pearl Harbor was led by the air group commander, Commander Mitsuo Fuchida. His force, launched 230 miles from Pearl Harbor,

---

Below: The aftermath. At a total cost of 29 aircraft of all types, the Imperial Japanese Navy crippled the US Navy's battle fleet. It was a mightly task even to clear away the wreckage.

Aircraft Strength in the Pacific, December 1941		
Country	Aircraft	Deployment
US Army and Navy	385	Hawaii and Pacific Fleet
	12	Midway
	180	Philippines
	12	Wake
RAF	330	Malaya
RAAF	165	Australia, Malaya, E. Indies and Solomons
Netherlands AF	200	East Indies
Allied total	1,284	
Japanese Army	550	For Malayan Campaign
	175	For Philippine Campaign
	600	China and Manchuria
	50	Japan
Japanese Navy	150	For Malayan Campaign
	300	For Philippine Campaign
	400	For Operation Hawaii
	325	Marshalls and Japan
	70	Seaplanes with Fleet
Japanese total	2,620	

US and Japanese Warplane Production

Year	United States	Japan
1941	19,433	5,088
1942	49,445	8,861
1943	92,196	16,693
1944	100,752	28,180
1945	Not known.	11,066

consisted of 50 bomb-carrying 'Kates', 40 torpedo-carrying 'Kates', 51 'Val' dive-bombers, and a fighter escort of 43 Zeros to tackle any interference from the Americans and press home ground attacks. This was followed an hour later by the second wave led by Lieutenant-Commander Shimazaki from the *Zuikaku*: 54 bomb-carrying 'Kates', 80 'Vals', and 36 Zeros. The first wave was actually picked up by American radar on Oahu, at a range of approximately 160 miles, but it was casually assumed that the huge plot on the screen was a flight of bombers from the American mainland which was expected to arrive that morning. Another reason for the ease with which the Japanese gained complete surprise during the run-in was that the Japanese formation was initially mistaken for air groups from the carriers *Lexington* and *Enterprise*, which were at sea.

Although the carriers were not in the anchorage the entire battle fleet was, and Fuchida commenced his attack at 0750 (local time) and it ranged virtually unchecked until 0825. As the first wave headed back to the carriers, *Utah*, *California*, *Arizona*, and *Oklahoma* were on the bottom, *West Virginia* was sinking, and *Tennessee* was blazing. The second wave forced the Americans to beach *Nevada* and severely damaged the *Pennsylvania* and *Maryland*. Ground attacks wiped out the entire effective strength of the US Navy scout-planes and flying-boats on Oahu. When the second wave finally left at around 1000 the strike force had lost only nine Zeros, 15 'Vals', and five 'Kates' out of the 354 that attacked. Crushing victory though this

Aircraft Losses in Pacific Carrier Battles			
Battle	Date	US	Japan
Coral Sea	May 4-8, 1942	39	61
Midway	June 4, 1942	147	332
E. Solomons	Aug. 24, 1942	20	90
Santa Cruz	Oct. 26, 1942	74	100
Philippine Sea	June 19-20, 1944	80	380
Leyte Gulf	Oct. 24-26, 1944	162	288

was, it was marred by Admiral Nagumo's decision not to search out and destroy the two American carriers—a decision which was to have fatal results for the Japanese in the crucial sea battles of 1942.

In the Japanese war plan, Pearl Harbor was a pre-emptive strike to win time for conquests elsewhere, and this aim was abundantly fulfilled. After the attack it was impossible for the US Navy to throw any major naval reinforcements into the desperate fighting in the western Pacific, and for a while the Pacific Fleet had to retire to the west coast of the United States. This enabled the Japanese to make a clean sweep in the western Pacific and air power was instrumental in their victories.

Even though bad weather delayed the Japanese strike on the airfields of the Philippines, their pilots were amazed to catch the American aircraft completely by surprise when they finally arrived five hours after the Pearl Harbor strike. By the end of the first day the Philippine air force had ceased to exist as a serious threat. The Japanese were able to turn to the elimination of the make-shift British battle fleet based on Singapore and consisting of the battleship *Prince of Wales* and the battle-cruiser *Repulse,* both of which, cruising without fighter cover, were over-

whelmed and sunk on December 10, 1941 by Japanese land-based naval bombers from Indo-Chinese airfields. This was achieved by their two standard types, the **Mitsubishi G3M**—'Nell'— and the **G4M**—'Betty'— both twin-engined machines with long-range striking capabilities.

Flying Fortress problems

Having swept the Pacific of every Allied battleship the Japanese could go ahead with their island-hopping campaign through the Dutch East Indies. For this air reconnaissance and protection were vital, and the Japanese retained both from the start. It soon became impossible for the surviving Allied cruisers and destroyers to move without being spotted by Japanese reconnaissance aircraft, most notably the **Kawanishi H6K**—'Mavis' — flying-boat with its impressive range of 3,107 miles. Meanwhile the Zero pilots ground down the dwindling Allied reserves of aircraft in the Dutch East Indies, coping easily with the Curtiss P-40 Warhawks and **Bell P-39 Airacobras.** However, the Boeing B-17 presented more of a problem. Its huge size and high speed caused much confusion at first and the gunsights of the Zero proved generally ineffective, causing many a capable Japanese pilot to misjudge his attack and miss completely. The B-17's ability to take punishment, plus its high defensive fire-power, were other points which the Japanese had to find out the hard way.

The Allies' chances of retaining a foothold in the Dutch East Indies were finally destroyed on February 19, 1942, by a wild day of dog-fighting over Java which cost the Allies nearly 75 fighters. It was the sort of day's fighting of which the Luftwaffe had dreamed during the Battle of Britain. Apart from the P-40s, the Japanese encountered **P-36 Mohawks** and **Brewster F2A Buffaloes** during this phase of the campaign, which shredded the last Allied pretence at fighter protection in the East Indies. By March the Japanese were already regrouping their crack fighter units at Bali before sending them east to Rabaul *en route* to the next target—the east coast of New Guinea, where hastily-seized airfields were to be the bases for the planned conquest of the vital Allied base at Port Moresby in New Guinea.

Between April and August 1942 New Guinea saw an intense air campaign, with the Allies operating from Port Moresby and the Japanese from their fields along the New Guinea coast. Physically separated by the Owen Stanley mountains, both sides came in for heavy air raids, with the Allies favouring attacks by the twin-engined **Martin B-26 Marauder.** During this phase the Japanese fighter wing based at Lae became the most successful Japanese air unit of the Pacific war

Top: Battle of Leyte Gulf. Japanese aircraft press home their attacks—often using the new Kamikaze tactics—through intense anti-aircraft shell-bursts. A doomed US ship burns fiercely.
Centre: Zero fighters—a contemporary Japanese painting of a carrier flight deck.
Bottom: Loss of a Havoc. While its bombs explode on shore at Karas, Dutch New Guinea, a Douglas A-20 Havoc, hit by anti-aircraft fire, plunges into the Pacific. Another flies close overhead.

—but its victories were hollow. Thousands of miles away the first carrier-versus-carrier battles of the war reversed the flood of Japanese victories and enabled the Allies to go over to the offensive.

A battle of errors

The first carrier clash took place in May 1942 and was part and parcel of the fight for New Guinea. It was fought by the Allies to thwart an amphibious Japanese assault on Port Moresby. This was achieved, resulting in an Allied strategic victory; but tactically the Battle of the Coral Sea (May 4–8, 1942) was an extremely confused affair. Both sides made mistakes which could have been disastrous. That they were not was due only to mutual inexperience in this novel form of warfare. American pilots sank the small Japanese carrier *Shoho* but missed the crucial target, the fleet carriers *Zuikaku* and *Shokaku*; the Japanese immobilised the American carrier *Lexington* which was lost because of inexperience in damage control. Both sides put in wildly inflated victory claims; identification was bad on both sides and at one stage in the fight Japanese aircraft even tried to land on the American carrier *Yorktown*!

unmasked the Japanese plan and superhuman efforts in the shipyards sent a carrier force to sea. This consisted of *Yorktown*, frantically patched up in 48 hours in Pearl Harbor after returning from the Coral Sea; *Enterprise* and the new carrier *Hornet*. Admiral Chester Nimitz, well aware of the terrifying superiority of the Japanese task forces committed to the Midway venture, relied on surprise to ambush the Midway attack force—and the all-important Japanese carriers.

The result was the Battle of Midway: June 4, 1942. Failure to surprise Midway meant that the initial attack was not enough to neutralise the island's defences, and Admiral Nagumo ordered his carrier planes to prepare for a second attack. While the aircraft were being rearmed he discovered that American carriers were in the vicinity and ordered his aircrews to prepare for a strike against the new menace. However, while the Japanese aircraft were still rearming on deck, the four Japanese carriers were surprised by American dive-bombers and three of the carriers—*Kaga*, *Akagi*, and *Soryu*—were set hopelessly ablaze. The surviving carrier, *Hiryu*, launched a counter-strike which crippled *Yorktown* (later sunk

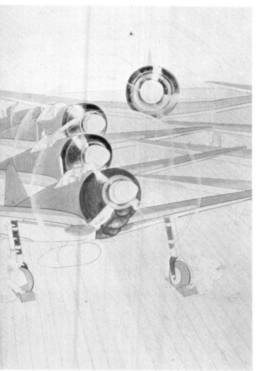

US AND JAPANESE CARRIER STRENGTH, DECEMBER 1941			
Carrier	Fighters	Dive bombers	Torpedo bombers
USA *Enterprise*	18 F4F Wildcat	36 SBD Dauntless	18 TBD Devastator
*Hornet**	18 F4F Wildcat	36 SB2C Helldiver	8 TBD Devastator 7 SBN
Lexington	18 F2A Buffalo	36 SBD Dauntless	18 TBD Devastator
*Ranger**	36 F4F Wildcat	36 SB2U Vindicator	—
*Saratoga**	18 F4F Wildcat	36 SBD Dauntless	18 TBD Devastator
*Wasp**	36 F4F Wildcat	36 SB2U Vindicator	—
*Yorktown**	18 F4F Wildcat	36 SBD Dauntless	18 TBD Devastator
*Long Island**	7 F2A Buffalo	13 SOC Seagull (scouting planes)	
Japan *Akagi*	21 A6M Zero	18 D3A Val	27 B5N Kate
Kaga	21 A6M Zero	27 D3A Val	27 B5N Kate
Hiryu	18 A6M Zero	18 D3A Val	18 B5N Kate
Soryu	18 A6M Zero	18 D3A Val	18 B5N Kate
Shokaku	18 A6M Zero	27 D3A Val	27 B5N Kate
Zuikaku	18 A6M Zero	27 D3A Val	27 B5N Kate
Hosho	11 A5M Claude	—	8 B5N Kate
Zuiho	16 A5M Claude	—	12 B5N Kate
Ryujo	16 A5M Claude	—	18 B5N Kate

*Operating in Atlantic waters.

The result of the Battle of the Coral Sea was that the Japanese lost a small carrier and were temporarily deprived of their best fleet carriers (*Shokaku* had been damaged and the air groups of both had been heavily depleted) but, for the loss of *Lexington*, the US Navy had stopped the Japanese from taking Port Moresby. This temporary stalemate in the south-west Pacific was followed by Yamamoto's attempt to force the decisive battle of the war by attacking an island objective which the US Navy could not afford to concede. This objective was the island of Midway, westernmost outpost of the Hawaiian group. By attacking Midway, Yamamoto was convinced that he could lure the last units of the Pacific Fleet to destruction by the guns of the Japanese battle fleet. He expected no opposition from American carriers, which he believed neutralised by the Coral Sea fight; and he was confident that his carriers would have surprise on their side in the initial smash at Midway's defences.

American code-breakers, however, had

by a Japanese submarine), but was subsequently eliminated by another American strike (on June 6). Midway wiped out the Japanese carrier supremacy at a stroke. Almost as important in the long run was the Japanese loss of some 250 aircraft and their practically irreplaceable crews.

Fight to a standstill

The next stage of the Pacific war opened in August 1942 when the Americans seized a foothold in the Solomon Islands by landing on Guadalcanal. The Japanese, based on Rabaul, were swift to counter-attack and the result was the six-month ordeal called the Battle of Guadalcanal. This struggle was unique: a land campaign which depended entirely on sea and air power. The Japanese cruisers and destroyers were supreme by night, while American naval air power retained a tenuous command of the sky by day. Two hard-fought carrier battles—the Eastern Solomons (August 24) and Santa

Allied Warplanes
of the Pacific Theatre

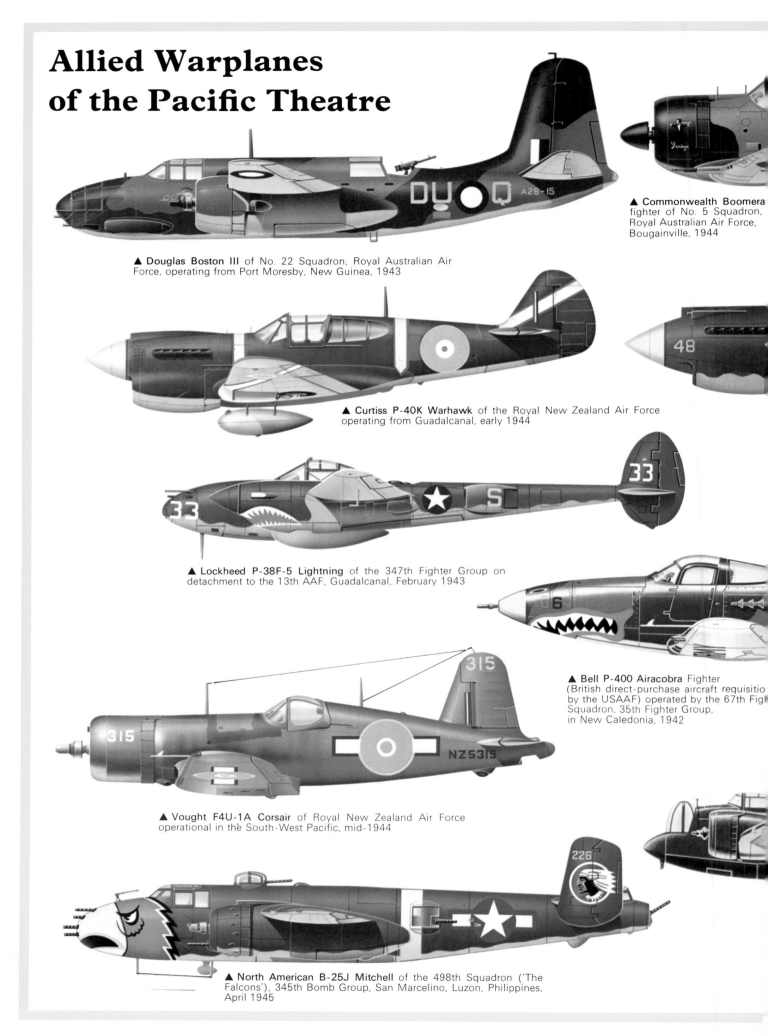

▲ Douglas Boston III of No. 22 Squadron, Royal Australian Air
Force, operating from Port Moresby, New Guinea, 1943

▲ Commonwealth Boomera
fighter of No. 5 Squadron,
Royal Australian Air Force,
Bougainville, 1944

▲ Curtiss P-40K Warhawk of the Royal New Zealand Air Force
operating from Guadalcanal, early 1944

▲ Lockheed P-38F-5 Lightning of the 347th Fighter Group on
detachment to the 13th AAF, Guadalcanal, February 1943

▲ Bell P-400 Airacobra Fighter
(British direct-purchase aircraft requisitio
by the USAAF) operated by the 67th Figh
Squadron, 35th Fighter Group,
in New Caledonia, 1942

▲ Vought F4U-1A Corsair of Royal New Zealand Air Force
operational in the South-West Pacific, mid-1944

▲ North American B-25J Mitchell of the 498th Squadron ('The
Falcons'), 345th Bomb Group, San Marcelino, Luzon, Philippines,
April 1945

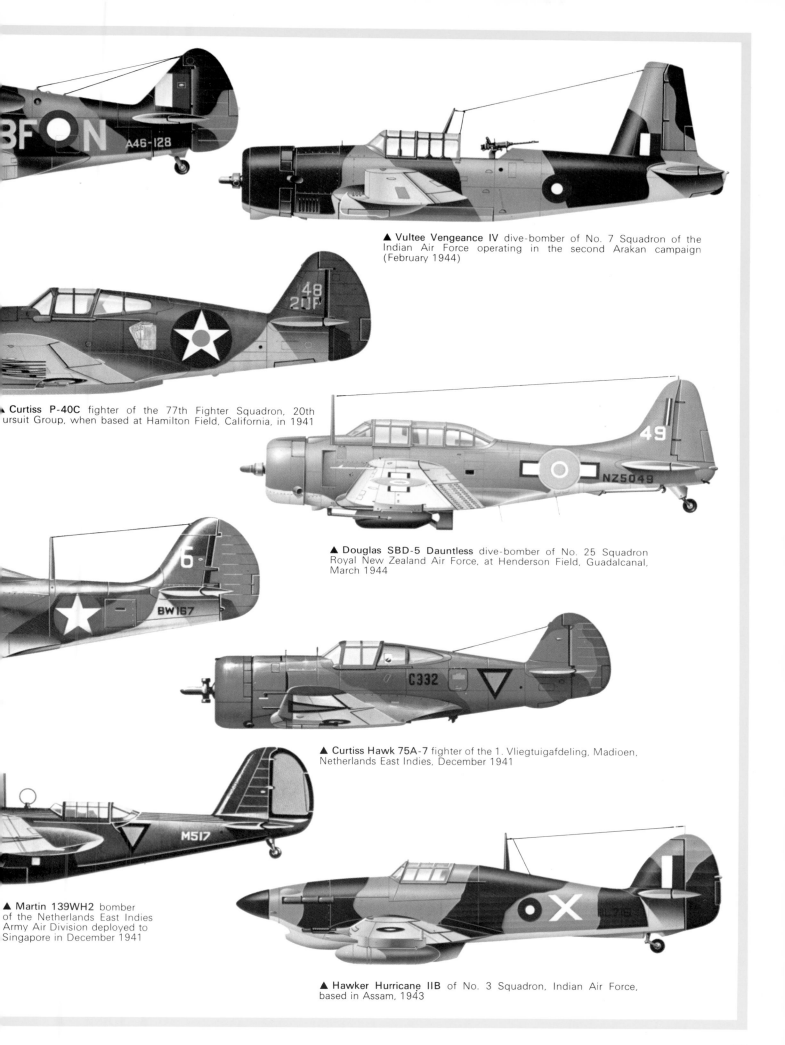

▲ Vultee Vengeance IV dive-bomber of No. 7 Squadron of the Indian Air Force operating in the second Arakan campaign (February 1944)

▲ Curtiss P-40C fighter of the 77th Fighter Squadron, 20th ursuit Group, when based at Hamilton Field, California, in 1941

▲ Douglas SBD-5 Dauntless dive-bomber of No. 25 Squadron Royal New Zealand Air Force, at Henderson Field, Guadalcanal, March 1944

▲ Curtiss Hawk 75A-7 fighter of the 1. Vliegtuigafdeling, Madioen, Netherlands East Indies, December 1941

▲ Martin 139WH2 bomber of the Netherlands East Indies Army Air Division deployed to Singapore in December 1941

▲ Hawker Hurricane IIB of No. 3 Squadron, Indian Air Force, based in Assam, 1943

139

PRINCIPAL PACIFIC WARPLANES 1942–45: BOMBERS

Country	Type	First ordered	Max. speed	Max. loaded range	Rate of climb	Ceiling	Bomb load armament	Crew	Number built
Japan	Nakajima P1Y1 'Frances'	1943	322 mph	2,700 miles ap.	9 mins 23 secs to 16,400 ft	33,135 ft	2,200 lbs; two 20-mm cannon	3	1,000 ap.
	Mitsubishi Ki-67 'Peggy'	1942	334 mph	1,245 miles	14 mins 30 secs to 19,865 ft	30,860 ft	1,760 lbs; four to five 12.7-mm mgs, one 20-mm cannon	6–8	700 ap.
United States	Martin B-26 Marauder	1939	315 mph	1,000 miles	12.5 mins to 15,000 ft	25,000 ft	5,800 lbs; five .50-in mgs	7	5,156
	Grumman TBF Avenger	1940	271 mph	1,020 miles	13 mins to 10,000 ft	23,000 ft	2,000 lbs of bombs or one 22-in torpedo or eight 5-in rockets	3	10,104
	Boeing B-29 Superfortress	1941	358 mph	3,250 miles	38 mins to 20,000 ft	31,850 ft	20,000 lbs; 12 .50-in mgs, one 20-mm cannon	10–14	3,970

Cruz (October 26) resulted in a tactical draw which passed the ball to the night operations of the surface warships. The Japanese lost the light carrier *Ryujo* and another crippling percentage of trained carrier aircrew; Japanese submarines torpedoed the carriers *Wasp* and *Saratoga* and torpedo-bombers sank the *Hornet*. In these two battles the American and Japanese carrier forces fought each other to a momentary standstill. The last key naval battles in the Guadalcanal saga were First Guadalcanal (November 12–13) Second Guadalcanal (November 14–15), and Tassaronga (November 30, 1942). By the time that the Japanese finally conceded defeat and evacuated Guadalcanal (February 7, 1943) the Imperial Japanese Navy had lost the equivalent of an entire peacetime fleet: two battleships, an aircraft-carrier, five cruisers, 12 destroyers, and eight submarines. Most of the fighting had been orthodox naval warfare: visual clashes between surface ships, almost entirely by night. But these engagements had been fought because the opposing carrier forces were unable to settle the issue by day. It was the last time that carrier units of the Japanese Navy were able to tackle their opposite numbers on equal terms.

During the Guadalcanal fighting the Japanese pilots got their first real taste of the new aircraft which would in time reverse the Zero's superiority for ever. The **Grumman Avenger** torpedo-bomber had just entered service in time for the Battle of Midway. It carried a power-operated dorsal turret and was an unpleasant surprise. The Japanese ace Saburo Sakai barely escaped death when he dived his Zero onto a formation of Avengers under the belief that they were Wildcats. Badly wounded, he managed to retain consciousness and return to Rabaul.

It was also during these campaigns that the Grumman F6F Hellcat showed its effectiveness. It remained the standard American carrier fighter to the end of the war, and enabled the American pilots to meet the Zero on virtually equal terms.

No parachutes—by choice!

A great advantage of the Allied machines which tangled with the Zero was their superior pilot and fuel tank protection. Magnificent aircraft though the Zero was, it was a death trap if hit in the fuel tanks. Another significant Allied advantage was the development of aircrew recovery. Air-sea rescue remained rudimentary on the Japanese side, depleting their vestigial reserves of trained aircrew still more. Ace pilots like Sakai, Ota, and Nishizawa preferred to fly without parachutes—simply because they found the harness irksome and felt that they could better become part of their machines without it. It was untrue that Japanese pilots were deprived of parachutes in order to make them fight. On the contrary, there was a standard order that parachutes should be worn, but this remained a matter of personal preference.

The year 1943 saw the Allies in the southwest Pacific take their first long step along the road to Tokyo, pressing home the counter-offensive in New Guinea and fighting their way along the Solomon Island chain to Bougainville and the doorstep of Rabaul. In this phase of the war no carrier battles took place but there was plenty of air activity. One of Yamamoto's last acts was to order the air reinforcement of the Solomons. He stripped the carrier air groups of strike aircraft and launched a massive air offensive on the Allied forces in the eastern Solomons

in April 1943. It was a failure, due to the changing balance in combat efficiency between the Japanese and American pilots.

On the very first day of the offensive—April 1—18 Zeros were shot down for the loss of a mere six American fighters. Yamamoto's pilots also grossly overestimated the damage they were inflicting, and when Yamamoto called off the offensive in mid-April he believed that the fortnight's fighting had sunk a cruiser and two destroyers and that his aircraft had shot down 175 Allied machines. In fact, the Japanese had only sunk a destroyer, a tanker, an anti-submarine trawler and a merchantman, and had damaged an Australian minesweeper.

Then, on April 18, 1943, Yamamoto was killed by a long-range ambush flown by **P-38 Lightnings** out of Guadalcanal. Intelligence of his movements had been culled from wireless interception, and the Admiral was shot down while flying from Rabaul to Buin. Removing Japan's greatest naval strategist, the man who had warned that he had absolutely no confidence of victory if the war should last more than a year, was a great asset to the Allies in the Pacific. And the failure of Yamamoto's air offensive was in stark contrast to the success of Allied bombing operations against Japanese attempts to reinforce New Guinea. In March 1943 the Battle of the Bismarck Sea had been fought—36 hours of intermittent bombing attacks against a Japanese convoy from Rabaul. This convoy consisted of seven transports, eight destroyers and a collier, and it carried 7,000 troops. By nightfall on the 3rd all the transports and four of the destroyers had been sunk and over 2,000 of the troops were lost—a crushing victory for the bombers. Only five Allied aircraft were lost in the attacks.

Superfortress: The First Atom Bomber

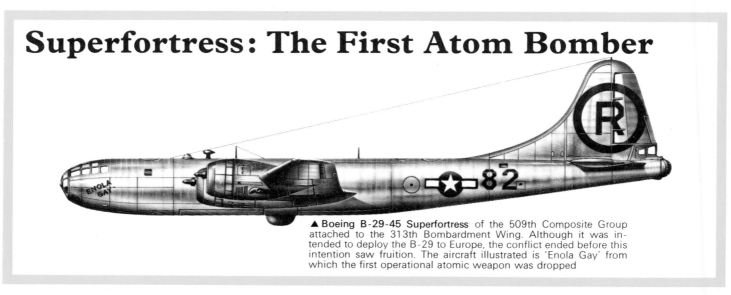

▲ **Boeing B-29-45 Superfortress** of the 509th Composite Group attached to the 313th Bombardment Wing. Although it was intended to deploy the B-29 to Europe, the conflict ended before this intention saw fruition. The aircraft illustrated is 'Enola Gay' from which the first operational atomic weapon was dropped

Above: A B-25 Mitchell Tokyo bound. On this daring raid Doolittle's lead aircraft had a take-off run of only 467 ft. as USS *Hornet* pitched in a 40 knot gale.
Right: Scratch one Mavis. After attack by US Navy fighters near Truk, one of the big Kawanishi H6K5 flying-boats starts to burn.

270 Kills in 2 days

In November 1943 the American drive in the central Pacific opened with the assault on the key atolls in the Gilbert Islands, Makin and Tarawa. The next objective was the Marshall group of islands with the main objectives neutralised by massive preliminary air strikes. After the taking of Kwajalein in the Marshalls by February 4, carrier aircraft strikes pounded the Japanese Combined Fleet's anchorage at Truk for two days, sinking two cruisers and four destroyers and accounting for 270 Japanese aircraft. The assault on Eniwetok, last objective in the Marshalls, was made with no intervention from the Japanese and the Marshalls campaign was over. The atolls of Wotje, Maloelap, Jaluit, and Mili were left isolated, and under sporadic air attacks—the Americans found that these by-passed Japanese garrisons were ideal for giving their raw pilots combat experience without undue risk.

The Japanese had no such facility. Frantic efforts to train more aircrews, sacrificing all the finer points of combat experience at the disposal of the seasoned instructors, failed even to keep pace with losses. The Japanese High Command could afford to lose the Gilberts and Marshalls but the next obvious objective on the Americans' list, the Marianas group, was vital to the defence of the Japanese homeland. The all-important battle of the central Pacific would be fought for the Marianas—the battle for which Japanese naval strategists had always yearned. To this end every effort had been made to reconstitute a fighting carrier fleet.

Only two veteran fleet carriers were left: *Shokaku* and *Zuikaku*. These had escaped the holocaust at Midway. A new fleet carrier, *Taiho*, had been commissioned. There were also six light carriers. Admiral

Ozawa, commanding the Japanese fleet, grouped his vessels into two task forces. Between them the Japanese carriers could operate 432 aircraft. The opposing carrier fleet—Admiral Marc Mitscher's huge Task Force 58—consisted of 15 carriers with a total of 900 aircraft. The invasion fleet for the Marianas was separate and it had its own air umbrella: 12 escort carriers with over 300 aircraft.

Terrifying odds

Despite the terrifying odds against them the Japanese were confident. Ozawa planned to fight the battle at long range, but he never had a chance. The Battle of the Philippine Sea took place on June 19–20, 1944. From the start every cardinal point of the Japanese plan was wrecked by superior American tactics and numbers. Ozawa had hoped to catch the Americans between hammer and anvil: trap them between the carrier aircraft of his fleet and the land-based aircraft from the airfields on the Marianas. The latter threat never materialised and Mitscher's fighters easily coped with the feeble attacks by the Japanese land-based aircraft. The Japanese carrier strikes were savaged by **Grumman F6F Hellcats**, successors to the Wildcats, 50 mph faster and with two additional heavy machine guns, and counter-attacks tore at Ozawa's fleet.

The Japanese carriers were shadowed by American submarines, which passed on accurate reports to the American carrier fleet. A Japanese pilot in the act of taking off from *Taiho* spotted a torpedo streaking towards his ship and instantly dived his plane onto it—an act of sacrifice which could not save *Taiho* from being hit by another. No serious damage seemed to have been done and *Taiho* steamed on, but lethal fuel fumes began to build up in her hull. At 1220 hours an American submarine torpedoed the *Shokaku*, which sank six hours later; and as she was going down the *Taiho* blew up. While Ozawa was shifting his flag to the cruiser *Haguro*, his last air strikes against the American fleet were being massacred. Some 373 Japanese aircraft had taken off from Ozawa's carriers on the 19th:

only 130 returned. With the Japanese land-based aircraft losses thrown in the overall Japanese loss was around 315, while the total American losses for the day were only 23 aircraft.

Frenzied dog-fight

On the 20th, the fleets were still in contact and a mass American strike of 131 aircraft set out to finish the job. A frenzied dog-fight over the battered Japanese fleet reduced the number of operational Japanese fighters to a mere 35, but the American strike only managed to inflict heavy damage on *Zuikaku* and the seaplane carrier *Chiyoda*. It was enough. Ozawa no longer had an operational carrier force and he retreated to Okinawa, leaving the American fleet free to cover the conquest of the key Marianas: Saipan, Tinian, and Guam.

The loss of the Marianas was an important milestone in the defeat of Japan. The result of Ozawa's defeat, plus the knowledge that the enemy was now at the gates of Japan with a vengeance, finally saw the frantic development of more modern fighters. The three most important types were the **Kawanishi N1K1-J** and **N1K2-J Shiden** ('George'), the **Mitsubishi J2M3 Raiden** ('Jack'), and—best of all—the **Mitsubishi A7M2 Reppu** ('Sam'). All four types finally abandoned the old Zero formula and offered Japanese pilots multiple cannon armament and armour protection. The standard Shiden had four 20-mm wing cannon often augmented by two 7.7-mm machine guns; its maximum speed was 362 mph at 19,360 feet and its service ceiling was 35,300 feet. A total of 1,435 Shidens of all versions were completed before the end of the war. The Raiden was a light interceptor which was unpopular with its pilots on account of engine troubles, structural failures and poor visibility; Saburo Sakai also thought it 'flew like a truck' compared to the old Zero. Only about 730 Raidens were built instead of the 3,700 planned. The **Reppu** (final Zero development, first flown in May, 1944) on the other hand, was a sensational machine with a story even sadder than that of the German **Me 262** jet. It could out-fly any

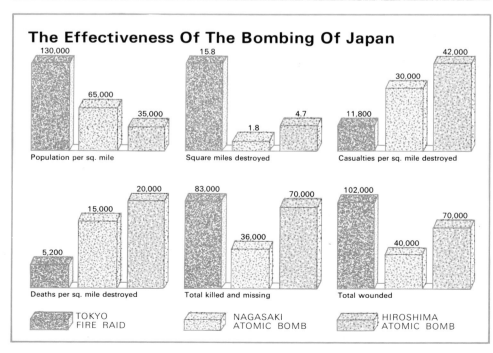

fighter the Americans had and could operate at over 40,000 feet—but only eight of these machines were completed by the end of the war. American bombers had wrecked the production-lines which should have turned the Reppu ('Sam') out in thousands.

Thus in the last months of World War II Japan's Navy pilots were still relying on the Zero, with the odds as heavily stacked against them as the Luftwaffe on the Eastern Front, and with the agonising knowledge that adequate weapons existed but too late and in insufficient quantities. And after Japan lost the Marianas a new menace faced the Japanese homelands: constant air raids by the biggest bomber of the war.

This was the **Boeing B-29 Super-fortress,** powered by four massive 2,200-hp Wright Cyclone engines. It could make 358 mph at 30,000 feet and normally carried 12,000 lbs of bombs over a range of 3,250 miles. The B-29 gave the Allies a weapon with which the long-awaited bombardment of Japan could be realised.

The first raids on Japan

The first B-29 raids on Japanese targets were made from China, a country which had battled on against the Japanese invaders ever since 1937 despite millions of casualties, the loss of all her key ports, and thousands of square miles of strategically-important territory. After the Japanese took Burma in 1942 and cut the 'Burma Road' across the eastern Himalayas, the bulk of Allied aid had to be flown into China 'over the Hump'.

Top left: Production at Nagoya. Girls at this aircraft plant are wearing headbands bearing the slogan Kamikaze (divinely sent hurricane).

Top right: Destruction at Yokohama. The sky is filled with high explosive and incendiary bombs as B-29s of the US 20th Air Force attack Japan's chief port.

Left: The F4U Corsair. Noted for its inverted gull wings, the Chance Vought Corsair was tough, powerful and superior to most Japanese fighters

---

Early and vital aid had come in the form of an airborne 'foreign legion' of volunteer fighter pilots: Claire Chennault's American Volunteer Group, the famed 'Flying Tigers'.

Chennault's men proved so important to the Chinese war effort that a major crisis of strategy arose with bitter arguments between the American ground forces adviser, General Stilwell, who argued that the Japanese could only be defeated in battle on the ground, and Chennault's contention that the key to victory over Japan lay in the air. In the event the Allies were able to operate from airfields in western China and it was from there that the first Superfortress raid on Tokyo was flown in June 1944. After a brief period of suspension the raids were resumed in November, this time from the new American bases in the Marianas. They met with little or no resistance over Japan, for no home-defence force had been created as yet. The increasingly heavier B-29 strikes began with a vengeance in December 1944. Every major city of Japan received pitiless fire raids. Japanese aviation factories were a major target from the start and the supply of new aircraft never rose above a trickle.

The Effectiveness Of The Bombing Of Japan

Population per sq. mile
130,000 / 65,000 / 35,000

Square miles destroyed
15.8 / 1.8 / 4.7

Casualties per sq. mile destroyed
11,800 / 30,000 / 42,000

Deaths per sq. mile destroyed
5,200 / 15,000 / 20,000

Total killed and missing
83,000 / 36,000 / 70,000

Total wounded
102,000 / 40,000 / 70,000

TOKYO FIRE RAID   NAGASAKI ATOMIC BOMB   HIROSHIMA ATOMIC BOMB

US Naval Aircraft of the Pacific War

▲Vought F4U-1D Corsair shipboard fighter from USS Essex (CV9) in April 1945

▲ Douglas SBD-5 Dauntless dive bomber of VMSB-231, Marine Air Group 22, South Pacific on combined operations with US Navy Task Force 58

▲ Curtiss SB2C-1 Helldiver dive bomber of VB-8 covering the Saipan operations, summer 1944

▲ Grumman F6F-3 Hellcat shipboard fighter of VF-9 flying as part of Air Group 5 from the USS Yorktown in attacks on Marcus Island, September 1943

▲ Martin PBM-5 Mariner maritime patrol flying boat, 1944-45. This was the final wartime production version of the Mariner

The Philippine Sea debacle was the last time that a Japanese carrier force met the American fleet head-on in battle, but it was not the last occasion that Japanese carriers put to sea. This occurred in October 1944 when the Americans landed at Leyte in the central Philippines. A complex Japanese naval plan was ordered into operation, which was aimed at decoying the American carriers away from the landing beaches while a concentrated Japanese battleship force got in among the landing fleet and destroyed the men on the beaches. The result was the Battle of Leyte Gulf (October 23–26, 1944)—a four-day epic which was the closest the Combined Fleet ever came to winning a major victory over the US Pacific Fleet. Air operations dominated throughout, and the total Japanese insolvency in air power was decisively proved.

Admiral Ozawa's carrier fleet consisted of four carriers with a pitiful total of 118 aircraft. This meagre parody of the superb task force which had struck at Pearl Harbor in December 1941 was now nothing more than a decoy duck to lure away the carriers of the American 3rd Fleet. The prime movers in the plan were the battleships: five of them, under Admiral Kurita, intended to break into Leyte Gulf through the San Bernadino Strait, and two under Admiral Nishimura, were to form the southern claw of a pincer movement by steaming through Surigao Strait and attacking from the south.

The fleets meet head-on

The Battle of Leyte Gulf breaks down into four main engagements. The first, Sibuyan Sea, saw the savaging of Kurita's battleship force as it approached San Bernadino Strait. Repeated American carrier aircraft attacks throughout the 24th finally sank the giant battleship *Musashi* but failed to halt the advance of the Japanese battle fleet. The second phase, Surigao Strait, was an orthodox night battleship action in the Strait which smashed Nishimura's force and averted the danger from the south. The third, Samar, saw Kurita's battleships surprise the light American escort carriers off the coast of Samar and put them to flight, only to throw away a decisive victory by withdrawing at the moment when it seemed that the fleeing carriers must be overwhelmed. And the fourth, Cape Engaño, saw the inevitable destruction of Ozawa's decoy carrier force by Admiral Halsey's pilots. Leyte Gulf was the greatest naval battle of World War II and was a clear-cut defeat for the Japanese. But it also ushered in a new phase of air warfare that is still unique: the Kamikaze strike, flown by dedicated pilots determined to sacrifice themselves by becoming human bombs and taking an enemy warship and its crew with them when they died.

The mentality behind the Kamikazes staggered Western minds and is still usually misunderstood. The legend itself was deep-rooted in the lore of Japan, for the Kamikaze was the miraculous cyclone (the word literally means 'Divine Wind') which had scattered Kublai Khan's invasion fleet in 1281 and saved Japan from a Mongol invasion. The Kamikazes of World War II were not fanatical suicides. Their motivation was 'one man, one warship'—an equation which offered Japan the only chance of whittling

down the vast American superiority in late 1944 and 1945.

A Kamikaze strike consisted simply of aircraft, single- or twin-engined, armed with bombs. Given fighter escort to the vicinity of the American fleet to be attacked, the Kamikaze pilot would then seek to crash his plane on an enemy warship—a carrier for preference. The ideal point was the flight-deck elevator, so that the exploding plane could create a holocaust in the carrier's hangers. Standard aircraft were used for the attack. Only one specialised Kamikaze aircraft was developed and this was more of a manned, stand-off rocket missile than a conventional aircraft — the **Yokosuka MXY-8 Ohka** ('Cherry Blossom')—which the Americans nicknamed *Baka*, or 'fool bomb'. Carried like an outsize torpedo beneath a bomber, the Ohka would pick up 200 mph of gliding speed for about 50 miles after being dropped at around 27,000 feet. The pilot would then fire his three solid-fuel rockets for his final dive onto the target at 570 mph. The Ohka's warhead consisted of a devastating 2,645 lb of high explosive.

1,900 Kamikaze sorties

The war had seen many examples of pilots deliberately crashing their machines onto enemy ships, presumably either desperately wounded or in the private knowledge that they stood no chance of escape; nor was this a prerogative of Japanese pilots only. But the first Kamikaze raids are accepted to have occurred during the running fight off Samar in the Battle of Leyte Gulf, when a land-based Zero crashed through the flight deck of the light carrier *St Lo* and sank her. In the last two major campaigns of the Pacific war, Iwo Jima and Okinawa, Kamikaze raids took over as the spearhead of the Japanese air defensive.

At Okinawa, the battle which carried the Americans to the very doorstep of Japan, about 1,900 Kamikaze sorties were counted (compared to 5,000 sorties by normal bombers). Their total score off Okinawa was 24 ships and landing-craft sunk (all of them American), and 202 damaged, of which four were British. Against the Kamikazes the armoured flight-decks of the British aircraft carriers proved an invaluable asset.

The Kamikazes made history in that they were the first really effective anti-shipping missile in the modern sense, but for all that they were a measure of desperation. Their impressive successes remained as low as they were because only skilled pilots could have singled out the really important ships to be attacked and crashed their aircraft at the most vulnerable spot—and the experienced pilots, typified by Saburo Sakai, regarded the Kamikazes as a waste of invaluable combat experience while respecting the motivation of those who actually flew such sorties. By the last months of the Pacific war, moreover, Japan's chronic shortage of aircraft and of fuel to fly them was making itself felt. Nevertheless the Allied planners knew that intense Kamikaze activity was only to be expected as they prepared for the last battle of the war: the decisive invasion of the Japanese homeland.

The latter was made unnecessary by the Japanese acceptance of surrender terms, an acceptance forced upon them by the two

atomic bomb detonations at Hiroshima (August 6) and Nagasaki (August 9). Both bombs were delivered by single B-29s flying from the Marianas, and were air bursts. The morality behind the use and even the necessity for using the atomic bomb against Japan has troubled humanity ever since 1945, but one fact is inescapable. The bombs used at Hiroshima and Nagasaki possessed only a tiny power compared with the weapons later developed in peacetime. Only two nuclear weapons have ever been used as weapons of war and those were the ones dropped on Hiroshima and Nagasaki. They were not only a deterrent to die-hard Japanese leaders who wanted to fight on to the end. For the years since 1945 their memory has proved one of the most decisive strategic deterrents in military history.

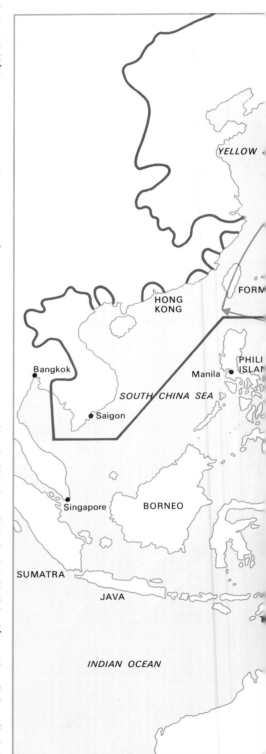

PRINCIPAL PACIFIC WARPLANES 1942–45; FIGHTERS									
Country	Type	First ordered	Max. speed	Max. loaded range	Rate of climb	Ceiling	Bomb load/ Armament	Crew	Number supplied
Japan	Nakajima Army 1 Ki-43 'Oscar'	1940	304 mph	750 miles	5 mins 30 secs to 16,400 ft	36,800 ft	Two 12.7-mm machine-guns; two 550-lb bombs	1	5,878
	Kawasaki Ki-61 'Tony'	1941	348 mph	1,185 miles	6 mins to 16,400 ft	32,800 ft	Two 20-mm cannon, two 12.7-mm machine-guns; two 550-lb bombs	1	2,753
	Nakajima Ki-84 'Frank'	1943	388 mph	1,815 miles	6 mins 26 secs to 16,400 ft	35,000 ft	Two 20-mm cannon, two 12.7-mm machine-guns; 1,100 lbs of bombs	1	3,500
	Mitsubishi J2M3 'Jack'	1943	380 mph	655 miles	5 mins 50 secs to 19,865 ft	37,800 ft	Four 20-mm cannon	1	about 500
	Kawanishi N1K2-J 'George'	1943	362 mph	890 miles	5 mins 50 secs to 19,865 ft	35,300 ft	Two 20-mm cannon, two 7.7-mm machine-guns; two 550-lb bombs	1	1,007
United States	Chance Vought F4U Corsair	1941	446 mph	1,562 miles	7.7 mins to 20,000 ft	41,000 ft	Six .50-in Browning machine-guns; two 1,000-lb bombs or eight 5-in rockets	1	12,681
	Grumman F6F Hellcat	1942	371 mph	1,495 miles	10 mins to 20,000 ft	37,300 ft	Six .50-in machine-guns	1	12,272
	Northrop P-61 Black Widow	1941	362 mph	600 miles	10 mins to 20,000 ft	33,100 ft	Four 20-mm cannon; four 0.50 in machine guns	3	704

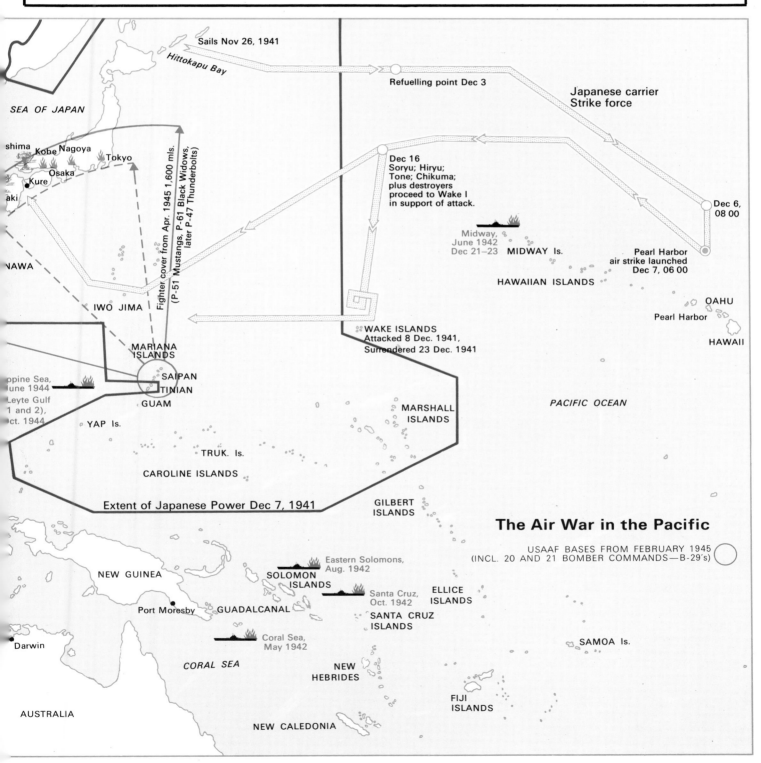

The Air War in the Pacific

The Elite

World War II produced a fighter ace, Erich Hartmann, with the incredible score of over 350 victories and the lionisation of fighter pilots, which began during World War I, was continued. But the rapid expansion of roles that aircraft were called upon to play demanded specialists in many other fields and inevitably some flyers mastered these new aerial skills better than others. These tank-busters, ship-busters and bomber pilots, along with the fighter aces, were the second air war's elite.

Inevitably, the first aces of World War II to hit the headlines were fighter pilots. They possessed all the glamour of the individualists who flew alone at almost unbelievable speeds and faced their enemy in personal combat. Just as naturally, the fighter aces held the limelight throughout the war. But between 1939 and 1945 the spreading intricacies of air warfare produced a crop of specialists, aces in lesser-known (and less glamorous) trades: dive-bombing, level bombing, ground strafing, and anti-shipping strikes.

The first fighter ace to emerge in Britain sprung to fame during the short-lived Battle of France: 'Cobber' Kain, a New Zealand-born fighter pilot who claimed 17 victories before being killed in a crash. The Battle of Britain soon produced more British aces. There was Douglas Bader, remarkable for the fact that he had lost both legs during a foolhardy stunting flight in a **Bristol Bulldog** in 1931 and had fought his way back into the RAF through sheer obstinacy. Then there was Robert Stanford Tuck, a master of aerobatics and a phenomenal shot, often to be seen fondling a penny buckled in his pocket by a German bullet. Bader and Tuck were both subsequently captured, Bader after a mid-air collision with a **Me 109** in 1941 and Tuck on a low-level attack in January 1942. Both later met in prison camp. Other British aces of the Battle of Britain who survived to become senior unit commanders later in the war included 'Sailor' Malan, Al Deere, and 'Johnnie' Johnson, the latter emerging as the top British fighter ace in Europe with 38 victories. As far as the Battle of Britain was concerned the top British scorer was an NCO: Sergeant Pilot James Harry 'Ginger' Lacey, with a score of 18 aircraft destroyed by the end of October 1940. Lacey was awarded a commission in January 1941 and ended the war in Burma, commanding No. 17 Squadron in operations against the Japanese.

The first Luftwaffe fighter aces emerged during the Spanish Civil War. That experience, plus the Polish and Scandinavian campaigns, meant that the Luftwaffe had the most battle-tested fighter pilots of any combatant nation in the European theatre in 1940. Germany's first air hero of World War II was Capt. Werner Mölders, who had won 14 victories in the Spanish Civil War and also evolved and introduced the loose 'finger-four' fighter combat formation. Mölders was the first pilot to exceed the top score of World War I, the 80 victories of the 'Red Baron', Manfred von Richthofen. On the Russian front in July 1941, Mölders became the first pilot ever to achieve over 100 aerial victories. He won Germany's highest award, the Knight's Cross of the Iron Cross with Oak Leaves, Swords and Diamonds. General of Fighters at the time of his death in 1941 with an overall score of 115 victories, Mölders was a legend. But his achievement was soon to be eclipsed.

Past the 300 mark

Adolf Galland took over from Mölders as General of Fighters and although he spent most of the rest of the war in stormy tussles with Hitler and Göring over fighter strategy he nevertheless ended the war with 104 victories, all scored in the West, having finally won approval for the formation of an élite combat fighter unit—far too late to reverse the Allied air supremacy. The first pilot to score 150 victories was Major Gordon Gollob, in August 1942. That record only stood for a month before being exceeded by Captain Hermann Graf with 200.

Another year was needed before the 250 mark was reached, with Major Walter Nowotny; and the magic figure of 300 was passed by Captain Erich Hartmann on August 24, 1944, on the Soviet front. Hartmann ended the war commanding I Gruppe of J.G. 52, the famous Luftwaffe fighter unit, with a personal score of 352 and the rank of major. Only one other pilot achieved over 300 victories: Gerd Barkhorn, Hartmann's close friend, with a personal score of 301.

Hartmann's amazing score has formed part of a stormy controversy over the accuracy of German victory claims, but has long since been vindicated. The immense numerical odds against the Luftwaffe meant that those who survived in Soviet Russia—on both sides—were formidable propositions in the air. Hartmann's own recipe for victory depended on careful assessment of the target and then a lightning attack, firing from as close in as possible. Like every other young fighter pilot (Hartmann was only 20 when first posted to Sovet Russia) Hartmann made stupid mistakes at the front before he learned his trade. But he was particularly fortunate by being coached by a wily collection of professionals who had learned to survive the hard way. And Hartmann was far from being a gifted individualist who operated on his own. In eight hundred combat missions he only once had his wingman shot down. When the war ended, and he and Hermann Graf were in danger of falling into Russian hands, Hartmann and Graf were ordered to fly out to the West but both declined to do so and accepted Soviet captivity with their comrades.

Hartmann's remarkable story must be compared with that of Hans-Joachim Marseille, the ace of North Africa. Flying with J.G.27—the *Afrika* fighter group—Marseille shot to fame as the undoubted Luftwaffe ace in the West in 1941/42, with a final score of 158. A master of deflection shooting, Marseille was adept in racking up multiple kills, his personal best for a day's hunting being 12. He lost his life over Alamein on September 30, 1942, flying one of the new **Me 109Gs** which suffered from engine trouble, filling his cockpit with smoke. Marseille was killed baling out. He had fought as a fledgling pilot in the Battle of Britain, and all his kills were against British-flown aircraft.

Uniting the élite

The latter point was of great significance in the German victory-registration system, for the Luftwaffe always accepted the superior technical and human skills encountered in combat in the West. But it has taken many years for the formerly neglected Soviet fighter aces to receive their due. As with their ground forces the Russians concentrated their élite into 'Guards' units, which put a constant edge on their morale. Russia's best pilots flew in these squadrons, men whose make-up was definitely above the ordinary. One such was Capt. Vladimir Lavrinenkov (who ended the war with 35 victories). Having downed an Me 109 and watched its pilot get away from the wreck in safety, Lavrinenkov landed nearby, tracked down the German pilot in the undergrowth, and strangled him with his bare hands before taking off again.

These 'Stalin Falcons', as they were known, were the Luftwaffe's most respected opponents on the Eastern Front. Their official top two aces were Ivan Kozhedub with 62 victories, and Alexander 'Sasha' Pokryshkin with 59. There followed Grigori Rechkalov with 58, Nikolai Gulayev with 57, and Kirill Yevstigneev with 52. Apart from these five '50-plus' Soviet aces, seven more were credited with more victories than the leading Anglo-American ace, Major Richard Bong, who scored his 40 kills in the Pacific against the Japanese.

The Japanese divided their air arm into Army and Navy, with the best weapons—particularly the fine Zero fighter—going to the Navy first. Its best pilots were not carefully watched and weeded out for rest periods when approaching the breaking point: they were kept on operations until they dropped. Nor was there any such system of decorations or regular promotion as was to be found in the air forces of the other

Hans-Joachim
Marseille, top
Luftwaffe ace in the
West, with a final
score of 158.

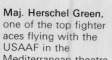

Gerd Barkhorn.
His 301 victories
make him only the
third pilot to
exceed a score
of 300.

Maj. Herschel Green,
one of the top fighter
aces flying with the
USAAF in the
Mediterranean theatre.

Douglas Bader,
the remarkable
British legless ace.

Adolf Galland, German
General of Fighters and an
ace with a score of 104.

Sgt. Pilot 'Ginger'
Lacey, top British ace
in the Battle of
Britain.

The Fighters of the Luftwaffe Aces

▲ Emblem of III/JG.2, and JG.2

▲ Bf 109F of Hauptmann Assi Hahn Kommandeur III/JG.2, St. Pol, summer 1941 with (right) detail of Hauptmann Hahn's 31 "kills". Major Hahn was shot down and captured on February 21, 1943 with total of 108 victories

▲ Emblem of IV/JG.51

▲ Bf 109F of Hauptmann Heinz Bär, Kommandeur IV/JG.51, Kerch, May 1942, with 113 "kills", and (right) detail of Bär's rudder marking

▲ Emblem of JG.1.

▲ Fw 190A of Major Heinz Bär, Kommandeur II/JG.1, Stormede, April 22, 1944, at time of 200th "kill" (rudder detail at right). Oberstleutnant Bär's final total was 220

▲ Emblem of I/JG. 27

▲ Bf 109F of Oberleutnant Hans-Joachim Marseille, Staffelkapitän 3/JG.27, Ain-El Gazala, June 17, 1942, with score of 101, and (right) detail of Marseille's rudder. Killed on September 30, 1942 with score of 158

▼ "Ace of Hearts" emblem on Fw 190 of Hauptmann Josef Priller, Gruppenkommandeur III/JG.26. Oberst Priller assumed command of JG.26 on January 11, 1943, and ended war with 101 victories

▲ Bf 109E of Oberleutnant Jochen Müncheberg, Staffelkapitän 7/JG 26, Gela, Sicily, February 12, 1941, at time of 24th "kill"—a Hurricane over Malta. Killed in action as Kommodore JG.77 in Tunisia, March 23, 1943, with 135 victories

▼ Tail of Oberstleutnant Gollob's Bf 109F (Kommodore JG.77) showing 107 "kills", Russia, June 24, 1942. Became Inspektor der Jagdflieger and ended war with 160 victories

▼ Major Hartmann retained the "Karaya" heart emblem of his old staffel, 9/JG.52, when he flew this Bf 109G as Kommandeur II/JG.52

▲Tail of Oberleutnant Erich Hartmann's Bf 109F (9/JG. 52) showing 121 "kills". Major Erich Hartmann ended war as Gruppenkommandeur II/JG.52 and Luftwaffe's top-scoring ace with 352 victories

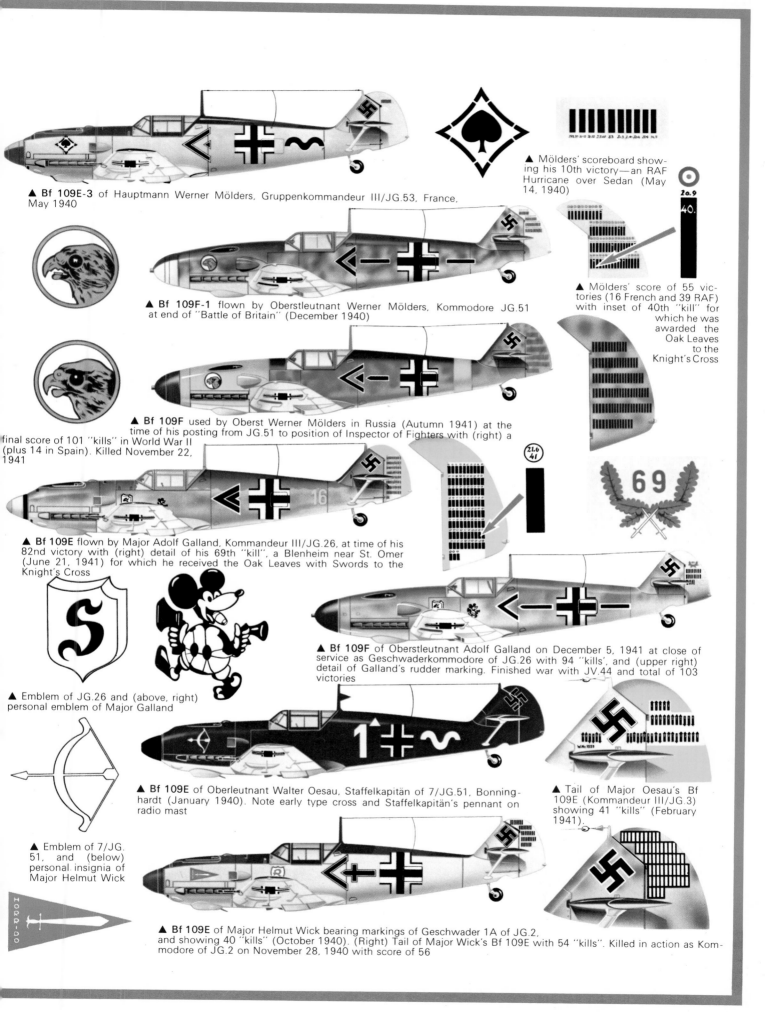

▲ Bf 109E-3 of Hauptmann Werner Mölders, Gruppenkommandeur III/JG.53, France, May 1940

▲ Mölders' scoreboard showing his 10th victory—an RAF Hurricane over Sedan (May 14, 1940)

▲ Bf 109F-1 flown by Oberstleutnant Werner Mölders, Kommodore JG.51 at end of "Battle of Britain" (December 1940)

▲ Mölders' score of 55 victories (16 French and 39 RAF) with inset of 40th "kill" for which he was awarded the Oak Leaves to the Knight's Cross

▲ Bf 109F used by Oberst Werner Mölders in Russia (Autumn 1941) at the time of his posting from JG.51 to position of Inspector of Fighters with (right) a final score of 101 "kills" in World War II (plus 14 in Spain). Killed November 22, 1941

▲ Bf 109E flown by Major Adolf Galland, Kommandeur III/JG.26, at time of his 82nd victory with (right) detail of his 69th "kill", a Blenheim near St. Omer (June 21, 1941) for which he received the Oak Leaves with Swords to the Knight's Cross

▲ Bf 109F of Oberstleutnant Adolf Galland on December 5, 1941 at close of service as Geschwaderkommodore of JG.26 with 94 "kills", and (upper right) detail of Galland's rudder marking. Finished war with JV.44 and total of 103 victories

▲ Emblem of JG.26 and (above, right) personal emblem of Major Galland

▲ Bf 109E of Oberleutnant Walter Oesau, Staffelkapitän of 7/JG.51, Bonninghardt (January 1940). Note early type cross and Staffelkapitän's pennant on radio mast

▲ Tail of Major Oesau's Bf 109E (Kommandeur III/JG.3) showing 41 "kills" (February 1941).

▲ Emblem of 7/JG. 51, and (below) personal insignia of Major Helmut Wick

▲ Bf 109E of Major Helmut Wick bearing markings of Geschwader 1A of JG.2, and showing 40 "kills" (October 1940). (Right) Tail of Major Wick's Bf 109E with 54 "kills". Killed in action as Kommodore of JG.2 on November 28, 1940 with score of 56

combatant powers.

A case in point was that of one of Japan's supreme air fighters, Saburo Sakai. A Navy pilot, he had left Japan for the China front in May 1938 (a reminder that by the time of Pearl Harbor Japan had even more combat experience than Germany, for her war with China had ground on without a break since 1937). Sakai started his war against the USA flying fighter sweeps out of Formosa against the Philippines. He later served during the conquest of the Dutch East Indies and was then transferred, with other crack fighter pilots, to a new Wing operating from an improvised airfield at Lae in New Guinea.

One-eyed killer

At Lae, flying in partnership with Hiroyoshi Nishizawa, who had achieved 101 confirmed kills at the time of his death in 1944, and Toshio Ota, Sakai became one of Japan's greatest Zero aces. Grievously wounded in the head during the fight for Guadalcanal, he managed to fly his Zero over 500 miles back to Rabaul and land in one piece. He lost his right eye and was declared unfit for combat flying, but was nevertheless hauled back onto operations by the desperate shortage of trained pilots. Shocked by the order to crash his bomb-laden Zero deliberately into an American warship, he was unable to do so, automatically accepting combat as the American fighters intercepted his suicide mission, and he survived the war with an accredited total of 60 kills. Honours unprecedented in the Imperial Japanese Navy were paid to Sakai. In 1944 he was promoted from warrant officer to ensign after 11 years' service. All other such honorary promotions had previously been made posthumously.

Examples such as this give a rough indication of the comparative intensity of the air fighting on the different fronts in World War II. First came the German–Russian front, then that of the Pacific theatre, which roughly tied with Western Europe. But the day fighters were not the only aces of the war.

Other specialists emerged such as Hans-Ulrich Rudel, Germany's ace Stuka pilot and tank-buster, with one Soviet battleship and 515 destroyed tanks to his credit, to say nothing of his 2,500 operational sorties! Then there were the night fighters, Germany's Helmuth Lent and Heinz-Wolfgang Schnaufer, with 110 and 121 confirmed victories respectively, and Britain's 'Cat's Eyes' Cunningham. America's Colonel 'Jimmy' Doolittle personally led the daring raid on Tokyo in April 1942, carried out by **B-25 Mitchells** taking-off from the flight deck of the carrier *Hornet* and flying on to China; Doolittle survived the raid and went on to become a leading American bomber general. Britain's own bomber hero, Guy Gibson, the man who led the now famous 'Dambusters', did not survive the war. He insisted on returning to operations and was killed over Holland in September 1944 after leading a raid from a Mosquito.

Then there were the élite units. Foremost among these was the Luftwaffe's J.G. 52, credited with over 10,000 air victories in four years. J.G. 52 aces included the world's three top-scorers: Erich Hartmann (352), Gerd Barkhorn (301), and Günther

TOP ACES OF WORLD WAR 2		
Country	*Ace*	*'Kills'*
Germany	Hartmann, Erich	352
	Barkhorn, Gerhard	301
	Rall, Günther	275
	Kittel, Otto	267
	Nowotny, Walter	258
	Batz, Wilhelm	237
	Rudorffer, Erich	222
	Bär, Heinz	220 (16 with Me 262 jet)
	Graf, Hermann	212
Great Britain	Pattle, M. P. st. J.	41+
	Johnson, J. E.	38
	Malan, A. G.	35
Soviet Union	Kozhedub, Ivan Nikitch	62
	Pokryshkin, Alexander Ivanovich	59
	Rechkalov, Grigori Andreevich	58
	Gulaev, Niklaev Dmitrievich	57
	Yevstigneev, Kirill Alekseevich	52
United States	Bong, Richard	40

Rall (275 victories). Together with Willi Batz (237), Hermann Graf (212) and Helmut Lipfert (203), these aces alone accounted for 1,580 Allied aircraft. The Luftwaffe's anti-shipping K.G. 26 *Löwen* wing, with torpedo-carrying **He 111s,** scored heavily during the destruction of Convoy PQ-17 in early July 1942.

The bomber heroes

Britain's No. 617 Squadron, 'The Dambusters', became the RAF's crack bomber unit, sinking the *Tirpitz* and carrying out other devastating pinpoint raids with the super-heavy 'Tallboy' and 'Grand Slam' bombs. As for the massed squadrons of the American 8th Air Force, which flew the terrible daylight raids over Germany, it is almost impossible to select any particular unit for particular gallantry.

Out in the Pacific, Sakai's Lae wing became the most successful Japanese fighter unit of the Pacific war. Between April–July 1942 constant air battles raged over New Guinea during the Japanese attempts to take Port Moresby and in those months the Zeros of the Lae wing reigned supreme, claiming 19 Allied fighters on June 16 alone—the record day for the period.

The Japanese custom of not awarding decorations to servicemen was unique. Public recognition of gallantry in the form of posthumous promotion was the norm. For every other combatant power in World War II, a lavish selection of medals paid tribute to the various grades of gallantry as officially recognised, and to the length of service in the various theatres of war.

The British had always followed a caste system which differentiated between officers and enlisted men. The supreme award for valour—the Victoria Cross—was an obvious exception: it was awarded both to officers and to non-commissioned men of all three services. World War II and the bombing by the Luftwaffe added a civilian equivalent created by King George VI—the George Cross. In 1942 the stubborn defence of Malta prompted the King to decorate the island of Malta with the George Cross in recognition of its heroic resistance to the bombs of the Luftwaffe and the Italian air force. After the Victoria Cross came the Distinguished Service Order (DSO), which was awarded to officers only, and then the Distinguished Flying Cross (DFC)—the RAF's equivalent to the Military Cross.

An amusing point of inter-service etiquette was thrown up during the Battle of Britain. The Navy's equivalent decoration to the DFC was the Distinguished Service Cross (DSC), and a Fleet Air Arm pilot, Sub-Lieutenant R. Cork, was awarded the DFC while

flying **Hurricanes** in Douglas Bader's 242 Squadron. Subsequent instructions from the Admiralty for Cork to replace his DFC ribbon with that of the DSC were overridden by Bader while Cork stayed with the

---

Far left, top: Scramble! Some of 'The Few'. The pilots of 19 Squadron.
Far left, bottom: Bomber Supremo. General Curtis LeMay, the man who directed the brave American bombing effort in Europe.
Left, top: The RAF's first ace. New Zealander 'Cobber' Kain who claimed 17 victories in the short Battle of France.
Left, centre: 'Cats Eyes' Cunningham, early night-fighter ace.
Below: Goering and Mölders. Goering, Luftwaffe overlord and World War I ace, made Mölders, the first man to score 100 victories, his General of Fighters.
Bottom: Stanford Tuck, a master of aerobatics and an incredible shot.

RAF, but the Admiralty won in the end when Cork returned to the Fleet Air Arm. For non-commissioned British aircrew the standard gallantry award was the Distinguished Flying Medal (DFM).

Diamonds for nine aces

The German equivalent to the DSO was the *Ritterkreuz*—the Knight's Cross of the Iron Cross. About 1,300 Luftwaffe men won the Knight's Cross in World War II. This basic decoration had three ascending 'bars': Oak Leaves, Oak Leaves and Swords, and finally the coveted Diamonds. Nine Luftwaffe aces won the Diamonds (including the two night fighter aces, Lent and Schnaufer) and 25 won the Oak Leaves and Swords—the 'cabbage and knives and forks' was its irreverent Luftwaffe nickname. Decorations of the Oak Leaves and above were normally awarded by Hitler in person. Below the Knight's Cross came the German Cross in Gold, then the Iron Cross itself, 1st and 2nd Classes.

The supreme American award was the Congressional Medal of Honor, with its pendant star worn suspended from a bar in the case of the army and army air force and from an anchor in that of the navy. Other leading American medals included the Silver Star, a handsome five-pointed decoration with a miniature silver star at its centre. For the air force the Americans, too, had their Distinguished Flying Cross: a cruciform bronze design bearing the emblem of a four-bladed airscrew. Other services cast unjustified sneers at the two American medals considered to be 'sent up with the rations'. These were the Air Medal for so many missions flown, and the Purple Heart for disabilities suffered while in contact with the enemy. The latter medal came in for much criticism—it was sometimes said that Purple Hearts were handed out for catching a cold while in a theatre of war. Merely to be hit by enemy fire was not the only qualification: it called for just as much courage, for example, for an unwounded B-17 gunner to stay in the shattered fuselage of his aircraft and in so doing contract frostbite.

Soviet Russia was lavish with awards. Apart from the coveted Gold Star of the Hero of the Soviet Union there were the Order of Lenin, Order of the Red Banner and the Order of the Red Star. Both Ivan Kozhedub and 'Sacha' Pokryshkin were three times decorated with the supreme Russian medal, the Gold Star.

The top three French decorations were the *Légion d'honneur*, the *Croix de Guerre*, and the *Medaille Militaire*. As for the Italian air force, the *Regia Aeronautica*, it held to the gold, silver, and bronze medals for valour.

Multi-national chestfuls of medal ribbons were not uncommon during World War II. There were, after all, very few combatant air forces without their foreign contingents. Americans, Poles, Czechs, and Free French flew with the RAF. Rumanians and Hungarians (and later Italians) served in Luftwaffe units as well as with their own national air forces. Theatre ribbons, too, helped to bridge international barriers. There were medals for service in the Pacific, on the Burma front, in North Africa, the European theatre of operations, and the Atlantic.

THRUST into a new era

The first jet-powered aircraft flew in Germany before the outbreak of World War II and, such was her lead, there is little doubt that had development been effectively pursued it could have virtually guaranteed Germany unassailable superiority in the air. As it was the Germans did manage to produce some frightening new weapons, including the first ballistic missiles and the world's first operational jet fighters and bombers. These early steps paved the way for the most significant advances in aviation history and put mankind on the threshold of a breakthrough into space.

In the history of air warfare, World War II was particularly important in that it saw the appearance of jet aircraft and rocket missiles, experiments which put mankind on the threshold of space. It also introduced the ballistic missile, under the shadow of which the world has lived ever since.

The principle of jet and rocket flight had been known for thousands of years: the thrust created by a 'slow-burning' explosion. Two basic methods of obtaining such an effect exist: the chemical rocket and the air-breathing jet engine. With the rocket engine the vehicle carries all its own fuel and burns it in a combustion chamber; with the jet, the engine draws in oxygen from the atmosphere.

The first practical experiments to produce such a reaction-thrust aircraft were made in Germany in the 1930s, starting with the familiar principle of the rocket. Towards the end of 1935, Prof. Ernst Heinkel began to experiment with rocket engines as aircraft power plants, working in collaboration with the young engineer Wernher von Braun, an employee of the German army's missile section. The first trials were made with a rocket mounted in the fuselage of a **Heinkel He 112** fighter.

These tests were carried out in the discouraging atmosphere of complete disinterest on the part of the Luftwaffe High Command and the first successful flight with the hybrid test-bed was made in the summer of 1937. Heinkel's next move was to build a properly-designed rocket aircraft and this he did with the **He 176,** powered by a Walter rocket with a duration of one minute. The first successful flight with the He 176 was made at Peenemünde on June 20, 1939, but met with great disfavour. Heinkel was an aircraft manufacturer: his first concern must be the production of orthodox machines for the Luftwaffe. Even a demonstration of the He 176 before Hitler and Göring on July 3, 1939, failed to obtain recognition for Heinkel's experiments, and his rocket aircraft was written off as nothing more than an interesting but time-consuming toy.

The same applied to Heinkel's experiments with turbo-jet engines, on which he had been working since 1936. Heinkel developed the jet experiments a young physicist, Pabst von Ohain, who had produced a workable engine by September 1937. By the summer of 1939 Heinkel was ready for flying tests with his specially-designed **He 178.** The first flight was made on August 27—five days before the outbreak of war. The demonstration, witnessed by Milch and Udet (Göring did not bother to attend) was a complete success. But again Heinkel found his work discounted by his superiors, the official attitude being that he was a 'bomber manufacturer'. A development contract for a jet engine went to Junkers, and Messerschmitt was given the job of evolving an airframe for it.

The realms of dream speeds

While working on the jet aircraft programme, Alexander Lippisch, a designer working with Messerschmitt, pressed ahead with his own ideas for a tail-less delta-wing aircraft, the product of his original experiments with sailplanes and various piston-engined designs. The result was the stocky **Messerschmitt Me 163,** shaped like a broad arrowhead. It was ready for flying trials by the spring of 1941, and behaved so well in its gliding tests that powered tests began at once, with Heini Dittmar as test pilot. Successive flights with increased amount of fuel in the tanks finally resulted in the first full-power test on Oct. 2, 1941, when the Me 163 passed the 1,000 km per hour (623 mph) mark—a 'dream speed' in those days. Despite this success, Dittmar experienced the first warnings of the threshold of the sound-barrier—the excessive build-up of pressure waves caused by an insufficiently streamlined aircraft travelling too fast. Violent tail flutter was followed by a headlong dive, but Dittmar was able to cut his rocket engine, recover control, and land safely. Experiments continued with the **Me 163A;** it had no undercarriage and landed on a skid, and Dittmar

Arado Ar 234B-2 Blitz bomber of 9. Staffel/Kampfgeschwader operating from Achmer in 1945

Heinkel He 162A-2 'Volksjäger' fighter of 3. Staffel/Jagdge-chwader 1 at Leck, Schleswig-Holstein, in April 1945

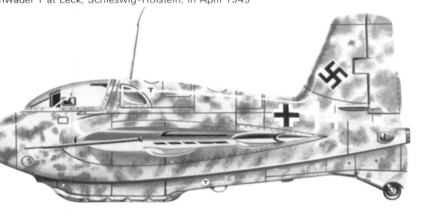

▲ Messerschmitt Me 163B-1a Komet rocket-propelled interceptor of 2. Staffel/Jagdgeschwader 400 at Brandis, 1945

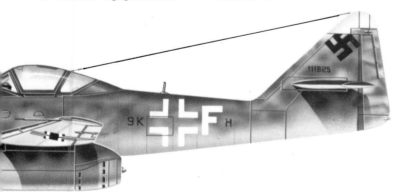

Messerschmitt Me 262A-2a fighter-bomber of 1. Staffel/ ampfgeschwader 51 at Achmer, spring 1945

dropped out after receiving severe spine injuries in a heavy landing. His place was taken by Rudolf Opitz, another famed sail-plane pilot. Test Commando 16 was formed at Bad Zwischenahn to work up the Me 163 and train the Luftwaffe's first rocket inter-ceptor unit to fly the operational version—the **Me 163B Komet,** or 'powered egg'!

It was an exceptionally dangerous task. The Komet was powered by volatile chemi-cals—'T-Stoff', a hydrogen peroxide and alcohol/hydrazine 'C-Stoff'—which explod-ed when mixed. Many fatalities were caused by the fuel dregs in the tanks igniting on landing a shade too 'hard'. The Test Com-mando 16 pilots started with gliding flights in the Me 163A, and then went on to 'sharp' (powered) starts before going on to the fully operational 163B. The engine of the latter had a full power duration of 8 minutes, but produced a phenomenal rate of climb, taking only 3 minutes 25 seconds to reach 39,370 feet. Twin cannon in the wing roots were the standard armament. Later experi-ments resulted in the adoption of vertically-firing shells triggered by light-sensitive cells in the wing roots and a battery of 24 R4M underwing rockets. The Me 163B was not a success in combat. Its pilots found that even its speed could not save it from the dense defensive fire of American B-17 formations and it was particularly vulnerable when gliding in to land. Allied pilots soon dis-covered this and took to having a brace of Mustangs waiting to shoot down the power-less and defenceless Komets as they turned in for their landing.

Sensational ideas betrayed

The story of the **Messerschmitt Me 262** jet fighter, though different in essence, was still that of a sensational idea betrayed by ignorance and indifference in high places. Messerschmitt's airframe, powered by an ordinary piston-engine, first flew success-fully in April 1941, but the first turbo-jet engines did not arrive from BMW in Berlin for another six months. Flying tests, begin-ning in March, 1942, revealed that the turbine blades of the first engines could not stand the strain and further delays followed until the arrival of the superior Junkers Jumo 004 turbo-jets. The Me 262's first successful test flight took place on July 18, 1942. At this stage it was still fitted with an orthodox tail-wheel undercarriage which compelled the pilot to apply the brakes at 110 mph to bring the tail up and take off. But its per-formance fulfilled all hopes.

Then, on August 17, 1942, an accident wrote off the only flying prototype of the Me 262 and retarded its development for months. FM. Milch at the Reich Air Ministry was not convinced at this stage that the 262 was anything more than a promising toy; in December 1942 its development was ap-proved at the rate of only 20 per month—for 1944! No real breakthrough came until General of Fighters Adolf Galland flew the Me 262 in May 1943 and immediately pressed for its adoption. For a time Hitler

◀ Germany's jet leadership. Four types, which could have given Germany un-challenged superiority in the air, had their potential been recognised earlier. But there were 'too few, too late' to change the Nazis' fortunes.

insisted that the 262 be developed as a 'blitz bomber', but at last the Me 262 joined the Luftwaffe as the most revolutionary fighter of the war.

The twin Junkers Jumo 004B turbo-jets gave the Me 262 a maximum speed of 540 mph at 19,684 feet. Its armament consisted of four 30-mm MK 108 cannon, augmented later by a devastating 'broadside' of 24 R4M rockets fitted under the wings. Used with the specially-developed EZ-42 gyro gunsight this gave the 262 an irresistible stand-off punch for use against the B-17 formations. The Me 262, Allied Intelligence believed when it appeared, could not fly on one engine, but Allied pilots often found of course, that this was a myth. The Me 262 was almost impossible to catch in a straight chase; its speed prevented Allied ground radar from tracking it, and the only way of bringing it down was by extremely hazardous power-dives which stressed the best Allied piston-engined fighters to the limit. German AA fire around the 262's airfields made the tactic of intercepting it as it turned in to land almost suicidal.

A desperation entry

The development of a successful jet engine in the Jumo 004B led directly to work on a fast reconnaissance bomber, the **Arado Ar 234 Blitz,** which the Allies first encountered after the Normandy landings in June 1944. It was a single-seat, twin-engined machine with a tricycle undercarriage. The **B-1** was an unarmed, photo-reconnaissance aircraft; the **B-2** could carry external bomb-loads: up to 3,086 lbs under the fuselage and up to 1,102 lbs beneath each of the engine nacelles. The Ar 234 was flung desperately into the battle on the Western Front in late 1944 and 1945 but only saw active service in small numbers. Its most celebrated appearance in action, together with bomb-carrying Me 262s, was in the frantic series of attempts to destroy the American held bridgehead across the Rhine at Remagen.

Before the end of the war a four-engined variant of the Ar 234, the **234 C-series,** had been ordered into production. This was powered by four BMW 003 turbo-jets and clocked a speed of 520 mph at sea level on test. The C-series variants consisted of a photo-reconnaissance machine **(C-1),** a straight bomber carrying a maximum load of 4,400 lbs of bombs **(C-2)** with a range of 472 miles, and the multi-purpose **C-3.** Another series, the **Ar 234, P-1, P-3, P-4,** and **P-5,** was under development by the end of the war

and these were night-fighter variants. But in general the story of the Ar 234 was that of the Me 262—too little and too late.

The Germans therefore produced the world's first rocket and jet fighters and the first jet bomber, but the British were hard on their heels. Frank Whittle's dogged work on turbo-jets finally resulted in the successful initial flight of the **Gloster-Whittle G-40 (E.28/39)** in May 1941, and work was pressed ahead on a twin-engined fighter. It was a tremendous technological leap for Glosters: their last RAF fighter had been the biplane **Gladiator,** Britain's standard fighter at the time of Munich. The final result was the **Meteor,** designed to Specification F.9/40; it was originally known as the **Thunderbolt,** but this was changed to avoid confusion with the **American P-47** piston-engined fighter of the same name. Experiments with Halford H1 and Metrovick F2 engines

Top left: An Enzian is launched. This was a very early ground-to-air missile.

Above: The Ju 248. Also known as the 8-263, this was a development of the Me 163, the pioneer rocket-propelled target-defence interceptor.

Top right: Gloster Meteor. Beating the Me 262 into action by about a week, the Meteor I was first used to catch and destroy 'V-1' flying bombs.

Centre right: Messerschmitt 262. Had it entered service early in 1944 this fine fighter would have wrought havoc. Hitler's insistence that it should carry bombs held back its operational career.

Bottom right: The Baka. The ultimate in suicide machines, this manned missile was released from the G4M2 carrier aircraft about 50 miles from its target. In the final dive the three-barrelled rocket was fired, and the Baka reached speeds over 600 mph.

OPERATIONAL JET WARPLANES									
Country	Type	First ordered	Engine(s)	Max. speed loaded	Max. range loaded	Rate of climb	Ceiling	Bomb load/ Armament	Number built
Germany	Messerschmitt Me 262A-1	1943	Two Junkers Jumo 004B turbojets = 1,980 lb.s.t.	528 mph	652 miles	6.8 mins to 19,686 ft	39,370 ft	Two 1,100-lb bombs; four 30-mm cannon; 24 R4M 50-mm rockets	1,400+
	Messerschmitt Me163B *Komet*	1942	Walter HWK 109 liquid-fuel rocket = 3,750 lb.s.t.	596 mph	8 mins full power	31,500 ft per min	54,000 ft	Two 30-mm cannon; 24 R4M 50-mm rockets	350+
	Arado Ar 234 *Blitz*	1943	Two Junkers Jumo 109-004B turbojets = 1,984 lb.s.t.	425 mph	416 miles	26.9 mins to 26,248 ft	28,873 ft	Max. bomb-load 3,086 lbs; two 20-mm cannon (when fitted)	210
	Heinkel He 162 *Volksjäger*	1944	BMW 003E-1 turbo-jet = 1,760 lb.s.t.	522 mph	620 miles	4,200 ft per min	39,400 ft	Two 20-mm or 30-mm cannon	116
Great Britain	Gloster Meteor F.3	1942	Two Rolls-Royce Derwent 1 turbo-jets = 2,000 lb.s.t.	458 mph	1,340 miles	3,980 ft per min	44,000 ft	Four 20-mm cannon	280

it over by a close pass or a tap with a wingtip was enough to upset the bomb's gyros and drop the missile to explode in open country.

The V-2 (official designation: A4) was a revolutionary weapon and there was no defence against it. A single-stage rocket, it produced many sub-variants, one of them being intended for use by U-boats against the American eastern seaboard. The V-2, housed in a special casing, was to be towed across the Atlantic and fired when within range. Submarine firings—the direct precursor of the modern Polaris missile—were made successfully before the end of the war, but the V-2's main use was against London. However, preliminary work was also started on the two-stage **A-9/A-10** variant, intended for use against the United States.

Tiny Tim and the Bat

The Germans also developed the first ground-to-ground tactical missiles, the two-stage **Rheintochter** and the four-stage **Rheinboote,** but their best work with missiles was in the field of air-to-ground projectiles. They developed successful glider-bombs and the **X-4** rocket missile, guided by signals from a trailing wire. Another type, the SD 1400X guided bomb, sank the Italian battleship *Roma* in September 1943 as she was on the way to Gibraltar. The constant search for an answer to the Allied bomber fleet led to experiments with ground-to-air missiles— **Enzian, Schmetterling,** and **Wasserfall** but none of these was ever developed to full operational status.

The Americans were equally concerned in the development of the missile—in their case the catalyst was provided by the demands of the Pacific war. The heavy casualties inflicted by Japanese strongpoints on every island attacked from Tarawa to Okinawa produced America's **Tiny Tim:** a massive air-to-ground missile that packed the punch of a naval shell. Far more sophisticated was the **Bat,** which was an air-to-sea anti-shipping missile in the form of a 12-ft long plywood glider with a 1,000-lb warhead. Carried by the PB4Y Privateer patrol bomber, Bats were used operationally in 1945, guided to their targets by radio.

On the human side, the problems of jet and rocket flight had to be tackled as they arose. The men of German Test Commando 16, for example, were classic guinea-pigs. The problems of such rapid exposure to high altitude and its effect on the human frame were totally unknown. Special high-altitude diet was provided for the Test Commando 16 pilots, to avoid the formation of excessive flatulence; the men were also subjected to punishing training in the low pressure chamber. The wildest rumours were current in the Luftwaffe about how pilots were punished by the unprecedented acceleration and deceleration in the new aircraft; the actual flying characteristics of the aircraft came as a pleasant surprise. But the advent of the jet produced one essential safety measure: the cartridge-fired ejector seat, first installed on several German aircraft, to shoot the pilot clear of his aircraft at high speeds. These seats were naturally regarded with as much initial mistrust as the first parachutes. Not until well after the war was a totally reliable ejector seat developed.

resulted in the selected power plant for the **Meteor Mk III** being the Rolls-Royce Derwent I centrifugal turbo-jet, giving a maximum speed of 493 mph at 30,000 feet. Armed with four 20-mm Hispano cannon, the first **Meteor Mk Is,** powered by Welland Is, entered service with No. 616 Squadron, RAF, in July 1944. The first interceptor missions were flown against **V-1** flying bombs, in company with the **Tempest V**—the RAF's top-performance piston-engined fighter at the close of the war. Later the more powerful Meteor IIIs were sent to the European mainland to try to combat the Me 262.

'People's Fighter' a terror

One other jet aircraft of World War II deserves mention. This was the **Heinkel 162 Salamander,** a measure of desperation. It was dubbed the *Volksjäger*—the 'People's Fighter'—and was a single-seat fighter made extensively of wood, armed with two cannon, and intended for flying by hastily-trained Hitler Youth pilot trainees. It had a tricycle undercarriage, and was powered by a single BMW 003E-1 turbo-jet mounted atop the fuselage. The Salamander was fast—522 mph at 19,680 feet—but a terror to fly.

Another German interceptor was an even more frightening concept. This was the **Bachem Ba 349 Natter**—'Viper'. It was a piloted rocket armed with a battery of R4M missiles in the nose which was intended to reach the altitude of B-17 formations, fire its rockets, and then break in two, the pilot parachuting to safety and its rocket engine coming down under another parachute for re-use. Its main problem was the prohibitive mortality rate among its test pilots.

The jet and the rocket produced the first weapons of the modern missile age: Germany's V-1 and **V-2.** V-1 (actually FZG 76) was a pilotless aircraft powered by an Argus As-014 pulse-jet, whose distinctive, guttural drone earned the machine its nickname 'buzz-bomb'. It carried a warhead of 1,870 lbs of high explosive and 150 gallons of fuel, expended at one gallon per mile. The V-1 was not merely used to bombard London in 1944: it was also used against Antwerp and as a tactical missile during the German offensive in the Ardennes of December 1944. British interceptors found that it was dangerous to explode V-1s with gunfire: tipping

NEW ALLIANCES

When World War II had been won, the victors found themselves in idealogical conflict with each other. New alliances were formed, and the lines redrawn for a different kind of battle; but the 'Cold War' was to last only five years before the two sides again resorted to arms in Korea. During that time were made some of the fastest advances in the history of aviation as the nations of both sides strove to build a jet air force.

immediate realities dominated the formation of postwar international alignment. In the Far East the United States had been the prime mover behind the defeat of Japan and in 1945 her forces dominated the Pacific and its seaboards. However, Soviet Russia's timely intervention in Manchuria on the eve of Japan's surrender, together with Chiang Kai-Shek's loss of the initiative to Mao-tse-Tung in China, meant that American policies in the Far East were met by a powerful Communist blocking influence.

In Europe, realities were harsher. In 1947, 6 western countries formed a committee to draft the American-inspired European Recovery Program (ERP), more familiarly known as the 'Marshall Plan'. The crowning event was the signing of the North Atlantic Treaty Association (NATO) between Britain, the United States, Canada, France, Belgium, Holland, Luxembourg, Italy, Portugal, Denmark, Norway and Iceland in 1949.

Meanwhile the Communist nations had not been inactive. The year 1947 saw the formation of the Communist Information Bureau (Cominform) between Soviet Russia, Yugoslavia, Bulgaria, Rumania, Hungary and Czechoslovakia. Yugoslavia effectively seceded from the new Communist power bloc, and was denounced accordingly by the Soviet Union and the other states in September 1949. Although the alignment of the Soviet powers was not formally defined until the formation of the Warsaw Pact in May 1955, all the elements of confrontation were active long before the outbreak of hostilities in

During this period the development of military aviation was effectively dictated by the *status quo* at the surrender of Germany and Japan, which had left the advantage decisively with the non-Communist Allied countries in 1945.

Piston power in the jet age

Britain led in jet development and the **Gloster Meteor F.3** and **F.4** were two of her standard post-war jet fighters, together with the **De Havilland Vampire** which entered service in 1946. The Vampire's best speed was 538 mph at 5,000 feet and it was armed with four 20-mm cannon.

American jet development started behind that of Britain but proceeded methodically and swiftly. At the close of the war the final marks of the **Mustang** and the **Thunderbolt—P-51H** and **P-47N**, were already being phased out and production of both had ceased by the end of 1945. Some American piston-engined aircraft, however, served on with distinction into the 1950s. Among them was the naval **Chance Vought Corsair F4U-4**, which saw service in Korea, and the **North American P-82** (later **F-82**) **Twin Mustang** and **Douglas A-26** (later **B-26 Invader,** both of which bore a major burden in Korea as tactical strike and reconnaissance aircraft. The B-26 (taking that designation when the **B-26 Marauder** was phased out) served in many roles in Vietnam also.

America's first really good jet fighter appeared in 1944: the **Lockheed F-80 Shoot-**

with its single engine carried in the fuselage. Next came the **Republic F-84 Thunderjet,** in 1947. This was another straight-wing design with the basic armament of six .5 in machine guns but it also carried underwing rocket projectiles. Performance of the **F-84B** was about the same as that of the Shooting Star. The **F-84G** version of the Thunderjet was equipped for air-to-air refuelling, a post-war development which transformed the operational mobility of military aircraft. It could also carry a tactical nuclear weapon, and was the first American fighter to be used extensively by minor air forces of the NATO bloc.

Swept-wing breakthrough

Redesigned in 1945 to incorporate German data on swept-wings, the **North American F-86 Sabre** of 1947, which with Russia's **MiG-15** fighter became the **Spitfire** and **Me 109** of the jet age, was the first swept-wing design to serve with the NATO air forces.

The MiG-15 provided Russia's big break-through in 1947. In engagements during the Korean War the MiG-15 was to prove that it had the edge over the American Sabre at heights above around 35,000 feet, but the Sabre, although out-gunned (the MiG-15 was armed with one 37-mm cannon and two 20-mm cannons) had a radar gunsight, could out-dive the MiG, and manoeuvred better at lower altitudes. The MiG-15 saw extensive service with the Warsaw Pact countries and

NEW AIRCRAFT

The bomber scene was far more confused in the immediate post-war period. The jet engine and the advent of the nuclear bomb stood traditional warfare, and with it the theory of air bombardment, on its head. One point, however, became clear: long-range aircraft of maximum endurance were essential to the world's two main power blocs, the Warsaw Pact countries and NATO; and so the basic format of the giant bomber lived on.

Super Superfortress

America's **B-29 Superfortress** had been the biggest bomber to see service in World War II and had achieved a number of 'firsts' which bridged the daunting technological gap between traditional bombers and those of the jet and missile age. These included an operation ceiling of over 30,000 feet, radar-controlled defensive fire system for the gun turrets, and all-round pressurisation for all crew positions. The B-29 remained as America's standard heavy bomber in the immediate postwar years and the backbone of Strategic Air Command (SAC). Some nine B-29 squadrons served in the Korean war and the aircraft was also supplied to RAF Bomber Command. A B-29 development, the **B-50**, powered by four Pratt & Whitney Wasp Majors, had a speed of over 400 mph. By 1951 the B-50 had replaced the B-29 in most front-line SAC squadrons.

The first **Convair B-36** flew in August 1946 and the first production aircraft started to enter service with the re-equipped 7th Bomb Group at Fort Worth in the summer of

1948. It was gargantuan in every sense. The wingspan of 230 feet housed six 3,500 hp Pratt & Whitney Wasp Major pusher engines. The fuselage, 162 feet long, housed a crew of 15. Maximum range was 10,000 miles; bomb-load was around 10,000 lbs over an 8,500 mile range. Maximum speed of the B-36 was 372 mph at 40,000 feet.

Subsequent development of the B-36 boosted the power by the addition of four jets set in pairs in underwing pods, giving this now ten-engined bomber a vital 10,000 feet increase in over-target height and a maximum speed increase of 58 mph. Overall production of the B-36 reached 350, and at its peak it equipped 33 SAC squadrons.

Awesome American Monopoly

Meanwhile, the Americans, Russians and British were developing their own jet bombers. The Red Air Force gained a slight lead over the RAF with the entry into service of the twin-engined **Il-28 'Beagle'** in 1950. Britain's **English Electric Canberra**, also twin-engined, followed in 1951. Neither the Red Air Force nor the RAF received heavy jet bombers until the mid-1950s.

This meant that for ten years after the close of World War II the United States held the monopoly of long-range, inter-continental strategic bombing aircraft.

America's leadership in military aviation was further reflected in the speed with which the world's first jet designed as a carrier fighter entered service. This was the Mc-Donnell FH-1 Phantom, which appeared

in 1946; a straight-wing design with two small Westinghouse turbojets buried in the wing roots. The Phantom's ceiling was 43,000 feet and it had a top speed of 505 mph at 30,000 feet.

Two other American naval jet fighters were in service by the end of 1949. These were the Phantom's successor, the **F2H Banshee** and the **Grumman F9F Panther**. The Banshee was a considerable improvement over the original Phantom design, with more powerful engines, increased tankage, and later provision for air-to-air refuelling. All this added up to more speed and more range; 642 mph maximum, ceiling 52,000 feet, and a normal range of 1,200 miles.

Grumman's F9F Panther used a single Pratt & Whitney J42 (later the J48) developed from the British Nene and Tay turbo-jets, giving a top speed of 630 mph. Like the Banshee, the Panther was armed with four 20-mm nose cannon, but could similarly carry up to 2,000 lbs of external bombs or rockets.

Irony in the new hostilities

Thus the five years between the surrender of Japan in 1945 and the outbreak of the Korean War in 1950 saw some of the fastest advances ever made in the history of aviation. With the former Allies against the Berlin/Rome/Tokyo Axis now estranged and re-grouping into two hostile camps, it was ironic that the last traces of the wartime alliance helped accelerate the new armed hostility known as the 'Cold War.'

The Last of the Piston-engined Fighters

▲ **Hawker Fury F.B. Mk. 60** served with No. 9 Squadron of the Pakistan Air Force until replaced by the F-104A Starfighter in 1960

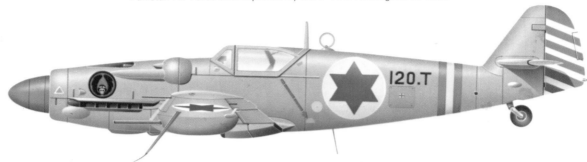

▲ **S 199,** the Czechoslovak-built Jumo 211F-engined version of the Messerschmitt Bf 109G, which equipped the first Israeli fighter squadron, No. 101, which began operations in June 1948 from Ekron

▲ **Grumman F8F-1 Bearcat** was operated by the Royal Thai Air Force into the 'sixties, that illustrated belonging to the 2nd Fighter-Bomber Wing

▲ **Messerschmitt Bf 109G-5/U2** of Finnish No. 31 Fight Squadron operating from Utti in 1948. This wartime fighter w finally phased out of Finnish service in 1954

▲ **Grumman F6F-5 Hellcat** served with Uruguayan Naval Aviation until 1961 at Laguna del Sauce

▲ **Lavochkin La-11** was the last piston-engined fighter to be produced in the Soviet Union, entering service in 1948 and being phased out in the early 'fifties

▲ **Supermarine Spitfire IX** of the Danish 725 Squadron, this type remaining in Royal Danish Air Force service until mid-1951

▲ **Hawker Tempest II** equipped five Indian Air Force squadrons (Nos. 3, 4, 7, 8 and 10) in the early 'fifties

▲ **North American F-51D Mustang,** captured in some numbers from the Nationalist Chinese, served with the Sino-Communists until supplanted by the MiG-15 in the early 'fifties

▲ **Hispano HA-1112-M1L,** the Spanish-built Merlin-engined development of the Messerschmitt Bf 109G, serving with the Spanish 71 Escuadron of the Ala núm 7 de Cazabombardeo in the mid 'sixties

The Early Jet Fighters

▲ De Havilland Vampire F. Mk. I of No. 247 Squadron, RAF (1946). The Vampire was the second British production jet fighter, having flown as a prototype on September 26, 1943

▲ North American FJ-1 Fury of the Naval Air Reserve, Oak California. Flown as a prototype on November 27, 1946, the served with only one US Navy Fighter Squadron, VF-5A, 1948

▲ Mikoyan-Gurevich MiG-9 (Fargo) was the first Soviet-designed turbojet-driven fighter to fly, achieving this distinction on April 24, 1946 and subsequently entering service in relatively limited numbers with the Soviet Air Forces

▲ Grumman F9F-4 Panther of US Marine Corps Squadron VMF-334. Flown as a prototype on November 24, 1947, the Panther entered service in May 1949 and saw action over Korea

▲ Dassault MD-450 Ouragan was the first jet fighter of French design to achieve production status but did not fly in prototype form until February 28, 1949. The example illustrated is an Ouragan supplied to the Indian Air Force in the mid-'fifties

▲ SAAB 21R serving with the Swedish Air Force's F7 (Skaraborgs Flygflottilj) in 1952. The SAAB 21R was a turbojet-powered adaptation of the piston-engined SAAB 21A and saw first-line service 1949–54

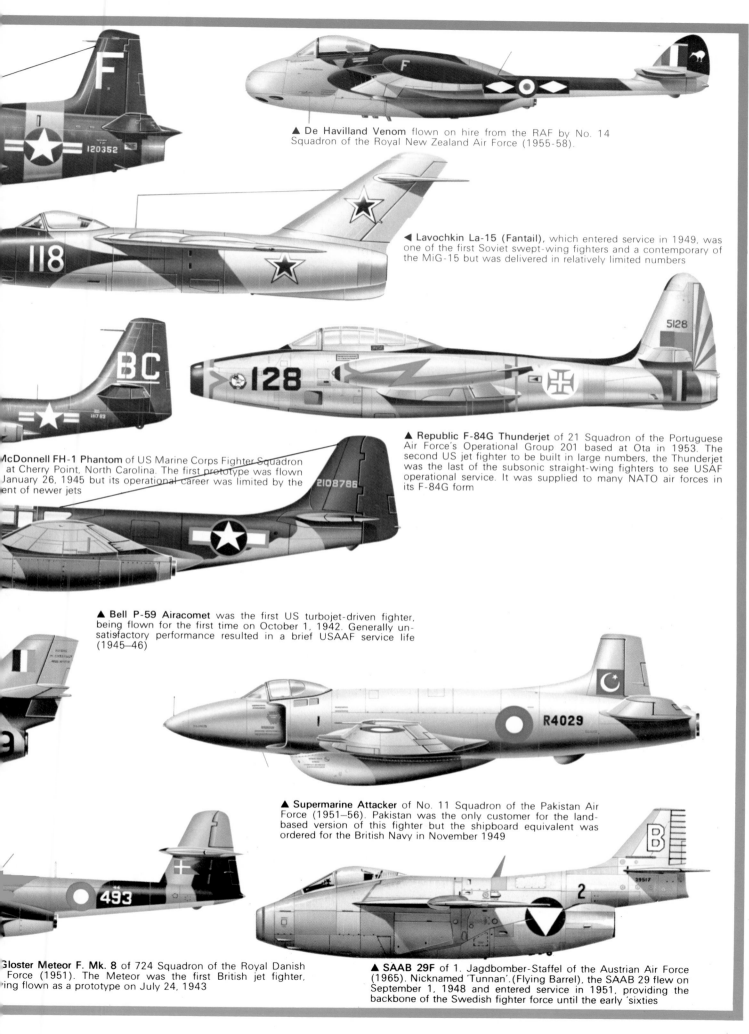

▲ De Havilland Venom flown on hire from the RAF by No. 14 Squadron of the Royal New Zealand Air Force (1955-58).

◀ Lavochkin La-15 (Fantail), which entered service in 1949, was one of the first Soviet swept-wing fighters and a contemporary of the MiG-15 but was delivered in relatively limited numbers

McDonnell FH-1 Phantom of US Marine Corps Fighter Squadron at Cherry Point, North Carolina. The first prototype was flown January 26, 1945 but its operational career was limited by the [adv]ent of newer jets

▲ Republic F-84G Thunderjet of 21 Squadron of the Portuguese Air Force's Operational Group 201 based at Ota in 1953. The second US jet fighter to be built in large numbers, the Thunderjet was the last of the subsonic straight-wing fighters to see USAF operational service. It was supplied to many NATO air forces in its F-84G form

▲ Bell P-59 Airacomet was the first US turbojet-driven fighter, being flown for the first time on October 1, 1942. Generally unsatisfactory performance resulted in a brief USAAF service life (1945–46)

▲ Supermarine Attacker of No. 11 Squadron of the Pakistan Air Force (1951–56). Pakistan was the only customer for the land-based version of this fighter but the shipboard equivalent was ordered for the British Navy in November 1949

Gloster Meteor F. Mk. 8 of 724 Squadron of the Royal Danish [Air] Force (1951). The Meteor was the first British jet fighter, [be]ing flown as a prototype on July 24, 1943

▲ SAAB 29F of 1. Jagdbomber-Staffel of the Austrian Air Force (1965). Nicknamed 'Tunnan'.(Flying Barrel), the SAAB 29 flew on September 1, 1948 and entered service in 1951, providing the backbone of the Swedish fighter force until the early 'sixties

AIRBRIDGE to BERLIN

The first major confrontation of the Cold War, with its ever-present risk of global conflict, came in the summer of 1948 when the Soviet Bloc denied the Western Powers their agreed right of access to the divided city of Berlin. The beleaguered and isolated city, still recovering from the ravages of war, had a desperate need of supplies that apparently far-outstripped the Allies ability to meet it. But quick improvisation and the methodical organisation of the most massive airlift in history saved the city and averted the very real possibility of a third world war.

The Cold War hardly ever erupted into actual fighting in Europe, but there was one event which threw the confrontation into sharp focus and which, had the West not possessed great statesmen, could easily have led to World War III. This crisis was overcome solely by the peaceful use of airpower, in the world's greatest and most sustained airlift.

In the summer of 1948 the Russians took a mighty gamble. Looking at the map they could see how the great city of Berlin, divided, like Germany itself, into sectors occupied by all four Allied powers, was isolated like an island in the heart of the vast Soviet Zone (today East Germany, or the DDR). It would need but a signature on a Red Army order for all communications with the city to be severed. Within days to weeks the Western Allies would see the Berliners starving. They would be forced to acquiesce to whatever the Russians demanded, which could be the removal of all Allied forces from the US, British and French Zones of Berlin so that the city would become completely a part of the Soviet Zone of Germany. Though this might not bring any great economic gain to the Soviet Union, it would be a huge moral victory in the Cold War. Once it was won, perhaps further bold strokes might win for Communism the whole of Germany.

So without the slightest warning Red Army troops closed the checkpoint on the Autobahn from Hanover to Berlin at Helmstedt, on the inter-zonal frontier, at dawn on June 25, 1948. Other forces closed all the other roads, railways and canals that formed the lifelines that kept the city alive. Berlin was still a shambles, the biggest heap of rubble the world had ever seen, but it was home to over 2,500,000 people (as well as to the Allied control commission and the Western occupying forces). Virtually no food or essential materials were produced within the city. It was totally dependent on its surface transport links for its survival. But the Russians merely announced that

there were 'technical difficulties' which necessitated the closure of all these routes.

While Western diplomats found it impossible to make any headway in talks with the Russians, Allied airmen began to fly a few of the most urgent necessities into the beleaguered city. Operation Vittles was begun by the US Air Force on June 26 when a **C-54 Skymaster** flew a priority cargo in from Frankfurt am Main. Operation Plain Fare was begun by the RAF two days later. It was evident that without aerial supply Berlin would have to be handed over to the Russians. Could such a huge and helpless city be kept alive solely by such a means? Nothing remotely like it had ever been attempted. The Allied commanders conferred hastily, discussed the use of bombers to augment the lift, of bringing in forces from the USA and British Dominions, of using gliders, parachuted supplies and civil aircraft. It was obvious the task would stretch the available resources to the utmost, and it would need urgent improvements to the extremely poor airfield and air traffic control network.

Nerve that would not break

By the end of June the US Air Force was operating a shuttle service with their modern and efficient C-54 Skymasters, while the RAF was using 50 Dakotas (**C-47** or **DC-3**) and 25 **Yorks** (transport development of the **Lancaster**). The British forces had organised a huge augmented ground organisation, and the Royal Army Service Corps were loading and unloading aircraft at top speed. Thousands of men and women found themselves doing unfamiliar duties, thousands of reservists were recalled, RAF scheduled

Round the clock. New equipment, such as this high-intensity runway light at Berlin-Tempelhof, helped the big lift to go on day and night, often in foul weather. The aircraft is a USAF C-54.

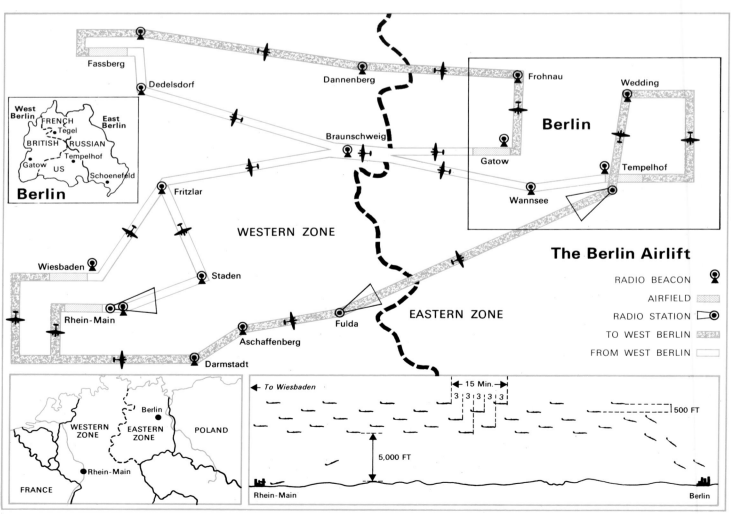

Fassberg

Dedelsdorf

Dannenberg

Frohnau

Wedding

Berlin

Gatow

Tempelhof

West Berlin FRENCH Tegel **East Berlin**

BRITISH RUSSIAN

Tempelhof

Gatow US Schoenefeld

Berlin

Braunschweig

Wannsee

Fritzlar

WESTERN ZONE

The Berlin Airlift

Wiesbaden

Staden

RADIO BEACON

AIRFIELD

RADIO STATION

TO WEST BERLIN

FROM WEST BERLIN

Rhein-Main

EASTERN ZONE

Fulda

Aschaffenberg

Darmstadt

WESTERN ZONE

Berlin

EASTERN ZONE

POLAND

Rhein-Main

FRANCE

To Wiesbaden

15 Min.

3 3 3 3 3

500 FT

5,000 FT

Rhein-Main

Berlin

164

services to the Middle and Far East were taken over by airlines, and the Berlin Airlift grew daily. The aircraft flew from four airfields in the Western Zones along the corridors, each 20 miles wide, which had been agreed by the four Allied powers at the end of World War II. They converged on the vital airfield of Gatow in West Berlin. Here the air traffic controllers worked around the clock, the hardstanding was quadrupled in size by German contractors who used rubble from the city—the one thing Berlin had in plenty—and the main runway was lengthened day-by-day to 6,000 feet. A new airfield was built at Fassberg in the British Zone, and in the French sector of Berlin another new airfield was urgently built at Tegel.

As the Soviet commanders in Berlin reported to Moscow on the streams of transport aircraft the Kremlin replied with

---

Airlift by Douglas. Towards the end of Operation Vittles the giant Douglas C-74 Globemaster came into service, carrying a load of over 20 tons. One of these monsters is seen opposite disgorging flour at Gatow; the bags were slid down a chute in the belly (upper right). The third photograph shows coal being manhandled out of a Dakota. The map shows how air traffic was organised between the busiest airfields. Though the system worked under constant strain it never faltered. Afterwards the NATO alliance built more than 100 new military airstrips in Western Europe.

---

an order to turn the screw harder. The Russians announced there would be 'great difficulties' caused by the Allied aircraft maintaining the Airlift; Soviet military aircraft would be 'carrying out exercises' through the corridors (which was expressly forbidden by the Allied agreement) and there was a blunt warning that 'the whole question of corridors will have to be reconsidered'.

RAF Group Captain H. M. S. Wright, of the Allied Control Commission, replied to the Russians: 'You cannot alter the four-power agreement; if you announce new regulations these will not be recognised by the other powers'. The Russians had hoped the West's nerve would break, and that the Allies would back down. But all that happened was that the lift grew day-by-day.

A further 70 C-54s arrived, to make a fleet of 130 of these capable giants. RAF **Sunderland** flying boats started shuttling from Finkenwerder to Havel Lake in West Berlin. American Overseas Airlines began operations on the corridor from Frankfurt with, at first, six round trips a week, then 25 and finally 39. Lancastrian fuel tankers of Flight Refuelling Ltd. began the British civil participation, which soon involved a motley force of nine types of aircraft owned by 26 mostly small and very new air charter companies and the big airline BEA, which co-ordinated the effort. Dakotas were hampered by spares shortages, and the civil fleet found the best workhorses were the **Halton** (converted **Halifax** bomber) and the **Tudor,** the latter carrying the biggest payload of all. In terms of weight the most important loads were flour, coal and petrol. Tudors, built to carry passengers in luxury,

acquired a reek of petrol and a black and white lining from the other two commodities.

Signing for 'hangers, one'

There was never a respite. Captain C. Treen, of Bond's Air Services, made six round trips (12 long flights) with his Halton in one 26-hour period, without a minute's sleep. An RAF Dakota flew 11,000 miles from the Far East, checked in with the controllers and was airborne with a load within three hours. Every day there were triumphs of improvisation. BEA, needing maintenance capability for dozens of aircraft that previously were all tended in Britain, asked the RAF for facilities and in 30 minutes the BEA German Manager signed a form assigning him 'hangars, one'. Meanwhile, tired pilots sketched on scraps of paper methods of wiping the bodies and blood of millions of insects from their windscreens, and of avoiding each other—and the hostile red-starred fighters—in the crowded corridors.

The original Allied target had been a lift of 750 short tons per day, but by the end of July 1948 the daily average was 215 British and 285 American loads per day for a total of 2,250 tons. General Lucius Clay, the US Military Governor of Berlin, announced the daily total could be sustained at 5,400 tons if necessary.

In that same month a most significant step was taken by the Allies. Major General William H. Tunner was appointed to command the Airlift. He was at the time undoubtedly the world's leading authority on airlifting, having learned the hard way by directing the Hump Airlift into China from August 1944. His first move was to raise the flagging morale of aircrew who were not aware of the strategic importance of their efforts and who were quartered in 'temporary' accommodation for months at a time.

No glamour—but no frenzy

Tunner's next move was to actually reduce the number of flights that aircrews were undertaking. In his opinion they were flying too many hours and, as exciting as their nonstop flying appeared to the Western press, to Tunner it meant that the operation was not being run efficiently enough. In his words 'the actual operation of a successful airlift is about as glamorous as drops of water on a stone. There's no frenzy, no flap, just the inexorable process of getting the job done'.

And there is no doubt that the flyers got the job done and done well. Day and night the piston-engined transports thundered along the disputed corridors, lurching at 160 knots through the rough air, braving electrical storms, torrential rain and blizzards, finally to come in on the primitive Ground Controlled Approach (GCA) technique and alight heavily on the runway at Gatow or at Tegel (opened in November). Scores of willing hands would heave out the tons of vital food or fuel, and usually put in some of Berlin's manufactured goods for the return trip. Officials would screen the queues of hopeful passengers and the aircrew, having just had time for a quick

cigarette and cup of coffee, were back in the cockpit. Queueing up for take off they would soon climb back into the gloom and murk.

One of the most notable achievements of the Airlift was the development of GCA landing techniques which were at the time used only at commercial airports and which took fifteen to twenty minutes to bring a plane in. The Military Air Transport Service (MATS) flew in two disassembled CPN-4 vans with 50,000 lbs of cathode ray tubes, radar and the most up-to-date ground control approach equipment.

During the Airlift the tower controller brought the planes down to 2,000 feet and, if visual landing requirements were below minimum, CGA would take over. Procedures were so improved in the course of the Airlift that CGA landings were made on the planes' regular three-minute headway and by late 1948 more CGA landings had been made at Templehof than at all the airports in the United States combined.

A record 12,840 ton day

By 1949 crews from the air forces of Australia, New Zealand and South Africa were at work, the main transport force had settled down as 200 C-54s, 40 Yorks, 40 Dakotas and 15 of the new **Hastings,** and there were eight all-weather dispatch airfields. An 8,000 ton day was not uncommon, and on April 16, 1949 a record 12,840 tons were flown in. Every day many hundreds of pilots would bring succour to the city, where the inhabitants were still weary and apprehensive but now filled with hope. Germany, a ruined nation outwardly with an exterior of darkness and devastation, was pulsing with life underneath. Not only the Allies but the Germans were toiling mightily to keep Berlin free. It was clear they could go on doing it indefinitely. So at midnight on Wednesday May 11, 1949, the Soviet troops suddenly raised all the barriers.

The lifting of the great blockade was a fact so stupendous it could not at first be comprehended. But the fleets of trucks, trains and barges that had been patiently waiting were suddenly allowed to move into the now rather frightening Soviet Zone and on to Berlin. The Airlift was no longer needed. In 10½ months the Allied aircraft had brought in 1,583,686 short tons for Berlin, as well as over 160,000 tons of material to build or improve airfields. The total number of round trips was a staggering 195,530 (today the same task could have been done with a mere 15,000), yet despite the appalling strain on man and machine the safety record was outstanding. The RAF, for example, made nearly 200,000 take-offs and landings on the airlift, yet suffered only four fatal accidents.

But the true significance of the Berlin Airlift went deeper. It showed what air transport can do for human good in a way that had never before been demonstrated. It showed the Germans they would not be abandoned. It showed the whole world that the Allies were not ready to be written off as spineless and weak. And it showed the leaders of the Soviet Union with crystal clarity that no gamble based on any kind of threat was going to come off. The Berlin Airlift was something they had never counted on happening.

KOREA

Against a backdrop of world-wide confrontation between the Communist and Capitalist nations, and with the very real possibility of a nuclear showdown, the Korean War broke out in June, 1950. For the first time the forces of the Western Bloc, ill-equipped for such a battle, faced defeat at the hands of the Communists.

Though the United States had pressed ahead faster than any other nation with the development of new combat aircraft after World War Two, the invasion of South Korea on June 25, 1950 caught it completely by surprise. The rather remote land of Korea had been Japanese, but in 1945 it was temporarily divided into a northern part, north of the 38th parallel of latitude (38°N), under Soviet Communist domination, and a southern part occupied by the Americans. The two parts were meant to be united into a single self-governing country, but this became bogged down in political arguments. Gradually the north and south grew to dislike and distrust each other, and eventually North Korea and South Korea were set up as separate states. They were self-governing,

but the North stayed Communist and the South kept US forces for its protection. On June 25, 1950 the North Korean army marched south across the 38th parallel, rolling up the weak South Korean army and expecting the Americans to keep out of the fight.

South Korea asked for US help, and eventually an Allied force was put together with land, sea and air elements from the USA, Britain, Australia, South Africa, Turkey and other countries. But despite desperate resistance the South Koreans were by November forced into a tiny region in the South-west around Pusan. Only one airfield was left outside Pusan, at Taegu; at Pusan itself were two crowded airstrips. The situation was grave. Much greater air forces

were available in Japan, but this was from 100 to 500 miles away and Japan-based fighter and attack aircraft could spend only limited time over the battlefield. Suddenly, in four months, Korea had changed from a sleepy backwater to the first-ever scene of military defeat of 'Western' forces at the hands of the Communists.

All this happened against a backdrop of global confrontation between the Communist and Capitalist nations. The Soviet Union had the atom bomb, was enormously strong in land forces and was believed to be fast building new jet aircraft. The West had also striven to put new types of aircraft into its front-line squadrons, but there was no sense of urgency and money was tight. And the aircraft industries had

Commonwealth effort with American aircraft. The British Commonwealth forces bore a major part of the Western Allies' burden on land, on sea and in the air. One of the luckiest units was No. 2 Sqn., South African Air Force, which flew the F-86F Sabre. These aircraft had four pylons, and so could undertake long-range attack missions with drop tanks and two 1,000 lb. bombs.

shrunk until there was no possibility of increasing output within a period of about two years at least. For example, the British industry's labour force had declined from 2,000,000 to a mere 140,000.

Problems for the new breed

Worse, the new types of aircraft were often ill-suited to the vitally urgent task of providing close-support firepower to the hard-pressed ground troops in South Korea. The new breed of jet fighters were fine and impressive aircraft, and such machines as the **F-80 Shooting Star, F-84 Thunderjet** and **F-86 Sabre** of the US Air Force and the **F9F Panther** and **F2H Banshee** of the Navy and Marine Corps appeared to be better than the scattered array of old World War II machines deployed by the North Koreans. Again, the **B-29** could provide heavy strategic striking power totally missing from the arsenal of the Communists, with range amply sufficient for missions from bases in Japan.

But all these aircraft were designed to operate either from aircraft carriers or from good paved runways at least 6,000 feet long. Carriers could steam up near the Korean coast—though the shallow sea bed off the east coast meant a big ship could not come nearer than about 70 miles, which is long enough when you are struggling back with severe battle-damage—but on the Korean mainland there were no good permanent airfields at all, except for the airport at Seoul captured by the North. Moreover, the jet fighters were designed for air combat. Though some could carry offensive stores in the form of 5 inch rockets and bombs of up to 1,000 lb, they suffered from long take-off and landing runs, rather sluggish performance when laden with ex-

ternal stores, and generally deficient range or endurance.

This left only the piston-engined machines, of which by far the best were the **F-51 Mustang**, and **F4U Corsair** and the **AD Skyraider**. These could operate more safely from the short Korean airstrips and carry good loads, and also had better flight endurance; but they were more vulnerable, and, when operated intensively, their pilots became exhausted. The Skyraider, with its marvellous weapon load carried on 15 attachment pylons, and flight endurance up to ten hours, was probably the best close-support machine available; but its pilots had to be lifted bodily from the cockpit for they were too exhausted to climb out themselves. The strain on the pilots was enormous.

During the early months of the campaign several American fighter squadrons gave up their shiny new F-80 Shooting Star jets and converted back to the old piston-engined F-51 Mustang. The Mustang was the most numerous Allied machine over the battlefield and it did great execution with its six 0·5 inch ('fifty calibre') guns in the wings and assorted loads of bombs and rockets. One of the most effective weapons against troops and 'soft-skinned' (unarmoured) vehicles was napalm, a streamlined container (often a drop tank) filled with a jellied mixture of naphtha and palm oil which upon hitting the ground was detonated to burst into a searing flame perhaps 50 feet wide and 200 feet long. The 5 inch rocket was often World War II stock, used with violent effect against armour, bridges, fortifications and other 'hard' targets. For specially hard targets an even punchier rocket had been developed, the 12-inch Tiny Tim, carried by the Skyraider.

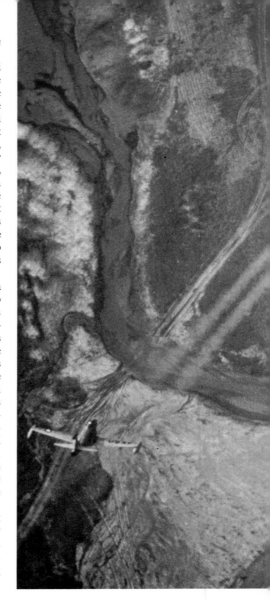

FAR EAST AIR FORCES SORTIES	
Interdiction	192,581
Close support	57,665
Counterair	66,997
Air supply	181,659
Other	222,078
FAR EAST AIR FORCES LOSSES AND CASUALTIES	
Sabres lost in air combat	78
Others lost in air combat	61
Killed in air operations	1,144
Killed in ground operations	36

US Navy fighter power. The US Navy fought in a coat of midnight blue. Two of its best aircraft were the Grumman F9F Panther jet (left, an F9F-2B) and Chance Vought F4U Corsair (right, an F4U-5N being bombed-up aboard USS *Philippine Sea*, with Panther jet fighters ranged on the flight deck further aft).

A motley mix of types

During the first months of the war a motley assortment of Allied aircraft operated much as had been done in Northern Europe in 1944–45, except that those in Korea were based on extremely poor makeshift airfields. The typical runway was pierced-steel planking (PSP) less than 5,000 feet long, with uneven surfaces, occasional bad bumps and rough patches that often caused burst tyres. Trying to operate the new jets from such strips was fraught with danger. Their laden weights were greater than for the piston fighters—say, 18,000 lb compared with 11,000—and their tyre pressures higher, making them highly unsuited to PSP laid on uneven ground. Their speeds at take-off and landing were higher—say, 160 mph compared with 120—and the early turbojet engines gave less thrust on take-off than big piston engines and propellers, so the run needed was much longer. To take-off quicker some jets used JATO (jet assisted take-off) bottles, which were solid-fuel rockets clipped underneath and jettisoned when the aircraft was airborne. These added to the cost and logistic supply problems. Like all jets, the basic problem remained that fuel consumption was very high at low altitudes. The jet fighters had been expected to do dogfighting at heights over 30,000 feet, but over Korea they were crawling over the battlefields at 1,000 feet or less to try to help the Allied troops.

In the Pentagon urgent discussions were held to attempt to find a specification for a superior kind of close-support aircraft tailored to the job. The Navy finally came out in favour of a twin-turboprop aircraft able to carry a huge ordnance load and, while still quite fast (about 450 mph), having far longer range and endurance, and better suited to use from short, rough strips, than the early jet fighters. No such machine was built, and the best answer was later found by Ed Heinemann, designer of the Douglas Skyraider, who quickly conceived a small and simple jet, the **A4 Skyhawk**—but Korea was over before it flew. So the campaign continued to be fought by a piston and jet mix of types that were all in some ways deficient. Many of the aircraft were of wartime vintage, as were nearly all the bombs and cannon shells.

Helicopter proving ground

Wartime aircraft, such as the **Martin Mariner** and **Short Sunderland**, carried out the vital task of ocean patrol, though they were backed up by the fine new **Lockheed Neptune** of the US Navy which was a great advance on such older land-based machines as the **Hudson** and **Liberator** in having better flight performance, much better radar and new kinds of submarine detection gear. And in two categories there had been major improvements since the war, and indeed since the Berlin Airlift. Strategic transport had been revitalised by the introduction of such big aircraft as the **Boeing C-97,** able to cross the Pacific at 300 mph while carrying 134 troops or more than 20 tons of cargo, and the even bigger **Douglas C124 Globemaster** which carried 200 troops or huge loads of cargo, including vehicles and other bulky items which previously could not be carried by air.

The other category where there was a major advance was the helicopter. In World War II this had been flimsy and experimental, but by 1950 there were several families of helicopter able to do a very useful military job. They were directly relevant to the Korean type of situation,

USAF fighter power. The US Air Force aircraft were almost all unpainted, apart from their markings. At first the most numerous jet was the Lockheed F-80C Shooting Star (above, rocketing North Korean tanks), but it was gradually replaced by the much faster North American F-86 Sabre. Below, two F-86Es of the 51st FI Wing take off for Korea.

SABRE 'KILLS'	
Tupolev Tu-2	9
Lavochkin La-9	6
MiG-15	792
Ilyushin Il-12	1
Others	2
Total:	810

because they could operate from any bit of level ground and could perform many vital trucking jobs right up to the front line. Later they also showed their value in bringing back pilots and crews from crashed aircraft, often far out to sea or deep in enemy-held territory.

During the autumn of 1950 Allied air attacks helped greatly in supporting the Allied armies as they broke out of their Pusan perimeter and flooded northwards again. Meanwhile, the B-29s undertook strategic bombing of North Korea, starting with precision attacks on major industrial targets and moving on to incendiary raids on towns similar to those that flattened the cities of Japan five years earlier. These raids were very effective, but nobody failed to understand that this was largely because of the lack of opposition. Times were changing. On the ground the Allies walked into a trap set by huge armies from the People's Republic of China, which had quietly crossed the Yalu river in the far north. In the air the Chinese had received supplies of a completely unknown Soviet type of jet fighter, the swept-wing **MiG-15,** very quickly designed in 1947 around the Rolls-Royce Nene jet engine supplied from Britain and later put into production on a huge scale. On November 1, 1950 the first of these silver arrow-like fighters was seen over Korea, and the air war was no longer one-sided.

First jet-to-jet combat

At the start the Communist pilots were obviously inexperienced and timid, but they gradually acquired boldness and skill. It was soon evident that the MiG-15 could completely outfly every Allied fighter, but early in December 1950 the US Air Force brought a wing of **F-86A Sabres** to Korea and these could fight the MiG on roughly level terms. Flight performance was similar, though the Communist fighter was much lighter and thus was superior in climb and manoeuvrability. The MiG-15 had two or three large-calibre cannon, capable of destroying an opposing fighter with a single good hit, but firing only one-third as many rounds in a given time as the six 'fifties' of the Sabre, but the combat was by no means equal because, while the Communist pilots were raw, the Americans were seasoned veterans.

Thus Korea became the scene of the first jet versus jet combat in aviation history when on November 7, 1950 an F-80 managed to destroy a MiG-15 in a diving attack. On December 17 the first Sabre pilot got a MiG in his sights. Over the following $2\frac{1}{2}$ years no fewer than 792 of the Chinese or Korean fighters were to be claimed by Allied pilots, the majority of them flying Sabres. True figures will never be known, but the Allied claims suggested a kill ratio of $12\frac{1}{2}:1$ in favour of the F-86 Sabre.

These aerial battles were exactly like those of World War II, though they could range up to 50,000 feet and reach speeds exceeding 700 mph. There was no ground control, no radar (except a radar ranging system in the Sabre's APG-30 gunsight), no missiles and nothing else that would not have been familiar to a pilot in the Battle of Britain. Navigation was by map-reading and dead-reckoning, fuel management was done by looking at the amount of fuel left and doing a quick mental sum involving the height and distance from base, and interceptions were made simply by seeing the enemy and chasing him. Once battle was joined, speed seldom rose much above about 450 mph unless one fighter tried to escape. Victory invariably went to the better pilot. The point should also be made that the American pilots enjoyed better and more lavish equipment than the Communists; but this was not always judged an advantage.

The APG-30 gunsight is a case in point. It was far more costly and complicated than the simple optical reflector sight fitted to the MiG-15, and might be supposed to have conferred a great feeling of superiority to the man using it. Yet to a considerable degree the reverse happened. Korea was a rough, tough place, and the American pilots often began to wish for rough, tough aircraft. The

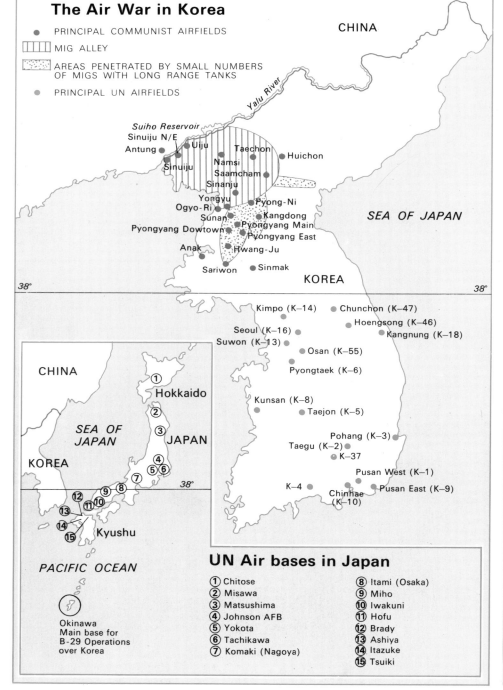

The Air War in Korea

- PRINCIPAL COMMUNIST AIRFIELDS
- MIG ALLEY
- AREAS PENETRATED BY SMALL NUMBERS OF MIGS WITH LONG RANGE TANKS
- PRINCIPAL UN AIRFIELDS

CHINA

Yalu River

Suiho Reservoir
Sinuiju N/E
Antung
Uiju
Taechon
Huichon
Sinuiju
Namsi
Saamcham
Sinanju
Yongyu
Pyong-Ni
Ogyo-Ri
Kangdong
Sunan
Pyongyang Main
Pyongyang Dowtown
Pyongyang East
Anak
Hwang-Ju
Sariwon
Sinmak

SEA OF JAPAN

KOREA

38°   38°

Kimpo (K–14)   Chunchon (K–47)
                    Hoengsong (K–46)
Seoul (K–16)
Suwon (K–13)   Kangnung (K–18)
            Osan (K–55)
    Pyongtaek (K–6)
Kunsan (K–8)
        Taejon (K–5)
            Pohang (K–3)
Taegu (K–2)
        K–37
                Pusan West (K–1)
K–4   Chinhae   Pusan East (K–9)
            (K–10)

UN Air bases in Japan

CHINA

Hokkaido ①

②

③ JAPAN

SEA OF JAPAN

KOREA

④
⑤⑥
⑦
38°
⑧
⑫ ⑨
⑬ ⑪⑩
⑭
Kyushu
⑮

PACIFIC OCEAN

⑯ Okinawa
Main base for
B-29 Operations
over Korea

① Chitose
② Misawa
③ Matsushima
④ Johnson AFB
⑤ Yokota
⑥ Tachikawa
⑦ Komaki (Nagoya)
⑧ Itami (Osaka)
⑨ Miho
⑩ Iwakuni
⑪ Hofu
⑫ Brady
⑬ Ashiya
⑭ Itazuke
⑮ Tsuiki

COMMUNIST MATERIAL LOSSES TO UN AIR ATTACKS 1950–53	
Troops killed	184,808
Tanks	1,327
Vehicles	82,920
Locomotives	963
Railway cars	10,407
Bridges	1,153
Buildings	118,231
Tunnels	65
Gun positions	8,663
Bunkers	8,839
Oil storage tanks	16
Barges and boats	593
Rail cuts	28,621

COMMUNIST AIRCRAFT LOSSES TO UN AIR POWER, 1950–53	
In the air	949
On the ground	89
Total	1,038

feeling grew that the hundreds of items of equipment carried by the American fighters often did little more than increase the cost, burden the aircraft with excess weight so that it could not outfly the MiG, keep the fighter on the ground through being continually unserviceable, and generally cause more trouble than they were worth.

The 'chuck it out' brigade

One of the leading American fighter designers, C. L. 'Kelly' Johnson (creator of such fighters as the **P-38 Lightning** and F-80 Shooting Star), went to Korea and

US winners. The US Air Force's superiority over the Mig-15 (seen right going down in flames) rested on pilot skill and experience. Major Vermont Garrison, below, shows his Lombard 'bonedome', face mask and ejection seat, in his F-86 Sabre. His unit was the famed 4th Fl Wing.

found pilots there were trying to remove from their fighters practically everything that could be unscrewed. The top-scoring US ace in World War II, Lt-Col. 'Gabby' Gabreski, added 6½ MiGs to his score flying a Sabre in Korea, but strongly belonged to the 'chuck it out' brigade. He discounted the value of the APG-30 radar sight and claimed: 'I'd rather sight my guns with a piece of chewing gum stuck on the windscreen.' Johnson returned to California musing on what had become known as the

US NAVY SORTIES AND LOSSES	
Sorties flown	167,552
Bombs dropped (tons)	120,000
Aircraft losses	814
US MARINES SORTIES AND LOSSES	
Sorties flown	107,303
Bombs dropped (tons)	82,000
Aircraft losses	368

'gum sight'.

In the long term this powerful feeling evaporated. It was bound to do so as soon as US engine designers could come up with engines of much greater thrust so that they could again outfly their opponents. Of course, by this time the Korean war was over, and for a decade there were no more dogfights with Russian-designed fighters. But it is a fact that the sudden appearance of the nimble MiG-15 was at least as unpleasant a shock as the **'Zero'** had been in 1941, and during the remainder of the Korean campaign American pilots were almost unanimous in thinking that the fighting capability of their aircraft would be improved if many components—even such useful ones as ejection seats and some of the guns—could be left off.

This wish for simplicity did not permeate the squadrons flying the extremely complicated B-29 heavy bomber, and though

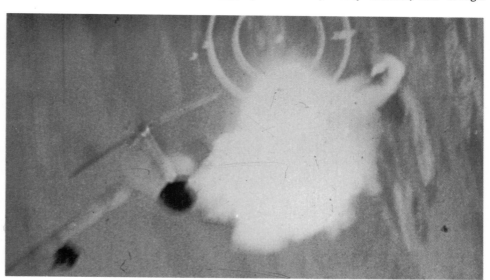

MiG against Sabre

▼ MIG-15, first flown in Korea in November 1950, could outfly all Allied fighters and was superior in climb and manoeuvrability to the F-86A Sabre

▼ North American F-86A Sabre, introduced into Korea a month after the MIG-15, and able to meet it on level terms because of the combat experience of the American pilots

U.S. AIR FORCE
91105
FU-105

many of these fell before MiG cannon fire they hit back hard and were able to destroy some of their speedy opponents. On the other hand, from the earliest days of the war some of the most important bombing targets had been bridges, especially the many road and rail bridges over the Yalu and other rivers in the north across which the Chinese Communists were pouring huge amounts of war material. Bridge-busting was discovered—or rediscovered—to be very difficult. Not only were the bridges very hard to hit, and little affected by a near miss, but they were surrounded by large numbers of light anti-aircraft guns able to throw up intense fire to heights of around 5,000 feet.

Strength versus stealth

Fighters would usually come in first to try to silence the flak with napalm, rockets, bombs and cannon fire. Then the main attack would be mounted, either by low-level fighter or attack aircraft or by B-29s flying level at about 15,000 feet. But it took hundreds of bombs or rockets to cut each bridge. In 1951 the B-29 squadrons began to use radio-guided bombs, the Razon and the 12,000 lb Tarzon, but these were not wholly successful. In any case the Communists soon showed that they were masters at stealthy movement, at keeping supplies moving under severe aerial attack and at immediately repairing damage to road or rail links and replacing bridges by under-water structures or removable pontoon crossings.

Though the technology of radars and countermeasures had not made much progress since 1945, except in the laboratory, much of the Korean air war took place at night. This was when Communist supply routes were more likely to be busy, and it was also judged safer for the B-29 to operate at night, with a matt-black under-surface. Night attacks by fighter and attack aircraft were often supported by special flare-dropping machines, some of them being **C-47 (DC-3)** transports carrying large numbers of flares to provide illumination over long periods. In 1952 the extremely effective **B-26 Invader** attack bomber was engaged against targets, mainly trains, illuminated by an 80-million candlepower searchlight (though this markedly increased the bomber's vulnerability and was eventually abandoned). It was painfully clear by 1952 that great progress had been made with Soviet radar, because fighters, search-lights and AA guns were all being obviously directed by radar against B-29 formations, and the latter's loss rate became as high by night as by day.

Allied airfields were ill-guarded against air attack, and a handful of Communist pilots were able to obtain disproportionately good results in individual night attacks using **Po-2** light biplanes, a 1926-vintage machine in the class of the **Tiger Moth.** Numerous costly US jets were destroyed by small bombs dropped by these venerable 90 mph attackers, and their slowness made them difficult to intercept by other aircraft. On one occasion the very latest jet night fighter, the US Air Force **F-94 Starfire,** put down its landing gear and flaps and slowed sufficiently to bring its 20 mm guns to bear. It

Swansong of piston engines. Early jets lacked flight endurance, and a heavy burden fell on more vulnerable piston-engined machines often built in World War II. The P-51D Mustang was the first combat type of the Republic of Korea AF (above). The Royal Australian Navy's carriers *Sydney* and *Melbourne* were equipped with the Fairey Firefly and Hawker Sea Fury (top), while the hardest-hitting strike aircraft of the US Navy was the Douglas AD Skyraider, a squadron of which destroyed the Hwachon Dam by using torpedoes (facing page). Even later, in Vietnam, piston-engined Mustangs and, especially, Skyraiders, were to prove valuable owing to their range, payload, endurance and good manoeuvrability.

THE KOREAN ACES		
Name and rank	Unit	Score
Capt Joseph McConnell	51st FIW	16
Lt-Col James Jabara	4th FIW	15
Capt Manuel J. Fernandez	4th FIW	14½
Lt-Col George A. Davis	4th FIW	14
Col Royal N. Baker	4th FIW	13
Maj Frederick C. Blesse	4th FIW	10
Capt Harold E. Fischer	51st FIW	10
Col James K. Johnson	4th FIW	10
Lt-Col Vermont Garrison	4th FIW	10
Maj Lonnie R. Moore	4th FIW	10
Capt Ralph S. Parr	4th FIW	10
Lt James F. Low	4th FIW	9
Lt Cecil G. Foster	51st FIW	9
Lt-Col James P. Hagerstrom	18th FBW	8½
Maj Robinson Risner	4th FIW	8
Col George I. Ruddell	51st FIW	8
Capt Clifford D. Jolley	4th FIW	7
Capt Leonard W. Lilley	4th FIW	7
Lt Henry Buttelmann	51st FIW	7

succeeded in destroying the enemy biplane but almost at once—perhaps slowed by the recoil of its guns—the F-94 stalled and crashed, killing the crew.

Wrong place for air power

Radar was also carried by the twin-jet **Douglas F3D Skyknight** of the Navy and Marine Corps, and the Vought Corsair F4U-5N. It was an uphill struggle to keep such aircraft serviceable. This was before transistors and other solid-state electronic devices had been put into production, and each radar contained hundreds of fragile, temperamental and individually fitted vacuum tubes. Though such complex equipment was necessary, it was impossible to avoid the feeling that Korea was the wrong place for the Allied air power; or, put another way, that the Allied aircraft had been designed for a different kind of war.

Korea is not a good place to deploy advanced combat aircraft. Its terrain is a mixture of abrasive sand and dust, waterlogged rice paddies and rugged mountains. Its climate is highly variable, and tens of thousands of Allied troops were put out of action by heat stroke and very nearly as many by severe frostbite. Typhoons and snow blizzards seemed to alternate with long periods of drizzle with cloud base at 1,000 feet or less. When this was added to the need to operate from rudimentary air-strips, which broke landing gears and lacerated multi-ply tyres, the problem of maintaining large-scale air operations can be seen to have been considerable. On top of all these problems was the fact that the industry supporting it all was on the other side of the world.

Korea was an unexpected and stern test which caught the big and technically superior Allied nations off-balance. They never did produce the ideal kind of aircraft for supporting a land war in difficult virgin territory. As soon as the war was concluded, on July 27, 1953, by an unsatisfactory armistice, the warring nations sat back to digest the many lessons. The Communists were able to refine still further their ways of deploying their huge advantage in army man-power. The capitalists did try to build aircraft incorporating Korean lessons, notably Heinemann's Douglas A-4 Skyhawk and Johnson's **F-104 Starfighter,** but most defence money was lavished on nuclear strategic weapons tailored to a totally different kind of conflict.

Allied Warplanes in Korea

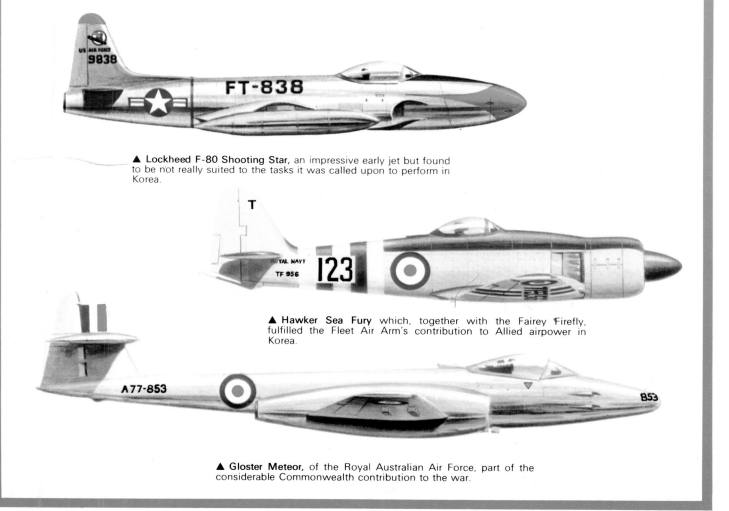

▲ **Lockheed F-80 Shooting Star,** an impressive early jet but found to be not really suited to the tasks it was called upon to perform in Korea.

▲ **Hawker Sea Fury** which, together with the Fairey Firefly, fulfilled the Fleet Air Arm's contribution to Allied airpower in Korea.

▲ **Gloster Meteor,** of the Royal Australian Air Force, part of the considerable Commonwealth contribution to the war.

THE JET TAKE

Korea was the first jet battleground and the real beginning of the jet takeover. As the threat of another world war loomed the security need of the major power blocs called for the equipping of the air forces of still more countries throughout the world. At the same time an increasing number of nations developed and built their own jet warplanes and the aircraft themselves became more sophisticated and more powerful as they reached near supersonic speeds.

Several of the World War II aircraft stayed in production after 1945. The **Vampire** day fighter became a multi-role tactical machine and was built in large numbers in Britain, France, Australia and Switzerland. The **Meteor** likewise adapted to new roles and was built by a consortium in the Low Countries. Agreeing with a widespread feeling that combat aircraft were becoming too complex, so that they would be too costly to buy and too difficult to keep serviceable, British designer Teddy Petter produced the **Folland Gnat,** weighing only 8,800 lb and armed with two 30 mm Aden cannon. This was not adopted by the RAF but was used in small numbers by Finland and Yugoslavia and put into large-scale production in India, where improved versions continued in production in the mid-1970s.

From the Vampire, de Havilland derived the **Venom,** with a more powerful engine (4,850 lb thrust instead of 3,300) and thinner wing. This was planned as a standard type to be made in vast quantities by many NATO nations, with much of the funding provided by the US taxpayer under the Off-Shore Procurement Program (OSP). OSP was a method whereby the US government paid for arms for its allies, even though they were not manufactured in the

United States, as an oblique way of defending itself and simultaneously building up its allies' manufacturing strength. Most of the European fighters of the period 1951–55 were put into production under OSP orders, but the programme was terminated when the European industries began to compete with the United States in commercial markets. In the event many of the huge Venom orders urgently placed in 1950–51 were cancelled, though the basic day fighter/bomber versions were built for many countries.

Britain took a very long time to produce modern transonic fighters. After five years of research and three years of flying swept-wing prototypes, the **Supermarine Swift** entered RAF Fighter Command in 1954. Production comprised small batches, each differing in wing shape, armament, engine or flight controls, and eventually the whole programme was abandoned, apart from a further small number built as reconnaissance machines.

The rival **Hawker Hunter,** however, was a great success. Entering RAF service in July 1954, this shapely day fighter was

bigger and much more powerful than the **F-86 Sabres** which were plugging the gap with Fighter Command and 2nd TAF in Germany, and had a much greater punch with a quickly replaceable package containing four 30 mm Aden cannon and ammunition. Eventually, by 1959, over 1,000 had been delivered to the RAF, while many others were built in the Low Countries. Several hundred were exported, main recipients being Sweden, India and Switzerland (to which country two batches of 30 were supplied as recently as 1972–73). From 1959 the Hunter became important chiefly as a tactical ground-attack machine, a role in which it has lasted very well.

Production of the **Lockheed F-80 Shooting Star** for the US Air Force and other countries had by 1952 been largely supplanted by the **T-33** trainer and **F-94** all-weather fighter.

Very large numbers were also made of the **Republic F-84 Thunderjet** (4,457 built in

174

OVER

five years) and the heavier and more powerful swept-wing **F-84F Thunderstreak** (2,711 built in three years). More than half these fighter-bombers were supplied to NATO nations in Europe, and many were then passed on to smaller countries around 1960. The vitally important North American F-86 Sabre developed through many versions, the Canadian-built types (1,815 made by Canadair) mostly having Orenda turbojets rated at 6,355 or 7,275 lb thrust, compared with 5,200 lb for the US machines, and the Australian version having the British Avon of even greater power as well as two 30 mm cannon. The next generation of US fighters were supersonic.

The Soviet **MiG-15** and its derivative, the **MiG-17,** were built in enormous numbers, probably exceeding that of any other jet (a figure of 19,000 has been mentioned unofficially). Both were built in China before the break with the Soviet Union in 1959, and both sources have exported to more than a score of countries. Other European fighters included the French **Ouragan,** sold to Israel and India; its derivative the **Mystere IIC** and **IVA,** sold to the same nations; and the supersonic **Super Mystere B.2** sold to Israel. In Sweden the **Saab J21R,** a jet conversion of a piston-engined pusher, was succeeded by the **J29,** an outstanding swept-wing fighter made in considerable numbers and sold to

Austria and Ethiopia. Saab's next product was the much further advanced **A32 Lansen** attack aircraft, with Swedish-built Avon

Supreme Hunter. Though it did not enter RAF service until mid-1954 the Hawker Hunter proved to be the finest of all subsonic fighters. Many hundreds are expected to be in service with many air forces until 1980 or even later.

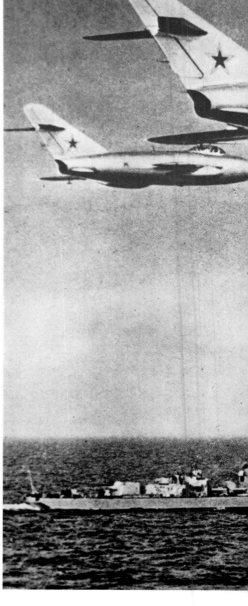

engine, and a faster all-weather fighter version, the **J32B.**

British all-weather and night fighters continued to adhere to the old philosophy that the navigator watched the scope of his AI (airborne interception) radar and told the power how to steer to intercept the enemy. The pilot then flew manually in a curve of pursuit until he could attack with guns or rockets. Aircraft built to this formula included the **Meteor NF.11, 12, 13 and 14,** the **Vampire NF.10,** the **Venom NF.2 and 3** and the nine marks of **Javelin.** Later versions of Javelin introduced the heat-homing Firestreak guided weapon, but still intercepted in the traditional way.

In the US Air Force the same method was used by the **Lockheed F-94 Starfire** family (the final version of which dispensed with guns and relied entirely on salvoes of rockets) and early versions of the much larger **Northrop F-89 Scorpion.** But the **F-89D** introduced a radical fire-control system comprising radar, computer and autopilot, with which a 'collision-course' attack could be made. The fighter continuously predicted future positions of the enemy, whilst attacking from any direction (even from head-on, if necessary). At the appropriate moment the armament was launched to hit the target at one of these future position/time calculations. The F-89D had 104 spin-stabilised rockets, while the **F-89H** replaced most of these by six Falcon guided missiles.

North American then fitted an even more advanced collision-course system into the single-seat **F-86D Sabre.** This carried rockets instead of guns, and had an after-burning engine to make it the fastest of the F-86 family. German and Italian companies collaborated to build an F-86D variant, the **F-86K,** armed with four 20 mm cannon. Later these all-weather Sabres were also given Sidewinder heat-homing missiles, and they serve in many air forces.

Other big all-weather fighters of the early 1950s included the French **Vautour,** supplied to Israel, the Soviet **Yak-25** family, and the Canadian **Avro CF-100** which developed through five main versions and was exported to Belgium. All had two

engines, and carried powerful radar, crew of two, autopilot and armament including rockets.

Supreme among tactical attack aircraft was the British **Canberra** which began life as a supposed strategic bomber but found its real niche with the multi-role **B(I).8** version armed with four 20 mm guns and an assortment of bombs and rockets. This and other marks were exported to numerous overseas airforces, largely owing to its docility and ease of training and maintenance. More recently the unique **Harrier** entered service with the RAF and US Marine Corps in the same tactical spread of roles.

The first jet bomber of the US Air Force, the **North American B-45,** was chosen because, having originally been a piston-engined design, it was produced very quickly. But it was only a stop-gap. The main attack machine in Korea was the **Douglas B-26 Invader,** which was still of great interest after 1960 as a multi-role machine for counter-insurgent (Co-In) and limited war operations. The British Canberra was built as the **Martin B-57** and in the mid 1970s was still emerging in new multi-role and specialised versions, and the **McDonnell Douglas B-66** tactical bomber eventually became more important in the sphere of various kinds of clandestine 'special reconnaissance' including ECM (electronic countermeasures) activity. Ultimately the most important US Air Force attack bomber became the **A-7 Corsair.**

European tactical machines included versions of the **Il-28 'Beagle',** the **Saab-17** and twin-engined **B18,** the French Vautour bomber versions and the **Fiat G91.** The latter, basically a scaled-down Sabre, emerged as the winner of a NATO international contest in 1957. In the event the French refused to have anything to do with it, their own designs having been the G91's unsuccessful rivals, and the G91 was finally adopted by Germany and Italy. Later many were supplied to other NATO countries.

Through the **Lincoln** strategic bomber continued in production in Britain and Australia until 1951 it was very soon useful only for limited-war operations, and from

1955 was replaced in the RAF by the **Valiant.** The first of three very similar 'V bombers', the Valiant introduced the concept of the large strategic bomber that, instead of guns, relied for its defence on height, speed and, later, advanced ECM. Though capable of only Mach 0.84, the Valiant was an excellent aircraft which at last gave the RAF a modern jet striking force. Most of the 108 production machines were tankers, reconnaissance or dual-role aircraft, but fatigue cracks caused sudden premature withdrawal of the type in 1965.

The **Vulcan** and **Victor** were built over a much longer time-period to a more challenging specification. Both served as bombers and reconnaissance aircraft, later variants appearing in service in 1960–61 with increased wing area, much more powerful engines and the capability of carrying the Blue Steel stand-off missile (the proposed Skybolt ballistic missile was not proceeded with, though each bomber could have carried two or four, in place of a single Blue Steel). The improved versions were intended to fly higher, but by the time they were in service this was no defence against surface-to-air missiles and the Vulcan and Victor were being forced to fly at tree-top height to try to avoid radar detection.

Air power at sea demands great contrasts in equipment. The Royal Navy de Havilland Sea Venom F(AW).21 making a belly landing (left) was a night and all-weather fighter engaged in the abortive Suez operation. The MiG-17s (above) were day fighters of the V-VS (Military Aviation Forces) in support of the Black Sea Fleet. The heavily loaded Douglas Skyraider (right) was an attack bomber taking off from USS Kearsage for targets in Korea.

In the USAF Strategic Air Command the **Boeing B-47** enjoyed success as huge as it was unexpected. It stemmed partly from the fact that the aerodynamic drag was an incredible 25 per cent less than predicted, so that on six 5,800 lb engines this 100-ton bomber could outrun all fighters save the F-86. Eventually, with range boosted by 'Flying Boom' aerial refuelling, the B-47 became the standard SAC medium bomber and over 2,000 were delivered by 1957. None were ever used by any other force.

The huge **B-52,** which entered SAC service in 1955, resulted from the development by Pratt & Whitney of a turbojet (the J57) giving 10,000 lb thrust with much better fuel economy than earlier US jets. It enabled Boeing to plan a 350,000 lb jet strategic bomber, with eight of these engines. The final models, introduced after 1960, had much greater fuel capacity, rendering aerial refuelling unnecessary, and more powerful fan engines which extended range to 10,000 miles when carrying two Hound Dog stand-off nuclear missiles. Structural difficulties followed the switch to low-level operations, and in Vietnam the main job was trucking up to 84,000 lb of conventional bombs. Like the B-47 the B-52 had a radar-directed rear gun turret, and the final modification was to equip the late **G** and **H** sub-types to launch the compact SRAM (short-range attack missile), with a 90-mile range and powerful nuclear warhead. About 200 of the 744 B-52s were SRAM-converted, each carrying up to 20 missiles as well as two Mk 28 thermonuclear bombs or two Quail ECM-carrying decoy missiles to fool enemy defence systems.

In 1956 the US Navy put into carrier service an entirely new species of aircraft, the seagoing long-range strategic bomber. This materialised as the **Douglas** (now McDonnell Douglas) **A-3 Skywarrior,** which could do most of the things a B-47 could but was appreciably more compact and lighter (83,000 lb). Carrying one H-bomb each, the Skywarriors of both the Atlantic and Pacific Fleets played a major role in the Cold War balance of power as they could attack in unexpected places with little warning. Like the later Mach 2 **A-5 Vigilante,** the A-3 later served mainly in reconnaissance, ECM and other roles.

The main medium bomber of the Soviet Union has since the early 1950s been the **Tu-16.** Powered by two 19,200 lb thrust turbojets in its original version, this is essentially a Valiant-class machine with half as many engines each of twice the power. It incorporates a complex defence armament derived from that carried by the **B-29,** which from 1946 until 1949 was built under licence as the **Tu-4** by the remarkable process of dismantling every part and working out the material specifications (76,000 of them) and production processes. B-29-derived armament was also applied to the remarkable **Tu-20,** powered by four very large turboprop engines and endowed with the extraordinary speed (for a propeller aircraft) of 560 mph. Weighing up to 375,000 lb this family of aircraft are typical of Soviet strategic bombers in being capable of development through numerous versions over a 20-year period.

The Tu-16 and Tu-20 both later appeared with a range of unusual radars, with stand-off missiles for attacks on cities or surface ships, with flight refuelling by the probe/drogue system, and ultimately in special reconnaissance versions with radically different avionic equipment, augmented crews and even, in some cases, early-warning radar. The **Mya-4** four-jet bomber has served in smaller numbers, but this too has been developed in flight-refuelled reconnaissance and ECM versions. Only the Tu-16 has been exported, in small numbers to the UAR and to Indonesia.

In the maritime role the problems in World War II were to develop effective ASV (air to surface vessel) radar and build shore-based machines with adequate range. The Americans led with both developments, and by 1945 such machines as the **PB4Y-2 Privateer** could do a good oceanic job. But thereafter progress was slow. The RAF **Shackleton,** starting with an airframe derived from the Lancaster, took more than ten years to work through three major sub-types with improved equipment, the final **3B** version having added jet engines to help the overstrained piston engines on take-off.

Similar technology went into the **Argus, Neptune** and early **Orion,** while the very efficient **Atlantic,** the winner of a NATO competition and built by a large international consortium, represents the pinnacle of this technology. Similar equipment, based on radars, MAD (magnetic anomaly detection) gear, sonobuoys and other sensing devices, were packaged into smaller carrier-based machines such as the British **Fairey** (Westland) **Gannet,** powered by a double turboprop running on ship's diesel fuel and designed to cruise with one engine-half shut down, and the American **Grumman Tracker** with two piston engines which was built under licence in Canada.

Second Generation Jet Fighters

▲ Canadair CL-13B Sabre Mk. 6 of No. 439 Squadron, Royal Canadian Air Force, at Marville, France, in 1957. One of the final production models of the North American F-86 Sabre clear-weather fighter which was flown as a prototype on October 1, 1947

▲ Gloster Javelin F.A.W. Mk. 9 of No. 64 Squadron, RAF (1960). The Javelin all-weather fighter flew as a prototype on November 26, 1951, and the type served with the RAF from 1956 until 1968

▲ Republic F-84FQ Thunderstreak of the Turkish 1st Tactical Air Force at Eskisehir (1970). Derived from the straight-wing Thunder-jet, the Thunderstreak was first flown on June 3, 1950, and the type was widely used by NATO air forces from the mid 'fifties through the mid 'sixties

▲ Folland Gnat of the Finnish Air Force (Squadron 11 at Luonet-järvi). The Gnat lightweight fighter was first flown on July 18, 1955, but apart from one squadron purchased by Finland, was only adopted by the Indian Air Force which has used it in the Indo-Pakistan wars

▲ Supermarine Swift F.R. Mk. 5 reconnaissance-fighter of No. 79 Squadron, RAF, 2nd Allied Tactical Air Force, Germany (1956). The Swift was the first British swept-wing fighter to enter service but was operated in the intercept role only from February 1954 to May 1955

▲ **Hawker Hunter F. Mk. 51** of 724 Squadron of the Royal Danish Air Force. The Hunter remained in Danish service from 1956 until 1974, and this type, which first flew on June 20, 1951, is expected to remain in service with some air arms until the 'eighties

◄ **Fiat G.91R.3** fighter-bomber of Leichtes Kamfgeschwader 43 of the Luftwaffe at Oldenburg (1970). Winner of a NATO contest for a light fighter-bomber, the G.91 first flew on August 9, 1956 and was adopted by Italy and Germany

▲ **Dassault Mystère IVA**, illustrated in service with the Indian Air Force, flew as a prototype on September 28, 1952 and entered service with the French Armée de l'Air in 1955

◄ **North American F-86D Sabre** of 726 Squadron of the Royal Danish Air Force. This all-weather variant of the Sabre remained in Danish service from 1958 until 1966

▲ **Republic RF-84F Thunderflash** of 717 Squadron, Royal Norwegian Air Force, at Rygge (1968). A reconnaissance-fighter derivative of the Thunderstreak with wing root intakes, the RF-84F was produced between 1954 and 1958

▼ **SAAB 32B Lansen** all-weather interceptor of the 1st Squadron of the Swedish Air Force Wing F12 at Kalmar. The interceptor version of the Lansen, flown for the first time on January 7, 1957, entered service in 1958 and was phased out at the beginning of the 'seventies

ikoyan **MiG-17F** of the Khmer (Cambodian) Air Force (1972). ed from the MiG-15, the MiG-17 flew in 1950 and entered ce with the Soviet Air Forces in 1952. It remains first-line ational equipment with a number of air forces

By 1959 a revolution was in the offing. The digital computer was reaching a degree of miniaturization such that airborne versions could be considered for complete control of the most complex combat situations. The US Navy developed the A-New anti-submarine weapon system, with extremely advanced avionics under digital control, and tailored the first version to fit a new Orion, the **P-3C.** The same system in much modified form was used as the basis for the most remarkable exercise in airborne packaging there has ever been, the **Lockheed S-3A Viking,** which, from 1973, replaced the old Tracker as the standard US shipboard ASW machine. Powered by two turbofans, the Viking is the smallest aircraft capable of carrying the crew of four, the range of radar/ MAD/sonics/emissions ASW sensing systems, and the computer control to enable

attacks to be made either alone or in partnership with other forces. Such operations involve the storage of millions of constantly changing items of data, and their instantaneous management. Steering the aircraft to drop AS weapons (chiefly homing torpedoes) is one of the automatic outputs.

With the excellent turbofan-powered **Nimrod** the RAF has an aircraft of great range and endurance which not only has all the new systems and digital control, as well as a completely separate analog computer serving different functions, but also retains the large crew needed to break into the automatic loops and direct the operation manually if necessary (though severe battle damage can be sustained without manual control being necessary). Compared with earlier oceanic aircraft the Nimrod has higher (475 knot) transit speed, far greater

crew comfort and superior weapon-system performance. Next aircraft in the same class will be the NATO **Atlantic 2** and **2B,** the **Boeing LRPA** (long-range patrol aircraft) and a new Soviet machine derived, like the Boeing and Nimrod (and the **Il-38**), from a civil airliner.

Flying boats are no longer used, though the Japanese have recently built small batches of four-turboprop boats for a wide range of maritime roles. Until 1955–59 flying

Communist co-operation. Red China laid the foundations of its air power with Soviet help. Since 1960 the construction of improved types of Russian fighter, notably the F-6 (based on the Mig-19) and F-9 (based on the Mig-21), has continued without Soviet aid. Both are cheap and effective fighters.

Red China's Air Power

▲ Mikoyan-Gurevich MiG-15bis of the late Korean War period. The MiG-15 was finally phased out of the first-line inventory in the early 'sixties when it was replaced by the Sino-Communist-built MiG-17F

▲ MiG-19SF built in China is currently the most important numerically of Sino-Communist fighters and has been supplied to other countries (e.g., Albania, Pakistan)

▲ Ilyushin Il-28 light bomber, Soviet-supplied, delivered before the onset of ideological differences between the Sino-Communists and the Soviet Union, has provided the backbone of Sino-Communist attack capability since the late 'fifties

boats such as the **Sunderland, Martin PBM Mariner** and **P5M Marlin** were widely used, and in 1950 the US Navy funded such very advanced boats as the four-turboprop **Convair P5Y Tradewind** (later converted to logistics transports) and four-jet 600 mph **Martin P6M Sea Master.**

Among carrier-based machines the profusion of types in the post-war period included a de Havilland series derived from land-based machines: the **Sea Mosquito,** the main version of which was a torpedo bomber; the **Sea Hornet,** the major version being a two-seat all-weather and night fighter; the **Sea Vampire,** built in modest numbers; the **Sea Venom,** the standard two-seat all-weather fighter of 1953–61, which was also built in modified form in France as the **Aquilon;** and the far bigger and more powerful twin-engined **Sea Vixen** all-weather fighter which entered service in 1959 armed with the curve-of-pursuit Firestreak guided missile and finally developed in **Mk 2** form with the collision-course Red Top missile able to intercept from any direction.

Other British carrier aircraft included the **Fairey Firefly,** a Griffon piston-engined two-seat fighter which grew a third seat as an anti-submarine attack aircraft; the 2,520 hp **Sea Fury** fighter-bomber, much used in Korea and supplied to other countries; the **Hawker Sea Hawk** day jet fighter and the similarly powered (5,000 lb Nene engine) **Supermarine Attacker;** the large **Blackburn Firebrand** torpedo fighter and its replacement the 4,200 hp turboprop **Westland Wyvern;** the **Supermarine Scimitar** transonic strike fighter with twin 11,250 lb Avon engines and four 30 mm guns; and the **Hawker Siddeley Buccaneer** transonic bomber designed for low-level under-the-radar penetration and capable of carrying a

16,000 lb load, of which 4,000 lb can be in an internal bay.

US Navy fighters in the Korean period included the powerful **Grumman F7F Tigercat,** with two 2,500 hp engines and various radar/crew options; the trim **F8F Bearcat,** used in small numbers; and the extremely important **F9F Panther,** used in huge numbers in Korea in many versions, and its successor the swept-wing **Cougar.** Vought made the evergreen 2,500 hp **Corsair,** post-war models (widely exported) having early wing-mounted radar; the odd **F7U** twin-jet **Cutlass** with no tailplane but two swept fins on the wing; and the Mach 1.7 **Crusader.**

Douglas provided the compact **F3D Skynight** radar-packed night and all-weather fighter, and the transonic **F4D Skyray.** North American developed the swept-wing F-86 into the **FJ-2 Fury** for the US Navy and Marine Corps, the more powerful, redesigned **FJ-3,** and the completely re-designed **FJ-4** and **FJ-4B** which could fly under automatic control and toss-bomb with nuclear weapons or launch Bullpup attack missiles. McDonnell followed the **FH-1 Phantom** with the excellent **F2H Banshee** and then, after having to switch engines through failure of the first choice, perfected the big transonic **F3H Demon,** the first naval fighter with guided missile armament.

Douglas kept the **AD Skyraider** family in production from 1945 for 12 years, and 3,180 were built in 28 versions (not counting 64 versions resulting from later changes). Powered by a big piston engine, the 25,000 lb Skyraider has great endurance and load-carrying capability, and variants can perform 32 distinct duties including ambulance, tanker, ECM surveillance, personnel transport and airborne early-warning, as well as

Under-the-radar-bomber. The Hawker Siddeley Buccaneer, later transferred to the RAF, was designed as a low-level ship-board bomber for the Royal Navy able to approach its targets beneath the enemy's radar screen.

---

all kinds of attack missions. The jet **A4D Skyhawk** has likewise continued in production, setting a remarkable 22-year record. Capable of 700 mph, this very compact machine has grown with more power, bigger loads and better avionics, and has found wide export sales for new and second-hand versions. Another carrier-based attack machine was the **Martin AM-1 Mauler,** a 3,500 hp load-carrier obsolete by 1957.

The aerial tanker is a vital adjunct to all major air forces and navies. Even the longest-ranged bombers often need aerial refuelling, and a very high proportion of the world's strategic and tactical aircraft could not fly all their designated wartime missions without using the technique. The Buddy pack, a streamlined container for fuel and a power-driven hose-reel, can convert almost any fighter or attack machine into a tanker, but the specialized tankers of the US Air Force were purpose-built. The **KB-29P** bomber conversion of 1949 was followed by a huge force of 888 **KC-97** tankers, which in turn yielded to 732 of the even bigger and more powerful **KC-135** (707 type) **Stratotankers,** not counting many built for transport and special reconnaissance roles. A further 14 KC-135s were delivered to France with the Flying Boom modified to trail a drogue matched to the **Mirage IVA** bomber. US Navy tankers include special versions of the A-3 Skywarrior and **A-6 Intruder.** RAF tankers have dwindled to a small force of rebuilt Victor bombers.

The Balance of Terror

As the large power blocs of the world edge their way cautiously towards detente, the peace is kept by the deterrent threat of nuclear war. This balance of terror is maintained by a complicated process of 'double think' whereby each side theoretically answers the others' theoretical strike with an even more devastating response, making the act of aggression unacceptable because of the resulting annihilation of both sides. The strong cards in this deadly game of bluff, with its constantly changing rules, are the air forces of the major powers. Upon their preparedness and their equipment depends the essential credibility of each side's position.

Nuclear weapons have introduced a new dimension to warfare; one of such scope and horror that the mind—and even the imagination—find it hard to grasp. A single nuclear bomb could ravage as many as 2,000 square miles by blast and fire. Up until the late 1950s, when significant advances in the control of the emission of radiation took place, a nuclear explosion would have infected the target with deadly radiation, making it poisonous for months or even years. To cap it all, the radiation, borne on wind or water, could have directly or indirectly killed or maimed thousands far from the site of the explosion.

Because of these terrible effects, nuclear strategy was founded and is still based on the concept of deterrence. Deterrence can be described as being so strong as to persuade a potential adversary that it is not worth his while to attack—a simple concept which has been adopted by states in one way or another for centuries. It also implies, and this is not quite so simple in the nuclear context, the ability to tell an opponent he should not do something you do not like, other than attacking you with armed force. The difficulty here, with nuclear weapons as the sanction, is whether one side can confidently threaten the use of nuclear attack if the other side has nuclear weapons with which it can strike back. This is the problem of 'credibility of the deterrent'. It is clear that whereas, in the past, war could be contemplated—and was often used—as an instrument of policy, nuclear weapons have added an awesome power to the clenched fist of deterrence.

It took some years for the strategic implications of nuclear weapons to sink in after 1945. Despite the US monopoly until 1949, when the Soviets exploded their first atomic device, and supremacy for some years after, the full implications of the threat of the atomic bomb did not really crystallise in military thinking until 1953. In

that year, both the US and Soviet Russia exploded thermonuclear devices (the hydrogen bomb). The immensely greater power of these weapons dissolved most doubts that a real revolution in warfare, and deterrence, had occurred.

Nonetheless, military planners continued for the rest of the decade to assume that a period of 'broken-backed war' would continue for an indefinite period after all nuclear weapons had been fired at the outset of a war. On all but the most sanguine assumptions about the ability of a defence to destroy nuclear weapon carriers before they arrived, it needed considerable imagination to decide who would be fighting such a war, what they would be fighting with, or indeed why they would be fighting at all. However, one must remember that it takes time for revolutions to mature; and that military thinkers are suspicious of those who claim that a new weapon renders all others obsolete; and that, if one avoids the trap of assuming that the next war will be like the last, it is exceedingly difficult without any experimental data (which can usually only be provided by another war) to deduce what the next war will be like.

Churchill's sublime irony

Despite these reservations, the deterrent value of the hydrogen bomb was popularly realised in the mid-1950s. For example, the British Defence White Paper stated in 1955 that 'the existence of the nuclear weapon may discourage overt armed intervention by the Communist powers such as occurred in Korea'; and in 1956 that 'the advent of

Nuclear reality. 'Survival is the twin brother of annihilation', said Churchill in a 1955 speech assessing the delicacy of the global nuclear standoff.

the hydrogen bomb has enormously strengthened the power of the deterrent and . . . the likelihood of global war has decreased'. In Churchill's famous words, delivered to the House of Commons in 1955: '. . . it may be that we shall, by a process of sublime irony, have reached a stage in this story where safety will be the sturdy child of terror, and survival the twin brother of annihilation'.

The deterrent theory, christened by some the balance of terror, can be condensed at its simplest to these propositions. Our opponent has aggressive intentions; he wishes to attack our territory or that of our allies, or he may attack targets which we and our allies consider to be vital interests, for example our communications or our sources of raw materials. He may threaten to do this by use of nuclear weapons. But, if we have nuclear weapons, we can cause an unacceptable amount of damage to his cities, industry, communications or maybe his armed forces. He will therefore decide that the game is not worth the candle.

While there has been no doubt, since the mid-50s, that nuclear weapons *per se* had the destructive power to back up these propositions, the theory depended—and still does—on two factors. First, that the weapons could be delivered to their targets. Secondly, that in the last resort there was a will to use them. Both these factors had a considerable effect on the power of deterrent forces and the development of nuclear strategy.

Until the end of the 1950s, the manned bomber was supreme as a carrier of nuclear bombs. The USAF had some hundreds of **B-29s** and later **B-47s.** Although the range of the faster and less vulnerable B-47s was not enough to allow intercontinental attack (that is, from the United States directly to the Soviet Union), the Americans had acquired rights to sufficient bases (in the UK, Spain and North Africa) within range of their targets to allow them to attack European Russia from the west and south. Air defence depended on manned fighter aircraft. Although radar and firepower as well as aircraft had improved since 1945—supersonic fighters such as the **F-100** and its successors and the **Mig-21** were introduced in 1955, they were unlikely at best to destroy more than a fraction of the attackers. The US alone, without the then very small British contribution, could deliver more than a hundred, possibly some hundreds, of nuclear weapons on Soviet targets. For their part, the Russians, while they could attack European targets, had then only a limited ability to attack the continental United States.

Counter counter confusion

But thanks to missile developments, the manned aircraft's supremacy was short-lived. During the late 1950s, the first anti-aircraft missiles (surface-to-air guided weapons or SAGW for short) appeared. These, faster than the bombers, with a much greater height and range than anti-aircraft guns, and able to follow a target aircraft whatever the latter's manoeuvres, seriously reduced the chances of the bomber getting through. True, the bomber could be fitted with electronic counter-measures, devices to deflect the missile from its target. But the missile in its turn could carry counter-

countermeasures. Overall the introduction of SAGW tilted the balance in favour of the defence.

Nonetheless, given that a comparatively small number of nuclear weapons on target (perhaps 10, perhaps 50, it was difficult to be precise) was enough to deter an opponent, the manned aircraft could perhaps have survived as a prime means of delivery in spite of probable heavy losses. Indeed, the US and Britain both planned supersonic bombers in the 1950s. One of the US aircraft, the **B-70,** never went into service; a British project by Avro was cancelled. Manned aircraft had certain advantages: they could be recalled after launch, be moved from base to base more or less at will, and be used for conventional warfare. But the bomber was vulnerable on the ground and might give considerable warning of its approach, of the order of half an hour or more. These disadvantages were exposed by the advent of the ballistic missile.

This weapon had been used, in a primitive form, when the Germans attacked London with V-2s in 1944-45. The V-2 was inaccurate, short range and had comparatively small high explosive warheads. In the scale of World War II they had little more than nuisance value. But direct defence against them was impossible at the time; and, although attempts were made to attack the launching sites, these were mobile and

Big bombers of the 1950s. The Soviet Tu-20 (above, carrying 'Kangaroo' missiles) weighs over 170 tons. The Boeing B-52H (right, with two Hound Dog missiles) weighs 244 tons.

almost impossible to find.

The ballistic missile as later developed was a very different weapon. Its range and accuracy were infinitely greater; earlier weapons, such as the US Thor and the cancelled British Blue Streak, in the late 50s and early 60s had ranges of the order of 2,000 miles and accuracies of about 1 mile; later weapons, such as Titan and Minuteman, had intercontinental range, 7,000 miles or thereabouts and greater accuracy. They could carry nuclear warheads and, thanks to their very high speed, they gave little warning of their approach. It was soon evident that, using elaborate and sophisticated radar systems, the United Kingdom could expect a maximum of three minutes warning of attack and the United States, thanks to its distance behind the radar screen, perhaps five times as much.

Balancing the balance

These warning periods, minute in terms of the time needed to take decisions and react, not only did not allow any time for the population to disperse or take shelter; they disturbed the deterrent balance. A surprise attack now had an excellent chance of destroying an aircraft force on the ground.

Earlier, liquid-fuelled, versions of the ballistic missile, sited above ground, were also vulnerable to nuclear attack, and a surprise strike had an excellent chance of neutralising an adversary's retaliatory power. The balance was, however, soon restored by later versions of the ballistic missile. These, solid-fuelled (which meant that they could be kept for long periods ready to go within the likely warning time), and sited either underground or at sea (which reduced their vulnerability), effectively eliminated the chance of an attacker destroying his opponent's nuclear force. The risk of counterattack causing unacceptable damage remained very high. This position was reached by the mid-1960s.

But the long-range manned aircraft still has a place in the strategic armoury, indeed the **B-1** is an indispensible part of the US nuclear strike strategy. The US still has a force of 442 **B-52s** and the USSR 140 **Tupolev Tu-20 'Bears'** and **Myasishchev M-4 'Bisons'** plus some 30 of the new variable geometry **Tupolev 'Backfire'** strategic bombers. The British and French also have strategic bombers and they have functions in situations other than global nuclear war. The strategic bomber can also add a third element, in addition to ground and sea-based missiles, to the nuclear force, thus complicating the task of an opponent. In the late 1950s and early 1960s, an attempt was made to extend the star role of the manned aircraft by developing a stand-off ballistic missile which would be launched from an aircraft. Over 7,000 SRAMs are now in service but the initial missile—Skybolt—was a failure and is mainly remembered because its cancellation led to a crisis of confidence between the British and

Americans and thus to the acquisition of Polaris (US designed, submarine launched missiles) by the British. During the last decade anti-ballistic missile defences (ABM) have been developed by the Soviets and the Americans. These are technically complex and enormously expensive to deploy on any scale. So far the only operational system known is a ring of 60 or so ABM sites round Moscow. The effect of this Soviet deployment on the deterrent balance is minimal, since the Moscow defences can be swamped by the large US missile force. However, the theoretical effect of widespread ABM defences is interesting.

If the 'balance of terror' is to remain stable, each side must be able to inflict unacceptable damage on the other. Equally, neither side should be able to eliminate the other's striking force by surprise attack. If therefore, ABM defences are put up over missile sites, the striking force becomes even less vulnerable and the balance becomes more stable. However, ABM defences of cities tend to reduce the chance of receiving unacceptable damage; and thus tend to make the balance less stable. It has been said that, for a solid and stable balance, '. . . hostages (by which is usually meant cities) must remain unambiguously vulnerable and retaliating forces must remain unambiguously invulnerable'.

Proliferating warheads

However, it looks as though the attack can retain a considerable lead over the defence. The first ballistic missiles carried one warhead. The next step was to put a number of warheads on one missile. This development complicates the task of ABM defences immensely since, even if all the warheads do not carry nuclear explosive, the defence cannot know which ones do; so all must be

destroyed. In the military jargon, these warheads are called MRVs (multiple re-entry vehicles). A further step was the MIRV (multiple independently-targeted re-entry vehicles); each of the pack of warheads carried by one missile can be sent to a different target, thus further complicating the task of the defence. Further possible developments are for the missile not to follow the usual ballistic trajectory (similar to that of a shell—but of course higher and further) but instead to go into orbit round the earth and thence descend on its target—this system is named FOBS, Fractional Orbit Bombardment System, and DICBM, a missile with a depressed trajectory. Both systems avoid part or all of ABM radars and thus reduce warning time and the effectiveness of ABM.

The credibility of a deterrent force depends not only on its technical ability to inflict an unacceptable degree of damage, but also on whether its owner is willing to use it. This is a difficult question and one which has provoked much debate. Fortunately, perhaps, it does not need to be answered in yes-or-no terms since, even if one is uncertain about an opponent's willingness to use his nuclear force, the risk that he will retaliate and inflict appalling damage remains.

During the 1950s the atomic bomb, and later the hydrogen bomb, appeared to provide the only counterbalance to the weakness of NATO in conventional forces. To those who believed that the Soviets were poised to overrun Western Europe with their large armies and tactical air forces, the large US strategic bomber force seemed to be the only shield. John Foster Dulles, then US Secretary of State, talked of 'massive retaliation' against Soviet aggression. Others referred to the NATO forces in Europe as 'a tripwire' which would respond to Soviet

incursion by triggering off devastation of the Soviet homeland. But, as the Soviet nuclear armoury grew, the question came to be asked: 'What Soviet aggression justifies pulling the nuclear trigger if that action means we are destroyed as well as the enemy?' A minor attack by small Soviet forces on a fringe target? An attempt to take West Berlin by force? A political coup in West Berlin? Or, do we only respond to an all-out conventional attack on NATO territory? If so, do we let fringe targets—or Berlin—go by default and thus be eaten piecemeal? A dilemma encapsulated in the question: 'Is it better to be Red than dead?'

Russia confronts the US

In 1955 some British military thinkers suggested a policy of 'graduated deterrence'. By that time a number of lower yield atomic weapons (i.e. with an explosive power of some kilotons as opposed to the megatons of the hydrogen or thermonuclear bombs) were being developed; and the policy proposed that these weapons (now called tactical nuclear weapons) should be used to attack enemy forces or local targets in the area of local aggressions. The punishment, as it were, would not only fit the crime but also be confined to the scene of the crime. Mutual national destruction could thereby be avoided for actions short of all-out war. The policy was not adopted, mainly because it was difficult to devise a scale of response. (It is worth remembering that 'lower yield' is a relative term: the Hiroshima bomb was a lower yield weapon but it killed 160,000 people and devastated 4 square miles of the city). However it served to heighten discussion of the 'trigger' problem and paved the way for the later theory of 'flexible response', evolved after the Cuba crisis of 1962.

The Cuban crisis is so far the outstanding confrontation of nuclear powers. The cause itself could be called 'nuclear': the stationing of Soviet missiles in Cuba, whence they could threaten American cities. For the Americans, this constituted a threat to their heartland and one which could not be tolerated. For the Soviets, their prestige and their position as Castro's patron and their power to assist or protect other states was involved. The crisis was resolved, thanks to communication between the two leaders, cool nerves, the use of carefully measured conventional force (the naval blockade), prudent negotiation—in that neither side was forced into a position from which there was no retreat—and above all a realisation on both sides of the consequences of nuclear war. The deterrent could be said to have been effective. To most, the message was comforting.

Nonetheless, several political problems associated with nuclear armaments remained. One, highlighted by Cuba, was the problem of control. Cuba was primarily a confrontation between the US and Soviet Russia: but it might have led to a third world war. America's allies complained that, although their interests were closely involved, they were not consulted during the crisis; they were only informed of US moves. On the other hand, during a fast-developing crisis there is rarely time for a dozen or more nations to reach common decisions. (In the

Technology of terror. US strategic weapons of the 1950s made bold strides into new technology. Nuclear submarines gave the city-destroying Polaris missile (above, a submarine launch of A3 model) a secure mobile launch pad deep in the ocean. The B-58A Hustler (prototype, right above) flew at Mach 2.

Long-serving bombers. The Tupolev Tu-22 'Blinder' (below) has an unusual layout; it is rather smaller and slower than the B-58 but has seen long operational service. So too has the Hawker Siddeley Vulcan (bottom, the B.2 version) which has good performance at very high or very low level.

Nuclear Bombers of Soviet Russia and the United States of America

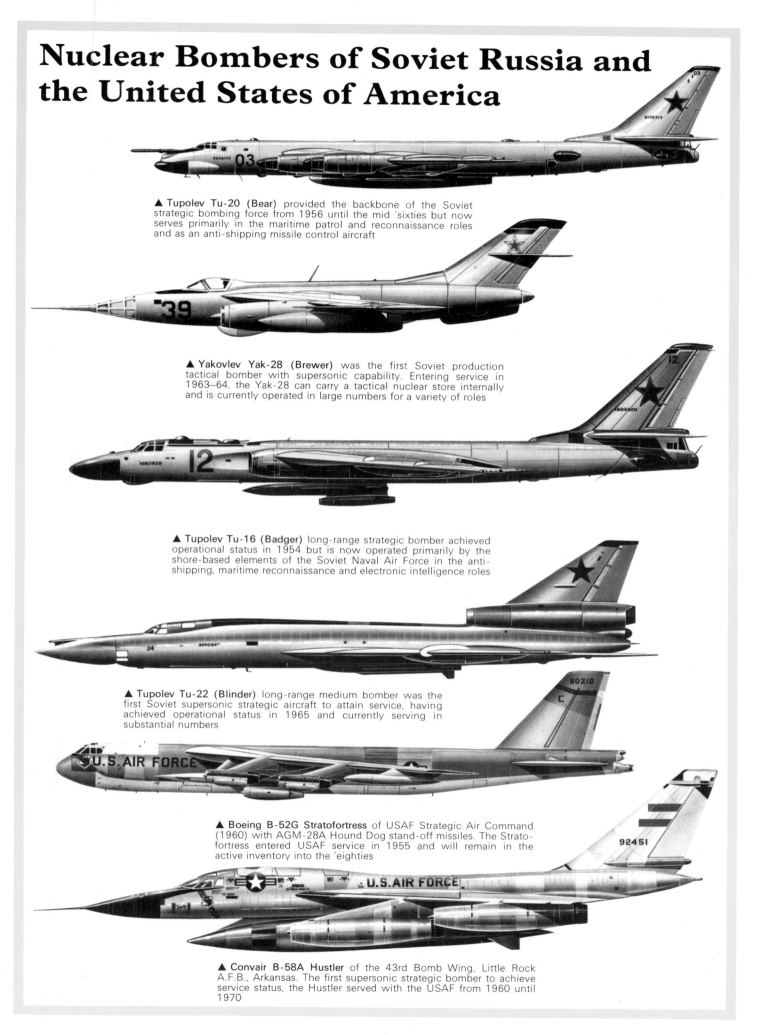

▲ Tupolev Tu-20 (Bear) provided the backbone of the Soviet strategic bombing force from 1956 until the mid 'sixties but now serves primarily in the maritime patrol and reconnaissance roles and as an anti-shipping missile control aircraft

▲ Yakovlev Yak-28 (Brewer) was the first Soviet production tactical bomber with supersonic capability. Entering service in 1963–64, the Yak-28 can carry a tactical nuclear store internally and is currently operated in large numbers for a variety of roles

▲ Tupolev Tu-16 (Badger) long-range strategic bomber achieved operational status in 1954 but is now operated primarily by the shore-based elements of the Soviet Naval Air Force in the anti-shipping, maritime reconnaissance and electronic intelligence roles

▲ Tupolev Tu-22 (Blinder) long-range medium bomber was the first Soviet supersonic strategic aircraft to attain service, having achieved operational status in 1965 and currently serving in substantial numbers

▲ Boeing B-52G Stratofortress of USAF Strategic Air Command (1960) with AGM-28A Hound Dog stand-off missiles. The Strato-fortress entered USAF service in 1955 and will remain in the active inventory into the 'eighties

▲ Convair B-58A Hustler of the 43rd Bomb Wing, Little Rock A.F.B., Arkansas. The first supersonic strategic bomber to achieve service status, the Hustler served with the USAF from 1960 until 1970

extreme case when enemy missiles are on their way, there is clearly no time at all).

The Kennedy solution

President Kennedy attempted to solve this problem, at least in part, when he proposed a multilateral nuclear force (MLF), composed of ships armed with ballistic missiles and manned by multi-national crews. The force, however, was not very viable—surface ships are vulnerable—and was to contain only a small part of the US deterrent. The proposal was not adopted. Since then, attempts have been made to improve the machinery for nuclear consultation in NATO. These are perhaps not perfect, but the problem, given the possibly divergent interests involved and the speed of reaction needed, is not easily solved.

Another problem is when to introduce nuclear weapons into a European conflict, assuming the Soviets do not start with a nuclear attack on the US or Europe. NATO conventional forces have remained inferior to the Russian forces available for attack in Western Europe. Most European nations did not wish to increase their defence expenditure for fear of harming their economies;

Nuclear bombers and electronic snoopers. The electronic side of the strategic war never stops. This Russian Tu-16 'Badger F' (top), with underwing electronic pods, was intercepted near Alaska. The USAF B-52C (right, being refuelled by a KC135) was photographed in the same area. The Blue Steel stand-off missile (far right) is being readied for installation beneath the Handley Page Victor B.2 of RAF Strike Command seen in the background. Constant readiness is all part of a nation's nuclear credibility.

European Nuclear Bombers

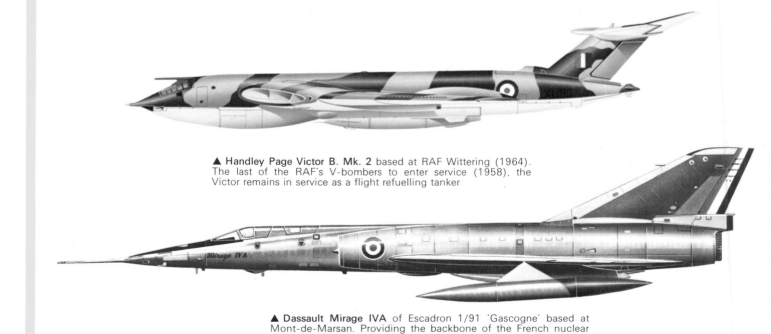

▲ Handley Page Victor B. Mk. 2 based at RAF Wittering (1964). The last of the RAF's V-bombers to enter service (1958), the Victor remains in service as a flight refuelling tanker

▲ Dassault Mirage IVA of Escadron 1/91 'Gascogne' based at Mont-de-Marsan. Providing the backbone of the French nuclear deterrent, the Mirage IVA achieved operational status in March 1968 and is currently scheduled to remain in service until 1980

they preferred to depend on the US nuclear umbrella with, for surety, the presence of US troops in Europe. Britain and France went further and developed nuclear forces of their own for a number of reasons including a belief that nuclear forces were more economical than conventional ones and a desire to have a larger voice in world affairs. Apart from the US umbrella, therefore, the conventional imbalance in Europe could only be corrected by 'tactical' nuclear weapons and these were deployed in Europe from the 1950s onwards, either on missiles such as Honest John, Sergeant and Pershing or airborne by, for example, the **Canberra** and the **F-105.** But the Soviets also deployed a force of tactical weapons, plus scores of MRBMs and IRBMs (medium- and intermediate-range ballistic missiles) which they could use in the European theatre. Any use of nuclear weapons by NATO was therefore likely to be answered in kind. The next step (in a process known as 'escalation') would probably be intercontinental bombardment between Soviet Russia and the US.

The Americans, drawing on their experience over Cuba, proposed in 1963 a policy of 'flexible response'. This envisaged more conventional forces in NATO to deal with at least the initial stages of a Russian conventional attack, thus giving more time for negotiation and increasing the number of options available to NATO before calling on nuclear weapons. The European allies have not all been enthusiastic about this policy, arguing that increased conventional forces lower the credibility of the deterrent, which should be sufficient in itself. Again, a cut-and-dried solution is not easy to find. No doubt more acceptable refinements of the strategy will evolve. In the meantime, the risks of taking action which might provoke nuclear retaliation remain high.

▲ Hawker Siddeley Vulcan B. Mk. 2 based at RAF Coningsby (1967). The Vulcan entered service (in its B. Mk. 1 form) in 1956 and is expected to be phased out in the early 'eighties

▲ Vickers Valiant B. Mk. 1 of No. 18 Squadron, RAF (1959). The first of the RAF's V-bombers, the Valiant served from 1956 until 1964

THE SUPERSONIC GENERATION

In October 1947 USAF Major Charles Yeager became the first man to fly faster than sound. Ten years later there were nine supersonic fighters in service in the United States and Soviet Union and Mach 2 and even Mach 3 fighters and bombers were already on order. It seemed logical to make aircraft fly faster and faster until combat experience clearly demonstrated the shortcomings of the pursuit of pure speed. Speed was not wholly abandoned but more attention was paid to manoeuvrability and equipment. The result was a number of exciting and efficient supersonic aircraft that proved their worth in Vietnam, the Middle East, the Indo-Pakistan War and in the routine conduct of affairs in the air forces of the world.

The development of the jet engine removed the restriction on aircraft speed which had been imposed by the piston engine and propeller. There was henceforth no obvious upper limit to the speed that might be attained, though there appeared to be obvious difficulties in flying faster than about nine-tenths as fast as sound (Mach 0.9, or about 595 mph at high altitude). At speeds greater than this the appearance of shock-waves caused rapid increase in drag, so that further increase in speed needed excessive additional engine thrust. Moreover, the shock-waves caused the airflow to become violently turbulent, leading to buffeting, control difficulties and such unpleasant symptoms as wing-dropping, nose-diving or uncontrolled pitch-up into a climb. It took years to overcome these fundamental problems. An American test pilot, Major Charles E. 'Chuck' Yeager of the newly formed Air Force, carved his name in history by flying a **Bell X-1** rocket experimental aircraft at Mach 1.06 (just faster than sound) on 14 October 1947, but he had a very rough ride. Supersonic fighters were obviously not just around the corner.

Over the subsequent six years progress was rapid. It is likely that supersonic flight was accomplished in the Soviet Union, but details have never been made public. What is known is that in the United States the Air Force and Navy raced each other up the Mach scale. The Bell X-1 reached 967 mph, and gave rise to the **X-1A** and **X-1B** capable of speeds up to Mach 2. Meanwhile the Navy's **Douglas D.558-II Skyrocket** passed Mach 1 and reached 1.88 before the end of 1951. Then in 1953 it went beyond Mach 2, or about 1,350 mph, while the Air Force **Bell X-2** sought still higher speeds and in a remarkable—but sadly fatal—final mission it reached Mach 3.2, or 2,094 mph. The X-2 was made largely of heat-resisting stainless steel, and could thus 'soak' at

speeds which would have made aluminium alloys dangerously weak as a result of 'kinetic heating'. At Mach 2 the airframe becomes heated to well over 100°C, and as high as 200° in places; at Mach 3 parts may reach 500°C, which is almost a dull-red heat. In the 1950s this meant using steel, but today it is possible to use titanium alloys—about as strong and little more than half as heavy.

Runaway cost of speed

Whatever materials are used, the airframe of a supersonic aircraft has to be quite different from that of a subsonic one. The wing has to be much thinner; the dominant factor is the thickness/chord ratio, the ratio between the depth and the distance from front to back. With piston-engined aircraft the t/c ratio might be 17 per cent for a bomber and about 14 per cent for a fighter, but for the supersonic aircraft it is hard to use anything greater than 5 per cent—thus the depth must be only one-twentieth or less of the distance from leading to trailing edge. With a conventional-shaped wing this meant a maximum thickness of only a few inches. What designers had to do was plan supersonic aircraft with wings of new and much broader shapes. Instead of sticking out far to each side the supersonic wing tended to be stubby and to cover a great distance from front to rear (i.e., to have a large chord). One of the ways of doing this was to make the wing roughly triangular, with a sharply swept-back leading edge so that at the root the wing extended most of the way from the nose to the tail of the fuselage. Other supersonic wings were just made very stubby. In any event the structure had to be quite new, with extremely thick slab skins sculptured by huge milling machines, and with major parts of the structure made of fine 'honeycomb' panels or from sheets chemically etched to the right form in acid baths. The

supersonic aircraft was obviously going to be extremely costly, and nations wondered if supersonic military machines would ever be bought in large numbers.

Their engines were also going to be very costly. They needed far more thrust than the early jet fighters, calling for bigger engines boosted by afterburners—jet pipes in which extra fuel could be injected to augment the thrust from 25 to 70 per cent. Use of an afterburner also demanded a complicated propelling nozzle. Whereas in early jets the nozzle was a plain hole, the supersonic nozzle was made of many large and complex parts, all able to function when red hot, which could close down the nozzle in low-speed flight, open it up for full power with afterburner and, in later aircraft, change the

NATO presence. Though far from new, the BAC Lightning F.2 interceptors of 92 Squadron, RAF Germany, were still among NATO's most potent combat aircraft in the mid 1970s. Their airspace was on the East–West borders.

profile and bring in various secondary airflows around the edges. In 1950 it was also wondered if supersonic aircraft would be safe in the hands of regular squadron pilots. Would they need special airfields? Could they fly in bad weather? Gradually the Americans found the answers.

Towards a supersonic force

By 1950 the leading nations were making the inevitable progress towards the supersonic air force. In 1952 the US Air Force had ordered not only a supersonic fighter but also a supersonic bomber; the Navy had ordered a supersonic fighter and was already flying one fighter, the bat-winged **Skyray,** which was at first prevented from flying faster than sound only through lack of its proper engine. In the Soviet Union the **MiG-19** was about to fly and three more supersonic fighters were on order. In Britain a supersonic research machine was being built that would later be developed into a a fighter. Supersonic fighter projects were under way in Sweden and France.

In 1953 the prototype MiG-19 day fighter exceeded the speed of sound, while the **North American F-100 Super Sabre,** the first of the US Air Force 'Century series' with fighter numbers over 100, went faster than sound on its maiden flight. In 1954 the Navy Skyray got its proper engine and went supersonic on its first flight. So did the **Vought F-8 Crusader,** yet another carrier-based fighter, on its first flight in 1955. By 1957 nine types of supersonic fighter were in service in the United States and Soviet Union, and the great **B-58 Hustler** bomber —twice as fast as sound—was well into its flight-test programme. This was dramatic enough, but much more was to come. Several more advanced fighters and bombers could fly at over Mach 2 (twice the speed of sound), and contracts had been let for a further generation of combat aircraft able to fly at Mach 3 (2,000 mph). Among the Mach 2 machines were the **Lockheed F-104,** the **Republic F-105 Thunderchief, Convair F-106 Delta Dart, McDonnell F-4 Phantom, Lightning, Mirage III, Saab 35 Draken, MiG-21,** and several lesser-known Soviet fighters. The Mach 3 machines were the **North American B-70,** a huge global bomber, and **F-108 Rapier** interceptor. It seemed logical to make aircraft fly faster and faster. To provide research back-up the United States bought three examples of a high-speed rocket aeroplane that was virtually a manned missile. The **North American X-15** could zoom out

into space more than 69 miles above the Earth, and could fly at over Mach 6 at speeds exceeding 4,000 mph.

Never had the speed of aircraft risen so swiftly. Between 1955 and 1960 the maximum level speed of fighters in service rose from 650 to 1,650 mph, a rate equivalent to 200 extra mph every year. This was due chiefly to the tremendous progress made in turbojet propulsion, with parallel improvements in airframe structures. At the same time great efforts were needed to make the highly supersonic aircraft compatible with existing airfields. Their wings needed advanced high-lift devices, with leading-edge slats or hinged droops, and with very effective trailing-edge flaps which were often more than doubled in effectiveness by being 'blown' by high-pressure hot air piped from the engine.

A quick step backwards

Flap blowing is a form of BLC (boundary-layer control), the objective of which is to keep the air flowing smoothly round the aircraft without breaking away into uncontrollable turbulence. The supersonic aircraft needed such assistance, because their very thin, sharp-edged wings were not suited to supporting the weight of the aircraft except at very high speeds. At low speeds the air tended to break away, and flap-blowing was one of the most powerful ways of preventing this. The high-pressure air was expelled at about the speed of sound through a thin slit just ahead of the flap (and sometimes behind the leading edge of the wing or tailplane as well). Rushing in a thin sheet over the metal

The First Supersonics

▲ Convair F-106A Delta Dart of the 94th Fighter-Interceptor Squadron, Selfridge AFB, Michigan (1969). Flown on December 26, 1956, the F-106A attained operational status in June 1959 and still provides the backbone of the manned fighter defence of metropolitan USA.

▲ Mikoyan MiG-21F of a Rumanian Interceptor Regiment (1967). The first Soviet fighter capable of M=2.0 performance to have entered service, the MiG-21 has been manufactured in a variety of versions and is currently the world's most widely used fighter

▲ Sukhoi Su-7BM (Fitter) ground attack fighter of the Czech FA. Developed in parallel with the Su-11, the Su-7 is widely used by the Soviet Air Forces and has been supplied to numerous other air arms, including those of Egypt and India

▲ Mikoyan MiG-19PM of the Polish Air Force (1965). The MiG-19 was the first Soviet production fighter capable of attaining super-sonic speeds in level flight. First flown late in 1953, the MiG-19 began to enter service early in 1955

▲ BAC Lightning F. Mk. 6 of No. 5 Squadron, RAF (1968). The first supersonic interceptor of British design to attain production, the Lightning, first flown on April 4, 1957, is now giving place to the Phantom and will be phased out over the next few years

▲ Dassault Super Mystère B2 of Escadron 2/12 'cornouailles' France's Armée de l'Air. The Super Mystère was first flown March 2, 1955 and was the first aircraft of European des capable of attaining supersonic speeds to achieve producti entering service in 1958

▲ McDonnell F-101B-100 Voodoo all-weather interceptor of the 2nd Fighter-Interceptor Squadron, USAF Air Defense Command, Suffolk County AFB, New York (1967). The F-101B first flew on March 27, 1957, entering service two years later

▲ North American F-100D-15 Super Sabre of the Turkish 1st Tactical Air Force based at Bandirma (1969). The world's first operational fighter with true supersonic capability, the Super Sabre first flew on May 25, 1953 and currently equips Air National Guard units as well as some Danish, French and Turkish squadrons

Convair F-102A Delta Dagger of the 526th Fighter-Interceptor Squadron, 86th Air Division, USAFE, at Ramstein, Germany. First flown on October 24, 1953, the F-102A serves with the Air National Guard and the Greek and Turkish air forces

▲ SAAB 35A Draken of Swedish Air Force Wing F 13 based at Norrköping (1963). Of 'double-delta' configuration, the Draken first flew on October 25, 1955 and entered service with the Swedish Air Force in 1960

▲ Yakovlev Yak28P (Firebar) was the first supersonic two-seat all-weather interceptor to attain service with the Soviet Air Forces. Flown in 1960 as a fighter variant of the basic Yak-28 (Brewer), it began to enter service in 1963–64

◀ McDonnell F-4B Phantom II of US Navy Squadron VF-84 operating from the USS Independence. First flown on May 27, 1958, the F-4 Phantom II has remained continuously in production for some 17 years and is currently the most widely-used of US-designed fighters

▲ Tupolev Tu-28P (Fiddler) is currently the largest and heaviest interceptor in operational service. Apparently flown in prototype form in 1957, the Tu-28P entered service with the Soviet Air Forces in the early 'sixties

surface it drew down the rest of the airflow with it, enabling the wing to give far greater lift at low speeds. The only snag was that the engine had to be run at high power, so its thrust had to be counteracted on landing, and part of its thrust was lost to supply the large airflow needed which reduced acceleration on take-off, or during an overshoot after a 'missed approach'. Flap blowing also made a dead-stick landing much more hazardous than before, because without the engine the aircraft had to be brought in at very much higher speed to avoid falling out of the sky like a brick.

Flap blowing was just one of the many extra features which helped to increase the price of supersonic aircraft. Whereas early jet fighters had cost £50,000 to £100,000 the supersonic machines cost from £500,000 upwards—and because of their huge fuel consumption, and need for swollen teams of maintenance engineers, they were much more expensive to operate. Supersonic capability was obviously not gained for nothing, and in many ways the supersonic aeroplane seemed to be a retrograde development. Its one advantage was its speed, and even this was not very obviously an advantage except in allowing it to catch hostile machines (or escape from them). The drawbacks were many. Cost was one of the greatest, and so was the logistic problem of supplying three times as much fuel as before.

Another handicap was that the supersonic machine had to take off and land at very high speed and thus needed a good level runway of great length. There was evidence by 1960 that operational runways needed to be almost twice as long as the bare minimum that could be used in test-flying. Emergency arrester barriers were installed to catch the sharp, speedy aircraft and prevent overruns, and it was found that even with a 10,000 feet runway barrier crashes were common. Not until the runway reached the length of 12,000 feet did such incidents disappear. Moreover the high-pressure tyres of most of the new fighters demanded a surface of thick concrete. What air forces wanted was something that could safely operate from a few hundred yards of fairly level grass or compacted earth. This need became ever keener, as armies equipped themselves with thousands of artillery rockets and tactical guided missiles each capable of rendering a conventional airfield useless.

Supersonic fighter war

Supersonic fighters took part in sporadic local operations over the Lebanon in 1958 and around Quemoy (off the coast of mainland China), and in 1962 reconnaissance versions were very busy over Cuba. At about the latter time supersonic interceptors began to be sent up to inspect unidentified aircraft approaching without an announced flight plan. Such aircraft were usually found to be engaged in the hazardous business of electronic reconnaissance, undertaken by the Soviet Union, by the United States and probably by Britain and other nations. Some of these 'ferret' aircraft would stay just on their own side of a land frontier, while others would keep over international waters. Big naval forces drew them like a magnet. Though they were packed with tons of

electronics rather than bombs they had to be intercepted and identified; indeed, one of their jobs was to test the readiness of the opposing defences. Thus it is that, since the early 1960s, thousands of supersonic fighter missions have been scrambled in frantic haste from land runways and carrier decks to take a look at these curious strangers. The Western fighters used have mostly been RAF Lightnings and F-4 Phantoms of the US Navy and Royal Navy or RAF, as well as US Navy F-8 Crusaders. This work has served to keep big supersonic interceptor forces constantly keyed-up to a high pitch of readiness, with small groups of aircraft at instant alert status, ready to take off on a mission (which might turn out to be a deadly combat) at a moment's notice.

The first full-scale war involving supersonic fighters was that in Vietnam. The first US element of combat aircraft in this conflict was an Air Force squadron of F-105 fighter/bombers detached there in 1962. In 1965 came the first outbreak of fighting between India and Pakistan, which was renewed in 1971. Both countries used many supersonic aircraft. The Indian Air Force used the subsonic **Gnat**, built in India, and the supersonic **HF-24 Marut** and MiG-21 (both built in India) and the bigger **Su-7** fighter/bomber. The Pakistani Air Force had a mixed bag of MiG-19s (bought from China where they were made), second-hand Lockheed F-104 Starfighters and new **Mirage IIIEP** all-weather fighter/bombers.

Many lessons were learned in the fierce fighting. One was that supersonic mattered little, because hardly any pilot ever exceeded Mach 1. In low-level ground-attack missions few aircraft can exceed Mach 1, and then only marginally. In dogfighting it is impossible to pull violent manoeuvres except at modest speeds below 500 mph. Thus the extra speed of the MiG-21, F-104 and Mirage was not used. On the other hand the older MiG-19 scored heavily, with its robust structure, good manoeuvrability and hard-hitting large-calibre guns, with very much greater propellant charge than the ammunition for the equal-calibre (30 mm) guns of the Mirage. This war also served to demonstrate, if proof were needed, that the supposedly dangerous F-104 can be operated safely under difficult conditions. It has a higher wing-loading than any other production aircraft ever built, yet in the first ten years Pakistan lost only three: one flew through the debris of its Indian victim and the pilot had to eject, the second did not pull out in time when strafing a surface target and the third was landing in a violent duststorm.

Troublesome little Gnat

Whereas Mach 2 suddenly seemed to be no great advantage, the ability to turn very tightly without losing speed became all-important. Supersonic aircraft need great engine thrust to overcome drag at full speed, so it follows that at lower speeds they have plenty of excess thrust. This can be used to help push them round sustained turns, or other manoeuvres, without the speed falling off. The little Gnat also did surprisingly well. Though it had a small engine, with no afterburner, it could manoeuvre very well and was so small it was very difficult to shoot

down. Thus the first real warfare between supersonic fighters showed that the 1950–53 vision of fighters streaking through the sky at over 1,500 mph was not coming to pass. Instead aircraft needed the traditional qualities of outstanding manoeuvrability, good resistance to battle damage and, by no means least, the ability to operate from short, rough, primitive forward bases and still stay serviceable.

Very small numbers of air-to-air guided weapons were used in the Indo-Pakistan wars, the chief type being Sidewinder and its Soviet counterpart known as Atoll. This was the first time that opposing air forces had both used missiles, but no dramatic change in tactics resulted; both missiles are quite short-ranged weapons, and they were used like an extension to gun armament with the advantage of not needing such precise aim.

But by 1960 there were many other air-to-air missiles in service which had brought about major changes in fighter capability and tactics. Early Sparrow missiles, Red Top, Falcons, the French R.530 and several Soviet types all proved lethal over ranges of around 10 miles, so to avoid being shot down ECM began to become even more important than flight performance, while to avoid the heat-homing weapons fighters tried to shield their heat sources or use thermal decoys. Missile interception, using both air-launched and ground-launched weapons, was vitally important in the 'Six-Day War' launched as a pre-emptive strike by Israel in June–July 1967. In this the majority of fighters were supersonic, the Israeli top-scorer being the **Mirage IIICJ** and the Egyptian and other Arab forces deploying large numbers of Soviet machines such as the MiG-17, MiG-21 and Su-7. The shattering effect of the opening Israeli attack on Arab airfields almost eliminated the Arab fighter squadrons, but Israel still lost many aircraft in air combat and as a result of the comprehensive air-defence system that the Arabs were beginning to bring into use, using Soviet radars, data links and SA-2 Guideline missiles.

Unused strategic bombers

When war broke out again in the Middle East in October 1973 the two sides had much more sophisticated air-defence systems, the Israeli one being mostly of US design and the UAR one wholly Russian. Until June 1972 large numbers of Russian technicians and 'advisors' were helping to install and man the UAR radar and missile sites, but by October 1973 most of these people had left and the system was being operated by Arab servicemen. In addition to the SA-2 the UAR had numerous units equipped with the SA-3 Goa, and infantry were equipped with the hand-held SA-7 which, though not unfailingly lethal in view of its small warhead, introduced a new factor into air affairs in being small enough for use by terrorists and subversive groups. Analysis of the results of the October 1973 war show beyond dispute that Arab losses were much heavier than Israeli losses even though most of the air combat took place over Arab territory. To some degree this bears out the precept that the best place to destroy enemy aircraft is on the ground, and the Israeli Air

Aircraft of the Pakistan Air Force used in the War with India

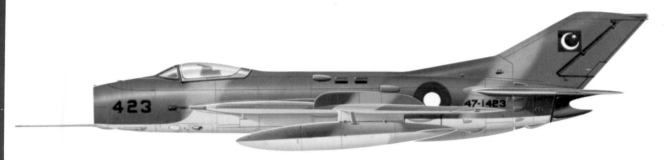

▲ Chinese-built MiG-19SF of the Pakistan Air Force

▲ Martin B-57B of No. 31 Bomber Wing of the Pakistan Air Force

▲ Canadair CL-13B Sabre Mk 6 of No. 17 Squadron, Pakistan Air Force, home-based at Mauripur

▲ Dassault-Breguet Mirage IIIEP of No. 5 Squadron, Pakistan Air Force

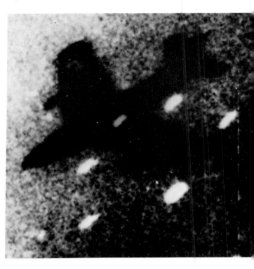

Force was far more active over hostile air bases than were UAR aircraft over Israel. The sizeable UAR forces equipped with Soviet-built strategic bombers were not used, so far as is known, and certainly not in any heavy strike on Israeli territory.

Besides appearing to bear out yet again that results tend to be overwhelmingly influenced by the training, experience and morale of the people involved, the October 1973 fighting reaffirmed the vital need for good ECM and a quick response to changing threats. The equipment carried by fighter and attack aircraft appeared to be much more important than the Mach number it could reach. Even quite early missiles can fly faster and turn more sharply than most fighter or attack aircraft, so there was little point in trying to outrun them. On the other hand there was every reason to try to defeat their guidance or homing systems, and even such lumbering machines as the old **Boeing C-97 Stratofreighters** demonstrated their vital importance as aerial ECM stations to detect, jam, confuse and distort the Arab radars.

Capability in electronics, infra-red and similar technologies appears today to be more important than possession of the fastest aircraft. During the 1950s, India, Egypt, Argentina, Australia, Canada, Spain and Yugoslavia all attempted to design and build their own jet fighter aircraft. Limited success was achieved by India and Spain, both of which brought their aircraft—the HF-24 Marut and **HA-200/220**, respectively —into full production and squadron service. The Jugoslavs developed their **Galeb** series of attack machines to the fully operational point, and then embarked on the development of a new combat jet in partnership with

The latest fighters of the Indian Air Force are of Soviet origin. The MiG-21FL (top) has been replaced in production at Hindustan Aeronautics by the MiG-21M with fatter straight-topped fuselage. Landing with drag chutes deployed is a Sukhoi Su-7B, a large but not entirely successful fighter bomber. The two air combat cinegun photographs purport to show an IAF Hunter being shot down by an aircraft of the Pakistan Air Force during the 1965 fighting.

Romania. None of the other countries brought their projects to a successful conclusion, and it is significant that today such advanced nations as Argentina, Brazil and Australia make no attempt to build combat aircraft of the supersonic type (except under foreign licence) and are more interested in utility machines which may be of greater and more immediate use. But an impressive number of supersonic aircraft have made their mark in service around the world with the forces of both smaller or poorer nations and those of the more technically advanced countries that design them.

Sweden's 'double delta'

For example, Britain's solitary homegrown supersonic aircraft, apart from handbuilt research machines, is the English Electric (since 1960, BAC) Lightning. Powered by two Avon afterburning turbojets arranged in an unusual superimposed way, it initially had very small fuel capacity but finally the maker was allowed to double the tankage and develop it as a multi-role machine which led to Middle East sales in both single-seat and side-by-side dual versions. Early

Lightnings had Firestreak pursuit-type missiles, but current models mainly have the collision-course Red Top.

Sweden's very unusual 'double delta' Saab 35 Draken, powered by one Avon, began life in 1958 as a crude manually flown day fighter with guns, and progressed through several versions ending with very fully equipped all-weather and multi-role variants, some of which launch heat-homing and radar-guided Falcon missiles made in Sweden. Denmark and Finland have bought many of the 600-plus delivered.

France's Mirage III likewise began as a simple day fighter, with two 30 mm guns or a primitive guided missile, and developed into an all-weather multi-role machine. It has been adopted by more countries than any other supersonic aircraft, and most recent sales have been of the **Mirage 5,** a stripped-down, low-cost version for nations that seldom suffer bad weather. The weight saved has been put to use by increasing the bomb load to 8,820 lb, though it then needs a very long concrete runway. In 1973 the first of a series of completely redesigned non-delta versions, the **F1,** entered service. Another Dassault tactical aircraft is the non-delta **Etendard,** a carrier-based attack, tanker and reconnaissance machine which will be replaced by the more powerful **Super Etendard** carrying a heavier load, radar and modern nav-attack avionics.

First of the US supersonic fighters, the F-100 was an advanced offspring of the **F-86** with more sweep (45°), more fuel capacity, a 15,000 lb afterburning engine (the 15,000 lb Pratt & Whitney J57) and four new 20 mm guns. It was able to reach about 800 mph, and later versions introduced underwing loads of offensive stores, an autopilot (later

Warplanes of the Indian Air Force

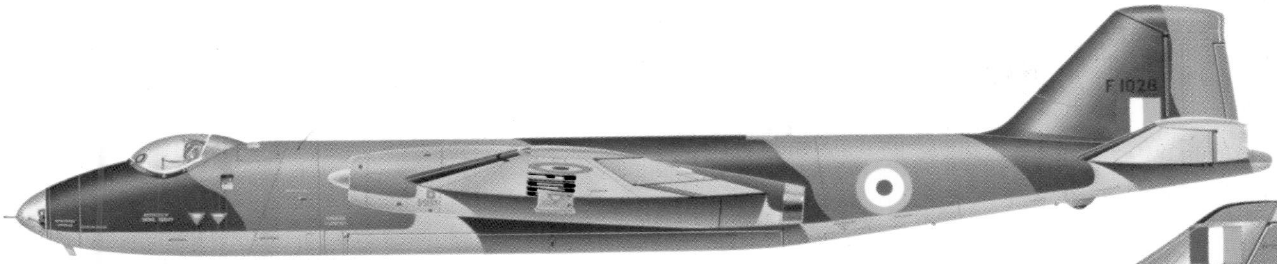

▲ English Electric Canberra B Mk 66

▲ Dassault Mystere IVA

▲ Hawker Hunter F Mk 56

▲ HAL Gnat Mk 1

▲ Sukhoi Su-7

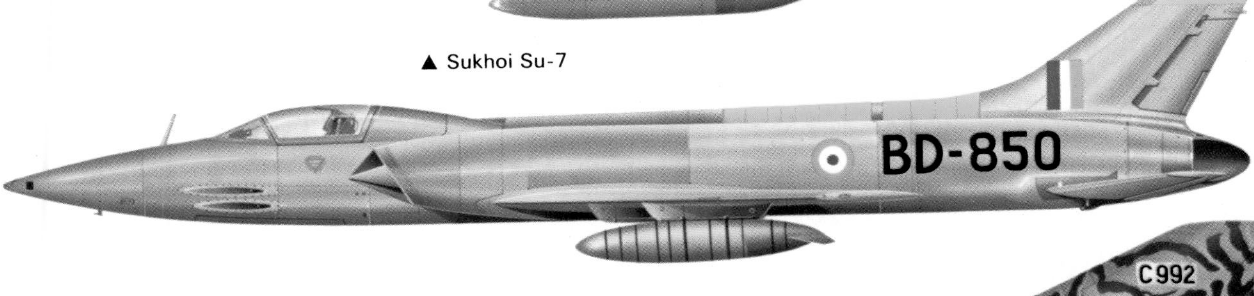

▲ HAL HF-24 Marut Mk 1

▲ MiG-21PFM

PRINCIPAL FRONTLINE SUPERSONIC FIGHTERS: WESTERN-BUILT

Type	Country of origin	First introduced	Primary role	Performance	Comments
North American F-100 Super Sabre	USA	1954	Fighter	(F-100C, D and F) — Max. speed, 864 mph at 35,000 ft. Initial rate of climb, 16,000 ft/min. Max. range, 1,500 miles	World's first operational supersonic fighter, did well in both ground attack and flying top cover as a fighter in Vietnam
Lockheed F-104 Starfighter	USA	1956	Interceptor and single-seat multi-purpose combat aircraft	(F-104G) — Max. speed, 1,320 mph at 40,000 ft. Initial rate of climb 50,000 + ft/min. Tactical radius (with 4 drop tanks), 690 miles	Originally intended as an air superiority fighter, the design was based on operational experience in Korea. Following dozens of seemingly inexplicable crashes when flown by German pilots gained some undeserved notoriety as 'Widow maker'
Convair F-106 Delta Dart	USA	1959	All-weather interceptor crew 1 or 2	Max. speed, 1,525 mph at 40,000 ft. combat radius, (clean) 575 miles	Evolved from the F-102 Delta Dagger, the latest versions of the F-106 carry multi-barrel cannon and are envisaged to continue in frontline service with the ADC until the late 1970s
Northrop F-5 'Freedom Fighter' and Northrop F-5E Tiger II	USA	1967	Air superiority fighter	(NF-5A) — Max. speed, 977 mph at 36,000 ft. Initial rate of climb (clean) 33,000 ft/min. Tactical radius with 1,500 lb ordnance, plus external fuel, 575 miles	A simplified supersonic fighter produced under US government or foreign contracts for many countries, as well as licence-built abroad. Saw limited operational service in Vietnam in 1965. A progressive intercept development known as Tiger II places emphasis on manoeuvrability rather than speed
McDonnell Douglas F-4 Phantom II	USA	1962	Supersonic multi-role fighter crew 2	(F-4E) — Max. speed, with external stores, 1,500 mph at 40,000 ft. Initial rate of climb, about 30,000 ft/min. Tactical radius (with 8 air-to-air missiles), 140 miles	Initially built as an all-missile armed naval fighter, the Phantom II was soon taken up by USAF. Became leading multi-role aircraft in Vietnam where it was perfected by adding a Gatling gun and wing slats. Without doubt the most effective two-seat interceptor and tactical strike fighter extant, flown and praised by hundreds of American and foreign pilots
BAC (English Electric) Lightning	UK	1960	Interceptor	(F Mk 6, approx.) — Max. speed, 1,500 mph at 40,000 ft. Initial rate of climb, 50,000 ft/min	First supersonic British interceptor to enter service. Standard equipment with RAF fighter–intercept squadrons in West Germany and the UK, and a formidable strike aircraft when necessary
Dassault-Breguet Mirage III	France	1961	Interceptor and close support fighter	(III-E) — Max. speed, 850 mph at sea level, 1,460 mph at 36,000 ft. Time to 36,000 ft, 3.0 min	Designed initially as a Mach 2.0 high-altitude interceptor requiring only small airstrips and capable of doubling as a ground support aircraft. A fine operational record in the Middle East
Dassault-Breguet Mirage F	France	1973	All-weather interception at any altitude	Max. speed (clean), 1,450 mph at 39,370 ft. Max. initial rate of climb (with afterburning), 42,000 ft/min. Range with max. external fuel, 2,050 miles	Developed by Dassault as a private venture concurrently with work on the Mirage F2, intended as an eventual replacement for the Mirage III. Met or exceeded all expectations during tests, now in series production
Dassault-Breguet Mirage 5	France	1970	Ground attack fighter	Max. speed (clean), 835 mph at sea level, 1,386 mph at 29,370 ft. Time to 36,000 ft, 3.0 min. Combat radius with 2,000 lb bomb load, 805 miles	Export version of the Mirage III-E long-range fighter/intruder version, optimised for the ground attack role and featuring simplified avionics
SAAB 35 Draken	Sweden	1960	Supersonic all-weather fighter	(SAAB 35X) — Max. speed, 924 mph at 36,100 ft. Initial rate of climb 22,650 ft/min. Radius of action, 395 miles	Designed to intercept bombers in the transonic speed range under all weather conditions. Standard equipment of the Swedish AF pending introduction of the SAAB 37
SAAB 37 Viggen	Sweden	1973	Supersonic multi-purpose fighter crew 2	(est.) — Max. speed (clean), 1,320 mph at 36,100 ft. Time to 36,000 ft, approx. 2.0 min. Tactical radius with external ordnance for typical hi-lo-hi mission, 620 miles	Designed as a basic platform which could be readily adapted to fulfill the four primary roles of attack, interception, reconnaissance, and training. Advanced 'double delta' configuration with STOL characteristics

PRINCIPAL FRONTLINE SUPERSONIC FIGHTERS IN SERVICE: EASTERN-BUILT

Type	Country of origin	First introduced	Primary role	Performance	Comments
Mikoyan MiG-19 'Farmer'	USSR	1955	Interceptor fighter	(MiG-19SF) — Max. speed, 902 mph at 32,800 ft; Initial rate of climb 22,640 ft/min; Service ceiling, 58,725 ft; Normal range, 864 miles	First Soviet fighter capable of supersonic speed in level flight. Large numbers still in operational service with the Soviet AF and elsewhere. Chinese copy of the MiG-19SF also in much evidence
Mikoyan MiG-21 'Fishbed'	USSR	1957	Multi-purpose fighter	(MiG-21MF) — Max. speed, 1,386 mph above 36,000 ft; Service ceiling, 59,055 ft; Range with max. internal fuel, 683 miles	One of the most successful (if controversial) combat aircraft of the 1960s, and unquestionably the world's most widely-used jet fighter
Mikoyan MiG-23 'Flogger'	USSR	1971	Interceptor fighter	(est.) — Max. speed, 1,520 mph at 39,000 ft; Service ceiling, 50,000 ft; Combat radius, 600 miles	First Soviet supersonic all-weather variable-geometry fighter designed as such to achieve operational status. Carries avionics reportedly comparable with those of the F-4J Phantom
Mikoyan MiG-25 'Foxbat'	USSR	1972	Interceptor and reconnaissance fighter	(est.) — Max. short-dash speed, 2,100 mph at 39,000 ft; Max. sustained speed, 1,780 mph at 39,000 ft; Time to 36,000 ft, 2.5 min; Normal combat radius, 700 miles	Designed as a Mach 3.0 high-altitude (75–80,000 ft) interceptor or fast strike aircraft, and possibly armed with 'snap down' missiles. One of the best interceptors in production today
Sukhoi Su-9 'Fishpot'	USSR	1962	All-weather interceptor fighter	(est.) — Max. speed (clean), 1,190 mph at 40,000 ft; Initial rate of climb, 27,000 ft/min; Service ceiling, 55,000 ft	Currently one of the most important Soviet AF air defence interceptors, deployed around the main industrial and population centres
Sukhoi Su-15 'Flagon'	USSR	1970	All-weather interceptor fighter	(est.) — Max. speed (clean), 1,650 mph at 39,300 ft; Range at subsonic cruise speed (with max. external fuel) 1,500 miles; Combat radius, 450 miles	Designed as a progressive Su-9 successor and reportedly deployed around the major Soviet centres. Next to the Su-9 the most important Soviet air defence interceptor
Tupolev Tu-28P 'Fiddler'	USSR	1963	Long-range all-weather interceptor fighter crew 2	(est.) — Max. speed (clean), 1,085 mph at 39,370 ft; Max. speed carrying four air-to-air missiles, 925 mph at 39,370 ft; Tactical radius for high-altitude patrol mission, 900–1,000 miles.	The largest and heaviest interceptor fighter in operational service, reportedly being phased out of first-line all-weather intercept units
Yakovlev Yak-28P 'Firebar'	USSR	1963	All-weather interceptor fighter crew 2	(est.) — Max. speed (clean), 760 mph at 39,370 ft; Max. speed with two air-to-air missiles, 695 mph; Service ceiling, 55,000 ft; Tactical radius for high-altitude patrol mission, 550 miles	Evolved parallel with the Tu-28P. Latest versions equipped with so-called Skip Spin air interception radar. Currently one of the principal interceptors used by the Soviet air defence regiments

The Starfighter

▼ **Lockheed RF-104G Starfighter** of the Aufklärungsgeschwader (Reconnaissance Wing) 52 of the Luftwaffe based at Leck in 1969. The reconnaissance version of the Starfighter has now been replaced in the Luftwaffe by the McDonnell Douglas RF-4E Phantom

with toss-bomb capability for nuclear bombs) and flight refuelling. Over 2,200 'Huns' were built, and their versatility gave them a leading role in Vietnam. Hundreds served with other air forces, mainly in NATO.

The **McDonnell F-101 Voodoo,** flown in 1954, amazed observers by having two of the very powerful J57 engines. This enabled it to fly with enormous fuel loads in its almost 70 feet long fuselage and though the first version carried four 20 mm guns and bombs, later versions had Falcon guided missiles, the Genie nuclear rocket and many other weapons. Most F-101s, bought by Canada and Nationalist China, have been employed in the interdiction role, but special all-weather interceptor and reconnaissance versions exist.

Smallest and thinnest yet

Powered by the same J57 engine, the delta-winged **Convair** (from 1962, General Dynamics) **F-102 Delta Dagger** is a single-seat all-weather interceptor. Marking the biggest technical jump in fighter history, it introduced the concept of an automatic system which could find the enemy, lock-on and track, and guide the fighter until spin-stabilised rockets or Falcon guided missiles could be unerringly launched. An internal

bay can house six Falcons, usually three heat-homing and three radar-guided, and most of the fuselage ahead of the wing is filled with avionics. In 1959 the US Air Force began to receive the redesigned F-106 Delta Dart, with the 23,500 lb thrust J75 engine and much more lethal radar and missiles. Speed was increased from 800 to almost 1,600 mph, and the F-106, which by 1961 equipped almost half the manned interceptor force of the Air Defence Command, is still in service.

Designed during the Korean war to meet the supposed need for a simpler, lighter fighter that could out-perform the enemy, Lockheed gave the F-104 Starfighter the smallest and thinnest wing of any production aircraft in history. Powered by a 15,000 lb J79 engine, the F-104 became dubbed 'the manned missile'. All versions carry a 20 mm six-barrel Gatling gun which raised the speed of fire of cannon to 6,000 rounds per minute. At first the F-104 was a day fighter, but the **F-104C** introduced equipment for ground attack, and the **F-104G** added comprehensive radar, an inertial navigation system and other changes for the whole spectrum of tactical missions. Though not adopted by the United States, the 104G, dubbed Super Starfighter, became the subject of an unprecedented global manufactur-

Fighters' roles. By the 1960s 'fighter' had little meaning. The McDonnell Douglas F-4C Phantom has been used mainly for ground attack. Much of its work has been at low level, but the group above are bombing North Vietnam in February 1966 from high level, the aiming being done by the B-66 lead ship. In contrast, the MiG-21PF, two of which are seen right taking off at night with full afterburner, is a true short-range interceptor.

ing programme. Canada, Japan, Germany, Italy, the Netherlands and Belgium produced more than 2,000 in 1961–66, and the advanced **F-104S** interceptor version, with big Sparrow missiles, is still being built in Italy.

Described as 'the one-man air force' the Republic F-105 Thunderchief is a very large Mach 2 aircraft powered by a 26,500 lb J75 engine and fitted with a Gatling and an internal bomb bay. Almost 900 F-105s were completed and later versions were developed with comprehensive equipment for multi-role operations in all weather, including nuclear toss bombing, and, unlike most other tactical aircraft, the 105 has an extremely high performance at high altitudes *and* good dogfight capability.

PRINCIPAL FRONTLINE SUPERSONIC BOMBERS IN SERVICE: EASTERN-BUILT					
Type	Country of origin	First introduced	Primary role	Performance	Comments
Tupolev Tu-22 'Blinder'	USSR	1965	Supersonic twin-jet strategic bomber	(est.) — Max. speed (clean), 990 mph at 39,000 ft Tactical radius on internal fuel, 700 miles	Successor to subsonic Tu-16, but insufficient range for intended strategic role, hence later conversion to missile/stand off bomb carrier
Tupolev 'Backfire'	USSR	1974–75	Supersonic twin-jet strategic bomber	(est.) — Max. speed, about Mach 2.3–2.5 at altitude Range, over 4,500 miles	First Soviet strategic bomber combining supersonic capability with sufficient range to hit targets in Continental USA

In Vietnam its importance as a multi-role aircraft was overshadowed only by the McDonnell Douglas F-4 Phantom, which is a classic among fighters. Powered by two J79 engines (Spey turbofans in British versions), the F-4 surpassed all other Western fighters of its day in flight performance, offensive load, range, endurance and radar capability. Originally a fleet defence fighter, it later became a multi-role land-based machine and the envy of every air force; every country that can afford it has bought it, including Britain, Israel, Iran, Australia, Germany, Spain, Turkey, Greece and Korea.

Fighter-bomber for 16 friends

Northrop developed the **F-5** light day fighter-bomber for nations friendly to the United States. Powered by two tiny J85 engines, the first F-5 versions were simple day fighter and ground attack aircraft carrying a 2,000 lb bomb load, two 20 mm guns and Sidewinder air-to-air missiles. More than 1,150 were supplied to 16 friendly countries, and in 1973 deliveries began of the greatly improved **F-5E Tiger II** version which in 1970 won the International Fighter Aircraft competition to choose an F-5 successor. The initial F-5E programme involved 325 aircraft, but over 1,000 are expected to be built before 1980.

Among US Navy fighters the Vought F-8 Crusader was supreme from 1956 until 1970, and a large-scale rebuilding programme has kept this Mach 1.7 single-seater competitive. At first a simple day fighter, it became an all-weather multi-role aircraft, and a STOL version was supplied to France. A later rival, the **Grumman F-11 Tiger,** was built in small numbers as a day interceptor.

Built in huge numbers like nearly all Mikoyan jets, the twin-engined MiG-19 was developed through several major versions in 1953–59, the final examples having new guns, all-weather AI radar and underwing racks for two types of air-to-air missile. These aircraft are still in use with many Eastern bloc air forces and in China where many were built.

Even larger numbers have been built of the MiG-21, a very small (even smaller than the Mirage III) Mach 2 day fighter which is a delight to fly and extremely simple and cost-effective. Again many new versions have led to introduction of AI radar, a new two-barrel rapid-fire gun and various bomb and guided-missile options. Several thousand have been exported, many of them to Egypt.

The similar but bigger and more powerful **Sukhoi Su-7B** and its variants is roughly a multi-role tactical counterpart of the F-105, though lighter and carrying a smaller load. Very large numbers have been supplied to at least eleven air forces. From it have been derived a considerable range of aircraft including fighters with two engines, lift jets, variable sweep and other advanced features.

Pride of place to Hustler

In its day the world's biggest fighter, the **Tupolev Tu-28P** has been a standard long-range interceptor since 1961. Powered by two large afterburning engines each rated at 32,800 lb thrust, it has an enormous fuel capacity and range of well over 2,000 miles. Speed of Mach 1.75 is combined with heavy cannon and guided-missile armament, there usually being two heat-homing missiles and two radar-guided weapons. The other long-established family of all-weather interceptors is by Yakovlev—the **Yak-25, -26** and **-27**

of 1955–60 having been superseded by the supersonic **Yak-28** family, which are quite new designs with increased fuel capacity, completely new radar and a mixed array of guided missiles. Few post-war basic combat aircraft have given birth to more variants and derivatives than the Yak-25.

Among supersonic bombers the General Dynamics B-58 Hustler has pride of place on account of being first. Powered by four J79 engines it was a 60° delta constructed largely of stainless-steel sandwich and carrying a fuel load equal to more than twice the total weight of the bare aircraft. Payload was carried externally, in an enormous mission pod much fatter than the fuselage and on small racks under the wings. The three-seat B-58 had a 20 mm Gatling gun in the tail and could fly over 5,000 miles on internal fuel. The B-58 was conceived to form about one-seventh of the SAC front line retaliation force, along with the **Stratofortress**.

In contrast the French **Dassault Mirage IVA,** powered by two 15,000 lb Atars, could barely fly 2,000 miles and thus adopted a difficult series of mission profiles based on extensive flight refuelling and, in extreme cases, failing to make the return flight but trying to reach neutral territory. This was on the assumption that, in any circumstances in which the Mirage IVA could be required to deliver its nuclear load, there would be no France left to return to.

In the Soviet Union the Mach 1.4 **Tu-22,** powered by two very large engines at the tail and weighing no less than 185,000 lb, is being supplemented by a later Tupolev bomber with variable-sweep and a speed of just over Mach 2. This is much larger and heavier, and is almost in the class of the US Air Force **B-1.**

PORTABLE ARMIES

The first aircraft specifically designed as troop carriers appeared at the end of World War I and in the two decades between the great wars the airborne army was a central factor in the policing of the lawless frontiers of the British Empire, though the number of troops involved was only a few hundred. Much bolder were the Blitzkrieg plans of the Nazis, which incorporated the concept of sudden massive assaults at carefully chosen points by huge armies conveyed by transport aircraft and large gliders. For even more sudden local assault a more radical arm was formed: parachute troops, dropped from the sky in tight 'sticks' over the smallest possible area of ground, possibly by night, with subsequent aerial resupply by parachuted stores.

After 1945 the glider and the paratrooper began to fade from the scene. On the other hand, great efforts were made to develop the military transport aircraft in all its forms, including long-range aeroplanes, short-haul STOL (short take-off and landing) aircraft, jet V/STOL (vertical or short) machines and helicopters. Much has been done with unmanned vehicles, and with RPVs (remotely piloted vehicles), which may in future also play a role in the increased mobility of land forces. And, of course, the development of such V/STOL combat aircraft as the **Harrier** has dramatically altered the dependence of tactical aircraft on permanent airfields, so that mobile armies can take their air support right along with them. Moreover, as such aircraft may be based far from any surface supply route, air supply is essential to keep them operating.

Routine peacetime operations of almost all armies involve much air transport, and for a nation with global commitments this involves running something like a very large airline. For straightforward movement of servicemen and families an ordinary long-range passenger transport can be used, though examples in military service in-

The biggest aircraft in service. The Lockheed C-5A Galaxy can lift up to 265,000 lb. of payload in more than 42,000 cubic feet of interior volume.

Hercules, Globemaster, StarLifter, Galaxy—the very names given to these aircraft betray something of the immensity of the problems involved in transporting and supplying a modern army. Big, versatile and tough aircraft are specially designed for the job and the picking-up and setting down of troops, equipment and supplies has become an essential aerial art.

PRINCIPAL TRANSPORT AIRCRAFT IN SERVICE

Type	Country of origin	First introduced	Primary role	Performance	Comments
Lockheed C-130 Hercules	USA	1956	Medium/long-range military transport	Range with max. fuel, 4,700 miles Max. speed, 384 mph Cruise, 350 mph	First operational USAF turboprop-powered transport, in service since 1956. Beloved by its crews, handled most of the tactical supply trucking in Vietnam. Numbers supplied to various foreign customers, including the RAF
Lockheed C-141 StarLifter	USA	1964	Long-range strategic transport	Range with max. fuel, 6,140 miles with 31,870 lb payload Max. speed, 571 mph at 25,000 ft Cruise, 520 mph	First jet-powered USAF strategic freighter, and mainstay of MAC, providing global range air lift capability. During the Vietnam conflict looked after logistic supply from the USA
Lockheed C-5 Galaxy	USA	1970	Long-range strategic freighter	Range with max. payload (265,000 lb), 2,950 miles Max. speed, 571 mph at 25,000 ft Cruise, 537 mph at 30,000 ft	Designed as a very large logistics transport for MAC, the G-5 Galaxy amply demonstrated its value for rapid movement of heavy equipment (tanks, etc.) during the Vietnam conflict
Short Belfast C Mk 1	UK	1966	Long-range strategic freighter	Range with max. payload (78,000 lb), 1,000 miles Max. cruise, 352 mph at 28,000 ft Econ. cruise, 336 mph	The only British-designed turbo-prop powered heavy freighter in service, cycled through extensive modifications since operational debut in January 1966
Antonov An-12 'Cub'	USSR	1960	Long/medium-range cargo and paratroop transport	Range, 2,110 miles with 22,050 lb payload and 1 hr fuel reserve Max. speed, 444 mph Max. cruise, 373 mph Max. payload, 44,090 lb	Currently the most widely used Soviet Air Force transport aircraft. Also supplied to Algeria, India, Iraq, and Poland
Antonov An-22 Antei ('Cock')	USSR	1967	Long-range troop and logistics transport	Range with max. payload (176,350 lb), 3,107 miles Max. speed, 460 mph Max. cruise, 422 mph	World's largest aircraft at the time of its appearance (1965), and the largest turbo-prop powered aircraft in service today. Can carry large missiles
Ilyushin Il-76 'Candid'	USSR	1973	Heavy freighter	Range with max. payload (88,185 lb), 3,100 miles Max. cruise, 528 mph at 42,650 ft	First operational Soviet four-jet heavy transport aircraft: larger, heavier, and more powerful than its earlier American counterpart, the Lockheed C-141 StarLifter
Douglas C-47 Skytrain (Dakota)	USA	1942	General-purpose transport	(C-47A) — Max. range, 2,125 miles Max. speed, 229 mph Cruise, 185 mph	Was probably the most widely known and -used aircraft during WW II years. Substantial numbers of C-47 variants (incl. licence-built Soviet versions) are still in service around the world. In Vietnam became the first heavily-armed 'gun ship' — a remarkably successful conversion
Transall C.160	France and W. Germany	1966	Medium-range tactical transport	Range with max. payload (35,270 lb), 730 miles Max. speed, 333 mph at 14,760 ft Cruise, 305 mph	The result of a joint French-German programme initiated in 1959, the Transall remains the principal *Luftwaffe* transport aircraft, and is also flown by the French, S. African and Turkish Air Forces
Antonov An-26 'Curl'	USSR	1969	Short/medium-range military freighter	Range with max. payload (11,023 lb), 807 miles Max. speed, 335 mph Long-range cruise, 273 mph	Intended as a versatile tactical transport with rough-field capability and featuring a unique two-position cargo/paratroop drop rear fuselage door
DeHavilland Canada DHC-4 Caribou	Canada	1959	Short-range tactical transport	Range with max. payload (8,740 lb), 242 miles Max. speed, 216 mph Cruise, 182 mph	A most successful Canadian design intended to operate from short, unprepared strips near the front line. Adapted by the US and twelve other air forces around the world

variably have large doors, stiffened floors and freight handling equipment so that part, or all, of the interior can be devoted to pre-loaded freight bins, pallets or small vehicles. For larger indivisible loads, such as heavy tanks, heavy artillery, dozers and scrapers, and such specialised equipment as that needed for sorting gravel and laying concrete roadways, there is no alternative to the very large strategic freighter. For economic reasons it would be helpful if these aircraft could be the same as their civil counterparts, but they cannot. Civil freighters are usually special freight or mixed-traffic versions of passenger transports but the military aircraft must be purpose-built. It has to be able to operate from short, rough airstrips, not more than 4,000 feet long, whenever it is in the battle area. Thus the entire design must be penalised in comparison with a civil machine tailored to a 10,000 feet concrete runway.

A transport with everything

Early logistic transports were just large piston-engined machines, often not wholly suited to their task. Typical of these was the **Douglas C-124 Globemaster,** which came into US Air Force service at the time the Korean war was raging in 1951. It was a low-wing machine distinguished by its huge fuselage, with over 10,000 cubic feet of cargo space. Vehicles could drive up ramps through the large nose doors, which left an entrance more than 11 feet square. Further back was a section of floor which could be lowered to the ground, loaded and electrically hoisted up again. On the other hand, the C-124 was too much like a civil airliner. Much could be learned by looking at such German wartime machines as the **Me 323** and **Ar 232,** which had a high wing, easier loading arrangements and multi-wheel soft-field landing gear.

In 1954, Lockheed flew the first **C-130 Hercules,** the aircraft which for the first time put together all the features necessary for an efficient military transport. It had a cargo hold of useful size, with an unobstructed section over 9 feet high and 10 feet wide, with a flat, level floor at the same height as a typical road vehicle floor so that nothing needed to be hoisted. In addition to large side doors the whole rear of the hold could open, and this could even be done in flight so that vehicles and huge freight pallets could be dropped by multiple parachutes. Four turbo-props gave a cruising speed over 300 mph for transoceanic range, and high-lift flaps and special landing gear suited the C-130 to operations from sand, mud, polar snow and ice and any other reasonably level surface. The well-liked 'Herky bird' has remained in production for 20 years and has lifted every kind of load in every kind of place.

Some are fitted with an aerial recovery system of the 'snatch' type, for picking up people where no landing is possible. The person to be snatched can be anywhere provided there is a clear space immediately in front for about 200 feet. A kit is dropped containing a harness and a balloon on a 500 feet nylon line. When the Hercules pilot sees the ballon he flies to intercept the line just below it. The balloon breaks away and the stretching nylon smoothly pulls the man at the other end off the ground. A winch swiftly winds the harness and wearer forward into the Hercules. Heavier loads can be picked up by the same method, and the Hercules can also retrieve parachuted loads such as returning space capsules.

In the Soviet Union the leading military transports have been designed by Oleg Antonov, whose C-130-class machines are

Special delivery. The aircraft demonstrating ground-level extraction of stores is a USAF Lockheed C-130 Hercules. The most successful and widely used tactical airlifter, the C-130 has served 36 nations. In contrast the Douglas C-124B (above, delivering a Thor missile) served only the USAF.

used in many countries. Today the giant **An-22** is the biggest Russian freighter, while the **Il-76** combines good speed and load with the ability to use 4,000 feet unpaved airstrips.

Larger, faster, further

Following the C-130, Lockheed built the **C-141 StarLifter,** which is larger and faster, and then the **C-5A Galaxy** which in the mid-1970s is the ultimate kind of heavy logistic freighter. It was designed to carry a 125,000 lb load for 8,000 miles, or 250,000 lb over shorter distances, and to take off from an 8,000 feet runway and land its load on 4,000 feet of battlefield airstrip (compacted earth or similar material). The C-5A is therefore fitted with very advanced high-lift wing flaps, and with a 'high flotation'

landing gear having 28 wheels. These aircraft provide about 43,000 cubic feet of interior volume and can carry almost every movable item of US military equipment at a cruising speed of 440 kt, or rather over 500 mph. One of the advantages of so large an aircraft is that it can be fitted with two decks, with troops on top and their heavy combat equipment below. Thus, for example, a complete armoured regiment or even a division can be airlifted thousands of miles in a few hours and go into action within minutes of its arrival. It is also significant that, whereas days or weeks in troopships and landing craft can leave troops prostrate with seasickness, and unfit for fighting for perhaps 24 hours, air transport leaves them fresh and ready for immediate action.

In quickly bringing major forces to the scene of an international incident, a political crisis or similar confrontation, air transport is today indispensable. Careful studies have also shown that it is almost always cheaper than surface transport, and that less is unusably locked up 'in the pipeline'. On the other hand the disposition of armies in battle areas cannot be so readily altered by air. Though front-line units can be supplied by helicopters, or by air dropping (either by

parachute or by extracting loads in a fly-past at minimum safe speed at very low level, with special shock-absorbing packaging), it is not easy to operate large transport aircraft from airstrips in battle areas owing to their vulnerability to enemy attack by mortars, artillery and tactical missiles. Even helicopters have to adopt the most extreme 'nap of the earth' flight path. Moreover, modern armies are almost certain to be well provided with anti-aircraft missiles, and even front-line infantry are likely to have shoulder-fired homing missiles capable of destroying any aircraft coming within a range of a mile or two. Thus armies are not air-portable actually on the battlefield except very locally and out of sight of the enemy. Even then, transport operations on any large scale are extremely difficult unless one holds almost undisputed command of the air.

Shockproof packaging

On the other hand, away from the scene of actual combat, the air is the most likely means of transport for all military forces. This has exerted a strong influence on the design of military equipment, further emphasising the need for lightweight, small

bulk, quick dismantling and foolproof re-assembly, and general compatibility with aircraft. Most of these tendencies are desirable in any case, but the need for air portability might, for example, result in a major item being made in light alloy instead of in cheaper steel. To take a particular example, it has had an influence on the materials used for armour, and it has had a very far-ranging effect on how ammunition and other items are packaged.

Packing is particularly important in the case of items intended to be air-dropped. Some stores, such as sacks of foodstuffs, can often be air dropped with no parachute and no special packaging, though this is most often done to alleviate famine after a crop failure or major earthquake when saving a few hours is better than getting a 100 per cent success with the delivery. With expensive military stores, shockproof packaging is often essential. The specifications for such packaging are severe, including resistance to water, fire, vibration, sudden violent impact (both by striking the ground at high speed and by being struck by a heavy, sharp object), and to such phenomena as sand-storms, salt-water spray and nuclear radiation. Air packaging is often custom-tailored to the item, and costly enough to be salvaged and

used again and again. Many methods are used for absorbing impact, and in the case of really large items the usual answer is flexible cushioning bags inflated with air or gas. Sometimes the bag is equipped with a ram air intake which automatically blows up the bag as the payload falls through the sky.

Parachute design has also been influenced by the need for sure and accurate delivery. Paratroops use round or square canopies provided with a 'blank gore' or other cut-out portion to enable the flight trajectory to be controlled by pulling asymmetrically on the shroud lines. As the numerous highly skilled sky diving teams have publicly demonstrated, the air portable army can arrive by parachute with very great precision. Though details are classified, there is no doubt that airborne troops can drop by night or in bad weather and home on to a ground beacon placed in the safe dropping zone. For special purposes a Rogallo wing type of support can be used instead of a parachute, this having the advantage of 'flying' rather than merely falling, so—depending on the height at which the glide starts—the final trajectory can cover several miles in complete silence. The Rogallo wing is a form of single-surface curving sail which behaves rather like some ship sails and slides

obliquely through the air under perfect control. Large wings of this kind can be packaged into a small volume and may be very useful for the precision delivery of heavy loads; at present it is not easy to steer heavy loads needing several conventional parachute canopies.

Delivering an army by air

Much research is still being done to discover the best ways of delivering armies by air. With rough tactical airstrips there is a vital need for near-perfect traffic control both in the air and on the ground, because there is unlikely to be room for more than one or two aircraft on the strip at any one time. Once a heavy transport is well down the glide-path it does not want to have to overshoot because there is another blocking the airstrip. Thus careful planning is essential so that the strip can be constructed (perhaps by an air-dropped engineer battalion), provided with radio communications and landing aids, air-traffic control brought into action, the first transport landed, positioned off the strip for rapid unloading and then taxied to the downwind end of the strip for take-off, while the second and third aircraft are landed and the fourth lined up on the

Tactical airlift is vital for almost all successful military operations. The impressive panorama shows Soviet paratroopers boarding a fleet of Antonov An-12s of the Soviet Air Force during the Dvina exercise in Byelorussia in March 1970. The lumbering Beverley C.1 (far left) of the RAF is thundering out of a forward strip near Aden. Turkish troops were airlifted into Cyprus by Agusta-Bell 204B helicopters (above) during the invasion of July 1974. French paratroopers are huddled in their Nord 2501 Noratlas (right) on their way to Port Said, during the Anglo-French Suez operation on 5 November 1956.

approach. Defensive guns or missiles may be on the first aircraft, together with such special supplies as drums of chemical to harden and compact the strip surface to keep it operative even in a tropical monsoon. Any strip likely to be used over a period may well be fitted with air-portable arrester gear, to prevent aircraft running off the far end. Fuel supplies may be flown in in huge flexible Dracones—long bag containers of rubberised fabric—which are extremely heavy when filled with tens of thousands of gallons of fuel. Despite this, if there is any possibility of air attack they may have to be hidden well away from the strip and coupled up to a refuelling hydrant system serving both aircraft and ground forces.

Armies need not only fighting troops and weapons but also such auxiliary services as central store depots, messes, hospitals, and headquarters equipped with the fullest communications and data links. Everything can be flown in and made operational very quickly, though the type of 'building' used may depend on the circumstances. Ambient temperature and precipitation may be those of tropical rain-forest or Arctic tundra, and in extreme cases it is today considered worth having full air-conditioning, especially for a hospital. Of course, many military transport aircraft are specially equipped as ambulances for casualty evacuation, with multi-tier litter (stretcher) installations and provision for in-flight medical attention, blood transfusions and, in emergency, even operations. Casualties would normally do the first few hundred feet of their journey on foot or carried on a stretcher, the next few miles (to an airstrip) in a helicopter and the rest of the journey by jet.

Civil engineering plays a major role in most battlefield operations. Disputed territory today is unlikely to retain existing facilities for long, and once a region has been captured (with the firm prospect of not immediately being lost again) it is likely that much effort will be devoted to building roads, railways, bridges, drains, water, electricity and other services, both for the occupying force and for any civilians. Usually almost everything needed for such work is flown in, until the surface transport system is once more functioning. Unlike civil air transport, sustaining an army tends to be a one-way operation, the return missions carrying little but casualties, empty packaging and possibly special prisoners.

In conclusion, special mention should be made of the aerial supply of fighting fleets at sea. The provision of fuel oil and most routine stores is done by fleet oilers and supply ships, but special cargo, personnel and items are sent by transport aircraft to one of the fleet's carriers. The COD (Carrier On-board Delivery) aircraft can fly hundreds of miles from a shore base direct to the designated carrier, and in wartime would have to use self-contained (inertial) navigation. COD transports are fully 'carrier compatible' but do not usually have to fold up to go down into one of the ship's hangars.

VIETNAM

War was never officially declared in Vietnam and the inconclusive 'peace' failed to halt the bloodshed. The anomalies are not confined to politics and history. The battleship was reborn and while, as in most wars of any length in this century, new aircraft and new combat techniques were introduced, some old and suprising aircraft, such as Dakotas, Skyraiders and Cessnas, found novel and effective combat uses in what was essentially a one-sided war in the air.

Conventional payloads for the B-52. The mighty Boeing B-52 Stratofortress was built to deliver nuclear weapons to distant enemies. In fact, its only combat function was to rain down 'iron bombs' (ordinary high explosive) on the Viet Cong. Here a well-worn B-52F of Strategic Air Command lets go a string of 750 lb. bombs on a coastal target in October 1965. Later many of these huge bombers were modified to carry loads of up to 70,000 lb. on each trip.

Whatever one's political views, it is undisputed that the Communist movement has frequently expressed its wish to dominate the world. Indeed the Chinese Communists have said they can accomplish this objective by themselves. In the past they have proved willing to spread their gospel by force, notably when the neighbouring country of Korea was artificially divided into two. Yet only a year after the end of the Korean War the decision was solemnly taken in Geneva to effect an exactly similar partition upon Vietnam, another country bordering China which, with Laos and Cambodia, made up the territory formerly called French Indo-China. The French had been astonishingly humiliated and defeated by the Communist Viet-Minh forces led by General Giap. Once the French had gone Giap planned a massive new Communist guerilla force to operate against South Vietnam, the state created south of the 17th N parallel. This force became known as the Viet-Cong (VC) or National Liberation Front (NLF).

Such moves were obvious. In the nuclear stalemate, which balefully suppressed thoughts of total war, subversion and guerilla activity were the natural, and publicly broadcast, objectives of the Communist Party in every land. Vietnam was well suited to such work. It combined trackless rice paddies, rugged mountains and triple-canopy jungle, with a climate of violent extremes equalling anything met in Korea. Infrastructure to support modern military forces was non-existent, but it was ideal country to infiltrate with people who by night maintained a systematic campaign of murder and intimidation yet by day were apparently peaceful farmers.

Western leaders took little notice when the VC campaign greatly intensified in 1957, but what was surprising was that the inefficient and corrupt South Vietnamese regime of Premier Diem showed little concern either, even though the countryside was in a state of planned anarchy. But in 1960, Diem appealed for US help, and special forces were sent as advisers. Meanwhile 'brush-fire wars' became a matter of sudden great interest in the Pentagon. The US Air Force

opened the Special Air Warfare Center at Eglin AFB, Florida, to explore hardware and techniques for anti-guerilla operations. A specification was written for the LARA/COIN aircraft (Light Armed Reconnaissance Aircraft, Counter Insurgency), calling for STOL performance and the ability to carry heavy armament loads and even evacuate stretcher casualties. The winner of the contest was the North American **OV-10 Bronco,** a unique machine which later served in Vietnam.

Controls prohibit success

Great efforts were applied to adapting existing aircraft to COIN operations in the absence of effective enemy air opposition. One of the stalwart types considered was, of course, the **A-1 Skyraider,** and these versatile veterans served not only with the Navy and Marine Corps but also with the Air Force and with the Air Force of South Vietnam. Another fine basis for a COIN was the **B-26 Invader** (by the same designer, Ed Heinemann), and a third was the **North American T-28** trainer which re-appeared with a far more powerful engine (a turboprop) and extensive provisions for weapons. Even helicopters were armed, and guns and rockets were fitted to **Bell UH-1A** (the first 'Huey' version) helicopters to 'keep the enemy heads down' while assault troops were being flown in.

In 1961, Lyndon Johnson, then Vice-President, announced that US 'advisors' could actually fight in Vietnam, provided that the VC fired first. Thus began a US involvement which bled the world's most powerful and most prosperous nation, involved millions of her young men and led to bitter controversy. At no time was there a state of war. The aim of the struggle became lost or forgotten, the Allied troops (which included not only all US forces but also units from Korea, Australia and New Zealand) had to obey strict rules which crippled their effectiveness, and the most detailed control of operations was exercised from Washington in a way that almost prohibited any Allied success, and in par-

ticular grossly diminished the effectiveness of Allied air power. In addition the US troops were inevitably regarded as foreigners, with foreign commanders; and the ARVN (Army of South Vietnam) was badly led, and had near-zero morale, and was ignored by the US leaders until seven years later.

US willingness to wage war

Things went from bad to worse. In 1963, Diem was assassinated, the Khanh regime took over, and 'Allied' control was reduced to a beleaguered existence in Saigon and a few other cities. The high-handed Civil Defence Corps and Civil Guards antagonised the few loyal civilians, the VC troops fought better than the better-fed, better-armed ARVN troops transported not on bare feet but in helicopters, and the torrent of US dollars seemed to disappear into the sink of Saigon politics. It looked grim not only for South Vietnam but for the whole Western world. As Mao said 'If the special warfare that the US imperialists are testing in South Vietnam can be overcome, this means that it can be defeated anywhere in the world.'

What the Communists did not count on was President Johnson's willingness to fight a war in all but name. VC attacks at Bien Hoa, at Pleiku, on the air base at Da Nang and on a US destroyer brought sudden major US responses, including air strikes from three US carriers in the Bay of Tonkin. US tactical airpower was increasingly brought into action, not only against VC forces (which usually were found not to be there) but also against bridges, communications and strategic targets. On March 8, 1965 US Marines landed at Da Nang and began the build-up of US ground forces, while a squadron of **F-105 Thunderchiefs** thundered in to a base in Thailand. There is not the slightest doubt that, had the US forces not arrived when they did, the South Vietnamese administration would have been annihilated.

Gradually the conflict escalated until the US forces alone were consuming ordnance four times faster than in the Korean war and slightly faster than the US forces in Europe in World War II. At least half the striking power was vested in the vital fighter/bombers: the A-1, which had great load-carrying capability, good range and endurance and the ability to survive punishment; the **F-100 Super Sabre,** which did well both in ground attack and flying top cover as a fighter; the F-105 Thunderchief, which in the first five years flew 75 per cent of the USAF attack missions; the **F-4 Phantom,** which was the supreme multi-role aircraft, yet desperately needed a Gatling gun and wing slats (and got both, by 1972); the **A-4 Sky-hawk,** perhaps the most cost-effective attacker of all; the **A-6 Intruder,** which alone could hit point targets by night or in bad weather; and the new **A-7 Corsair II** which arrived later in the war with both the Navy and Marines and, in 1970, with the Air Force. These aircraft bore the brunt of combat missions during the ten years of the US involvement in Vietnam.

Iron bombs and fast movers

At first these aircraft just fired their guns, if they had them (and, while the F-4 wanted a gun for air combat, the A-6 wanted one for flak suppression) and dropped 'iron bombs' (ordinary free-fall high-explosive). A great deal of the ordnance was far from new. Dropping clustered thousand-pounders at jet speeds, the fuses became armed in three seconds; then the bombs might jostle each other, detonate and blow the aircraft that dropped them to bits. Urgently newer ordnance was supplied, and guided missiles were brought into action.

First of the missiles was Bullpup, itself a concept 10 years old. Though it was soon being launched not only from attack aircraft but also from the **SH-34 (S-58)** helicopter, the Bullpup had to be steered all the way to the target. At first VC air opposition and AA fire was negligible, but by 1966 many thousands of very effective Russian guns and guided missiles were being dispersed very

cleverly, and even 2,000 riflemen could make life most uncomfortable for attacking pilots. It was soon judged that, while a short-range stand-off missile might enable attacking aircraft to avoid the target itself, they could not avoid the well-sited defensive fire. Indeed, Bullpup and some other early tactical attack missiles required extended exposure to defensive fire, and it was officially judged that 'attrition due to the launch constraints of some missiles could be double that suffered in dive bombing or strafing runs.'

When dropping iron bombs or napalm, fixed-wing 'fast movers' (the jet fighter-bombers) typically made passes at about 400-450 knots in dives from 25° to 60°, or—especially with napalm—dropped on the level at about 200 feet at the same speed. In nearly all missions, and especially when the target was close to friendly troops, a FAC (forward air controller) was essential.

Sometimes the FAC was on the ground, but usually he was in a **Cessna O-2** or similar lightplane. The FAC might boldly trail his coat to draw VC fire, but his main role was to point out the precise location of the target, marking it with smoke or flares and giving R/T instructions on how many feet away and in which direction the attacking jet should aim. The FAC job, which also involved many other duties, was hazardous in the extreme. Later the push-pull **Cessna O-2TT** became available, and controllers had many special tools including some of those needed for the 'psy-war' (psychological warfare) role, which included loudspeakers, leaflets and broadcast equipment. But by 1968 the job of FAC was often being under-

Low-speed Supersonics. In Vietnam supersonic fighters were usually employed at 350 knots at low level trying to hit unseen ground targets. The McDonnell Douglas F-4C Phantom (top) has just fired a salvo of 2.75 inch rockets; the stalwart F-100D (right) has released napalm tanks.

PRINCIPAL AIRCRAFT USED BY THE US IN VIETNAM

Type	Role	Comment
North American F-100 Super Sabre	Fighter and ground attack	Acquitted itself well in both roles
Republic F-105 Thunderchief	Fighter and ground attack	In the first 5 years flew 75% of the USAF attack missions. Numbers based in Thailand from March 1963 onwards
McDonnell Douglas F-4 Phantom II	Tactical strike fighter	Was the supreme multi-role aircraft, yet desperately needed a Gatling gun and wing slats (and got both, by 1972)
General Dynamics (Convair) F-111	Tactical strike fighter	First detachment arrived in March 1968. Most efficient, despite some adverse publicity due to a few early crashes
Northrop F-5	Air superiority fighter	For some reason only one squadron operational for a short while in 1965
Douglas A-1 Skyraider	Tactical attack and strike aircraft	Had great load-carrying capacity, good range and flight endurance, and the ability to survive battle damage. Proved to be the ideal close-support aircraft for some time
Douglas A-4 Skyhawk	Carrier- or land-based attack bomber	Could be described as the most cost-effective attacker of all. Two-seat TA-4J also did good work around the battlefield
Grumman A-6 Intruder	Carrier-borne low-level strike aircraft	The only aircraft that could hit 'point targets' by night or in bad weather. Used to mine Haiphong harbour in North Vietnam in 1973.
Vought A-7 Corsair II	Tactical attack aircraft	Arrived later in the war, first with the US Navy and USMC, then (1970) with the USAF
North American OV-10 Bronco	Counter-insurgency and forward fire-control aircraft	Winner of the LARA/COIN (Light Armed Reconnaissance Aircraft, Counter-Insurgency) contest calling for STOL performance and ability to carry heavy armament loads and evacuate casualties. Reached operations with USMC and USAF units in 1967
Cessna O-2	Forward fire-control aircraft	Of invaluable service in close country and confused fighting.
North American RA-5C Vigilante	Carrier-based reconnaissance aircraft	The most sophisticated reconnaissance aircraft in Vietnam, able to provide instant and total multi-sensor surveillance of targets. Also surveyed the entire territory of both N. and S. Vietnam so that accurate maps could be prepared to serve the whole campaign

taken by skilled pilots of fighter-bombers who knew every inch of the terrain and, for example, once blasted a VC armoured car off the face of the earth when it was disguised as a bush that the FAC knew was not growing there. The fast-mover FACs usually flew the F-100 or F-4, though the two-seat **TA-4J** also did good work. These men were skilled and experienced, and operated as freelance controllers able to call up devastating forces in a matter of minutes.

VC fear of the hated B-52s

Logistic supply from the distant United States was mainly by ship or by the MAC fleet of **C-141 StarLifters,** while the beloved **C-130** handled most of the tactical supply trucking. A vast army of helicopters was built up, mainly by the US Army, for forward supply, casualty evacuation, aircraft and vehicle recovery and, increasingly, armed participation in the land battle. The most numerous helicopter was the Huey, but the big **CH-47 Chinook** did heavy trucking and brought back downed aircraft, the **CH-54 Skycrane** force paid for itself ten times over and was swiftly augmented, and huge orders were placed for the **Hughes OH-6** light observation machine. Lockheed began work on the AAFSS (advanced aerial fire suppression system), which materialised as the fantastic **AH-56 Cheyenne,** a helicopter as complicated and expensive as the **B-52** but which never entered service. Instead, thousands of Huey-cobra (armed Hueys) were bought, though some considered these merely a very costly two-seater that could easily be shot down with a rifle from either of its defenceless flanks.

Eventually VC troops learned to lie low when helicopters were around, because in the absence of an enemy they might go away. But the VC hated the B-52s, early models of which were painted green/brown camouflage above and black below and, operating from Guam and Thailand, rained down torrents of bombs to demoralise and

destroy. On many occasions fighter-bombers operated in the same way, releasing hundreds of tons of ordnance in straight and level formation flight at about 12,000 feet, often with a **B-66 Destroyer** serving as pathfinder and master bomber. B-66 versions also accompanied more and more raids into North Vietnam to operate in the ECM role, while an increasing force of **KC-135** tankers was kept busy topping up fighters and attack aircraft that were 'below bingo' (below the fuel state to reach base).

The vital role of reconnaissance was flown by many types. The most sophisticated machine was the Navy **RA-5C Vigilante,** which, operating from the giant supercarriers, was alone able not only to provide instant and total multi-sensor surveillance of targets, but also surveyed the entire territory of North and South Vietnam so that accurate maps could be prepared to serve the whole campaign. Tactical reconnaissance was handled mainly by the **RF-4C Phantom,** which was especially valuable in assessing post-strike damage in North Vietnam, and the **RF-101 Voodoo** and Army **OV-1 Mohawk** family of multi-sensor STOL turboprops. Some of the Mohawks carried SLAR (side-looking aircraft radar) with MTI (moving target detection) to spot, say, a moving man seen against the fixed ground and in-flight processing and readout of the resulting pictures. ECM and 'electronic reconnaissance' became increasingly important as the North's capabilities increased. Many types handled this tricky work, including special **RB-57s, RA-3B Skywarriors** of the Navy, the specially designed **EA-6A Prowlers, EB-66s** and even **RC-47 Dakotas.**

Deadly Magic Dragons

The shelter afforded by the extensive areas of forest and jungle assumed serious proportions, and great research efforts were made in the United States to try to perfect methods of detecting troops, metal objects (such as

Boeing B-52 Stratofortress	Strategic bomber	Operated from bases in Guam and Thailand almost immune until the situation began to change dramatically after mid-1972. This led to some urgent re-thinking regarding its combat potential and resulted in hurried rearmament with SRAM missiles
Douglas EB-66 Destroyer	Electronics countermeasures aircraft	Often served as pathfinders and master bombers. Also accompanied B-52 raids into N. Vietnam operating in the ECM role
McDonnell RF-101 Voodoo	Reconnaissance	Together with the RF-4C Phantom II handled most of the battlefield reconnaissance
Grumman OV-1 Mohawk	STOL observation aircraft	A whole family of these aircraft were in operational service, some with SLAR (Side-Looking Aircraft Radar) with MTI (Moving Target Detection) —able to spot a moving man against the fixed ground.
Martin RB-57 Douglas RA-3B Skywarrior Grumman EA-6A Prowler Douglas RC-47	Electronics countermeasures aircraft	In addition to the EB-66s a number of other types did this work—becoming more important as the North grew more capable of using sophisticated anti-aircraft defence systems
Fairchild C-123 Provider	Medium tactical assault transport	In addition to its intended transport role was used to spray forests with special chemicals to defoliate trees
Douglas AC-47 Fairchild AC-119G AC-119K Lockheed AC-130 Hercules	Large aircraft converted into heavily-armed 'gunships'	A development of the Vietnam war, and remarkably successful in suppressing VC attacks. Became operational in 1970
Boeing KC-135 Stratotanker	In-flight refuelling tanker	An increasing force was kept busy refuelling fighters and attack aircraft
Lockheed C-130 Hercules	Medium/long-range transport	One of the most beloved aircraft there; handled most tactical supplies
Lockheed C-141 StarLifter	Strategic transport	Looked after logistics from the USA

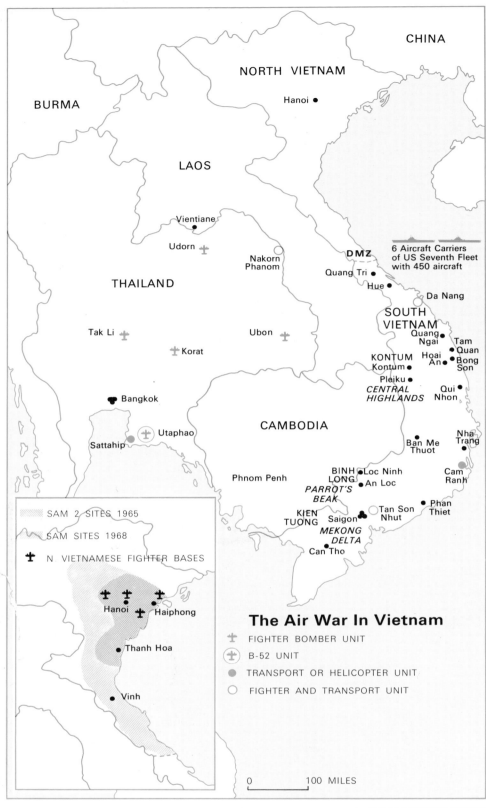

CHINA

NORTH VIETNAM

BURMA

Hanoi •

LAOS

Vientiane •

Udorn ✚

Nakorn
Phanom

THAILAND

DMZ

Quang Tri •

Hue •

Da Nang

6 Aircraft Carriers
of US Seventh Fleet
with 450 aircraft

SOUTH
VIETNAM

Tak Li ✚

Ubon ✚

Quang,
Ngai •

Tam
Quan •

Korat ✚

KONTUM

Hoai
An •

Bong
Son •

Kontum •

Bangkok ♦

Pleiku •

Utaphao ✚

CENTRAL
HIGHLANDS

Qui
Nhon •

Sattahip ●

CAMBODIA

Phnom Penh

Ban Me
Thuot •

Nha
Trang •

BINH
LONG •

Loc Ninh

An Loc

Cam
Ranh ○

PARROT'S
BEAK

KIEN
TUONG

Tan Son
Nhut ○

Phan
Thiet •

Saigon ●

SAM 2 SITES 1965

SAM SITES 1968

MEKONG
DELTA

✚ N. VIETNAMESE FIGHTER BASES

Can Tho •

✚ ✚ ✚

Hanoi ✚ Haiphong

Thanh Hoa •

The Air War In Vietnam

✚ FIGHTER BOMBER UNIT

Ⓧ B-52 UNIT

● TRANSPORT OR HELICOPTER UNIT

○ FIGHTER AND TRANSPORT UNIT

Vinh •

0   100 MILES

PRINCIPAL HELICOPTERS USED BY THE US IN VIETNAM

Type	Role	Comment
Bell UH-1, etc. 'Huey'	Multiple	The most numerous helicopter, a real 'maid of all trades'
Huey-Cobra	Gunship	Armed 'Huey'. After convincing trials and despite vulnerability to ground fire thousands of these were acquired instead of the very expensive AH-56 Cheyenne
Hughes OH-6	Observation	Good performance under operational conditions, leading to large production orders. 'Silent' version of the OH-6A undertook clandestine reconnaissance
Boeing/Vertol CH-47 Chinook	Transport	Brought in heavy goods where needed and picked up shot down aircraft; a strong and reliable machine
CH-53	Transport	Carried various loads to far-flung fire bases, etc.
Sikorsky CH-54 Skycrane	Transport	Did most of the 'heavy lifting', including complete helicopters—even a CH-47 Chinook. A most useful machine, and much appreciated. Numbers in action swiftly increased
Sikorsky UH-34	Multiple	In Vietnam since Spring 1962, and proved to be an exceptionally rugged machine capable of taking numerous hits

rifles) and other unnatural materials when hidden beneath the lofty canopies of leaves. While these projects bore some fruit, defoliation became the order of the day, helicopters and such fixed-wing machines as the **C-123** being used to spray the forests with chemicals which would cause the leaves to wither and fall. As this was likely to kill the tree this action triggered off a wave of protest by conservationists who had been unmoved by the human slaughter, and from 1967 onwards the whole Vietnam war became increasingly a matter of heated and often bewildered debate in the United States. As for the new sensing programmes, these eventually embraced 'people sniffers', remote sensor-transmitters, and conventional sensors conveyed in RPVs (remotely piloted vehicles).

The RC-47 was not the only venerable **DC-3** variant to play an active role in Vietnam. Another was the **AC-47,** known as Puff the Magic Dragon. It carried heavy armament, smacking of the B-17, firing through the left cabin windows; typical armament would be three GE Miniguns each firing up to 6,000 rifle-calibre rounds per minute from huge boxes of ammunition

Most sorties flown against the Viet Cong were directly in support of surface forces. The big Boeing-Vertol Chinook helicopter (top left) has brought in the troops of the Royal Australian Regt.; the colour illustration shows the streams of fire—up to 18,000 rounds per minute—pouring from an AC-47 gunship; at upper right is a shattered rail siding near Thanh Hoa after attack by US Navy A-4 Skyhawks and A-6 Intruders in 1966; and the large picture shows the view from a US Navy UH-IE gunship helicopter looking for the Viet Cong who rocketed the burning patrol boat.

filling much of the fuselage. The AC-47 operated at night and often worked with a FAC or multi-sensor reconnaissance aircraft. As soon as a ground target was discovered the pilot would sight on it by pointing the left wing at it, lining up with an optical sight in the left cockpit window. This automatically put the AC-47 into a banked turn to the left. Then, either blind or using a bright, blinding searchlight, the area would be raked with fire; and it was significant that the circling 'Dragon ship' fired from all directions.

This seemingly crude technique proved remarkably successful, and before long the modification of large transport aircraft to provide this orbiting fire was one of the main methods of night interdiction and suppressing enemy attacks. All that was needed was a big weight-lifter. Some of the most successful conversions were **Fairchild AC-119Gs** (the twin-boom freighter of the Korean war), which were fitted with four Miniguns, a pallet-mounted airborne illuminator, a light-intensifying night observation system, a flare launcher, special electric generators, analog gunfire control and protective armour. Then came the **AC-119K,** with extra thrust from added jet pods, and infra-red sensors, radars and two 20 mm cannon. Hardest hitters of all were the **AC-130E Hercules,** with four 20 mm Gatlings, four Miniguns

and every conceivable kind of target sensing system. These became operational in Vietnam in 1970.

AX—simply devastating

In 1967 the first OV-10A (COIN) aircraft reached the operational Marine Corps and Air Force units in Vietnam, and though having only a modest performance they did fine work and were liked by their crews. Their role was one of armed FAC, but in the Pentagon a much later specification was drawn up, called AX, for yet a further purpose-built ground attack machine for limited wars. It was now thought a better engine than the turbo-prop might be the turbofan, and emphasis was placed on

Radar bombing through low cloud. Four Republic F-105D Thunderchiefs release 3,000 lb. bombs guided by an RB-66.

simplicity, the ability to deliver devastating firepower (where the COIN fell short) and to survive enemy anti-aircraft fire. Thought was also spared for the hazards of the FAC mission, and experiments were made with the OV-10, the Armed Porter, the **O-2TT** and other types. None proved wholly successful, while the less vulnerable fast-movers were costly, ill-adapted to visual observation at either low or high speeds and relied almost entirely on crew skill and experience.

In March 1968 a detachment of six **F-111As** was sent as a special exercise from Nellis AFB to duty in Vietnam to

prove that this controversial swing-wing attacker was fit for service. Within three weeks half the force had been lost, and with another crash at Nellis the F-111 was grounded. This was sheer bad luck. The losses were not due to enemy action (the only two that were available for post-crash inspection were found to have been due to failure of a weld in the tailplane drive), and when one looked behind the headlines the F-111 could be seen to have flown dangerous missions deep into North Vietnam operating quite alone, without the support from tankers, ECM and radar jammers, and top-cover fighters needed by other attack machines—and they could unerringly find and hit their targets. Their effectiveness was far greater than, for example, the little

Northrop F-5 a 'squadron' of 12 of which briefly operated in Vietnam in 1965.

By 1968, penetration of major target areas in the North was no picnic. Vast numbers of guns and guided missiles, supported by a very thorough radar control and reporting network, made the defences a tougher proposition than anything previously encountered in World War II or at any other time. The air-launched guided missile became urgently wanted in improved forms. While the aged Bullpup continued to be used, the tactical pilots wanted a 'launch and leave' capability that freed the carrier aircraft from the need to loiter in the target area (or even five miles from the target, where defensive firepower might be even heavier). In 1965 the Shrike ARM (anit-radar missile) was hurriedly brought into use, with disastrous results. By 1968, Shrike was doing better, homing automatically on to enemy radars, but to take out other kinds of target frantic work went ahead on the TV-guided Maverick missile and on Hobos (homing bomb system). A great profusion of types of so-called 'smart' weapons were in the laboratory, many of them having semi-active homing by laser light (the laser being mounted on the ground or in the launch aircraft). A further powerful weapon was the Navy's Condor, with TV guidance from more than 40 miles away, but like the other point-target missiles it did not reach Vietnam in time to be effective.

The battleship returns

So hazardous did attacks on the North become that in 1968, after three years of urgent pleas from the US Army and Marines, the Navy de-mothballed a 16 inch-gun battleship (at a cost equal to about six crashed F-4s) and used her to bombard targets in the North (over 1,000 of which were in her range); then the ship was again mothballed just before the final massive Communist offensive at Easter, 1972, when such firepower along the DMZ (the demilitarised zone supposedly

established between the two sides during armistice talks) was urgently needed. The only bright spot in the situation—apart from the long-term facts that the VC no longer existed, and the enemy was the legitimate army of North Vietnam—was that the old SA-2 missile was erratic, could be fooled by ECM and with luck could even be evaded by a manoeuvrable aircraft flown to the limits. The enemy air force put up a few **Mig-21s** but never challenged the US armadas seriously.

In late January 1968 the Communists launched a huge Tet (lunar new year) offensive, and air supply helped Marines beleaguered at Khe Sanh to survive—though at least one-third of the supplies were grabbed by the enemy. While the US forces continued to fight according to very rigid and restrictive rules—expressed by President Johnson as 'They don't dare bomb an outhouse without my say-so'—the heaviest air assaults on targets in the North did not weaken the North Vietnamese will to fight, and attacks on the Ho Chi Minh supply trail merely delayed the passage of food and ammunition without stopping it. By 1969 some of the newly invented devices were in use. One was the Igloo White remote sensing system. The whole area of the Ho Chi Minh trail, and other truck routes, was sprinkled with things like 'land sonobuoys'—small canisters which could detect vibration due to a vehicle and transmit a signal by radio. Used in conjunction with special receiver aircraft, these sensors enabled watch to be kept on the position of every truck on the road. The People Sniffer was also worth having, though it was useless in rain or some other conditions. Carried by helicopters, it measured ammonia in the atmosphere, and if it happened to be exactly downwind of troops the concentration rose by one or two parts per million (the Communists took to hanging urine jars on trees as decoys).

Another major new development was the previously mentioned RPV, which by 1970 was becoming important in the field. Some were radio-controlled reconnaissance machines, feeding back information in various ways, while others were intended later to replace attack aircraft which needed a crew riding on board; **BQM-34A** RPVs, for example, were used to launch Maverick, Hobos, Shrike and other missiles against

the Fan Song radars, mock-up SA-2 missile sites and similar targets. Yet a further new line of development was the Quiet Aircraft, for surveillance of enemy forces at close range. Aircraft such as the **Q-Star,** and special helicopters such as The Quiet One (a much modified **OH-6A**), were made so quiet that they could hardly be heard even at close range, and they were then operated over enemy targets in brief autorotative flight while gathering information with multiple sensors. By January 1969 there were 549,500 US troops in Vietnam. Most were conscripts with an effective stay of about four months so that, in a war where experience counted for everything, every US unit was constantly being deprived of its only experienced personnel). The Army's force of some 4,000 aircraft included over 3,600 helicopters, rather more than the number lost in Vietnam during the previous seven years. This force played a central role in winning the land battle. It enabled a system of fire-support bases (forts) to be set up, as the French had done in the same territory, and constantly supplied. The French had pushed about one convoy a month along Route 19, and most had been ambushed (the last and biggest was wiped out almost to the last man). In 1970 there were five convoys a day on the same route, travelling by air. The **CH-47C, CH-54A** and **CH-53** were carrying huge loads, and Gunship helicopters provided protective fire support. Helicopter pilots sometimes flew 13 hours in one day, and their choppers frequently exceeded 200 hours a month.

In 1970 the end was in sight. The most fundamental thing was that the purpose of the war had at last been enunciated, the South Vietnamese people apparently understood and approved, the economy of the country had been rebuilt and the ARVN (army of South Vietnam) had been rebuilt and properly trained. Even a South Vietnamese air force had been brought to the status of a formidable permanent force. By no means least, the Communist rest and resupply areas of Cambodia and Laos were entered, mopped up and sealed.

The final chapter opened with a huge and reckless invasion of the South in 1972 which almost cost Hanoi its regular army. By this time half-hearted armistice talks had been going on for years, but what turned the talks into genuine two-sided horsetrading was the final series of carefully planned, relentlessly executed bomber (mainly B-52) attacks against Hanoi and its port of Haiphong. These final raids, in November 1972-January 1973, were costly in aircraft and crews; about 29 B-52s were lost, and rapid conferences were held to re-think the ECM situation and improve defence against the more formidable SA-3 missile. But the attacks shut Haiphong and virtually halted Hanoi's ability to wage 'big war', and thus accomplished their political objective of compelling the Communists to seek a conclusive solution at the conference table.

Despite the loss of heavy bombers, these final raids were one of the very few occasions in the long and bloody Vietnam war in which air power was not only effective but also cost-effective. Often, despite the combination of superior equipment and great crew skill and courage, Allied air power in Vietnam was both extravagant and aimless.

Unusual aircraft of the Vietnam War. North Vietnamese MiG-21PF day fighters (left) did little to hamper the massive US air effort. McDonnell Douglas A-1H Skyraiders (below) of the 6th Special Operations Sqn. escort a Sikorsky HH-3E 'Jolly Green Giant' rescue helicopter.

SKY-HIGH SEA POWER

World War II conclusively proved that maritime air power was essential for the survival of the major countries. Technological advances since then have made it more difficult for the world's maritime air arms to fulfil their multiple roles, even though events have shown that without their effectiveness every nation, no matter what its size, is vulnerable.

Thirty years after the end of the Second World War the argument still rages over which is the most effective form of a country's vital maritime air arm. It can be defined either as the air element of sea power or as the maritime element of an independent air force according to the defence dogma which has the most influential following in the country concerned. It is not purely a matter of semantics. The accepted definition may decide the essential naval and air policy of a country.

The roles played by the world's maritime air arms have not changed greatly but technological advances have made them more difficult to fulfill. But these air arms still reconnoitre for enemy naval forces outside the range of a fleet's surface scouts; provide a striking power beyond the range of the fleet's guns or surface-to-surface missiles; provide fighter defence against hostile bombers, supplementing the fleet's surface-to-air missile system; reconnoitre for enemy submarines and, either on their own or in conjunction with surface warships, hunt and destroy them.

In theory, all these roles can be adequately played by shore-based aircraft, taking advantage, where necessary, of inflight refuelling. Naval opinion is doubtful, to say the least, of this proposition. It suspects the capacity of a fighter defence or defensive air strike not under its sole control and operating, perhaps, at very large distances from its base.

This naval view has prevailed in the United States, in Soviet Russia and in France, where the navies concerned have retained their own air arm, both shore-based and ship-borne, responsible for all aspects of maritime air operations though, until recently the Soviet Navy has not taken the consequent step of providing itself with ship-borne tactical aircraft.

The Royal Navy, on the other hand, lost control of its own element when the Royal Air Force was founded in 1918. In 1937, control of the ship-borne air element was restored to the Navy but the Air Force continued to provide the long-range, shore-based squadrons operating in maritime roles. Their operations such as ASW and shipping surveillance, are controlled through Joint RN and RAF Maritime Headquarters ashore. A similar arrangement holds good for the Australian, Canadian, New Zealand and Italian navies.

US cuts 80 carriers

Since 1968 the Royal Navy has abandoned to the Royal Air Force the provision of fixed-wing maritime air operations previously operated from carriers while phasing-out the carriers themselves, as a result of a government decision to accept the feasibility of such a concept.

When the Second World War came to an end, the maritime air element of the Allies comprised an enormous force of aircraft. The United States Navy alone had 99 aircraft carriers of all types in commission as well as a large force of naval and marine land-based aircraft. The Royal Navy of her British ally was advancing a programme to increase her carrier force from its current 14 (excluding escort carriers) to 38, while under control of the British and Dominion Air Forces there were 51 Anti-Submarine Squadrons (684 aircraft) and 24 Maritime Strike Squadrons (414 aircraft). By the end of 1947 the USN's carrier force had been reduced to 20 with a corresponding reduction of its shore-based air element: the British, suffering an agonising economic recession, had only three carriers in commission. The strength of the maritime wing of the Royal Air Force had been reduced to nine Anti-Submarine Squadrons (about 70 aircraft), distributed world-wide, and no Strike Squadrons. The weaker naval powers were in process of developing naval air power by the acquisition of carriers from Great Britain or the United States.

Vista of naval air power. Ranged on the vast flight deck of the US super carrier **Saratoga** are A-1 Skyraiders, A-3 Skywarriors, A-4 Skyhawks, F-3 Demons, F-8 Crusaders, E-1 Tracers and a Boeing Vertol HH-25 rescue helicopter.

Maritime Patrol Aircraft of the NATO Countries

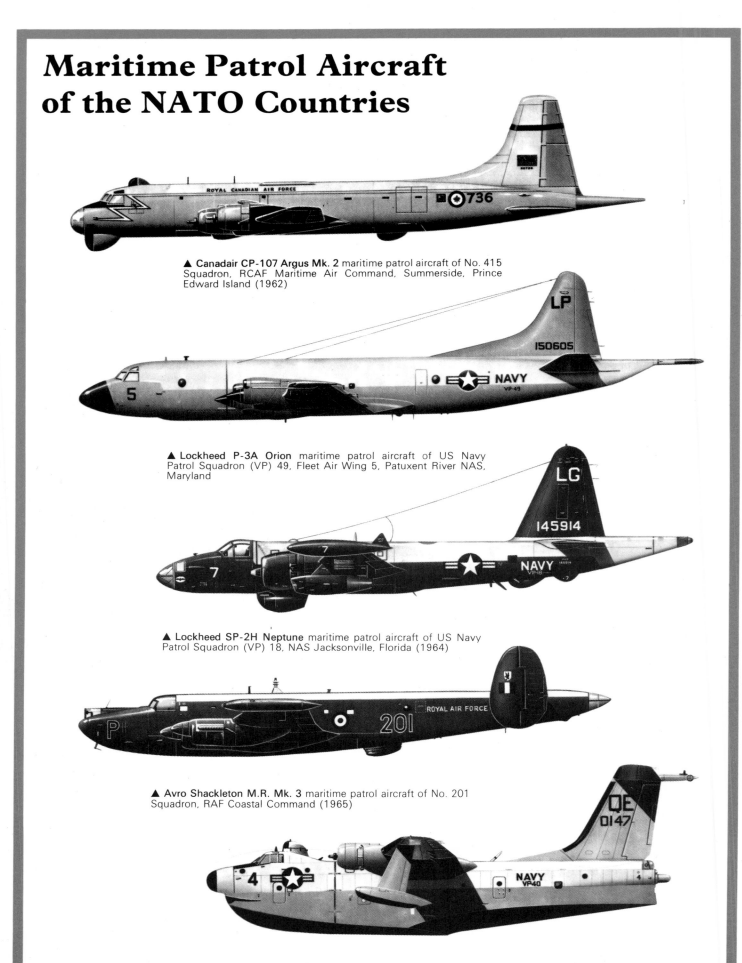

▲ **Canadair CP-107 Argus Mk. 2** maritime patrol aircraft of No. 415 Squadron, RCAF Maritime Air Command, Summerside, Prince Edward Island (1962)

▲ **Lockheed P-3A Orion** maritime patrol aircraft of US Navy Patrol Squadron (VP) 49, Fleet Air Wing 5, Patuxent River NAS, Maryland

▲ **Lockheed SP-2H Neptune** maritime patrol aircraft of US Navy Patrol Squadron (VP) 18, NAS Jacksonville, Florida (1964)

▲ **Avro Shackleton M.R. Mk. 3** maritime patrol aircraft of No. 201 Squadron, RAF Coastal Command (1965)

▲ **Martin SP-5B Marlin** maritime patrol flying boat of US Navy Patrol Squadron (VP) 40, NAS Sangley Point, Philippine Islands (1965)

The French, involved in their war in Indo-China with the communist Viet Minh, bought the escort carrier *Biter*, the light carrier *Colossus* and, later, the *U.S.S. Langley*; under their new names, *Dixmude*, *Arromanches* and *Lafayette*, they were were effectively used in support of French land forces until 1952. The Netherlands, Canadian, Australian, Indian, Brazilian and Argentinian navies each bought a British-built carrier.

During the 1950s the major military powers of the world crystallised into the two power blocs with the Western Alliance (developing into NATO) on the one hand, and the Warsaw Pact countries, dominated by the USSR, on the other. Up to that time Soviet Russia had contented itself with being simply the world's greatest land power with a limited, defensive role for its navy. Now it took the first steps in the rapid construction of a Soviet Navy which within 20 years would reach a parity with that of the United States and even, in some respects, a superiority. It did nothing, at first, to provide itself with any ship-borne air arm, but a parallel growth in the Soviet naval shore-based air force was begun.

'Badger' gives way to 'Bear'

To provide long range maritime reconnaissance in combination with a strike capability, the **Tupolev Tu-16** (NATO codename 'Badger') twin jet-engined, reconnaissance-bomber was brought into service in 1954. It had an operational range (calculated as $\frac{2}{3}$ of the absolute range, taking advantage of in-flight refuelling) of some 2,400 nautical miles. Like the 'Beagle', the 'Badger' is still in service with the Soviet naval aviation and has also been supplied to Egypt and Indonesia. A number of differently equipped versions of the 'Badger' have been produced, some carrying six to eight 23 mm cannons and up to nine tons of bombs or air-to-surface missiles as well as the necessary radar sets for navigation and bomb-aiming for a 'ship-strike' role; others armed with the cannons only, but equipped with a wider range of electronics, function as collectors of electronic intelligence (ELINT) or for electronic counter measures (ECM) as well as long range surveillance.

In the following year there came on the scene an aircraft with more than double the operational range (5,126 nautical miles). This was the **Tu-20 'Bear'**, powered by four turbo-propeller engines. The functions of most of these aircraft are confined to reconnaissance and electronic warfare and they carry no 'strike' weapons. It is rare for a NATO maritime exercise to take place anywhere in the world without surveillance by aircraft of this type; the movements of US fleets on foreign stations are similarly kept under regular observation. There is also an anti-submarine version of the Tu-20,

equipped with sonobuoys, depth charges and homing torpedoes.

Another type of reconnaissance aircraft in service since 1963 is the shorter-range but supersonic **Tu-22 'Blinder'** powered by two large jet engines. Employing in-flight refuelling and flying at supersonic speeds, it has a range of some 900 nautical miles increasing to 1,200 nautical miles at subsonic speeds.

Russia takes the lead

Two types of aircraft equipped wholly for anti-submarine warfare and in service since 1967 and 1969 respectively are the amphibian **Beriev Be-12 'Mail'** and the **Il-38 'May'**. The 'Mail', powered by two turbo-propeller engines has a range of some 600 nautical miles, the 'May', a four-engined turbo-propeller landplane, has an endurance of twelve hours and a range of 1,600 nautical miles.

These six types of fixed-wing aircraft are all that the Soviets have thought necessary to provide as air support to their huge, and still expanding navy—now the largest, in many respects, in the world. No ship-borne fighter aircraft are included in the list, for the Soviet Navy has only recently acquired aircraft-carriers, relying in the past upon its

surface-to-air missiles and gunfire for anti-aircraft defence of its fleet. Vertical or Short Take-off and Landing (V/STOL) aircraft and the constantly changing capabilities of helicopters could bring about a change in Soviet thinking. Already the *Moskva*, the first of several big V/STOL carriers, has been in commission since the late 1960s.

The great expansion of the Soviet Navy from 1950 was one of the causes of the state of nervous tension which came to be called the 'Cold War' in the relations between the Warsaw Pact countries and those of the Western Alliance which, with the accession of the United States became the North Atlantic Treaty Organisation. From the Cold War came the shooting war in Korea in which the multi-national naval forces of the NATO countries played an important role.

After the outbreak of the Korean War in June 1950, the US Navy's carrier force in commission had dwindled to only 15 vessels of all types. This was now increased to 39, comprising three of the large *Midway*-class, 14 modernised *Essex*-class veterans of the Second World War, five light and 17 escort carriers, by bringing out a number of ships from the reserve. They were to play an important part in the Korean war in collaboration with British Commonwealth

Eyes—and teeth—of Soviet maritime air power. The Beriev Be-12 'Mail' (above) has a range of 600 nautical miles and is equipped for anti-submarine warfare. The Myasishchev M-4 'Bison' (right, being shadowed by RAF Lightnings) is employed as a long-range reconnaissance aircraft.

Carrier Combat Aircraft

▲ Vought F-8E (FN) Crusader of Flottille 12F of France's Aéro-navale (1965). Flown on March 25, 1955, the Crusader featured a variable-incidence wing and entered US Navy service in 1957

▲ Douglas F4D-1 Skyray of US Navy Squadron VFAW-3. Of modified delta design, the Skyray flew on January 25, 1951 but test problems delayed acceptance of the aircraft which did not enter service until 1956, being finally phased out in 1964

▶ McDonnell F2H-3 Banshee of Royal Canadian Navy Squadron VF 870 (1958). The Banshee shipboard fighter first flew on January 11, 1947 and was operated by the US Navy from 1949 to 1959

▲ Hawker Siddeley Sea Vixen F.A.W. Mk. 2 of No. 766 Squadron, the Naval Air Fighter School at RNAS Yeovilton. The non-naval first prototype was flown on September 26, 1951, and the Sea Vixen entered service in 1959

▲ Hawker Siddeley Buccaneer S. Mk. 2 strike aircraft of Royal Navy Squadron No. 801 embarked aboard HMS Victorious (1965)

▶ Grumman F11F-1 Tiger of US Navy Squadron VF-21 (1958). The US Navy's first supersonic fighter, the Tiger flew on July 30, 1954, entered service in 1957 and was reallocated to Advanced Training Command from 1959

▼ Douglas A-3B Skywarrior shipboard attack bomber of Heavy Attack Squadron (VAH) 2 'Royal Ramparts' of the US Navy, home-based at NAS Whidbey Island, Washington (1961)

▼ Grumman S-2E Tracker shipboard anti-submarine warfare a craft of US Navy Anti-Submarine Squadron (VS) 26 aboard USS Randolph (1964)

◀ **Vought A-7A Corsair II** shipboard attack aircraft of US Navy Squadron VA-174

▲ **Grumman F9F-6 Cougar** was a swept-wing development of the Panther and was first flown on September 20, 1951, entering service with the US Navy late 1952 and serving throughout the remainder of the 'fifties

Vought F7U-3M Cutlass shipboard fighter of the US Navy. Of ly unconventional design, the Cutlass first flew on September 1948 and served with the US Navy from 1954 until 1957

▲ **North American FJ-4B Fury** of US Navy Squadron VA-151. A progressive development of the FJ-2 Fury, a shipboard derivative of the F-86 Sabre, the FJ-4B was the final version of the Fury and, first flown on December 4, 1956, was an attack fighter and was finally phased out in 1962

▲ **Dassault Etendard IVM** shipboard fighter of Flottille 15F of France's Aéronavale. The semi-navalised Etendard IVM prototype flew on May 21, 1958, and the type entered service with the Aéronavale in 1962

▲ **Vickers Supermarine Scimitar F. Mk. 1** of No. 803 Squadron, Royal Navy. Flown as a prototype on January 20, 1956, the Scimitar attained operational status in 1958 but was retired in the early 'sixties

▲ **Grumman A-6A Intruder** shipboard attack aircraft of US Navy Attack Squadron (VA) 42 'Green Pawns', Oceana NAS, Virginia (1963)

▼ **McDonnell F3H-2M Demon** of US Navy Squadron VF-112. The prototype flew on August 7, 1951 but the type suffered protracted teething troubles and did not enter US Navy service until 1956, finally being phased out in 1964

PRINCIPAL LAND-BASED MARITIME AIRCRAFT

Type	Country of origin	First introduced	Primary role	Performance	Comments
Lockheed P-2 Neptune	USA	1946	Maritime reconnaissance and patrol bomber	(P-2H)—Normal range, 2,200 miles; Max. speed, 403 mph; Patrol speed, 173–207 mph	A most successful (and record-breaking) design from the start; front-line use by US Navy ended in 1970 but in operational service with other air forces
Lockheed P-3 Orion	USA	1962	Long-range maritime patrol aircraft	(P-3B, -3C)—Max. mission radius at 135,000 lb, 2,383 miles; Max. speed, 473 mph at 15,000 ft	Developed version of the civil Electra airliner; carries very comprehensive search and destruct equipment (including nuclear depth bombs)
Lockheed EC-121 Warning Star	USA	1970	Electronic reconnaissance	(RC-121D)—Range, 4,600 miles; Max. speed, 321 mph at 20,000 ft	USAF Air Defense Command relies upon EC-121Hs (modified RC-121Ds) for early warning and command control duties; linked with NORAD SAGE installation
Canadair CP-107 Argus	Canada	1958	Long-range maritime reconnaissance	Patrol endurance, 12 hrs; Max. speed, 315 mph at 20,000 ft; Cruise, 223 mph	Designed as a replacement for Lancaster MR Mk 10; in operational service with Maritime Command of Canadian Armed Forces
Avro Shackleton AEW Mk 2 and 3	UK	1952 1972	Airborne early warning aircraft	(MR Mk 3)—Range, 3,660–4,215 miles; Max. speed, 302 mph at 12,000 ft	Derived indirectly from the Lancaster bomber via the Lincoln, a number, extensively modified, remain in operational service
Hawker Siddeley Nimrod MR Mk 1	UK	1969	Long-range maritime patrol aircraft	Typical flight endurance, 12 hrs; Econ. transit speed, 490 mph; Max. speed, 575 mph	Derivative of the Comet 4C; carries active and passive sonobuoys, plus a full range of ASW weapons
Bréguet 1150 Atlantic	France	1965	Long-range maritime patrol aircraft	Max. endurance, 18 hrs; Max. range, 4,950 miles; Max. speed 409 mph at altitude	One of the earliest specially-designed and -built maritime patrol aircraft; early product of real European co-operation
Kawasaki P-2J	Japan	1970	Maritime patrol and anti-submarine patrol aircraft	Range with max. fuel, 2,765 miles; Max. cruising speed, 250 mph	Basically a turbo-jet powered derivative of the Lockheed P2V-7 Neptune, but with much improved search and control equipment
Tupolev Tu-16 'Badger'	USSR	1955 (bomber)	Maritime reconnaissance crew 5–6	(est.) Range, 4,000 miles with 6,600 lb useful load; Patrol speed, 400 mph at 35,000 ft	Evolved from the first Soviet strategic jet bomber; world's first jet-powered maritime reconnaissance aircraft
Tupolev Tu-20 'Bear'	USSR	1959	Long-range maritime reconnaissance	Max. range, 7,800 miles; Max. speed, 480+ mph at 36,000 ft	Largest turbo-prop aircraft to achieve operational status; now known to be an important anti-shipping missile control aircraft
Tupolev 'Moss'	USSR	1967	Airborne early warning and control system (AWACS) aircraft	(est.) Max. unrefuelled range, 4,000+ miles; Max. continuous cruise, 460 mph	Essentially a modified Tu-114 commercial transport, with provision for in-flight refuelling. Carries very extensive electronic equipment
Ilyushin Il-38 'May'	USSR	1970	Long-range maritime patrol aircraft	(est.) Max. range, 4,500 miles; Patrol endurance, 12 hrs	Evolved from the Il-18 commercial airliner and operational with the Soviet Navy from early in 1970
Myasishchev M-4 'Bison'	USSR	1964	Long-range maritime reconnaissance aircraft	Max. range, 7,000 miles; Max. speed, 560 mph at 36,000 ft	Developed from the first operational Soviet four-jet strategic bomber; to keep track of Western naval moves (particularly nuclear submarines)
FLYING BOATS					
Beriev Be-6 'Madge'	USSR	1952	Maritime reconnaissance and general purpose	Range, 3,000 miles; Max. speed, 258 mph at 8,000 ft	Most widely used Soviet flying boat in the late 1950s; large numbers still remain for various duties, particularly in the Arctic
Beriev Be-12 'Mail'	USSR	1965	Maritime reconnaissance	Range, 2,485 miles (max.); Max. speed, 389 mph at 10,000 ft	World's largest amphibian flying boat in military service in the early 1970s; standard equipment of Soviet naval aviation units

carriers, providing tactical air power beyond the reach of the US Air Force's shore-based fighter-bombers, and interdicting the North Korean lines of communication.

New US super carriers

A principal feature of the Cold War, however, was the United States policy of using her then superior nuclear bomb capability as a deterrent threat in the face of any Soviet aggressor. One of the means of delivery was to be nuclear bombers such as the **Douglas Skyraiders** and **Skyhawks** and, in the late 1960s, the **Vought Corsair II** flown off from the carriers of her Strike Fleet operating in the Atlantic. To rejuvenate and strengthen this carrier force, a number of super-carriers was approved by Congress, the first of which, the 59,650 ton *Forrestal*, was commissioned on 1 October 1955. She was followed at roughly yearly intervals by the *Saratoga, Ranger, Independence, Kitty Hawk, Constellation* and the nuclear-powered 72,500 ton *Enterprise*.

The maritime air power represented by carrier forces is not only strategic and offensive, however. The main task for the navy of any sea power must be to ensure for its sea-borne traffic the free use of the oceans by defending its merchant shipping. Carrier forces, therefore, also operated tactically using **Grumman Tracker** anti-submarine aircraft, **Tracer** reconnaissance planes and **Crusader** fighters—later superseded by **Phantom IIs.**

They also provided support in the form of distant reconnaissance against enemy submarines and surface ships, with the ability to hunt the former with shore-based multi-engined aircraft similar in scope to those in use with the Soviet Navy. From the end of the Second World War until the early 1950s, these were mainly long-range **Consolidated** **Privateer** aircraft. These were being replaced from 1947, however, by the specially developed **Lockheed Neptune,** which was to continue in service with the USN until 1965 and, indeed, is still in service with a number of other navies. It was finally superseded by the **Lockheed Orion,** an aircraft powered by four turbo-propeller engines which can carry an assortment of weapons—mines, nuclear depth-charges, anti-submarine torpedoes and sonar buoys—to a total of 17,000 lb. It has been supplied also to the Australian, New Zealand, Norwegian and other air forces.

Britain's new Ark Royal

British carrier strength at the time of the Korean War was mainly the eight light carriers of the *Glory*-class, ships of between 13,190 tons and 13,350 tons, operating obsolescent, propeller driven aircraft; and it was ships and aircraft of these types, including *HMAS Sydney*, which made up the chief part of the British Commonwealth naval contribution to the United Nations forces throughout that war. During the Cold War, however, Britain was anxious to play her part in the NATO naval effort by contributing aircraft carriers and nuclear strike aircraft to the American Strike Fleet. Thus during the 50s the new fleet carriers *Eagle* and *Ark Royal* joined the modernised

The prohibitive cost of maritime air power. Only the super powers can today afford aircraft carriers. The two photographs at left were taken in the Gulf of Tonkin during the Vietnam war and show launch of a Grumman E-1B Tracer from USS *Coral Sea* and an A-7A Corsair from USS *Constellation*. The Tupolev Tu-16 (above) wheels over the helicopter carrier *Moskva*. The new Lockheed S-3A Viking (below) is undergoing fleet evaluation trials. In 1974 the Hawker Siddeley Nimrod (facing page) was among the best land-based ocean patrol aircraft, though awaiting new systems.

PRINCIPAL CARRIER-BASED AIRCRAFT IN SERVICE

Type	Country of origin	First introduced	Primary role	Performance	Comments
Vought (LTV) F-8 Crusader	USA	1957	Carrier-borne fighter	(F-8J)—Max. speed, 1,120 mph at 40,000 ft; Combat radius, 600 miles	Standard US Navy single-seat carrier-borne jet fighter for over ten years, and still a very useful back-up weapon
McDonnell Douglas F-4 Phantom II	USA	1962	Carrier-borne all-weather fighter and strike aircraft	(F-4B)—Max. speed, Mach 2.5 at 40,000 ft; Combat radius, 900 miles	A carrier-borne attack fighter that, at the time of its appearance, was superior to most land-based counterparts, and was soon adopted by USAF
Grumman F-14A Tomcat	USA	1973	Carrier-borne variable-geometry multi-purpose fighter	(est.) Max. speed with four Sparrow missiles 910 mph at sea level, 1,564 mph at 40,000 ft	The first supersonic 'swing wing' fighter intended for shipborne use from the outset; the most advanced naval aircraft in the world
McDonnell Douglas A-4 Skyhawk	USA	1956 (A-4A) 1970 (A-4M)	Carrier- or land-based attack aircraft	(A-4M)—Max. speed (clean), 670 mph at sea level; Tactical radius (with 4,000 lb bombs), 340 miles	Very agile; can carry an amazing external payload for its size, extending to several hundred variations; saw early action over Vietnam
Grumman A-6 Intruder	USA	1963	Strike and reconnaissance aircraft	(A-6A)—Max. speed (clean), 685 mph at sea level; Range with max. internal fuel and four Bullpup missiles, 1,920 miles	Originally a long-range, low-level carrier-borne strike aircraft, developed into anti-radar missile carrier and night intruder
Vought (LTV) A-7 Corsair II	USA	1967	Tactical light attack and interdiction aircraft	(A-7D)—Max. speed (clean), 698 mph at sea level; Tactical radius with internal fuel and 3,600 lb external weapon load, 700 miles	A most useful subsonic attack aircraft, able to carry a very wide range of offensive stores, and with a fine combat record in Vietnam
Douglas EA-3B Skywarrior	USA	1960	Electronics counter-measures	(A-3B)—Max. speed, 610 mph at 36,000 ft; Tactical radius, 1,050 miles	Largest carrier-borne aircraft in the world at the time of its appearance, many modified for ECM, seeing extensive service in Vietnam
Grumman S-2 Tracker	USA	1954 (S-2A) 1972 (S-2G)	Carrier- or land-based anti-submarine	(S-2E)—Range, 1,300 miles; Max. speed, 265 mph; Cruise, 150 mph	S-2G (modified S-2E) was introduced in 1972 for operations until 1976, until finally replaced by the Lockheed S-3A Viking
Lockheed S-3A Viking	USA	1974	Anti-sub-marine aircraft	(est.) Combat range, 2,300 miles; Max. speed, 506 mph; Cruise, 185 mph	Developed as replacement for the Tracker; carries comprehensive range of underwater weapons; capable of detecting and destroying 'quiet' submarines
North American Rockwell RA-5C Vigilante	USA	1964	Reconnaissance	Max. speed, 1,360 mph at 40,000 ft; Tactical radius, 1.000 miles	Designed to operate from largest US Navy attack carriers; reconnaissance version was most sophisticated aircraft of this class in Vietnam
Grumman E-2 Hawkeye	USA	1964 (E-2A) 1973 (E-2C)	Airborne early warning	(E-2C)—Max. speed, 374 mph; Cruise, 310 mph	E-2C carries radar able to detect airborne targets in a land-clutter environment and carrier airborne inertial navigation system
Grumman EA-6B Prowler	USA	1972	Electronic warfare air-craft	Max. speed, 595 mph at sea level; Cruise, 466 mph	Developed from the Grumman A-6 Intruder; used to detect, locate, classify, record and jam enemy transmissions
Dassault Etendard IV-M	France	1962	Carrier-borne fighter and tactical re-connaissance	Max. speed, 673 mph at 36,000 ft; Tactical radius, 435 miles at 43,000 ft	Entered service in 1962 and has been the standard French shipboard strike fighter ever since. Replacement scheduled for 1976–77
Breguet Br 1050 Alize	France	1959	Carrier-borne anti-submarine attack	Max. speed, 285 mph at sea level; Flight endurance (search configuration), 5 hr 12 min	Forms the equipment of three French naval aviation squadrons; no fixed-wing replacement is foreseen after it is phased out
Sikorsky S-58 Sea Bat Sea Horse	USA	1954	General purpose	Max. speed, 123 mph at sea level; Range, 280 miles	Originally designed as a carrier-borne anti-submarine helicopter. Modified version built in Britain as Westland Wessex
Sikorsky S-61 Sea King	USA	1961	Amphibious all-weather anti-sub-marine helicopter	(SH-3D)—Max. speed, 155 mph at sea level; Range, 620 miles	The first helicopter to combine the 'hunter' and 'killer' roles in a single machine; substantial numbers in service with the US Navy and other air forces
Kaman SH-2 Seasprite	USA	1962	All-weather search, ASW, and rescue helicopter	(SH-2F)—Max. speed, 168 mph at sea level; Range, 445 miles max.	From 1970 US Navy assigned the Seasprite force to Light Airborne Multi-Purpose System (LAMPS) program for ASW and anti-missile defence

World War II carrier *Victorious* and were eventually equipped with the **Blackburn Buccaneer** strike aircraft. Meanwhile, the light carriers *Centaur*, *Albion* and *Bulwark* of the *Hermes*-class joined the fleet between 1953 and 1954 to operate mainly in the tactical role; the *Hermes* herself was delayed until 1959 when she was completed with greatly more sophisticated and effective electronic and other equipment and emerged as a small 'strike' carrier rather than a light carrier.

In the Suez operation in November 1956, aircraft from the British carriers *Eagle*, *Albion* and *Bulwark* and the French carriers *Arromanches* and *Lafayette* launched fighter-bomber air strikes to neutralise the Egyptian Air Force. Operating close off the Egyptian coast, their attacks complemented the high-level night bombing by **Valiant** and **Canberra** bombers and the low-level attacks by fighter-bombers of the Royal Air Force which had to operate from as far away as Cyprus.

The early 1960s saw the carrier strength of the European powers at its peak with the British operating the strike carriers *Eagle*, *Ark Royal* and *Hermes* and the light carrier *Centaur*, the French commissioning the new carriers *Foch* and *Clemenceau*, while the Americans had commissioned seven super carriers, including the nuclear-powered

---

Western naval air power is dwindling. The Harrier (far left, seen embarked on a Commando carrier during an assault by Wessex 5 helicopters) is not being developed by Britain for the obvious naval roles, but the AV-16 version goes ahead in the United States. The F-4K Phantom (left, making a finely judged recovery) entered service with the Royal Navy in 1969. The US Navy Phantom (below) is launching one of its four Sparrow air-to-air missiles, during trials at Point Mugu firing range in California. Relative to the Soviet Union, western naval and maritime air superiority has fallen sharply since 1965.

Enterprise, with two more, conventionally-powered, under construction.

Cumbersome but workable

The shore-based element of British and British Commonwealth maritime air power was provided by the independent Air Forces of the various countries and its operations controlled by senior officers of their own service in conjunction with naval commanders in Joint Maritime Headquarters ashore. The Italians have a similar system. It has created difficulties inside NATO where the Americans, in particular, view it as cumbersome and inefficient. With good-will, however, it has been made to work.

From the end of the Second World War until the 1950s, British Commonwealth Air Forces relied for long range, maritime reconnaissance upon adaptations of the wartime **Lancaster** bomber. These were then superseded with the Royal Air Force by the four-engine, propeller-driven **Shackleton** which, in its turn, has now been replaced by the jet-engined **Hawker-Siddeley Nimrod.** The Australian and New Zealand Air Forces and those of other NATO or western-aligned countries adopted the American Neptune, followed in due course by the Orion. The Canadian Armed Forces adopted the Canadian **Argus,** which, powered by four Wright turbo-compound radial piston engines has a range of more than 4,000 miles at a speed of 194 knots. The Europeans also developed a long-range maritime aircraft of their own, the twin-engined **Bréguet Atlantic** powered by Rolls Royce Tyne turbo-propeller engines. It has an endurance of 17 hours which gives it an operational range of 4,300 nautical miles. All these aircraft carry the multifarious equipment and weapons necessary to hunt and attack submarines.

New roles for helicopters

To this world-wide deployment of the maritime air power of the middle 1960s was

added a new element—the ship-borne helicopter. Since this had first come to sea during the 50s for air-sea rescue service its role had expanded. It was used as a transport vehicle to carry assault troops from ship to shore and it had also been adapted to operate submarine hunting equipment in the shape of the 'dipping sonar' and submarine attack weapons such as homing torpedoes. For these functions it had eventually become borne by most warships as well as in amphibious warfare ships such as commando carriers. The Soviet Navy progressed along the same lines and in 1967 and 1968 two specially designed helicopter carriers, the *Moskva* and *Leningrad* joined their Black Sea Fleet.

Helicopters, of course, are too slow and too vulnerable to gunfire to take on all the functions of fixed-wing maritime aircraft and helicopter-carriers cannot fulfil the functions of fixed-wing aircraft carriers.

Therefore, when the question of replacement of the British ships at the end of their useful life came under consideration, and the ever-increasing cost so daunted successive British governments that they finally come to the decision in 1968 to allow the carrier force to phase-out as ships reached the end of their lives, it was necessary to accept the controversial thesis that shore-based aircraft of the Royal Air Force could provide all the air support necessary.

Russian change of heart

But one essential task of ship-borne aircraft under the immediate control of the naval tactical commander must be to strike against submarines and fast patrol boats poised to launch surface to surface 'cruise' missiles. Instant response to a call for action against such a threat was essential and an aircraft based perhaps hundreds of miles from the scene could never provide this. To some extent a fleet's own surface-to-surface missiles could fill the requirement; but the Royal Navy had no such weapon and it turned to the French Exocet missile.

Fortunately at this time a new development occurred—that of an effective V/STOL aircraft, the **Hawker Harrier.** Able to take off without the aid of catapults and to land on without arrester gear, the Harrier can operate from much smaller, cheaper carriers. Construction work began on the first of these, the *HMS Invincible*, in the early 1970's. It is officially classified as a 'through-deck' or 'multi-role' cruiser and the committment to equip the Royal Navy with Harriers is not necessarily total, though it is in service with other navies and air forces. The corresponding class of vessel in the US Navy is the Sea Control Ship, a low-key carrier without catapults or wires but equipped for jet V/STOL aircraft and other weapons systems.

It may be the advent of the fixed-wing V/STOL type of aircraft that has inspired the early 70s they began the construction at Nikolayev of two carriers, but until they are observed at sea it will not be known whether the Russians are going to give their ever-growing fleet the highest performance air support of fixed-wing carrier aircraft or the more modest but more simply provided air support of V/STOL aircraft.

AERIAL
Reconnaissance

The Soviet capture of the luckless Gary Powers and the destruction of his high-flying U-2 'spyplane' in 1960 made the world aware of the extent and importance of aerial reconnaissance. Observation had been the very first military duty of aircraft and reconnaissance had been refined to a specialised field during World War II, but it was only the uncertainty of the Cold War, with its attendant threat of nuclear annihilation, that brought about the building of purpose-built, high altitude reconnaissance aircraft.

Long before aircraft were used for any kind of fighting role they were being used for reconnaissance. In 1794, only a year after men first flew in a balloon, aerial observers were helping the French army to win the battle of Fleurus in Belgium. In 1911, a mere eight years after the first flight of the Wrights, an Italian officer near Tripoli was making detailed reports of the enemy Turkish forces as he flew near them in his **Bleriot** (similar to the aircraft in which Bleriot himself crossed the English Channel two years earlier). During World War 1 reconnaissance was one of the most important and ceaseless duties of every type of flying machine, both over the land battles and over the seas where range limitations became accute.

Between the wars aerial reconnaissance grew in stature and it was increasingly realised that it had to be done in depth. Future wars would involve not only air operations in direct support of land and sea battles but also strategic bombing deep in the heart of enemy nations to strike at war industries and transport—and, perhaps, directly at cities and civil populations. Such operations would be of little value without extensive and detailed aerial reconnaissance to find out, firstly, what targets existed and where, and, secondly, how badly they had been hit in the subsequent attack. This called for the development of large aerial cameras fitted in long-range high-flying aircraft which might stand a good chance of making lone penetrations hundreds of miles across the hostile land. In fact it was only when the RAF bombers themselves began to be fitted with cameras, arranged to expose their film at the same time as their flares lit up the ground and their bombs exploded, that the unpalatable truth was discovered that hardly any aircraft were getting anywhere near their targets.

By 1945 reconnaissance had become an exact science. Special fast, high-flying aircraft, such as versions of the **Spitfire, Mosquito** and **P-38 Lightning**, raced across Europe either at about 40,000 feet or else at less than 100 feet, to bring back sharp and clear photographs of every kind of enemy activity, or the results of Allied attacks. Such work made it increasingly difficult for a warring country to conceal any major activity, unless it could prevent even single aircraft from penetrating its airspace. Aerial reconnaissance gave the Allies advance information on German ground radars, the V-1 flying bomb, the V-2 rocket and all the new and radical kinds of jet aircraft for the Luftwaffe.

Eisenhower's 'open skies'

After World War II the descent of the 'Iron Curtain' around the Communist nations introduced a new element into peaceful co-existence. Increasingly the Communist East and Capitalist West confronted each other in a 'cold war', with the terrifying existence of nuclear weapons as a deterrent to any actual fighting. Both sides sought information about the other, and this was especially true of the West because what went on behind the Iron Curtain was almost completely unknown. Snippets of information were brought through the Curtain by intelligence agents (who were few in number) or by defecting Communists, but the Western nations were largely in the dark about Communist accomplishments and activities. In July 1955 the US President, General Eisenhower, made a remarkable proposal called Open Skies. He suggested that both sides should throw open their territories to detailed aerial photography, so that each should know what the other was doing. He claimed this would 'ease the fears of war'. The Soviet Union did not buy this idea, and perhaps regarded it as a big confidence trick because they already knew almost all that went on in the United States just by reading the papers, and so the proposal would have been of far greater benefit to the USA.

Probably the Americans never expected

the proposal to be accepted. Certainly, before it was made, plans were afoot to go ahead and take pictures over the Soviet Union anyway. The USAF Strategic Air Command was becoming strongly equipped with large long-range reconnaissance versions of its great global bombers; the **RB-36, RB-47** and **RB-52** were equipped with batteries of large cameras and special navigation and electronic equipment for flights over hostile territory. But these were judged too vulnerable for clandestine 'overflights' except fairly limited penetrations around the Communist frontiers. What the Americans intended to do was carry cameras right across the huge Communist heartlands in a vehicle that could not be intercepted. They thought of huge rockets, but such things were far in the future (though nearer than most experts thought). The best answer seemed to be a new kind of aeroplane able to fly higher than any fighters or anti-aircraft weapons could reach.

'Skunk works' U-2

The original specialist high altitude reconnaissance aircraft was the amazing **DFS 228** built by the Germans during World War II. It was a rocket-powered glider that could operate at 60,000+ feet and the prototype planes were taken to the United States after the war. A similar project was conceived just after the Korean War by one of the top American designers, C. L. 'Kelly' Johnson, of Lockheed Aircraft. At first his idea was rejected, but in December 1954 the urgent need for an invulnerable aerial spy-plane had been appreciated and Lockheed was given an unpublicised contract to build one. It was allotted a meaningless 'utility' designation, being called the **Lockheed U-2.** It was secretly designed and built in Johnson's 'Skunk Works' in California which devoted all its time to confidential defence studies and experimental hardware.

The first U-2 was flown in 1955. It was essentially a jet sailplane. The big Pratt & Whitney J57 engine was the one massive item. Everything else was constructed for extreme lightness. There were two small landing gears under the fighter-like fuselage, and two simple 'pogo wheels' under the wings, to stop the aircraft rolling over, which were jettisoned after take-off. The great 90 foot wing was amazingly slender and arched and flapped almost like the wing of a great bird.

The U-2 was not meant to fly very fast, nor penetrate clouds or rough air, nor per-

US lead in specialist reconnaissance machines. By far the most remarkable and most costly reconnaissance aircraft, the Lockheed SR-71A can fly 2,000 miles in one hour. Many far-ranging operational missions have been made by these Strategic Air Command machines. In contrast, most Soviet reconnaissance aircraft are conversions. The Tupolev 'Moss' (top) is an early-warning and control development of the Tu-114. The Yakovlev 'Mangrove' (centre) is a tactical reconnaissance version of the Yak-25 all-weather fighter. The 'Badger E' version of the prolific Tu-16 (bottom) was photographed shadowing exercising NATO ships.

form any save gentle manoeuvres. The one thing it could do was climb to more than 80,000 feet and fly more than 3,000 miles. Later, with the more powerful J75 engine, it exceeded 90,000 feet and could fly 4,000 miles. To fly such a mission was no small ordeal for the lone man secured in his pressure suit in the tiny cockpit, who navigated the frail craft and operated the extremely advanced camera installations—one of them being a huge instrument able to reveal objects no larger than coins or golf balls from the operating height of some 16–17 miles. The U-2 also carried extensive ECM (electronic countermeasures) which could detect and record almost all the radio and radar signals coming up from the territory far below.

For years the U-2s operated completely illegally yet very successfully over many Iron Curtain lands. They were flown by civilian pilots of the Central Intelligence Agency, and their aircraft bore no markings.

Gary Powers is captured

On May Day 1960 a U-2 took off from Peshawar, Pakistan, to fly right across the Soviet Union to Bodo in Norway. About half-way through the mission the U-2 was shot down by a surface-to-air missile near Sverdlovsk. The pilot, F. Gary Powers, escaped unhurt and was eventually given a ten-year sentence after a rather theatrical trial in Moscow. No more long U-2 overflights took place across Soviet Asia, but they went on at full pressure elsewhere. One of the places regularly photographed was Cuba, which since 1953 had maintained close ties with the Soviets.

In August 1962 a U-2 picture taken over Cuba showed a surface-to-air missile site of a well-known Russian type. U-2 surveillance was stepped up, and, on October 14, one brought back pictures of a frightening new development: Russian long-range ballistic missiles were being emplaced on the island.

have been plotted flying over Canada, Alaska and Japan and plenty of more legitimate activity has been recorded. Almost every day, for many years, long-range aircraft such as the **Tu-16 'Badger'**. **Tu-95 'Bear'** and **Mya-4 'Bison'** have made extensive missions close to the UK, North America and Western naval forces to test the alertness of the defences, sense and record radar and other signals, take photographs and generally gather as much information as possible. Every mission (so far as is publicly known) has been intercepted by Western fighters, which have then accompanied the big Soviet machine on its sophisticated reconnaissance task.

Sophisticated snooping

Today the outstanding reconnaissance aircraft is the **Lockheed SR-71,** able to fly at well over 2,000 mph for two hours at a height of over 80,000 feet. In addition,

When the existence of the U-2 could no longer be denied it was described as a harmless research machine working for the extremely respectable National Advisory Committee for Aeronautics (who later insisted they did not know its true role). In 1956, U-2 units based in West Germany and Turkey began missions at very great heights along the Communist frontier taking photographs and recording electronic transmissions. On occasion they also took samples of radioactive fallout from Soviet nuclear tests which, when analysed, told almost everything about the type of bomb, its power, its 'dirtiness' and where the test had taken place. In 1957 a third U-2 detachment began working from Japan. By this time dozens of out-and-return overflights had been made, yielding among other things vital pictures suggesting that, while Soviet emphasis on huge bombers was merely an exercise in misleading propaganda, frightening progress was being made with ICBMs.

They menaced a large area of the USA and Central and South America. Reconnaissance was stepped up still more. President Kennedy put the US war machine on an instant alert status, and then challenged the Soviet Union. Any Cuban missile shot, he said, would unleash America's nuclear might against the Soviet Union. It was a time of agonising tension. A few days later a high-flying U-2 was shot down over Cuba by a missile similar to that fired near Sverdlovsk $2\frac{1}{2}$ years earlier. But Kennedy did not unleash his nuclear armada. The busiest American unit was squadron VFP-62 of the US Navy, whose **RF-8A Crusaders,** unarmed reconnaissance versions of the supersonic fighter, raced across the island at low level bringing back miles of film. It was a Crusader that first provided evidence that the Cuban missile sites were being dismantled. Thus did aerial reconnaissance reveal a new arms threat, control it and secure its removal.

On the Soviet side reconnaissance planes

reconnaissance versions have been produced of such fighters and bombers as the **F-101 Voodoo, F-104 Starfighter, F-111, F-4 Phantom, A-3 Skywarrior, A-5 Vigilante, B-57, Vulcan, Valiant, Victor, Mirage III, G91, Draken** and **Viggen,** as well as multi-sensor reconnaissance pods which could be attached beneath combat aircraft.

A multi-sensor pod carries more than just a camera. It may have batteries of optical cameras of different sizes and focal lengths, arranged to give a pin-sharp picture even of terrain rushing past a mere 100 feet away. The film is often of 'false colour' types which, instead of portraying how things look to human eyes, picks out different kinds of material in contrasting colours. Such film can defeat any normal camouflage, and instantly pick out things that a human observer would miss. The cameras can be arranged to point forwards, vertically or obliquely to either side. In addition, there may be various kinds of radar, such as a SLAR (side-looking airborne radar) which can provide a highly detailed picture of the whole terrain beneath and far out to each horizon. Yet another device is IR (infra-red) linescan, which measures the temperature of everything it sees and converts the result into a continuous picture. Cold things appear dark and hot things white. Thus it is possible to see not only which car in a park has its engine running, and which factory chimney is warm, but also the warm patch of ground where a truck was parked until it darted for cover on hearing the aircraft approach!

In Vietnam all these methods were used, together with even stranger ones involving remote sensing devices left in enemy territory to broadcast warnings. Another new technique used in that conflict was quiet aircraft. When quietness is the over-riding design aim it is possible to make aeroplanes very nearly silent. The Americans wondered

hard to destroy—something carrying just the sensing systems and no crew. Thus the reconnaissance mission is one of the main duties of the RPV (remotely piloted vehicle), a set of initials that is slowly revolutionising warfare. Whereas in 1957 the British foolishly thought the combat aeroplane was about to be made obsolete by the missile, it can now be seen that there is room for both, as well as for the RPV which lies midway between them.

There are many kinds of RPV. Some, such as the big **Compass Cope** aircraft of the US Air Force, are operated like manned aeroplanes, taking off and landing from their airfield runway (and having the ability to do so in all kinds of weather). Others are carried most of the way under a 'mother aircraft', which then releases them for their mission past or across the hostile territory. The information gathered may be sent back to the mother aircraft or direct to the home base, or it may be brought back with the RPV.

towards the area to be reconnoitred, cruising on a tiny jet engine at about the speed of sound, and, either follows a pre-programmed route, or else is guided by a remote pilot (hence the description 'remotely piloted'). At the conclusion of the mission the tiny spy comes back, spreads parachutes, and sinks to the ground ready for its cameras or other

Contrasts in reconnaissance. Lockheed U-2s were at first operated by civilian pilots and carried no markings; after they were unmasked, when Gary Powers was shot down over Russia, some were used openly by the 4080th Wing USAF in an upper-atmosphere sampling programme (far left). The six-bladed, wooden propeller-driven Lockheed YO-3A (top centre) was an ultra-quiet spy aircraft of the US Army. The Boeing E-3A AWACS (bottom centre) carries 20 tons of electronics. A Tu-20 'Bear D' (below) is intercepted by RAF Phantoms.

if it would be possible to make small reconnaissance aircraft that could fly by night very close to Vietcong forces and bring back photographs and other information without ever being detected! This seems like an impossible requirement, but in fact it was successfully done. Lockheed built a series of aircraft driven by piston engines in sealed boxes, driving large, slow-turning propellers, which could not be heard when they flew—or glided—over at 100 feet. Just how far this development has gone is now highly classified.

The RPV—a radical change

There are now two other radically different kinds of reconnaissance vehicle. Bearing in mind that the purpose of a reconnaissance aircraft is to gather information over enemy territory and bring it, or send it, back to a friendly base, the job can be done by flying fast and high, or by something so small it is

Sending back the information can be done using TV, computers, and high-capacity data links—which may have to be 'secure', so that the information cannot be intercepted by anybody but the intended recipient. Compass Cope RPVs have long slender wings of 85 to 95 feet span, giving long range and the ability to cruise at 70,000 to 90,000 feet for perhaps 24 hours. Such craft can undertake missions more hazardous than would be considered reasonable with manned aircraft, and they are much harder to shoot down. Many other RPV types are used for electronic reconnaissance, sensing, recording and jamming enemy radio and radar transmissions.

Small RPVs are used at short ranges over land or sea battles. Some are free-flying missiles, such as the Canadian USD-501 used by Canada, Britain and West Germany. This has a streamlined body only 13 inches diameter and measuring about 12 feet long with its rocket launch booster. It is fired

sensors to be unloaded. A quite different species of reconnaissance RPVs are tethered platforms which lift cameras and other sensors hundreds or thousands of feet into the air where they can see the entire battle area. They are the modern equivalent of the reconnaissance balloon of 1794.

There is another quite different kind of aerial surveillance system which could be said to be part of air warfare. Sputnik 1 was launched in October 1957, and by 1960 both the USA and Soviet Union were busily launching military satellites equipped with amazing cameras and other sensing systems. Some were used for monitoring missile launches, but many have been assigned to long-term multi-sensor reconnaissance of huge areas of the Earth from heights between 90 and about 500 miles. Spy satellites as big as two buses are at work today for the Russians and Americans. Each side has shown it can shoot the other's satellites down, but the work goes on.

WARS of SURVIVAL
The Middle East

The emotive and fervid religious and patriotic overtones of the conflicts between the young state of Israel and her Arab neighbours have aroused emotional involvement throughout the world, and tended to obscure some of the important military lessons to be learned from the three major clashes between the two sides. Each in their way has confirmed the paramount importance of air power and powerfully demonstrated a different aspect of it—the first because the superiority was always totally one-sided; the second because a classic, rehearsed strike led to the instant destruction of one side's air forces on the ground; and the third because it provided conclusive proof of the effectiveness of a strategically sited missile screen.

Airpower has been a major determining influence on the course of the three most important wars in the Middle East since 1945; those between Israel and Egypt in 1956, and Israel and the Arab States in 1967 and 1973. In the first two, Israel enjoyed—through its own efforts or those of others—virtual air supremacy. This, added to greater drive, morale and tactical sense on the ground, enabled her to gain crushing victories in about a week. In the last, her advantages both in the air and on the ground were by no means so marked: the war lasted longer—18 days—and neither side gained an outright military victory.

It is useful to remember the small scale of these wars. They did not last long; small forces—by the standard of European wars—were engaged; the battleground was limited. In Sinai the main battle area measured about 140 miles from west to east and, at its mid-point, 100 miles from north to south. In the north, the Israel-Syrian border is only 40 miles long. The common border with Jordan is much longer, some 250 miles, but Jordan's population is small and its forces relatively weak.

Israel itself is a tiny country, with a sea-coast of only 130 miles and a width varying from 60 miles to—before the 1967 war—as little as ten miles in the Jerusalem sector. Its cities are only about 5 minutes flying time from airfields in Sinai and about 20 minutes flying time from bases in Egypt. A prime element in its strategy has therefore always been to neutralise enemy air forces and to gain space for manouvre where possible on the ground. This was possible in Sinai to the south-west, but difficult to the north-east, where both political and military factors weighed against invasion of Syria.

Complex political factors have conditioned the timing, the duration and the military results achieved in these wars but, in simple terms, the major powers, for political and economic reasons, had an interest in the survival of both sides. Broadly speaking, the Americans have leaned to the side of Israel and the Russians to the Arabs, with the Europeans attempting both to protect

Hotting up the Middle East. A brace of McDonnell Douglas A-4E Skyhawks of the Israel Defence Force/Air Force add their quota of napalm to an already awesome conflagration during a fire-power demonstration.

what they conceived to be their interests and to influence the super-powers. At the same time, both Russia and the US wished to avoid direct confrontation. Hence the prominent part played by the United Nations, as a safety-valve for debate, as an instrument for engineering an end to the fighting and as a useful, if fragile, sentry on the boundaries. The fundamental causes of the conflicts, the existence of Israel and the Palestinian question, appear on the surface to be problems that cannot be solved by military action but military achievements are, in the long run, political bargaining counters in the negotiations for any solution.

Assault on the Canal

President Nasser nationalised the Suez Canal on July 29, 1956. After abortive attempts to

Middle East combatants. The Mil Mi-6 helicopter was used by the Egyptian AF. The Hunter F.6 was one of the first batch supplied to Jordan. Israeli fighter power: an F.4E Phantom and a Vautour IIA.

reach a political settlement, the French and British determined to mount an armed assault on Egypt to gain control of the canal. The Israelis, goaded by constant armed raids by their neighbours, alarmed by signs of a joint Egyptian-Jordanian-Iraqi armed threat, and unable to tolerate the closure of the Straits of Tiran by Egypt, decided in October to attack in Sinai. There is evidence that the timing of the Israeli assault was fixed in collusion with the British and French to provide an excuse for the attack.

The most important dates are:
October 29 Israelis launch their attack at 1600 hours and parachute a battalion into the Mitla Pass area.

October 30 Anglo-French ultimatum to Egypt and Israel to cease operations within 48 hours. Israeli offensive develops in Sinai, cutting off southern part.

October 31 Nasser orders Egyptian forces to retreat from Sinai and tells his Arab allies to stay out of the fight. First attacks at night against Egyptian airfields by British **Valiants**

and **Canberras.**

November 1 Anglo-French air attacks on airfields continue, mounted from Malta (Valiants), Cyprus (RAF Canberras and **Venoms,** French **Thunderstreaks**), and carriers (RN **Seahawks** and **Sea Venoms,** French **Corsairs**). Israelis fight Battle of Mitla Pass and begin breakthrough in centre and north.

November 2 Anglo-French air attacks continue against airfields and other military targets (radar, barracks, tank and troop concentrations) and are maintained until the 4th. Israeli troops advance to within 10 miles of the Suez canal. Egyptians complete withdrawal from Sinai.

November 3 Israelis mop up in Sinai and Gaza strip. This is followed by a lull in the ground fighting for two days.

November 5 Israel captures Sharm-el-Sheikh and opens the Straits of Tiran. Israeli operations are now suspended. An Anglo-French parachute force drops at Port Said and Port Fuad, followed the next day by a seaborne force. Fighting continues that day

The Changing Shape of Israel

PRE-1967 ISRAEL
1967 CEASE-FIRE LINES
OCCUPIED TERRITORIES
1973 CEASE-FIRE LINES
1973 ARAB GAINS
1973 ISRAELI GAINS

Beirut
LEBANON
Damascus
Golan Heights
Haifa
SYRIA
Nazareth
Tel Aviv
West Bank
R. Jordan
MEDITERRANEAN SEA
Amman
Port Said
Gaza
Jerusalem
Suez Canal
Ismailia
Beersheba
Bitter Lakes
ISRAEL
JORDAN
Cairo
R. Nile
Suez
Eilat
Aqaba
Sinai
EGYPT
SAUDI ARABIA
R. Nile
Sharm el Sheikh

Arab Aircraft of the Yom Kippur War

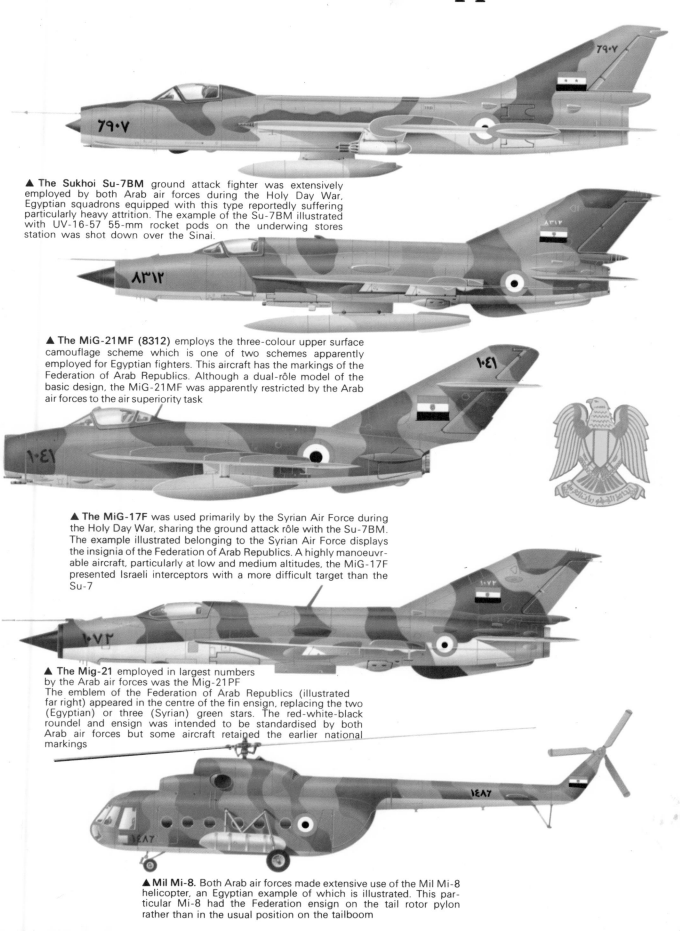

▲ The **Sukhoi Su-7BM** ground attack fighter was extensively employed by both Arab air forces during the Holy Day War, Egyptian squadrons equipped with this type reportedly suffering particularly heavy attrition. The example of the Su-7BM illustrated with UV-16-57 55-mm rocket pods on the underwing stores station was shot down over the Sinai.

▲ The **MiG-21MF (8312)** employs the three-colour upper surface camouflage scheme which is one of two schemes apparently employed for Egyptian fighters. This aircraft has the markings of the Federation of Arab Republics. Although a dual-rôle model of the basic design, the MiG-21MF was apparently restricted by the Arab air forces to the air superiority task

▲ The **MiG-17F** was used primarily by the Syrian Air Force during the Holy Day War, sharing the ground attack rôle with the Su-7BM. The example illustrated belonging to the Syrian Air Force displays the insignia of the Federation of Arab Republics. A highly manoeuvrable aircraft, particularly at low and medium altitudes, the MiG-17F presented Israeli interceptors with a more difficult target than the Su-7

▲ The **Mig-21** employed in largest numbers by the Arab air forces was the Mig-21PF
The emblem of the Federation of Arab Republics (illustrated far right) appeared in the centre of the fin ensign, replacing the two (Egyptian) or three (Syrian) green stars. The red-white-black roundel and ensign was intended to be standardised by both Arab air forces but some aircraft retained the earlier national markings

▲**Mil Mi-8.** Both Arab air forces made extensive use of the Mil Mi-8 helicopter, an Egyptian example of which is illustrated. This particular Mi-8 had the Federation ensign on the tail rotor pylon rather than in the usual position on the tailboom

in the area, but troops advance down the Canal.

November 7 British and French order their troops to cease fire, in response to American and United Nations pressure. Allied troops halt after advancing 23 miles down the Canal.

The dominating feature of the air war was the destruction of the Egyptian Air Force by the Anglo-French attacks on airfields, completed, in the view of the Anglo-French commanders, by the morning of November 2. At the outbreak of the war, the Egyptians had (excluding transports) 175 combat aircraft, of which 44 were **Il-28** twin-engined bombers. But of these only 57 fighters (**MiG 15s, Vampires** and **Meteors**) and 12 Il 28s were reckoned to be operational. Apart from an air strike by fighters on the Israeli advanced forces near the Mitla pass on October 30, the EAF contribution to the battle was minimal. Israeli casualties from air attacks in Sinai were insignificant; and single Il 28s made only two raids on Israel, dropping their bombs on open country.

The Israelis had a mixed bag of fighters— **Mysteres, Ouragans, Meteors** and **Mustangs**—82 operational in all; plus 16 **Mosquitoes** and 17 **Harvards.** During the first two days of the war, they shot down 4 Mig 15s, 3 Vampires and a Meteor in dog fights over Sinai. Thereafter, with air supremacy assured thanks to the British and French, the Israeli airforce could range at will over the battlefield, providing air support to the army. In this role, it had, according to General Dayan, a decisive effect on the battle, particularly against armour and during the Egyptian retreat.

A devastating opening attack

After Suez, the Israelis withdrew from Sinai, the Gaza strip and Sharm-el-Sheikh in 1957; and were replaced in these areas by a United Nations policing force. No permanent solution was found to the Palestinian problem. Both sides received modern armaments, the Arabs from Russia, the Israelis from France and the US. Palestinian commando raids and Syrian artillery attacks escalated during the 60s. In late 1966 and early 1967, Israel delivered sharp reprisal attacks on Jordan and Syria. Nasser, as prime leader of the Arab world, decided to intervene to bolster his allies and, in May, 1967, requested withdrawal of the UN force. U Thant, the UN Secretary General, agreed. On May 22, the Egyptians closed the Straits of Tiran. On May 30, Egypt and Jordan signed a defence pact. On May 31, Iraqi troops moved into Jordan in support. Believing themselves threatened from all sides, the Israelis decided to attack and opened what has become known as The Six-Day War with a pre-emptive air attack of devastating efficiency.

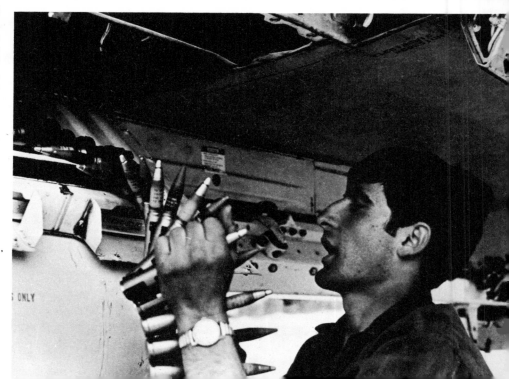

June 5 At 0745, the Israeli Air Force, flying low to avoid radar, attacked 10 airfields in the Canal Zone and Sinai. Further waves followed at 10 minute intervals. In two hours and 50 minutes, the IAF attacked 19 airfields and destroyed, it is estimated, 300 out of 340 serviceable Egyptian combat aircraft, including all 30 long range **TU16**

'**Badger**' aircraft. At 0815, the Israeli army launched its attacks in Sinai in the north, the centre and to the south. Progress was rapid, and the Abu Agheila stronghold was captured by dawn the next day. Fighting broke out on the Jerusalem front during the morning. After a Syrian raid on Haifa, the Air Force attacked Damascus airfield. The Jordanian Air Force was destroyed on the ground at midday. During the afternoon 23 Egyptian radar installations were put out of action. Further attacks were made on the Egyptian airfields visited in the morning and on SAM-2 sites.

June 6 Fighting continued in Sinai, Jerusalem and on the West Bank. The IAF continued its attacks on airfields and radar installations and provided ground support in Sinai and on the West Bank. The Syrians began shelling settlements from the Golan heights and made three minor ground attacks.

June 7 The first Israeli troops reached the Canal (in the North). At 1100 the Egyptians abandoned Sharm-el-Sheikh. The Old City of Jerusalem was taken by 1400 and the West Bank was cleared by nightfall. On the central axis in Sinai, Israeli troops reached the Mitla pass, which had been blocked at its western end by Israeli airstrikes.

June 8 The remains of the Egyptian Air Force made two or three minor airstrikes in Sinai. The Israeli army continued to roll forward and reached the Canal by 0200 the following morning. The Israeli air force turned its full attention to Syrian gun emplacements on the Golan heights. Egypt agreed to a ceasefire late that night.

June 9 Although a ceasefire had been agreed for 0320 on the Syrian front, fighting continued. The Israeli Air Force attacked bunkers on the heights continuously and at 1130 Israeli ground forces attacked the heights, establishing two bridgeheads by nightfall.

June 10 Israeli air and ground offensives continued on the Golan heights. The IAF pursued retreating Syrians up to a self-imposed limit of 25 miles from Damascus. A ceasefire became effective on this front at 1930.

Classic, rehearsed strike

It is no exaggeration to say that the war was won on the first day by the Israeli strikes on the Arab air forces. The attacks on the Egyptian airfields, carefully thought out, meticulously planned and rehearsed, have been described by one writer as 'a classic among classics'. The choice of time for the first raid can serve as an example of the quality of planning. 0745 was some three hours after dawn (the orthodox time for attack). It was chosen because the Egyptian

Fluctuating Israeli fortunes. The F-4E Phantom (top) was all-powerful in the October War. In 1967 many Russian SA-2 missiles were captured by Israel in the Sinai (centre). The 20mm shells are being loaded into an A-4 Skyhawk. The last seconds of an Arab Mig-21 and an IDF/AF wreck.

dawn patrol would be returning to refuel, the morning mist would have burnt off, the Israeli pilots would be more refreshed, and the Egyptian High Command and government leaders would be on the way to their offices and thus enable to react at once.

Four fighter bombers—**Mirage IIIs, Super Mysteres** or **Vautours**—attacked each airfield after an approach at extremely low level either over the sea or directly across Sinai. 'Dibber' bombs—slowed after release by retro-rockets and then driven into the ground by booster rockets—were used on

---

Missiles provide the balance. The Syrian MiG-17 (below) landed by mistake on an Israeli airfield in 1968. At that time Arab pilots were often inexperienced but even by the time of the October War in 1973 they were still no match for skilled Israeli pilots in the powerful and versatile Phantom (bottom). An extensive ground-to-air missile defence (right) made up for any deficiencies. Built and partly manned with Soviet supervision the missile box around the Canal filled the West Bank.

runways; cannon and rockets on parked and taxiing aircraft. The interval between successive waves on the same target was ten minutes; 7½ minutes were allowed over the target. Turnround times at base were very fast, about 7 minutes; each aircraft could thus be over its target within one hour of its last attack. Sortie rates were high; more than 1,000 sorties were flown during the first two days of the war and some pilots did 8 sorties per day. Arab losses were 415 aircraft in the first two days—in effect the virtual destruction of the Egyptian, Syrian and Jordanian air forces. The Egyptians had some Soviet SAM-2 missiles but these were unable to deal with low-level attacks. Israeli losses during these intensive attacks amounted to 26 aircraft out of a strength of some 240.

The overwhelming success of the initial strikes allowed the Israeli Air Force to give priority to the ground battle in Sinai and the West Bank on the second and third days of the war. In consequence, progress on the ground was rapid and army operations in these two areas were virtually complete by the end of the third day. During the first two

days the Syrians had contributed nothing to the battle except one air raid, for which they were rewarded by the loss of their air force on the ground. They only began ground operations on the third day. On the fourth, fifth and sixth days, the Israelis could use against Syria their whole air force and a ground force augmented by units which had finished their tasks in Sinai. The relatively slow advance in Golan was due to the mountainous ground and the strength of the Syrian defences, concrete bunkers and protected gun emplacements.

The Six Day War was one of those occasions, rare in war, where everything could be said to have gone according to plan, where surprise was unblemished, the right force was concentrated in the right place at the right time, blows struck were precise, and the enemy—where he might have been somewhat awkward—obligingly fitted in with the timetable.

Outrage and diplomacy

In contrast to their post-Suez action, the Israelis did not withdraw from the territories

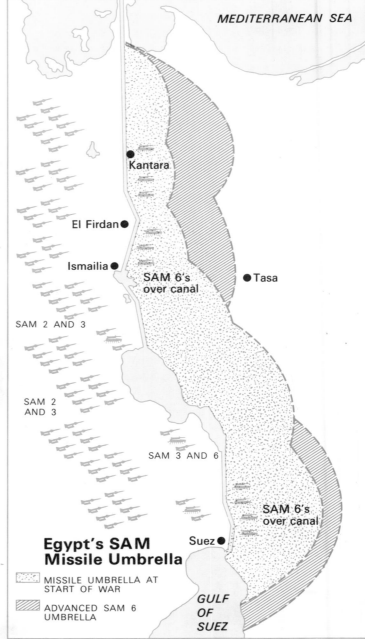

Egypt's SAM Missile Umbrella

MISSILE UMBRELLA AT START OF WAR

ADVANCED SAM 6 UMBRELLA

MEDITERRANEAN SEA

Kantara

El Firdan

Ismailia

SAM 6's over canal

Tasa

SAM 2 AND 3

SAM 2 AND 3

SAM 3 AND 6

SAM 6's over canal

Suez

GULF OF SUEZ

Israeli Aircraft of the Yom Kippur War

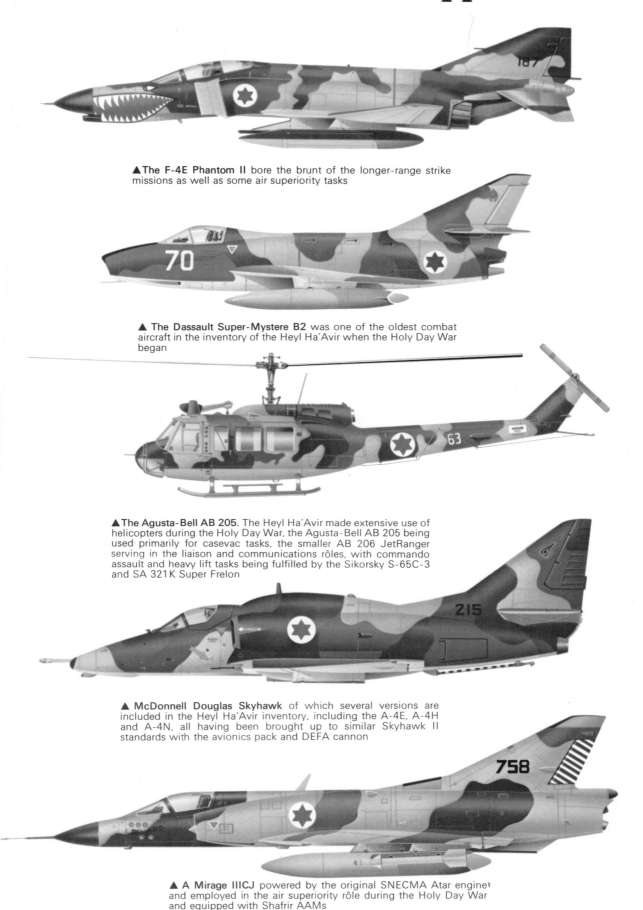

▲The F-4E Phantom II bore the brunt of the longer-range strike missions as well as some air superiority tasks

▲ The Dassault Super-Mystere B2 was one of the oldest combat aircraft in the inventory of the Heyl Ha'Avir when the Holy Day War began

▲The Agusta-Bell AB 205. The Heyl Ha'Avir made extensive use of helicopters during the Holy Day War, the Agusta-Bell AB 205 being used primarily for casevac tasks, the smaller AB 206 JetRanger serving in the liaison and communications rôles, with commando assault and heavy lift tasks being fulfilled by the Sikorsky S-65C-3 and SA 321K Super Frelon

▲ McDonnell Douglas Skyhawk of which several versions are included in the Heyl Ha'Avir inventory, including the A-4E, A-4H and A-4N, all having been brought up to similar Skyhawk II standards with the avionics pack and DEFA cannon

▲ A Mirage IIICJ powered by the original SNECMA Atar engine and employed in the air superiority rôle during the Holy Day War and equipped with Shafrir AAMs

Israeli Counter Measures Against SAM 6 Missiles

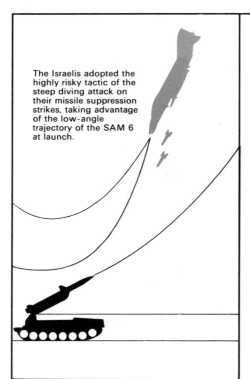

The Israelis adopted the highly risky tactic of the steep diving attack on their missile suppression strikes, taking advantage of the low-angle trajectory of the SAM 6 at launch.

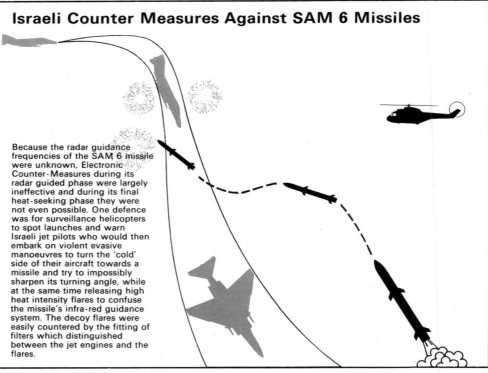

Because the radar guidance frequencies of the SAM 6 missile were unknown, Electronic Counter-Measures during its radar guided phase were largely ineffective and during its final heat-seeking phase they were not even possible. One defence was for surveillance helicopters to spot launches and warn Israeli jet pilots who would then embark on violent evasive manoeuvres to turn the 'cold' side of their aircraft towards a missile and try to impossibly sharpen its turning angle, while at the same time releasing high heat intensity flares to confuse the missile's infra-red guidance system. The decoy flares were easily countered by the fitting of filters which distinguished between the jet engines and the flares.

—Sinai, the West Bank and the Golan heights—which they occupied in 1967. In their view, they had been threatened and attacked far too often since 1948 for them to surrender these assets without a secure and lasting peace settlement. For the Arabs, the return of the territories was the condition for beginning peace talks. The United Nations, and on occasions the United States, spent the next six years trying to reconcile these two points of view and bring the two sides to talks which would lead to a permanent settlement. The Israeli standpoint was hardened by the increasing activity of the Palestinian guerillas, whose terrorist attacks multiplied in scale and scope. For their part, the Arabs were outraged by the Israelis founding settlements on the West Bank.

In 1968, the Israelis started to construct the Bar-Lev line—a series of defensive strong points designed to prevent Egyptian incursions across the Canal. The Egyptians, to prevent construction, shelled these positions. The Israelis replied in kind. The Egyptians made commando raids. So did the Israelis, who added air raids on towns and military targets. These actions, the so-called War of Attrition, lasted until 1970, when the United States managed to get both sides to agree to an uneasy ceasefire.

Nasser died in September, 1970. His successor, Anwar Sadat, showed himself willing to make moves towards peace, but each broke down on the timing of Israeli withdrawal. In 1972 it was clear to Sadat that the increasing detente between Russia

and the US meant that the Russians would not support him in any armed action and that, failing a settlement, he would have to fight in order to protect his own position, both at home and throughout the Arab world.

In July of that year, he therefore expelled his Russian 'advisers' who, since they manned many of his military installations, had an effective veto on his military plans. In October, he began to plan for war, while still maintaining diplomatic initiatives in parallel.

The latter failed and, on October 6th, 1973, Egypt and Syria attacked simultaneously on two fronts, across the Canal and in the Golan heights. It was to be a vastly different war from those in 1956 and 1967. The Israelis, thanks partly to an

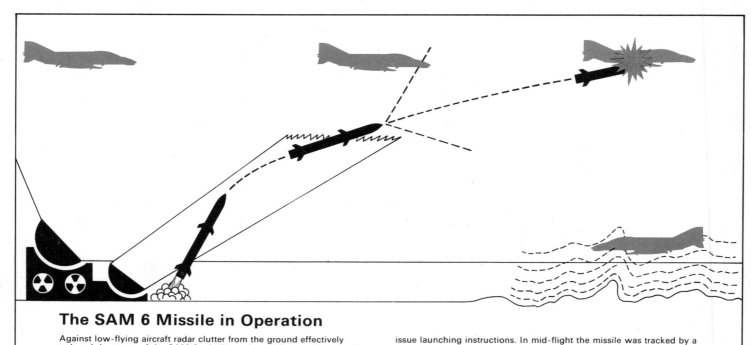

The SAM 6 Missile in Operation

Against low-flying aircraft radar clutter from the ground effectively reduced the range of the SAM 6 missile to about 15 miles. However its slant range was about 25 miles, an approaching aircraft being detected by the targeting radar. An associated computer would then calculate and issue launching instructions. In mid-flight the missile was tracked by a second ground radar and guided towards its target. In the final phase the heat-seeking device of the missiles own guidance system would direct it towards the infra-red radiation from an aircraft's jet exhaust.

obsession with the Palestinian guerillas and partly to contempt for Arab forces, were unprepared. The Egyptian and Syrian forces were far tougher fighters than anyone had expected. And they had much more formidable weapons, especially anti-aircraft and anti-tank missiles.

On the 'wrong' sides

The October, or Yom Kippur War, so-called because it was launched on the Jewish Day of Atonement when most Israelis were either holidaying or at their devotions, lasted from the 6th to the 24th October.

It can be divided roughly into three phases. During the first, until the 10th October, the Israelis were taken by surprise and the Egyptians obtained a bridgehead, up to 10 miles deep, virtually the whole length of the canal, and the Syrians, having very nearly driven the Israelis off the Golan heights on the 7th October, were pushed back to roughly the original start lines.

During the second phase, until the 15th October, the Egyptians first consolidated their positions in Sinai and then attacked towards the Mitla Pass. But their bridgehead was narrow, they made no progress, and lost a great number of tanks. In Syria, the Israelis advanced 10 km, and dealt with Iraqi and Jordanian attacks in the south of the Golan sector.

In the third phase, until the ceasefire, the Israelis, by a combination of luck and daring, established a bridgehead on the west of the canal, encircled Suez town, and cut off the Egyptian Third Army. This complex and dangerous situation, with each contestant on the 'wrong' side of the Canal, stimulated the US and Russia to organise a ceasefire. The first, on October 22nd, broke down. The Israelis took advantage of this to complete the encirclement of the Third Army before the final ceasefire on October 24th.

At the outbreak of the war the Israeli Air Force had 330 front rank aircraft, including about 130 supersonic **Phantoms** and Mirages, against the Egyptian and Syrian paper total of 520 supersonic **MiG-21s, Su-7s** and 180 subsonic **MiG-17s**.

The Israeli forces suffered heavily, especially during the first phase when they were caught unprepared. Reserves had not been mobilised. They were very heavily pressed in Golan for the first two days, and did not get a grip on themselves in Sinai until the 8th. During the whole war, they are estimated to have lost 800 tanks, 115 aircraft and 2,412 dead; around a third of the Arab losses but still very heavy for a country of Israel's size and much worse than her losses in the two previous wars.

On the ground, the Israeli Army was seriously strained by the enemy armoured forces. The Egyptians had some 1,800 tanks and the Syrians 1,200, as opposed to the Israeli's 1,700. The Arabs handled them with determination and often in large numbers—the Syrians are estimated to have used 700 tanks in their first assault on the Golan lines. And the Israelis suffered heavy losses from the Russian-made Snagger and Snapper anti-tank wire-guided missiles.

Denial of air supremacy

But the major factor affecting the battles was the denial to the Israelis of the air supremacy they had enjoyed in the earlier wars. This was due to the Egyptian and Syrian missile systems, deployed in the Canal Zone and in the Golan area and backed up by AA guns, including mobile Russian-made ZSU-23s. In the first afternoon of the war (the assaults began on both fronts at 1400 hours) the Israelis lost 30 **Skyhawks** and 10 Phantoms, mostly over Golan. In the first week, they lost 80 aircraft, about two-thirds, over Golan. There was no question of eliminating the opposing air forces by a swift and devastating attack as in 1967. Not only was there no chance of surprise but the Israelis were hard put to give support over their front lines.

The missiles used by the Arabs were the SAM-2, SAM-3, SAM-6 and SAM-7. SAMs 2 and 3 are two-stage (solid fuel launch and liquid fuel in flight), command radar guided (controlled from the ground), and have only limited mobility—it takes at least 8 hours to dismantle and get on the move to a new site. SAM-2 is used against high-flying aircraft, SAM-3 can tackle low fliers. But SAM-6, mounted on a tracked vehicle, is highly mobile. Moreover, although it uses radar in the early stages of flight, it has its own infra-red heat tracking device for the final homing onto its target: it is thus more difficult to jam or throw off the scent by counter-measures. SAM-7, smaller and carrying a lighter warhead, is even more mobile. It can be carried and fired by a man, or, as in a version used by the Arabs, up to 8 can be mounted on a vehicle and fired in salvo, thus reducing the effect of evasive action by the aircraft and increasing the chance of a hit.

Israeli pilots tried various counter measures; steep attacks, anti-radar metallised strips, electronic counter measures, evasive manoeuvres and hot flares. These sometimes worked. But steep attacks brought aircraft within range of the efficient AA guns; evasive action involved two planes and had to be well coordinated; and, towards the end of the war, counter-counter measures were being devised.

Vital missile cover

The success of the Egyptian crossing of the canal owed much to the extensive missile screen. Without this it is very doubtful whether the Egyptians, crossing at three points in daylight and very vulnerable to air attack, could either have got more than a fraction of their force across or have consolidated their bridgeheads as they did. In the event, they had over 500 tanks in Sinai on the second day. The value of the missiles is also shown by the success of the Israeli force which crossed the Canal during the last phase of the war. Although this force had great difficulty in crossing and was in peril for nearly two days, once it got going and began to overrun missile sites, it received unimpeded close air support and its momentum accelerated.

The Arab air forces, though very active in close support of their troops, appear to have played a less important role in determining the balance of advantage between the two sides. Their combined losses amounted to some 450 aircraft, mostly to fighters and AA fire. The Israelis had the edge outside the missile screens. Indeed, they claim to have lost only four aircraft in dog-fights. It is also notable that the Egyptians did not attack Israeli cities. This was no doubt due to Sadat's objectives being almost certainly limited to regaining some territory and inflicting severe losses on the Israelis, thus getting good cards with which to force a settlement. It is probable that for the same reasons the Egyptian Army did not exploit its bridgehead sooner and more vigorously.

The three wars illustrate the value of control of the air, especially to a state with limited resources facing greater odds on the ground. In 1956 and 1967, the Israelis, secure from air attack and with their strike forces unimpaired, could call the tune. In 1973, thanks in the main to the Arab SAM defences, they were very hard pressed in the early stages. In the first phase, fighting on the defensive on the ground and in desperate straits in Golan, they were most worried by the losses of aircraft and pilots to the missiles. Without an effective air striking force, their army would have been in great danger from the numerically superior Arab forces fighting on two fronts.

ARAB AIRCRAFT LOSSES AT END OF DAY TWO OF SIX DAY WAR			
Country	Type		No.
Egypt	Bombers:	Tu 16	30
		Il 28	27
	Fighters:	Su 7	10
		MiG 21	95
		MiG	20
		MiG 15 and 17	82
	Transports:	An 12	8
		Il 14	24
	Helicopters:		13
Iraq	Bombers:	Tu 16	1
	Fighters:	MiG 21	9
		Hunter	5
	Transports:		2
Jordan	Fighters:	Hunter	21
	Transports:		5
	Helicopters:		2
Lebanon	Fighters	Hunter	1
Syria	Bombers:	Il 28	2
	Fighters:	MiG 21	32
		MiG 15 and 17	23
	Helicopters:		3

HELICOPTER WARFARE

During World War II the performance limitations of helicopters meant that they were of little practical value. By the time of the Korean War they were immensely useful but still vulnerable and it was not until the Vietnam War that they were able to take their place in the forefront of military aircraft. Continuing developments show that their versatility is apparently endless and that they are capable of fulfilling many specialist roles that are beyond the capabilities of fixed wing aircraft.

In World War II the helicopter was fragile and deficient in all aspects of performance except for its one great virtue of VTOL (vertical take-off and landing). It needed no airfield, and could even hover above a chosen spot. By the Korean war (1950–53), helicopters could rescue a downed pilot from 100 miles inside enemy territory and still stand a good chance of bringing him back without suffering engine failure or some other malfunction. But the whole concept of the helicopter is quite unlike the aeroplane in that primary structures spend their life whirling and threshing about in a way that can soon induce breakage or fatigue. Turning the helicopter into a reliable vehicle was a massive task that demanded enormous engineering effort.

During the Vietnam war the helicopter really came of age. It had already grown markedly in size, and in the Soviet Union from 1957 the **Mi-6** set records by lifting loads exceeding 44,000 lb and also, with less load, by flying at over 200 mph. From the **Mi-6** was developed the **Mi-10** crane version, with the ability to straddle large loads such as the biggest commercial vehicles, mobile hospitals and other items up to a length of 65 feet 7 inches, width of 32 feet 10 inches and height of 10 feet 2 inches. Large numbers of these very capable vehicles were in use by 1963, many of them in military logistic roles. Later, in 1969, the Soviet Union displayed the **Mi-12,** a collossal helicopter with two Mi-6/Mi-10 engine and rotor groups arranged side-by-side. The Mi-12, also called **V-12,** set a world record by lifting a payload of 88,636 lb.

No other nation has a helicopter remotely approaching this capability, which is necessary only for special lifting duties, many of them in connection with heavy construction

Helicopters have revolutionised war at sea. Far from land, a Kaman UH-2C Seasprite alights on the helicopter pad of a surface vessel of the US Navy.

work and nearly all of them over short distances. In Vietnam the most capable helicopter was the **CH-47 Chinook,** which nominally has a payload of some 6,000 lb in its original form and seats for up to 44 troops. In emergencies Chinooks carried as many as 147 civilians and their possessions, and they also paid for themselves many times over by retrieving more than 11,500 aircraft which had been shot down or disabled, thus saving a book value exceeding $3,000 million. About 600 Chinooks were used in Vietnam, but the number of **Bell 'Huey'** helicopters used in SE Asia ran into thousands. The Huey, a large family of related machines, is the outstanding example of a sound basic design giving rise to special-purpose offshoots. Nearly as many varieties exist of the **Sikorsky S-61** family, developed in the same timescale of 1957–73.

Equipped for special roles

Many of both these types of helicopter are used for traditional tactical duties such as battlefield transport, liaison, rescue and assault. Specially equipped versions can fulfil other roles. The S-61 was originally built to carry extensive ASW (anti-submarine warfare) gear, and homing torpedoes or depth charges. Other S-61 versions have been used to carry bulky freight, to pick up astronauts, to fly tricky ECM (electronic countermeasures) missions and to fly MCM (mine countermeasures) sorties. The MCM mission involves sweeping mines by towing any of several kinds of MCM gear, and the size of helicopter needed for this work has grown. The **S-64** and **S-65,** both with more than 8,000 horsepower, have been found very useful for minesweeping, and in some circumstances they have acted as tugs for manoeuvring surface vessels in confined spaces.

In 1965 a completely rebuilt version of the Huey flew for the first time. Called the **Hueycobra,** it was much slimmer; instead of having a large cabin it had a tandem-seat cockpit for a crew of two, usually a pilot and a gunner, seated lower down in front. The new Cobra version was designed as the first 'gunship' helicopter for armed missions. The number of weapon options is considerable. Typical equipment includes a remotely trained Minigun firing either 1,600 or 4,000 rounds per minute, a 20 mm re-

Towards specialisation. Gradually the helicopter learned how to participate in every land battle. Its first task was merely to fetch and carry—a Wessex HAS.I brings Italian 105mm pack howitzer (right). By 1962 the Bell UH-IB was firing the French SS.II anti-tank missile (far right) and in 1966 the US Navy Seawolf version of the same helicopter was a fully armed battle vehicle patrolling the Mekong Delta area (bottom).

DEVELOPMENT OF THE HELICOPTER FROM 1945

Year of Introduction	Type	Country of Origin	Primary Role	Comments & Performance
1946	Bell Model 47 (OH-13E, etc.)	USA	Light utility	First helicopter to receive a Type Approval Certificate (in 1946) for commercial use. Variations of this basic model have been built ever since, the total production in the US and (under licence) abroad amounting to over 5,000 machines. Cruise, 90 mph; range, 300 miles
1949	Sikorsky S-55 (UH-19B, etc.)	USA	General purpose	Was one of the most widely used of Sikorsky helicopters. Licence production in Japan and (in slightly modified form) in the UK, as Westland Whirlwind. Cruise, 85–90 mph; range, 400 miles
1948	Mil Mi-1 'Hare'	USSR	Light military transport	First Soviet helicopter to enter large-scale production. Widespread military and civil use. Now largely replaced by the Mi-2 but substantial numbers still in service. Cruise, 84 mph; range, 340 miles
1949	Hiller 12 series (H-23 Raven, UH-12A, etc.)	USA	Light utility	Stanley Hiller's most successful design, more than 2,000 examples being built until production was terminated in 1967. Most of the first 100 production machines were used operationally in Korea. Cruise, 90 mph; flight endurance, 3.2 hrs
1951	S.E.3120 Alouette	France	Light utility	Developed from the first original French post-war helicopter design, S.E. 3101, the Alouette became the first version of the most successful French helicopter designed and built to date. Originally a piston-engined 3-seater, progressive development led to the turboshaft-engined Alouette II of 1955 and Alouette III of 1959
1951	Yakovlev Yak-24 'Horse'	USSR	Military transport	Notable as the world's largest helicopter at the time of its official appearance in 1955, and a number of international records established same year. Cruise, 96 mph; range, 125 miles
1952	Mil Mi-4 'Hound'	USSR	General purpose	Comparable to Sikorsky S-55 in design—no doubt to reduce development time—and the most produced Soviet helicopter to date. In Soviet Air Force service since 1953, and sold to more than 20 other countries. Cruise, 99 mph; range, 250 miles
1953	Sikorsky S-56 (CH-37, etc.)	USA	Assault transport	First twin-engined helicopter designed to USMC specifications calling for an airborne assault transport. In operational service from 1955
1954	Sikorsky S-58 (UH-34, etc.)	USA	General purpose	One of the most successful 'heavy' helicopters, with over 1,800 produced and used by the US and several foreign services. Was one of the first special anti-submarine helicopters. A slightly modified version built under licence in the UK as Westland Wessex. Cruise, 98 mph; range, 190–250 miles
1955	Sud Alouette II	France	Light utility	Turbo-shaft powered 5-seat development of the original Alouette. About 1,300 have been bought by various customers all around the world. Cruise, 112 mph; range, 400 miles
1955	Kamov Ka-15 and Ka-18 'Hen' and 'Hog'	USSR	Light utility	The only successful co-axial rotor helicopters of post-WW II era, built in some numbers for the Soviet Navy, Army and Aeroflot use. The Ka-15 established several international records in 1958. Cruise, 70 mph;
1951–56	Bristol Type 192 Belvedere	UK	General purpose	Britain's first tandem-rotor helicopter. Much use was made of Sycamore components to speed up development but the design ran into prolonged teething troubles. Eventually operational with three RAF squadrons. Cruise, 75 mph; range, 150 miles
1956	Bell Model 204B (HU-1, UH-1A, -1B, etc.)	USA	Utility	This 10-seat utility machine was destined to become the most widely used and known American helicopter in Vietnam under its nickname 'Huey' (from the original designation HU-1). Armed UH-1As went into service in Vietnam in October 1962, and 'Hueys' of various versions formed the bulk of equipment used by the 1st Air Cavalry Division of the US Army—the first such unit in the world (to Vietnam in 1965). Led to the development of Bell Model 209 Hueycobra of 1965. Cruise, 126 mph; range, 260 miles
1957	Mil Mi-6 'Hook'	USSR	Heavy transport	World's largest helicopter until the appearance of Mi-12 in 1969. Designed as a heavy and bulky load carrier (incl. large missiles), and had remarkably trouble-free development. Operational with Soviet and several other air forces. Led to the development of the Mi-10 'flying crane'. Cruise, 168 mph; range, 310 miles
1958	Westland Scout and Wasp	UK	General purpose	Designed as a private venture, this light helicopter was evolved into a very efficient anti-tank weapon (Scout) and anti-submarine warfare helicopter (Wasp). In addition to service with British military forces and aboard RN frigates, Wasps have been supplied to various foreign customers. Cruise, 122 mph; range, 320 miles
1958	Kaman K-600 Huskie (H-43)	USA	Crash rescue and utility	First US twin turbine helicopter. Often known as 'Pedro', the HH-43 serves on crash rescue duties at all USAF bases. Also supplied to several other nations
1959	SA 316 Alouette III	France	Light utility	Developed from the Alouette II of 1955, continuing the success of its predecessors: already over 1,000 built or on order, as well as licence-production agreements (incl. Rumania)
1959	Kaman SH-2 Seasprite	USA	All-weather search and rescue	First real all-round helicopter, with retractable undercarriage and 'floating' hull. Carries auto stabilising equipment. From 1970 the US Navy Seasprites are used on anti-submarine warfare and missile defence. Cruise, 155 mph; range, 445 miles (max.)
1960	Kamov Ka-22 Vintokryl 'Hoop'	USSR	Troop and freight transport	An experimental Soviet convertiplane design that did not advance beyond the record-breaking and trial stages. Most unusual in having two turboprop engines fitted at the wing tips driving tractor propellers and rotors
1960	Mil Mi-10 'Harke'	USSR	Flying crane	Evolved from the Mi-6 heavy transport helicopter. Can carry very bulky loads—even small houses, etc. Established a series of international records in 1961. Appeared 18 months before the very similar Sikorsky S-64 Skycrane. Large numbers in use. Cruise, 120 mph
1960	Sikorsky S-61 Sea King	USA	Anti-submarine, ASR and transport	Designed as a combined 'Hunter' and 'Killer' anti-submarine helicopter with all-weather capability. In Vietnam became known as 'Jolly Green Giants' on account of their green/brown camouflage; on operations have rescued many hundreds of downed airmen and more than a billion (US dollars) worth of damaged aircraft. Cruise, 120 mph; range, 250 miles
1961	Boeing-Vertol CH-47 Chinook	USA	Medium transport	Standard medium transport helicopter of the US Army, in service as battlefield mobility machine since 1962. Irreplaceable in Vietnam, where about 600 Chinooks were used on a wide variety of tasks. Cruise, 150 mph; radius with 12,000 lb external load, 200 miles
1962	Sikorsky S-64 (CH-54 Tarhe)	USA	Heavy flying crane	Evolved from the S-60 and generally known as Skycrane, the S-64 has a strong superficial resemblance to the Soviet Mi-10. Did great service in Vietnam, where this 'heavy lift' force was swiftly augmented. Also good for minesweeping tasks and even as a tug for smaller ships in confined waters. Cruise, 110 mph; range, 190 miles
1962	SA 321 Super Frelon	France	Heavy duty multi-purpose	Large and very efficient helicopter derived from smaller Frelon prototypes. Has a boat-type hull and is produced as a fully amphibious anti-submarine warfare or ordinary transport version. Powered by three turbine engines. Operational with French and several other air forces. Cruise, 143 mph; range, 440 miles
1965	Bell Model 209 AH-1G Hueycobra	USA	Gunship	Evolved from the highly successful Bell UH-1 utility helicopter series which were used operationally in Vietnam armed with various combinations of weapons. The Hueycobra 'chin turret' can be fitted with a wide variety of offensive armament, from guns to grenade throwers. Was the first helicopter designed solely as an aerial weapons' platform, and thousands of Hueycobras were ordered instead of the very expensive and complicated AH-56 Cheyenne developed for ground support
1966	Hughes OH-6/ Model 500 Cayuse	USA	Light utility	Winner of a US Army contest in 1965 for a light observation helicopter, and a popular and very agile machine. Over 1,400 built in the US, with many more under licence in Japan and Italy. Proved very efficient in Vietnam leading to large production orders
1969	Mil Mi-12 'Homer'	USSR	Heavy transport	World's largest and heaviest helicopter, powered by four turboshaft engines, and present holder of the international weight lifting record (88,636 lb). Evidently designed to carry loads similar to those taken by the fixed-wing Antonov An-22 Antei
1971	Westland/ Aerospatiale WG.13 Lynx	UK	Multi-role	An Anglo-French project, developed in several versions for the British Army, Royal Navy and French Naval aviation. An incredibly agile helicopter, and one of the very few that can be rolled and looped. Cruise, 176 mph; range (with 10 passengers), 173 miles

motely trained cannon, a 40 mm rapid-fire grenade launcher, various kinds of rockets, and tubes for eight TOW anti-tank guided missiles. Infra-red, optical and radar with MTI (moving-target indication) can all be fitted for sighting at night.

Despite the mass of equipment, the extensive armour and the bristling exterior, the Hueycobra is much faster than the transport Hueys, reaching about 220 mph. It can be manoeuvred like a fighter, and heralded a completely new sort of helicopter that can take care of itself over a battlefield or even in air combat by reason of its equip-

Rescue role. Stabilized by drogue parachutes, an OV-IOA Bronco twin-turboprop tactical aircraft is 'rescued' by a powerful Sikorsky CH-53 Sea Stallion.

The Versatile Helicopter

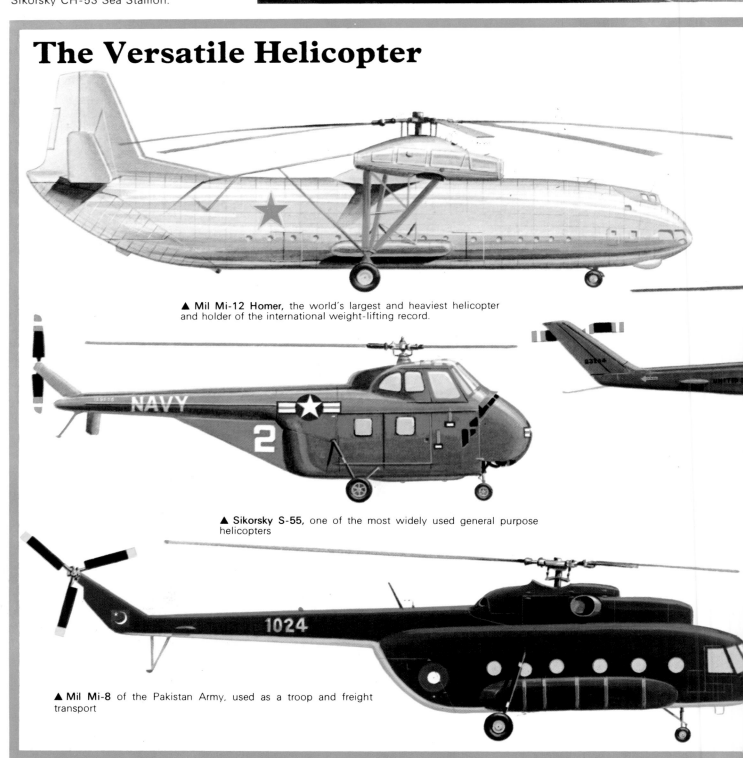

▲ **Mil Mi-12 Homer,** the world's largest and heaviest helicopter and holder of the international weight-lifting record.

▲ **Sikorsky S-55,** one of the most widely used general purpose helicopters

▲ **Mil Mi-8** of the Pakistan Army, used as a troop and freight transport

ment and agility. Nevertheless, the gunship helicopter tries to stay out of trouble.

Anti-tank pop-up

One of its main roles is anti-tank fighting. For this it can operate in two ways. In one mode it carries guided weapons arranged to fire forwards, sighted by the second crew-member. The tactic is for the helicopter to creep along behind any natural cover, searching for its prey with the crew's eyes, with radar and with infra-red. When it finds armoured forces it pops up for a few seconds to fire a missile and guide it to its target. It may only be visible for about three seconds; then it dashes sideways behind cover and lies low for a few seconds before engaging another target from a different place. Alter-

natively an anti-tank helicopter may be of the traditional transport type, carrying a section of anti-tank infantry and their missiles. The soldiers may set up and fire well away from the helicopter, but they can also return to it to pick up fresh missiles.

During the 1960s Lockheed built an extremely advanced and complicated attack helicopter, the **Cheyenne.** Its development was eventually stopped, for technical and financial reasons, but not before it had demonstrated the amazing breadth of things a fully equipped armed helicopter can do in a land battle. Its place is being taken by the **AAH,** Advanced Attack Helicopter, which is simpler and can be bought in much greater numbers, the AAH target price being the relatively low one of $1.4 to $1.6 million. The two-seat AAH will be primarily

a tank-killer, firing guided missiles, but it will also have a 30 mm gun firing 1,000 rounds per minute and many other weapons for the close support of ground troops. A British helicopter in the same class is the **Westland Lynx,** being manufactured in partnership with Aérospatiale of France. The Lynx is a multi-role helicopter with incredible agility. Its novel rotor and control system enable it to move in any direction with extraordinary speed, while very comprehensive equipment allows the crew to devote almost all their time to the operational tasks instead of merely flying the helicopter. Lynx is one of the few helicopters to have been rolled and looped.

Like several earlier battlefield helicopters the Lynx also exists in a naval version. This can be carried by frigates and similar-sized

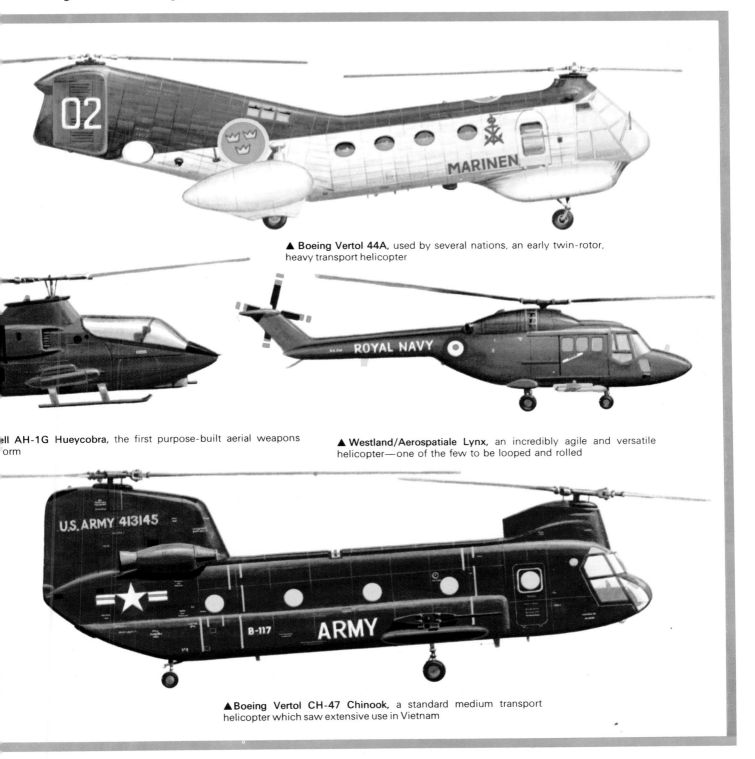

▲ Boeing Vertol 44A, used by several nations, an early twin-rotor, heavy transport helicopter

ll AH-1G Hueycobra, the first purpose-built aerial weapons orm

▲ Westland/Aerospatiale Lynx, an incredibly agile and versatile helicopter—one of the few to be looped and rolled

▲ Boeing Vertol CH-47 Chinook, a standard medium transport helicopter which saw extensive use in Vietnam

ships, and though it will operate primarily in the ASW role, and for general ocean surveillance, the naval Lynx will also have a formidable capability against surface ships. One of its weapon options is the BAC Sea Skua missile, which can be used against targets still over-the-horizon to the parent frigate.

Destruction above and below

The Lynx makes use of an advanced radar, the Seaspray, which is able to detect small fast patrol boats, air-cushion vehicles and hydrofoils, any of which could carry dangerous anti-ship missiles, when they are still invisible to the naked eye on the extreme horizon. The return radiation, though very faint, can be sensed by the guidance receiver in the nose of the Sea Skua missile. Once the missile has acquired the target, and locked-on, it can be launched towards the enemy vessel. Swooping down to the sea, the missile is pulled out of its dive by its radio altimeter which then keeps it running just above the surface of the sea, homing on the enemy ship with ever-increasing certainty and accuracy. The overall result is that the enemy

Left: The beginning. The first useful transport helicopter was the Sikorsky S-55, which was later developed into the British turbine-engined Whirlwind.

ship cannot escape destruction, without the helicopter having to approach within range of defending guns or short-range missiles. The parent frigate would never see the enemy vessel at all.

In the very important ASW role the helicopter has a unique ability to shadow the enemy closely. No surface vessel has much hope of outrunning a modern nuclear submarine, and a fixed-wing aeroplane goes too fast; but the helicopter can stay close and move immediately in any direction according to the signals received from the detection gear. It has a further advantage in that it can 'dunk' a sonobuoy in the water, listen to try to pick up the sound of a submerged submarine, fish it up and dunk it again in a different place. Thus the helicopter need carry only one or two sonobuoys, whereas an aeroplane must carry dozens and wastefully use each once only. Indeed, the economy of the dunking sonar technique means that a large ASW helicopter can use sonobuoys of a particularly large and powerful type, either active or passive, giving greater range and fidelity than the small Class A sonics dropped in profusion by the ASW aeroplanes. Other naval helicopters have been equipped with such missiles as Sparrow and Sidewinder to defend the fleet against enemy aircraft, with minelaying gear, with equipment for retrieving aircraft

and for towing ships. Many kinds of radar have been fitted, some of them having large-aperture aerials rotating inside inflatable radomes blown up in flight by air bled from the engine.

But possibly the most novel military rotorcraft is the **Aercab** (Aircrew Escape/Rescue CApaBility) developed by the American Kaman Co. This folds up to fit inside a specially designed fighter ejection seat. With a normal ejection seat the occupant may leave the stricken aircraft successfully only to find himself in another dangerous situation, for he may land among flaming wreckage and in any case be in enemy territory. With Aercab he ejects in the normal way; then a drogue slows the seat, allowing rotor blades to unfold. Within four seconds the seat converts into a rotor glider. Two further seconds and a tiny turbofan engine springs to life to provide forward thrust. With the rotor spinning freely the pilot could then fly up to 57 miles at 115 mph, the hope being that this would bring him at least to a suitable landing spot and preferably to one in friendly hands.

Lifting men in—lifting off without! Israeli paratroopers are flown in by Bell 205 (right); the Gyrodyne QH-50C (below), a pilotless anti-submarine system, was tested in 1960 with a pilot.

NEW POWER in the skies

The rising cost of development and production of new aircraft has led to a new philosophy, not only in their design, but also in their sales. Increasingly, the less powerful nations of the world are being involved in the production of the latest warplanes which are then used by their air forces. But the United States and the Soviet Union still easily lead the world in the design, building and deployment of the increasingly diversified and sophisticated aircraft and weapons systems—some with the most astonishing capabilities—which almost every nation sees as essential to its security.

The most important trends in military aviation since the 1950s have been: use of engine power for short take-off, fast climb and manoeuvrability, instead of speed; steadily increasing diversity and dominance of avionics, ECM and similar mission equipment; need for independence from long paved runways; and ceaseless escalation in costs, even compared with the universal rise in the cost of living, thus placing more and more desirable items beyond the reach of more and more defence staffs. The situation appears to be being reached where no nation can afford more than a fraction of its ideal defence equipment, so that its air force becomes increasingly a fine exercise in compromise.

Curiously, the number of nations attempting to build any type of military aircraft is as high as ever (except, perhaps, for the 1930s), though advanced combat aircraft are a planning, design and development task quite beyond all but five or six countries. In many cases aircraft have been designed and developed by two or three nations in partnership. This procedure, followed mainly in Europe, has a US rival technique in which the powerful US industry designs and develops an advanced combat aircraft and then looks for other nations prepared to come in with a controlled share of the programme, or—in some cases—to build the whole aircraft under licence.

Almost all US fighters of recent years have been designed wholly by the parent company yet offered to other nations not only as a product to buy but also as a programme in which to share. In 1974 the two next-generation fighters of the US Air Force and Navy were being 'sold' as hard as possible to Australia and various European countries as subjects of partnership programmes in which the buyer's own industry would share. Other deals involve raw materials, manufactured commodities and many other considerations having nothing to do with aviation yet making an appeal to the buyer or vendor.

The **McDonnell Douglas F-15 Eagle,** for example, was for quite some time the subject of increasingly detailed discussions with the Australian government and industry to see whether the latter would be interested in making the forward fuselage, pylons, engine parts and other items 'without strings' (hoping, justifiably, that the RAAF could then hardly fail to buy the F-15 as its next standard fighter). The F-15 was planned in 1966–69 as an answer to the Soviet **Mig-25 Foxbat** and, though much later in concept, the F-15 is slower than the Mig-25, but more manoeuvrable. The two Pratt & Whitney F100 reheat turbofan engines were rated at 23,400 lb thrust each in the first F-15s, flown in the early 1970s but later engines are expected to have thrusts up to about 30,000 lb. With the full thrust the ratio of total engine thrust to aircraft gross weight will be 1 : 1, and such ratios are not untypical of modern fighters in which the excess power is used to drive the fighter round very tight sustained turns without loss of speed.

Engage, lock-on and fire

The F-15 is a single-seater with a fixed-sweep wing, a very broad fuselage, slab tailplanes carried on fuselage extensions outboard of the engine nozzles, and vertical fins above the same fuselage extensions. The big engines are fed by sharp-edged wedge intakes which can tilt downwards to improve efficiency at high angles of attack. Just outboard of the right intake is the gun, which for production Eagles is a completely new 25 mm weapon firing caseless ammunition. In the nose is the solid-state phased-array radar by Hughes with a lookdown capability for seeing aircraft at tree-top height against the ground. The F-15 can engage, lock-on and fire missiles against enemy aircraft about 70,000 feet above or below its own flight level. In a dogfight the radar feeds a symbolised picture to the IBM head-up display (HUD), which is a feature of almost

all tactical aircraft used for attacks on all aerial or surface targets. The F-15 also has three pylons stressed to carry a 660 US gallon tank or 3,940 lb weapons (though it would be rare to carry this load on each of the three pylons at once), as well as recessed attachments on the fuselage for four Sparrow air-to-air missiles and outer-wing pylons for ECM pods.

Price per copy for the F-15 is likely to stabilise at about $10 million, though early examples have cost far more (because of their large share of the research and development burden). The US Air Force plans to buy a total of 749, including about 70 tandem-seat TF-15 trainers. Major features of the F-15 are its great size (significantly larger than a Phantom, though somewhat lighter), its emphasis on radar and weapons for fighting other aircraft and its refusal to be in any degree degraded in order that more should be bought with the available funds.

Dramatic contrast in costs

Budgetary problems have loomed large in the history of the US Navy's counterpart, the **Grumman F-14 Tomcat.** Indeed for two years the maker refused to continue production because he was losing too much money, even at prices in excess of $16 million per copy, and Grumman claim to have lost $190 million on the first five production batches for a total of 134 aircraft. Even in the supremely well-managed US programmes this kind of financial catastrophe appears to be extremely hard to

avoid, and in the long term it is bound to whittle down still further the number of nations or organisations able to produce advanced military aircraft.

Unlike the F-15 the Navy fighter is optimised as a true multi-role aircraft, fulfilling surface attack missions as well as air superiority fighting. It has tandem seats for pilot and radar intercept officer, a very complex and extremely refined high-lift wing with sweep variable from 20° to 68°, twin TF30 reheat turbofan engines each rated at about 21,000 lb thrust, and slab tailplanes and slightly canted twin fins. Armament comprises a Vulcan 20 mm multi-barrel cannon, racks for four Sparrow or four Phoenix missiles fired by the extremely advanced Hughes AWG-9 radar and fire-control system, and a very wide range of external armament or fuel tank options. Perhaps the most remarkable armament is the big Phoenix missile which can single out its quarry 100 miles away. At the other extreme of range, the Agile air-to-air missile can be fired from within half a mile of its target in the most violent manoeuvres, typifying the new breed of close-range dogfight missiles. The first Tomcat flew in December 1970, and squadrons VF-1 and VF-2 were formed in 1973.

Forming a sharp contrast with the big and costly F-14 and F-15 are the two LWF (light-weight fighter) prototypes, the **General Dynamics YF-16** and **Northrop YF-17.** Both have been built to demonstrate extreme manoeuvrability and simple, cost-effective dogfighting performance. Both are

single-seaters with limited ordnance load and no attempt to break new ground in the all-weather attack of surface targets, though several weapon pylons (up to seven) can be fitted and ground attack is one mission that will be evaluated by the Air Force. Both aircraft have a fantastic ratio of thrust to weight: the YF-16 has a design combat weight of 17,500 lb and an F100 engine rated at 25,000 lb, while the YF-17 weighs about 21,000 lb and has two engines rated at 15,000 lb each. Thus they will almost certainly out-manoeuvre everything else in the sky, apart from missiles, and should also prove attractive to secondary countries.

Europe's underweight F-111

Europe's first advanced combat aircraft is **MRCA,** the multi-role combat aircraft, being developed by the UK, Germany and Italy working together in a tri-national company called Panavia. This programme has the firm prospect of initial sales amounting to more than 800 to the three sponsoring governments, split into about 380 for the RAF—165 for air defence and 215 for strike —as well as 322 for the Luftwaffe and Kriegsmarine and 100 for the Regia Aeronautica. MRCA is the most refined and most versatile military aircraft of its day, being designed for short rough-field performance, tremendous load-carrying ability, extreme efficiency and economy, and outstanding performance at all flight levels. The two Turbo-Union RB.199 three-spool reheat fan engines are a vital factor in this remarkable flexibility, and the swing wings, electrical signal flight controls and advanced mission equipment also play their part. It can perform most of the missions of an **F-111,** though much smaller and under half as heavy.

In France the only modern combat aircraft is the **Dassault Mirage F1,** derived from the familiar delta-wing Mirage but having a high-mounted wing of conventional shape, with advanced high-lift systems, and a tailplane. Powered by a 15,800 lb Atar 9K-50 engine the F1 can exceed Mach 2.2, carry a bigger load much further than earlier Mirage fighters, and has roughly double the range. Dassault expect to be able to offer the larger **Super Mirage** powered by two more efficient M53 engines and capable of Mach numbers in the range 2.4–2.6. This, derived from the swing-wing **Mirage G8,** is expected to be a single-seater with a fixed wing swept at about 55° and having a higher aspect ratio (more slender) than most other fighter wings.

Super fighters. The appearance in April 1965 of the Mikoyan MiG-25 'Foxbat' (below) gave Western defence staffs a profound shock. To rival this 2,000 mph fighter the US Air Force has contracted with McDonnell Douglas for the F-15A Eagle (above) which, though slower, is an outstanding all-round combat aircraft with the world's most advanced interception radar and fire control.

The future. Tactical aircraft are going to have to operate from dispersed make-shift sites. First jet to do this is the V/STOL Harrier, with vectored thrust to lift or propel the aircraft. These Harrier FGA.3 attack aircraft of RAF Strike Command are dispersed in a dense wood. Despite the lack of support facilities, sortie rates are very high.

An exercise in packaging

Advanced carrier machines are typified by the **Lockheed S-3A Viking** and a range of jet V/STOL multi-role attack fighters such as the developments of the **Harrier** and the **Rockwell XFV-12A.** The Viking is basically an exercise in packaging, because in an extremely small airframe it finds space for four men and an amazing quantity of ASW sensing and attack systems, and weapons, as well as fuel for a combat range of over 2,000 miles. Powered by two quite small fan engines, the Viking has STOL performance and extreme flight efficiency, and is sure to appear in a transport form for COD (Carrier On-board Delivery) to supply carriers at sea.

The jet V/STOLs contrive to combine the flight performance of an air-superiority fighter — certainly in the matters of manoeuvrability, climb and dogfight performance— with near-zero field length, varied weapons capability, multi-mode (air/air or air/surface) radar, and general compatibility with small surface vessels equipped with small, flat operating platforms.

The Soviet Union long ago displayed a crude V/STOL prototype, called 'Freehand' by the West, which is thought to have been developed into a maritime V/STOL jet fighter. Such aircraft can be operated from any ship with a platform, which need not be larger than 80 feet square (though in practice it would usually be larger, for use by several machines, and backed up by a hangar and small maintenance shop).

Various designs of 'through-deck cruiser' and 'sea control ship' have been schemed for vessels which, among other roles, could fly off jet V/STOLS to command the local airspace, strike enemy surface vessels far beyond the horizon and fulfil many other functions within a radius of 200 or more miles. Small numbers of aircraft and consequent high unit costs have seriously delayed the West in this field, despite obvious evidence of rapid Soviet progress in all forms of maritime power. The Soviet Union, incidentally, are almost alone in still using flying boats, the **Beriev M-12 (Be-12)** being a fine multi-role twin-turboprop which

The whale-like Galaxy

Among transports there is no hint of anything bigger than the whale-like **C-5A Galaxy,** of which 79 are in use with USAF Military Airlift Command, though much bigger special-purpose machines have been considered for flying petroleum from remote oilfields. More effort is going into making transports that can use smaller fields and operate with greater efficiency. Military forces can often afford more complicated equipment that would not appeal to a cost-conscious civil operator, and the USAF's two possible replacements for the **C-130** are a case in point. Called AMST (advanced medium STOL transport), they are the **Boeing YC-14** and **McDonnell Douglas YC-15.**

Both are about as big as a C-130, and have high wings and similar rough-field landing gear. Each has a novel STOL high-lift system which makes use of engine power to help lift the aircraft in order to hold the field length down to a mere 2,000 feet. The YC-14 has 'upper-surface blowing': the two big fan engines discharge across the top of the wings and, in the high-lift regime for STOL, blow down across the wide-span trailing-edge flaps to give superior lift to anything attainable by other methods (apart from those using special lift engines). The YC-15 has four smaller engines tucked close below the wing to discharge right into the lowered wing flaps, which are of titanium and graphite composite materials to bear the tremendous high-temperature blast. Such aircraft will combine jet speed with

2,000 feet field length, and carry 20–25 ton loads including 150 troops, vehicles or bulky cargo. Later they will pave the way to superior civil transports.

In the maritime field there are several duties, any of which may be performed by large long-range shore-based aircraft or smaller machines able to operate from a carrier. One of the most vital missions is ASW (Anti-Submarine Warfare) which today involves such varied sensing systems for finding submerged submarines as special radar, MAD (magnetic anomaly detection) to detect distortion in the Earth's magnetic field, sonar systems using active or passive sonobuoys, exhaust-gas sniffers and other methods. Large shore-based machines, such as the **Nimrod,** combine all these methods in complex systems controlled by computers which link all the sensors, the navigation systems, the flight-control system and the crew information-display systems so that the aircraft can fly accurately over featureless ocean, seek and find targets, and attack them with precision.

Many other things are possible; for example the computer memory of an aircraft whose patrol time is up can in a fraction of a second be transmitted by radio to the memory of the relieving aircraft so that the latter instantly has a complete picture of the operational scene. Future ocean patrol aircraft are likely to be either much smaller, with fewer crew and more computers, or else even larger and to combine the ocean ASW role with that of general surveillance, mapping, logistic transport, resource survey and tanking or flight refuelling.

The Harrier

▲ Hawker Siddeley (AV-8A) **Harrier** of US Marine Corps Squadron VMA 513

has gained numerous world class records—largely because there is nothing else in the same class, apart from the Japanese **SS-2** family of ASW or ASR (air/sea rescue) boats of which small numbers have been delivered since 1968.

Flying boats appear to be out of fashion, but every air force in the world needs robust, simple aircraft able to fly attack missions against surface targets—either against an enemy in war, or to maintain internal law and order, or merely as a 'presence' to avoid armed challenge from any quarter. Many air forces use old jet fighters, or even piston-engined machines, for this all-embracing role.

Trainer that packs a punch

Increasing importance is being attached to modern military jet trainers, which are invariably available with armament options for both training and offensive use. Examples of aircraft long used for both roles are the **Macchi MB.326, BAC Strikemaster** and **Potez/Fouga Magister.** The Italian MB.326 is notable in that it has been mass-produced in Brazil, the Republic of South Africa and Australia, and has been developed into a single-seater used more for attack than for training. Since 1960 much thought has

been devoted to a new generation of trainer and attack machines, and modern examples are the **Alpha Jet, HS.1182 Hawk** and **Saab 105G.** All reach very nearly 600 mph and carry up to 5,000 lb of external stores—a weight greater than the maximum load of any bomber in service in 1939. Such aircraft can operate from airfields with a field-length of about 4,000 feet, which are common everywhere, and they are financially not too much of a burden for small nations to buy and operate.

There are other multi-role tactical aircraft both higher and lower in the price scale. The cheapest of all are lightplanes, often derived from civil aircraft, which combine very STOL performance and minimal cost with effective weapons for use against any kind of air or surface targets unlikely to hit back. Of course the advent of cheap shoulder-fired guided missiles may in future rule out such an assumption, and in any case it is advisable to have some protection against small-arms fire. A minimal attack machine of this type is the Swedish **MFI-17.** A larger aircraft able to carry not only weapons but also a small section of infantry, or army supplies, is the **Britten-Norman Defender,** derived from the **Islander** light civil transport.

In a class above this is an interesting

species of aircraft purpose-built for the tactical ground attack role and making no pretensions to be a fighter, trainer or anything else. Here the accent is squarely on the ability to survive hostile ground fire, to manoeuvre well and safely in tight corners, to carry a huge ordnance load and to deliver the latter with precision. By far the most carefully planned machine in this class is the **Fairchild A-10A** of the US Air Force, winner of the AX competition arising from America's involvement in Vietnam. This is virtually a twin-turbofan transport able to operate from a 4,000 feet rough strip whilst carrying no less than 16,000 lb of stores on eleven pylons. It also mounts a multi-barrel 30 mm gun, the most powerful gun ever fitted to an aircraft, to punch through armour or other hard targets.

Lesser powers have also seen the value of a versatile ground-attack machine. In 1974, Argentina took a lead when her air force took delivery of the twin-turboprop **Pucara,** smaller than the A-10A, but following the same formula in carrying guns and a heavy external weapon load out of very short rough airstrips. Such aircraft are bound in the long term to be judged more cost-effective than elderly jet fighters and they are the most likely kind of aircraft to be used in future wars.

▲ SEPECAT Jaguar A tactical strike fighter of the Armée de l'Air

Co-operative success. Product of the first collaborative programme for a combat aircraft, the SEPECAT Jaguar is a most successful design. The A-model of the Armée de l'Air (left) has great range and load and is simple and cheap, the RAF Jaguar GR.1 (below) is more costly, with inertial navigator, laser target seeker and many other advanced features. Though small, it carries as much load as a Phantom or a Lancaster over extremely long ranges.

Another outstanding European combat aircraft is the **Saab 37 Viggen,** with a unique canard configuration with a high-mounted flapped foreplane and broad low-mounted delta wing. Powered by a Swedish-US RM8 reheat turbofan of 26,000–28,000 lb thrust, the Viggen entered service as the **AJ37** attack machine in 1971. Subsequent versions include the **SK37** trainer, **SF37** land reconnaissance aircraft, **SH37** maritime surveillance and attack and the considerably revised **JA37** fighter version. All Viggens are designed to operate from rough emergency airstrips and straight sections of highway, and to be maintained by inexperienced, conscript ground crews.

World's best interceptor

In the Soviet Union the dominant fighter bureaux continue to be those of Artem Mikoyan and Pavel Sukhoi. The **MiG-21** is still in full production after two decades, and has probably been built in much greater numbers than any other contemporary fighter. Although very small it handles beautifully and is well-liked, though the latest multi-role version, the **MiG-21MF,** is somewhat heavier and can carry four sets of air-to-air missiles, rocket pods, bombs or tanks, in addition to the basic armament of a twin-barrel 23 mm cannon.

The variable-sweep **MiG-23 'Flogger'** is in service in much smaller numbers, and is seemingly fast (Mach 2.5) and efficient, though at 28,000 lb only half as heavy as a Phantom. It is quite different in layout from the big **MiG-25 'Foxbat'**, which appeared in 1965 and at once set about demolishing world records and causing consternation among Western defence staffs. With a stubby fixed wing, it set the fashion later followed by the F-15, with a wide body, two big reheat engines fed by wedge intakes, and canted twin fins for good manoeuvrability at all Mach numbers. Armed with a gun and various kinds of missile, the MiG-25 can reach Mach 3.2 and exceed 80,000 feet, and early in 1973 the USAF Secretary described it as 'probably the best interceptor in production in the world today'. In the Middle East these aircraft have maintained surveillance over Israel with immunity to interception by the Mirage or Phantom.

In the field of strategic attack one aircraft demands pride of place: the **Rockwell B-1** is the only aircraft known in this class. It was popularly believed in the late 1950s and 1960s that the large manned bomber was dead, but examination of the situation in the absence of bombers showed a horrifying possibility for the United States. An enemy missile attack could be timed to hit every US ICBM simultaneously, so that the nation would be shattered and lose all retaliatory power other than the submarine-borne Polaris and Poseidon. The ICBMs dared not be fired upon radar sighting of the oncoming missiles because the latter might not contain warheads, but (perhaps) just leaflets! The risk dared not be taken of unleashing thermonuclear war; yet waiting to see if it was a real nuclear onslaught would wipe out much of the United States and all its ICBM force. But with a bomber force there was no problem. Bombers could be sent out the moment an enemy attack was detected, and recalled if for any reason there had been a false alarm. Moreover, contrary to what many experts had imagined, the bomber of the 1970s could be made to penetrate enemy airspace as surely as could jet bombers in the pre-missile era.

The United States has placed its faith in the **B-1** which, instead of trying to fly fast and high, is most likely to fly fairly fast and very low. At high altitude it can fly slightly faster than Mach 2, and at sea level it can fly at about Mach 0.9. It is roughly the same size and weight as the **Concorde** airliner, but its four GE F101 reheat fan engines are less powerful. Variable wing-sweep gives the B-1 outstanding short-field capability, it being a basic requirement that the force should be able to disperse to thousands of remote airstrips to avoid being caught on the ground. It was also vital that the B-1 should be unfailingly able to leave the ground within minutes of an alarm; any longer time and the bomber could be destroyed by an enemy missile. Thus the B-1 has special rapid-start systems, computer control and checkout, and the ability to operate in a nuclear environment (which affects many hundreds of engineering features, such as the two main computer memories which are of plated-wire that is not affected by radiation). The B-1 has LARC (low-altitude ride control) vanes on each side of the nose which, operated by a motion-sensing control system, damp out vertical undulations and the response due to atmospheric gusts to reduce structural stresses and give the crew a smoother ride through low-level turbulence at full speed.

Radar cross-section (apparent size to a radar) of the B-1 is about one-twentieth as large as that of a **B-52.** The bomber carries two kinds of decoy, as well as the most sophisticated ECM ever invented. The BDM (bomber defence missile) can also be carried and, in dire emergency, launched to act as a protecting fighter. In the final run to the target the B-1 would fly as close to the earth as possible, riding on its TFR (terrain-following radar) to follow the undulations of the ground and thus stay as far as possible under defending radars. It has three big bomb bays, each of which can carry a wide range of stores including a rotary dispenser (like a revolver cylinder) for eight SRAMS (Short Range Attack Missiles). Thus 24 SRAMS can be carried internally, plus eight more externally, all programmed for separate targets if necessary. SAC (Strategic Air Command) expect eventually to deploy a force of 241.

The only other bomber in a remotely similar category is Russian and codenamed **'Backfire'** in the West. Not much is known about it beyond the fact that it is smaller than the B-1 but also has a swing-wing. Apparently powered by two (or more) reheat fan engines in the shallow but broad fuselage, the Backfire is a product of the Tupolev bureau and has that designer's 'trade mark' in that the six-wheel main gears fold into large streamlined boxes projecting behind the fixed parts of the wing. This bomber is thought to have entered squadron service in 1972 and to be matched with at least one new type of rocket-propelled air-to-surface missile. Like every modern strategic aircraft it is equipped for flight refuelling, the Soviet method being a copy of the British probe/drogue system.

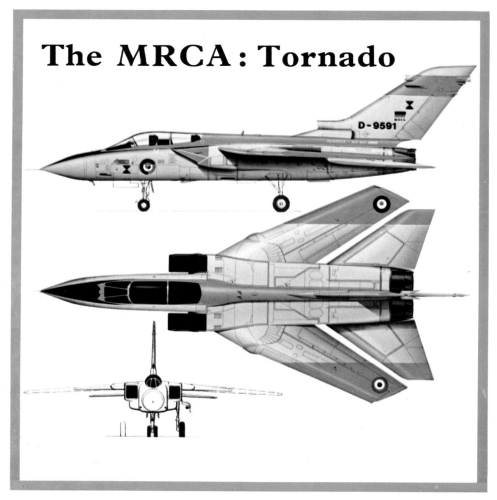

The MRCA: Tornado

D-9591

Index

Picture Credits

The publishers wish to thank the following photographers and organisations who have supplied photographs for this book.

Photographs have been credited by page number. Where more than one photograph appears on the page, references are made in the order of the columns across the page and then from top to bottom.

Some references have, for reasons of space, been abbreviated as follows:

The Imperial War Museum: IWM

United States Air Force: USAF

Associated Press: AP

Etablissement Cinematographique et Photographique Des Armées: ECPA

References to pictures are shown in bold type. References to aircraft types within charts and tables are shown in italic.

Page 1: IWM. 2: Camera Press Ltd. 6: IWM. 8: USAF-J. Taylor-RHL/IWM. 9: IWM/IWM. 10: IWM. 18: IWM/IWM/IWM/IWM. 20: IWM/IWM/IWM. 21: IWM/IWM. 22: IWM. 23: IWM/IWM/IWM. 24: IWM/IWM/IWM. 25: IWM. 26: IWM. 29: IWM. 30: IWM/IWM. 32: IWM. 34: IWM/IWM/IWM. 35: IWM. 36: IWM/IWM/IWM. 38: IWM/IWM. 39: IWM. 40: IWM. 41: IWM/IWM. 42: IWM/IWM. 44: IWM. 46: IWM/IWM. 48: IWM. 50: Flight International. 54: John Taylor-RHL/John Taylor-RHL. 55: USAF-John Taylor-RHL/USAF-John Taylor-RHL/USAF-John Taylor-RHL. 56: RHL. 60: RHL/RHL. 61: RHL/RHL. 64: IWM/IWM. 65: IWM. 67: IWM/IWM/IWM. 68: IWM/Flight International/IWM. 69: IWM. 70: IWM/Bapty & Co/RHL/USAF. 76: USAF/USAF. 77: Gaston Berelemont-RHL/USAF. 78: RHL. 79: Bapty/IWM/Bapty/Blitz Publications. 84: Bapty/RHL. 85: IWM. 86: Bapty. 87: IWM/Bapty/Blitz. 90: Bapty/IWM/IWM. 92: IWM. 94: IWM/USAF/USAF/USAF. 98: USAF/USAF. 99: IWM. 100: IWM. 106: IWM. 112: IWM/IWM/Novosti Press Agency. 116: Bapty/IWM/IWM/IWM. 119: Blitz/IWM. 121: IWM/IWM. 122: IWM. 124: IWM/IWM. 126: Bapty/Bapty. 127: IWM/USAF. 128: IWM/IWM/IWM. 130: Fujifotos, Tokyo/Fujifotos. 134: US Navy/US Navy/RHL. 135: US Navy. 136: Fujifotos/RHL/US Navy. 141: IWM/IWM. 142: Fujifotos/USAF/IWM. 147: RHL/USAF-RHL/IWM/IWM/IWM/IWM. 150: IWM/USAF. 151: IWM/IWM/IWM/IWM. 154: Deutsches Museum, Munich/IWM. 155: IWM/IWM/IWM. 156: General Dynamics. 162: USNA-RHL. 163: USNA-RHL/USNA-RHL/USNA-RHL. 166: USAF. 168: US Navy/US Navy/USAF. 169: USAF. 171: USAF/USAF. 172: IWM/USAF. 173: US Navy. 175: RAF, Air Historical Branch. 176: Air Historical Branch/Novosti. 177: US Navy. 181: RAF Stanmore. 182: RHL. 184: Novosti. 185: USAF. 186: US Navy/Novosti/RAF Stanmore/USAF. 188: USAF/USAF. 189: Air Historical Branch. 190: RAF Stanmore. 196: Pilot Press/Pilot Press/AP. 200: USAF. 201: Novosti. 202: USAF. 205: USAF/Air Historical Branch. 206: Novosti/Air Historical Branch/AP. 207: ECPA. 208: USAF. 210: USAF/USAF. 213: Australian Information Service/USAF/US Navy/US Navy. 214: USAF/Pilot Press. 215: USAF. 216: Camera Press. 219: Pilot Press/RAF Stanmore. 222: RAF Stanmore. 223: US Navy/US Navy/Lockheed Corporation/RAF Stanmore. 224: RAF Stanmore/Royal Navy. 225: US Navy. 226: Lockheed. 227: Pilot Press/Pilot Press/Pilot Press. 228: USAF/Lockheed/USAF. 229: RAF Stanmore. 230: Camera Press. 232: Pilot Press/Pilot Press/Pilot Press/Camera Press. 234: Camera Press/Camera Press/AP/Camera Press. 236: Camera Press/Camera Press. 240: US Navy. 243: USAF/US Navy/Air Historical Branch. 244: US Navy. 246: Air Historical Branch/US Navy. 247: Camera Press. 248: McDonnell Douglas. 249: Pilot Press. 250: RAF Stanmore. 251: Robin Adshead.

Acknowledgements

The Publishers wish to acknowledge their indebtedness to the following books which were consulted for reference or as a source for illustrations:

The First and the Last by A. Galland published by Methuen & Co. Ltd.

Bridge in the Sky by Frank Donovan, published by Robert Hale & Co., London and David McKay, New York.

Airwar over Korea by Robert Jackson, published by Ian Allen 1973.

Insight on the Middle East War by the Insight Team of the Sunday Times/Times Newspapers Limited, published by Andre Deutsch 1974 (diagrams and maps on the Middle East wars).

KOREA (SOUTH) KUWAIT LAOS LEBANON

LIBYA MALAGASY MALAYSIA MALI

MAURITANIA MEXICO MONGOLIA MOROCCO

NEPAL NETHERLANDS NEW ZEALAND NICARAGUA

NIGER NIGERIA NORWAY OMAN

PAKISTAN PANAMA PARAGUAY PERU

PHILIPPINES POLAND PORTUGAL QATAR

RHODESIA RUMANIA RWANDA SALVADOR